Contents

Foreword

**Part One
From the Romance languages up: Phonological reconstruction**

0 Introduction: Orientation to the comparative method	1
0.1 The basic requirement: Regular cross-language correspondences	1
0.2 Exclusion of interlanguage borrowings	3
1 The reconstruction of Proto-Southwestern Romance: A demonstration	5
1.0 Introduction	5
1.1 The Proto-Southwestern (PSW) consonants	7
1.2 The Proto-Southwestern vowels	18
1.3 Recapitulation of Proto-Southwestern phonology	24
1.4 Reconstruction of the corpus in Proto-Southwestern	25
1.4.1 Residual categories	25
Notes for Chapter 1	27
2 The reconstruction of Proto-Romance: A guided exercise	29
2.0 Introduction	29
2.1 Reconstruction of the Proto-Romance (PRom) phonemes	30
2.2 Reconstruction of the corpus in Proto-Romance	33
Notes for Chapter 2	34
3 The confrontation of Proto-Romance with attested Latin	36
3.1 The corpus in Latin	36
3.2 The phonemes of Latin	37

3.3 Reconstruction and reality   38
Notes for Chapter 3   39

Part Two
From Latin down: Phonological changes

0 Introduction: Orientation to the diachronic view   41

0.1 The differentiation of language and dialect   41
0.2 Phonological criteria for language change and split   43
Notes for Introduction   46

1 The Latin language becomes the Common Romance language   47

1.0 The phonological inventory of Latin   47
1.1 Modification of stress rules   48
1.2 Syncope involving certain vowels   48
1.3 Monophthongization of diphthong /ay/ (AE)   50
1.4 Phonetic laxing of the short vowels   50
1.5 Modification of vowel length   50
1.6 Loss of the consonant /h/ (H)   51
1.7 Other dialectal changes   51
1.8 Summary of the changes, and inventory of Common Romance   52
1.9 Equating Proto-Romance with Common Romance   53
    1.9.1 Extrapolating the unreconstructible items of the corpus   53
    1.9.2 Residual discrepancies between Latin and Common
           Romance   53
Notes for Chapter 1   60

2 Common Romance splits into Southern, Eastern, and Italo-Western Romance   61

2.0 Introduction   61
2.1 Preliminary changes   61
    2.1.1 Phonetic laxing of postvocalic consonants   61
    2.1.2 Fusion of nonlabila consonants with a following yod   62
    2.1.3 Dialectal merger of /č/ with /c/   62
    2.1.4 Dialectal merger of /kw/ with /k/   62
2.2 The crucial change: Lowering of the lax high vowels and
      consequent dialectal mergers   62
2.3 Summary of the split, and inventory of Italo-Western
      Romance   63
2.4 Residual discrepancies   64
    2.4.1 In Southern Romance as reflected by Sardinian   64

A Course in Romance Linguistics

Volume 2: A Diachronic View

Erratum

An historical comparison
of the major Romance languages
with a reconstruction
of their common source
and a chronological account
of their development
through changes and splits

Frederick B. Agard

Georgetown University Press, Washington, D.C. 20057

Discussion in the Introduction to Part Two closely follows appropriate sections (many passages being taken verbatim) of Agard 1975, 1976, 1980, and is reproduced with permission of the respective publishers, as follows:

Agard (1975). Toward a taxonomy of language split (Part 1: Phonology). Leuvense Bijdragen 64:293–312.

Agard (1976). The genealogy of Modern Spanish. In: Proceedings of the Second International Conference on Historical Linguistics. Edited by W.M. Christie. Amsterdam: North-Holland Publishing Co.

Agard (1980). The genealogy of the French language. In: Contributions to historical linguistics. Edited by van Coetsem and Waugh. Leiden: E.J. Brill.

Copyright © 1984 by Georgetown University Press

All rights reserved

Printed in the United States of America

Library of Congress Cataloging in Publication Data
(Revised for volume 2)

Agard, Frederick Browning, 1907–
A course in Romance linguistics.

Includes bibliographies.
Contents: v. 1. A synchronic view—v. 2 diachronic view.
1. Romance languages—Grammar. I. Title.
PC61.A3 1984   440   83-20817
ISBN 0-87840-088-5 (v. 1)
ISBN 0-87840-089-3 (v. 2)

Contents / v

2.4.2 In Eastern Romance as reflected by Roumanian	65
2.4.3 In Italo-Western Romance as reflected by Italian	72
Notes for Chapter 2	73

3 Italo-Western splits into Italo-Dalmatian and Western Romance — 74

3.0 Introduction	74
3.1 Preliminary changes	74
3.1.1 Dialectal fusion of geminates into single, tense consonants	74
3.1.2 Dialectal merger of postvocalic /w/ with /ḅ/	74
3.1.3 Semivocalization of the coda /g/	75
3.2 The crucial change: Semivocalization of the coda /k/	75
3.3 Summary of the split, and inventory of Western Romance	76
3.4 Residual discrepancies in Italo-Dalmatian Romance as reflected by Italian	76
Notes for Chapter 3	80

4 Western splits into Unshifted Western and Shifted Western Romance — 80

4.0 Introduction	80
4.1 The crucial changes	80
4.1.1 Dialectal merger of the lax with the tense obstruents	81
4.1.2 Dialectal merger of the lax voiceless with the tense voiced obstruents	81
4.2 Summary of the split, and inventory of Shifted Western Romance	82
Notes for Chapter 4	83

5 Shifted Western splits into Northwestern and Southwestern Romance — 83

5.0 Introduction	83
5.1 Preliminary changes	83
5.1.1 Dialectal merger of /č/ with /c/	83
5.1.2 Dialectal merger of /ž/ with /z/	84
5.2 The crucial change: Dialectal merger of the lax with the tense resonants, and subsequent gain of vowel length	84
5.3 Summary of the split, and inventory of Southwestern Romance	85
5.4 Residual discrepancies in Northwestern Romance as reflected by Old French	86

vi / Contents

5.5 The confrontation of Southwestern with reconstructed
    Proto-Southwestern Romance   89
Note for Chapter 5   90

6 Southwestern splits into South Gallo-, East Ibero-, and West Ibero-Romance   91

6.0 Introduction   91
6.1 Preliminary change: Dialectal raising of /a/ before codas /y/
    and /w/   91
6.2 The crucial changes   91
    6.2.1 Dialectal merger of /ð/ with /z/   91
    6.2.2 Dialectal merger of /ð/ with /z̪/   91
    6.2.3 Dialectal loss of /ð/   92
6.3 Summary of the split, and inventory of West Ibero-Romance   92
6.4 Residual discrepancies   93
    6.4.1 In South Gallo-Romance as reflected by Occitan   93
    6.4.2 In East Ibero-Romance as reflected by Catalan   96
    6.4.3 In West Ibero-Romance as reflected by Spanish and/or
          Portuguese   97

7 West Ibero-Romance splits into Castilian, Asturian, and Galician   99

7.0 Introduction   99
7.1 Preliminary changes   99
    7.1.1 Dialectal loss of the lax resonants /l̪/ and /n̪/   99
    7.1.2 Dialectal nasalization of vowels   99
    7.1.3 Dialectal merger of /ž/ with /z/   100
    7.1.4 Dialectal shift of /ʎ/ to /ž/   100
    7.1.5 Dialectal loss of codas /y/ and /w/   100
    7.1.6 Dialectal cleavage of /t/ into /t/ and /č/   100
    7.1.7 Dialectal raising of /ɔ/ before palatal onset   101
    7.1.8 Dialectal diphthongization of /ɛ/ and /ɔ/   101
    7.1.9 Dialectal merger of /l/ with /ʎ/ postvocalically   101
7.2 The crucial change: Partial dialectal mergers of the onset
    clusters /pl kl fl/   101
7.3 Summary of the split, and inventory of Castilian   102
Notes for Chapter 7   104

8 Castilian splits into Toledan and Burgalese   106

8.0 Introduction   106
8.1 Preliminary change: Backing of [f] to [h]   106

8.2 The crucial change: Dialectal borrowing of new [f] and consequent gain of /h/	106
8.3 Inventory of Burgalese Castilian	107

9 Burgalese Castilian splits into North Castilian and South Castilian — 108

9.0 Introduction	108
9.1 Preliminary change: Shift of /c ẓ/ to /ṣ ẓ/	108
9.2 The crucial change: Partially intersecting dialectal mergers of /ẓ/	108
9.3 Summary of the split, and inventories of North Castilian and South Castilian	109
9.4 The amalgamation of North Castilian and South Castilian as Spanish and the inventory of this language	109
9.5 Residual discrepancies in Castilian and/or Spanish as reflected by Spanish	111
Notes for Chapter 9	115

10 Galician splits into Gallegan and Portuguese — 116

10.0 Introduction	116
10.1 Preliminary changes	116
10.1.1 Fusion of final vowel strings	116
10.1.2 Denasalization in nasal-plus-oral vowel strings	116
10.1.3 Shift of /c ẓ/ to /ṣ ẑ/	116
10.2 The crucial change: Partially intersecting dialectal mergers of /ẓ/	117
10.3 Summary of the split, and inventory of Portuguese	117
10.4 Residual discrepancies in Galician and/or Portuguese, as reflected by Portuguese	119
Notes for Chapter 10	122

Part Three
From Latin down: Grammatical changes

Stage 1:
A grammar of Latin, together with diachronic changes in its popular dialects

viii / Contents

0 Introduction	125

Nominal structures

1 The common-noun phrase	**125**
1.0 Internal structure of the common-noun phrase (CNP)	125
1.1 Common nouns as heads	126
1.2 Gender and inflection of nouns	126
1.2.1 Gender	126
1.2.2 Inflection	127
1.3 Determiners in the CNP	128
1.3.1 Adjectival/adverbial words	128
1.3.2 CNPs functioning as quantifying determiner	131
1.3.3 Determinative expressions of evaluation, result, comparison	131
1.4 Modifiers in the CNP	131
1.5 The CNP and discourse factors: Substitution and reduction	131
2 The proper-noun phrase	**132**
2.0 Internal structure of the proper-noun phrase (PNP)	132
2.1 Person names as heads	132
2.2 Modifiers with person-name heads	132
2.3 Reduction of the PNP	133
2.4 Place names as heads of PNPs	133
2.5 Modifiers with place-name heads	133
3 The pronoun phrase	**133**
3.0 Internal structure of the pronoun phrase (ProP)	133
3.1 Pronouns as heads	133
3.2 Modifiers in the ProP	134
4 Dependent nominals functioning as modifiers in larger nominals	**135**
4.3 Genitive modifiers	135
4.3.1 The replacement of possessive genitives	135
4.3.2 The reduction of genitive modifiers	136
4.6 Coordinated nominals	136

Adjectival structures

5 The adjective phrase — 137

5.0 Internal structure of the adjective phrase (AdjP) — 137
5.1 Adjectives as heads — 137
5.2 Quantifiers in the AdjP — 138
5.3 Complements in the AdjP — 139

6 Dependent adjectivals functioning as modifiers within NPs — 139

Adverbial structures

7 The adverb phrase — 139

7.0 Internal structure of the adverbe phrase (AdvP) — 139
7.1 Adverbs as heads — 139
7.2 Complements in the AdvP — 140
7.3 Quantifiers in the AdvP — 140

Verbal structures

8 The verb phrase — 141

8.0 Internal structure of the verb phrase (VP) — 141
8.1 Verbs as heads — 141
8.2 The attributes of aspect and voice — 141
    8.2.1 The perfective aspect — 141
    8.2.2 The passive voice — 142
    8.2.3 Cooccurrence of perfective and passive — 142
8.3 The negator — 143
8.4 Coordinated verbals — 143

Clausal structures

9 The clause: A general overview — 144

9.0 Internal structure of the clause (Cl) — 144
9.1 Verbals as predicates — 144
9.2 Subjects — 144
9.3 Complements — 144
    9.3.1 Transitive verbs and their complements — 144
        9.3.1.1 Transitive-1 verbs — 144

	9.3.1.2 Transitive-2 verbs	145
	9.3.1.3 Transitive-3 verbs	145
	9.3.1.4 Transitive-4 verbs	145
9.3.2	Linking verbs and their complements	146
9.3.3	Intransitive verbs and their complements	146
	9.3.3.1 Intransitive-1 verbs	146
	9.3.3.2 Intransitive-2 verbs	146
9.4 Modifiers in the clause		147
9.5 Modality		147
9.5.1 The tense/mood system		147
9.5.2 Semantics of the moods and tenses		148
9.6 Subject-predicted linkage by person/number inflection		149

10 Special types of clauses — 149

10.1 Clauses with indefinite underlying subject	149
10.2 Clauses with null subject	150
10.3 Passive clauses	150
10.4 Imperative clauses	150
10.4.1 The subject in imperative clauses	151
10.4.2 Prohibitions	151
10.5 Negative clauses	151

Clauses and discourse

11 Movement and reduction transformations — 152

11.1 Extraposition of subjects and of complements	152
11.2 Reduction of subjects	152
11.3 Reduction of complements	152

Dependent clauses

12 Dependent clauses with full modality — 153

12.0	Introduction	153
12.1-3	As subject or complement within a higher clause	153
	12.3.1 As protasis in a conditional clause	154
12.4-5	As modifier within a NP	155
12.6	As modifier within an AdvP	155
12.7	As object within a PrepP	155

13 Dependent clauses with reduced modality — 156

13.0 Introduction — 156
13.1 The infinitive suffix -RE — 156
13.2 Other suffixes — 157

14 Dependent clauses in expressions of comparison — 157

14.0 Introduction — 157
14.1 Comparisons of inequality — 157
14.2 Comparisons of equality — 159

Sentential structures

15 The sentence — 160

15.0 Internal structure of the sentence (S) — 160
15.1 Clauses as segmental constituents — 160
15.2 Intonation contours as prosodies — 160

16 The sentence as speech act — 161

16.0 Introduction — 161
16.1 Declarations and exclamations — 161
    16.1.1 Purely declarative speech acts — 161
    16.1.2 Additionally exclamatory declarative speech acts — 161
16.2 Questions — 162
    16.2.1 Yes/no questions — 162
    16.2.2 Information questions — 162
16.3 Commands/requests — 162
Diachronic recapitulation — 163
Notes for Stage 1 — 163

Stage 2
The grammar of the Common Romance language, together with diachronic changes in its Southern, Eastern, and Italo-Western dialects

0 Introduction — 168

Nominal structures

1 The common-noun phrase — 168

1.2 Gender and inflection of nouns — 168
  1.2.1 Gender — 168
  1.2.2 Inflection — 168
1.3 Determiners in the CNP — 170
  1.3.1 Adjectival/adverbial words — 170
1.5 The CNP and discourse factors: Reduction — 170

3 The pronoun phrase — 170

3.1 Pronouns as heads — 170

4 Dependent nominals functioning as modifiers in larger nominals — 171

4.3.1-2 The replacement and reduction of possessive genitive modifiers — 171

Adjectival structures

5 The adjective phrase — 171

5.1 Adjectives as heads — 171

Verbal structures

8 The verb phrase — 173

8.0 Internal structure of the verb phrase — 173
8.1 Verbs as heads — 173
8.2 The perfective aspect — 173

Clausal structures

9 The clause: A general overview — 175

9.0 Internal structure of the clause — 175
9.2 Subjects — 175

9.3 Complements	175
9.3.1 Objects	175
9.3.2 Datives	175
9.3.3 Equivalents	176
9.5 Modality: The tense/mood system	176

10 Special types of clauses   177

10.1 Passive clauses	177
10.4 Imperative clauses	178

Clauses and discourse

11 Movement and reduction transformations   178

11.1 Extraposition of subjects and complements	178
11.3 Reduction of complements/modifiers	179

Dependent clauses

12 Dependent clauses with full modality   181

12.0 Introduction	181
12.3 Conditional clauses	181
12.4-6 Relative clauses	181

13 Dependent clauses with reduced modality   182

13.1 The infinitive suffix -rę	182
13.2 The gerund suffix -ndo	182

14 Dependent clauses in expressions of comparison   183

Diachronic recapitulation	183
Notes for Stage 2	184

Stage 3
The grammar of Italo-Western Romance, together with diachronic changes in its Italo-Dalmatian and Western dialects

Nominal structures

1 The common-noun phrase — 187

1.2 Gender and inflection of nouns — 187
  1.2.1 Gender — 187
  1.2.2 Inflection — 187
1.3 Determiners in the CNP — 188
  1.3.1 Adjectival/adverbial words — 188

3 The pronoun phrase — 188

3.1 Pronouns as heads — 188

4 Reduction of possessive genitive modifiers in higher CNPs — 190

Verbal structures

8 The verb phrase — 190

8.2 The perfective aspect — 190

Clausal structures

9 The clause: General — 190

9.5 Modality — 190

10 Special types of clauses — 191

10.4 Imperative clauses — 191

Clauses and discourse

11 Reduction transformations — 192

11.3 Reduction of complements/modifiers — 192

Dependent clauses

12 Dependent clauses with full modality — 192

12.4-6 Relative clauses — 193

14 Dependent clauses in expressions of comparison	193
Diachronic recapitulation	193
Notes for Stage 3	193

Stage 4
The grammar of Shifted Western Romance, together with diachronic changes in its Northwestern and Southwestern dialects

Nominal structures

1 The common-noun phrase	195
1.3 Determiners in the CNP	195
1.3.1 Adjectival/adverbial words	195

Clausal structures

9 The clause	195
9.5 Modality	195
Diachronic recapitulation	196
Notes for Stage 4	196
Appendix 1: The corpus of Romance lexical cognates	198
A subset of Latin lexical items (not in corpus) for downtracing	242
Appendix 2: Independent projects in diachronic phonology and morphosyntax	247
Appendix 3: The Romance *Stammbaum*	250
Bibliography	253

Foreword

This second volume of *A Course in Romance Linguistics* is as strictly diachronic—that is to say, historical—as the first volume is synchronic. It is divided into three principal parts.

The first part, *From the Romance languages up: Phonological reconstruction*, involves application of the Comparative Method with a view to protolanguage reconstruction. After an initial step-by-step demonstration of the method, utilizing a corpus of modern Spanish, Portuguese, Catalan, and Occitan lexical cognates as input, and resulting in a phonological reconstruction of 'Proto-Southwestern Romance', the student is guided through a 'do-it-yourself' exercise in the reconstruction of 'Proto-Romance' using the Old French, Italian, Roumanian, and Sardinian cognates of the same lexical items as new input. This part of the book then concludes with a confrontation of the reconstructed output with attested Latin.

The second part, *From Latin down: Phonological changes*, records diachronic phonology chronologically, illustrating the changes with items of the corpus, evaluating them in accordance with a set of criteria for identifying *language* change and/or split, and thus establishing step by step, through a series of splits, the genealogy (or, more graphically, the *Stammbaum*) of the present-day Romance languages. The branching from Southwestern Romance down to Spanish and Portuguese is fully detailed; in an independent study project of the sort suggested in the Appendices, the student may be encouraged to trace from other intermediate languages down to other present-day descendants.

The third part, *From Latin down: Grammatical changes*, starts with a grammatical sketch of Latin based on the phrase-structure model utilized in Volume 1. There then follow statements of changes and of consequent restructurings in the grammars of the languages intermediate between Latin and Western Romance. In one or another independent study project, as suggested, the student may endeavor to trace grammatical changes from Western down to French, Spanish, or Portuguese; or from Italo-Romance down to Italian; or from Eastern Romance down to Roumanian.

Part One
From the Romance languages up: Phonological reconstruction

0. Introduction
Orientation to the comparative method

0.1 The basic requirement: Regular cross-language correspondences. With the design of reconstructing the common source of a given group of languages, the basic requirement of the comparative method is a treasury of regular cross-language CORRESPONDENCES of formal elements. Such a fund of data is available only in a set of languages with empirically observable similarities of structure. An attempt to operate the comparative method on, say, English, Arabic, Japanese, and Eskimo would founder at the outset because these languages fail to share any corpus of lexical items with patterned resemblance to one another in both form and meaning. It is of course a truism that all human languages share items containing the same sememe(s)—for example, a word meaning 'friend'—but only in certain clearly delimited sets of languages do the words for 'friend' also have similar phonetic shapes—e.g. English *friend*, Dutch *vriend*, German *Freund*, etc., or Fr *ami*, Sp/Po *amigo*, It *amico*, Ro *amic*. Shared items of this nature are said to be COGNATES, and a group of languages sharing a body of cognates meeting certain further criteria are classed as cognate languages. The further criteria may be stated as follows.

- The number of shared cognates must be significantly larger than that shared by one member of the group with some other language from another group. Thus, for example, English and French share numerous items such as *beef/boeuf* or *letter/lettre*, including a very considerable number of the type *form/forme, just/juste, pure/pur*, etc.; but such items are far fewer in number than those shared among French and Spanish, Spanish and Italian, Italian and Roumanian, and so on all around.

• Within the storehouse of shared items there must exist regular phonological correspondences—that is to say, matching, congruent sets of phonemes across the board, and in a like position in the word, such as the initial set /b/b/b/b/b/ in Fr *bon*, Sp *bueno*, Po *bom*, It *buono*, Ro *bun*. To qualify as a regular correspondence a given set must recur in a sizeable number of items, as we can easily verify that this particular set indeed does.

The method assumes that a significantly large number of regular correspondences is precisely what betrays a single, common source language existing at an earlier point in time—one which, in evolving from one into several languages via linguistic changes and splits, nevertheless transmitted sounds which remained 'the same' (like the /b/'s in the above example) in their respective distributions, or else were modified in one or another position in one or more of the languages, though always predictably across items and never randomly as in one item but not another—i.e., as the theory underlying the method has it, sound-change operates with thorough regularity, affecting all items containing a given sound in a given position—or, put another way, the laws of sound-change do not exempt individual items. This on the face of it is a gross oversimplification, however, inasmuch as there do exist innumerable apparent exceptions. Such deviations as seem to constitute exceptions must then be accounted for in terms of special sociolinguistic circumstances that inhibit the global application of a sound-change law (or 'rule') in identifiable instances—for example, the contextual interplay of specific words, such that the shape of one influences the shape of another, perhaps by the pressure of some speech taboo; or the prevalence of an item from one dialect (subject to Law X) within the territory of another dialect (subject to Law Y), particularly in the vicinity of isoglosses where opposing changes, spreading out from different focal areas, meet and clash.

Be this as it may, the comparative method cannot operate without accepting the immutability principle as basic. Thus, to illustrate, if the original stressed nucleus in our same example ends up as /ué/ in Spanish, we must expect this language to have /ué/ in all other items that had started with that original nucleus. The corollary assumption which flows from regularity of correspondence is, then, that any two correspondence sets which *differ* in any way at all in exactly the same phonotactic position reflect *different* phonemes in the source, or 'proto-', language. So for example:

• If word-initial /b/b/b/b/ is established as reflecting one particular protophoneme (presumably */b/!), then /b/b/b/v/ (or /b/b/v/v/, or

/b/v/v/v/, or whatever) in the same position, though partially overlapping, must reflect a different protophoneme just as surely as, say, /v/v/v/v/ in that position would. On the other hand, however, if /b/b/b/b/ is a word-initial set, while /v/v/v/v/ or the like is a word-medial, postvocalic set, then the two sets are in NONCONTRASTIVE DISTRIBUTION and hence may or may not reflect different protophonemes: the determination will depend on other factors in the context of the entire corpus of items under scrutiny.

• If /k/k/k/k/ is a word-initial correspondence occurring before a set of vowels reconstructible as a back vowel (say */u/), while /č/č/č/č/ or so is also a word-initial correspondence occurring before a set of vowels reconstructible as a front vowel (say */i/), then the two sets are in COMPLEMENTARY DISTRIBUTION and will be assumed to reflect one and the same protophoneme (presumably */k/) unless there is clear-cut evidence to the contrary.

0.2 Exclusion of interlanguage borrowings. The method also recognizes that some of the evident cognates within a given group of languages must be ruled out of consideration because they are, or can be, due to the cultural borrowing of lexical items from one language by another, rather than to their uninterrupted evolution from a single source language. This happens very frequently in two situations: (1) the conquest and colonization, by speakers of Language A, of the territory inhabited by speakers of Language B; (2) a renascence of learning and letters, accompanied by the enrichment of one or more languages through the borrowing of concepts, and therefore of terminologies, from a learned source. When unrelated languages are brought into contact by conquest, and words are borrowed by the dominant language (the *superstratum*) from the dominated language (the *substratum*) or vice versa, correspondences among resultant cognates are not dependably regular. But in a revival of learning, where vocabulary is borrowed from an absent and perhaps dead source in written form, rather than via living languages in contact, the correspondences are indeed regular, as in the case of the Latin (and later Greek) borrowings into the Romance languages and English. Even between French and English there are innumerable regular correspondences in items ending in derivational suffixes such as **-ion** (*nation, solution, profession, occasion, religion* . . .), **-té/-ty** (*liberté/liberty, charité/charity* . . .) **-ifie/-ify** (*vérifie/verify, solidifie/solidify* . . .), **-ure, -ique/-ic**, and so on; whereas among the Romance languages there are literally thousands of across-the-board correspondences of the sorts exemplified in Fr *cycle*, Sp/Po/It *ciclo*, Ro *ciclu*, or Fr *téléphone*, Sp *teléfono*, Po *telefone*, It *telefono*, Ro *telefon*, or Fr *religion*, Sp *religión*, Po *religião*, It *religione*, Ro *religiune*. In a number of correspondences there turns out to be a suspicious uniformity, such as the consistent /t/'s in Fr *minute*, Sp/Po/It *minuto*, Ro *minut*, as compared to the regular set /∅/d/d/t/t/ in Old Fr *mu*, Sp/Po *mudo*,

It *muto*, Ro *mut*, which reconstructs as Proto-Romance */t/ (*mūtu-*), and this discrepancy enables the comparatist to sift out many a borrowed item. In general, the greater the uniformity within a set, the more likely that the item is borrowed rather than inherited, since borrowings are lifted unchanged from their lending language while the original words have undergone changes prior to the moment of borrowing—changes therefore not reflected in the borrowed item. In the final analysis, however, the certain identification of items inadmissible to the reconstructed protolexicon depends also on the linguist's knowledge of the external history of the input languages. As for the Romance languages, we are familiar with their entire sociocultural history. A matter of record are, indeed:

- The diffusion of Latin as the dominant spoken and written language throughout the Roman Empire;

- The dissolution of that empire in the wake of invasions by Teutons, Slavs, and other aggressors speaking other languages;

- The multilingual chaos of the Dark Ages, with the Romance vernaculars geared to the expression of a relatively primitive society, their vocabularies consisting largely of concrete and nontechnical terms, while the small number of scholars (mostly clerics) clung to Latin for learned discourse either spoken or written;

- The gradual emergence, in medieval times, of the impoverished Romance tongues as vehicles of literary expression;

- The 15th and 16th century spirit of achievements since known as the Humanistic Renaissance, when the national languages were found less and less adequate to the needs of an increasingly complex culture and life style;

- The attendant pressure to abandon Latin as a means of advanced expression and to raise the vernacular tongues to a status where they themselves would be capable of expounding on all phases of national activity;

- The consequent self-enrichment of the several languages through the borrowing, in wholesale quantities, of abstract and technical terms from their very ancestor, Latin, which in its classical form had an extraordinarily rich lexicon including a highly developed system for word-derivation from basic roots; thus not only were innumerable words borrowed intact, but also new, technical terms for designating wholly new phenomena were created by derivative compounding out of ideological roots. The process of parallel borrowing and creating by the various languages, to meet expressive needs which transcended national and linguistic boundaries, is still going on today and thus it is that Fr *motocyclette,* Sp/Po *motocicleta,* It *motocicletta,* for example, are cognates naming one and the same artifact of modern civilization.

Chapter 1
The reconstruction of Proto-Southwestern Romance: A demonstration

1.0 Introduction. Beyond the foregoing basic assumptions by, and constraints upon, the comparative method, further procedural steps will best be expounded in an actual demonstration of its operation on an organized body of data. For this purpose we select as input to our experimental reconstruction four very closely related Romance languages, namely, Spanish (Sp), Portuguese (Po), Catalan (Ca), and Occitan (Oc).[1] The relevant cognates are stored in a preselected corpus of 475 lexical items, displayed on the even-numbered pages of Appendix 1. The items are numbered consecutively, each is glossed in French/Spanish, and each is written in both its orthographic and its surface-phonemic notation, the latter enclosed between the conventional slashes. Stressed-vowel phonemes are printed with an accent-mark over them only where they occur (i) in the antepenultimate syllable of the word, as, for example, in Item 241, the entry for 'larme/lágrima', or (ii) in the ultimate syllable of the word, as, for example, in Item 11, the Catalan and Occitan entries for 'amour/amor'. Elsewhere, in any of the four languages, the stress may be read as inhering in the penultimate vowel if the word is vowel-final, and in the last vowel if the word is consonant-final; so, for example, in Item 5, stress is to be read as occurring on the second vowel in all four languages.

The corpus is large enough to guarantee the occurrence of all but the rarest correspondence sets a suitable number of times and thus attest to their regularity; a more extensive corpus would only serve to exemplify the highly frequent correspondences cumbersomely often. All items are bare stems,[2] i.e. without inflectional morphemes of plurality, concord, or modality attached to them. The presence of such suffixes introduces the problem of morpho-

1 Reconstruction of Proto-Southwestern Romance

phonemic processes, and such processes becloud the comparative picture if they are not actually irrelevant to it, with each language obeying its own rules for pluralizing a noun or whatever.[3]

In order to evaluate the numerous and partially overlapping correspondences with sufficient perspective, it is necessary to have available the phonemic inventory—and also, ideally, the phonotactics in terms of syllable structure—of each input language.[4] We therefore present, for convenience of reference, a panoramic overview of the four phonemic systems, listing consonant units, consonant clusters, vowel units, and vowel clusters (i.e. diphthongs); beyond this PARADIGMATIC display, attention will be called to one or another SYNTAGMATIC detail only where particularly relevant, as we proceed.

```
C  U   Sp  p b t d      č  k g f   θ s         x m n ñ l ʎ r R y w
O  N   Po  p b t d         k g f v   s z š ž     m n ñ l ʎ r R y w
N  I   Ca  p b t d      č  k g f     s z š ž     m n ñ l ʎ r R y w
S  T   Oc  p b t d c ẓ č ǧ k g f     s z         m n ñ l ʎ r R y w
O
N  C   Sp  pr br tr dr kr gr fr        pl bl kl gl fl
A  L   Po  pr br tr dr kr gr fr vr     pl bl kl gl fl  kw gw
N  U   Ca  pr br tr dr kr gr fr        pl bl kl gl fl  kw gw
T  S   Oc  pr br tr dr kr gr fr        pl bl kl gl fl
S

V  U   Sp  í é    á    ó ú                      i e a o u
O  N   Po  í é ɛ́ á ɔ́ ó ú    ĩ ẽ ã õ ũ           i e a o u    ĩ ẽ ã õ ũ
W  I   Ca  í é ɛ́ á ɔ́ ó ú                        i   ə   u
E  T   Oc  í é ɛ́ á    ó ú ǘ                     i e a o u ü
L
S  C   Sp  yé yá yó yú    wí wé wá wó    ye ya yo yu    wi we wa wo
   L   Po
   U   Ca
   S   Oc  yɛ́
```

A correspondence of phonemes to be characterized itself as phonemic, or 'emic', as we shall say, is a distinctive one which reflects one protophoneme as distinct from all the other reconstructed phonemes. Just as a phoneme may have phonetic, or 'etic', variants (i.e. allophones) in complementary distribution, so also may an emic correspondence have etic variants which differ solely by virtue of being in complementary distribution relative to the correspondences which reflect the surrounding protophonemes.

We shall reconstruct the Proto-Southwestern (PSW) Romance consonants first, and the vowels afterwards, because the distribution of the consonant correspondences is discernible in terms of their position in the syllable, and does not depend to any significant extent on the contiguous vowels. The vowels are to be reconstructed after the consonants precisely because the etic subsets of vowel correspondences vary more in accordance with their consonantal environments, than vice versa.

1.1 The Proto-Southwestern (PSW) consonants. It is useful to keep separate not only the two consonantal positions in the syllable—onset and coda—but also initial vs. noninitial syllables and, among the latter, postcoda vs. postnuclear distribution, the latter either final or nonfinal in the word. Hence we shall be tracking consonant correspondences through a hierarchy of five noncontrasting positions as arranged in the following schema:

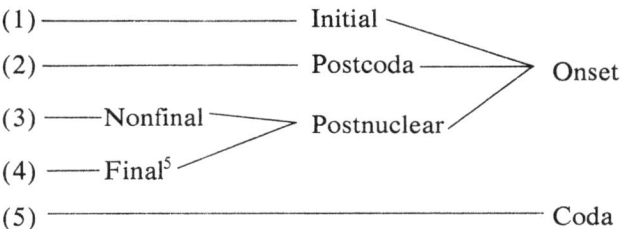

We shall start with the reconstruction of the PSW unit consonants, after which separate correspondences will be adduced for reconstructing certain clusters which, like the units themselves, function as syllable onsets though not as codas.

Displayed first is the relevant input for the PSW obstruents.

A1 Position	(1)	(2)			(3)		(4)	(5)
CEx	323	149	416	53	98	48	none	none
Sp	p-	-p-	-p-	-p-	-p-	-p-		
Po	p-	-p-	-p-	-p-	-p-	-p-		
Ca	p-	-p-	-p	-∅	-p-	-p		
Oc	p-	-p-	-p	-p	-p-	-p		
PSW	*p-		*-p-		*-p-			

The basis of complementary distribution (CD) for Position (Pos.) 2: in Catalan, a stop does not occur word-finally after a nasal coda.

We have no hesitation in reconstructing */p/'s for all three positions and conflating them into a single class of voiceless bilabial stops functioning as syllable onset but not as syllable coda.

8 / 1 Reconstruction of Proto-Southwestern Romance

A2 Position	(1)	(2)	(3)		(4)	(5)
CEx	27	32	68	256	none	none
Sp	b-	-b-	-b-	-b-		
Po	b-	-b-	-b-	-b-		
Ca	b-	-b-	-b-	-p		
Oc	b-	-b-	-b-	-p		
PSW	*b-	*-b-	*-b-			

For the basis of CD in Pos. 3, see A4.

We reconstruct */b's for all three positions and conflate into a single class of voiced bilabial stops functioning as onset but not as coda.

A3 Position	(1)	(2)			(3)				(4)	(5)
CEx	429	369	332	282	208	236	59	251	none	none
Sp	t-	-t-	-t-	-t-	-t-	-č-	-t-	-č-		
Po	t-	-t-	-t-	-t-	-t-	-t-	-t-	-t-		
Ca	t-	-t-	-t	-∅	-t-	-t-	-t	-t		
Oc	t-	-t-	-t	-t	-t-	-č-	-t	-č		
PSW	*t-	*-t-			*-t-					

The basis of CD for Pos. 2: in Catalan, same as A1. The basis for Pos. 3: in Spanish and Occitan, although /t/ and /č/ are separate phonemes in either language, a /č/ occurs in either where the preceding nuclear correspondence is any one of those followed by the set /∅-y-∅-∅/.[6] Thus it is that while in some cases the conditioning factor lies merely in the phonotactic constraints of the particular language itself, in other cases it can only be identified in terms of an entire contiguous correspondence set.

We therefore reconstruct */t/'s for all three positions and conflate into a single class of voiceless alveodental stops functioning as onset but not as coda.

A4 Position	(1)	(2)			(3)		(4)	(5)
CEx	130	92	342	376	51	370	none	none
Sp	d-	-d-	-d-	-d-	-d-	-d-		
Po	d-	-d-	-d-	-d-	-d-	-d-		
Ca	d-	-d-	-t	-∅	-d-	-t		
Oc	d-	-d-	-t	-t	-d-	-t		
PSW	*d-	*-d-			*-d-			

1.1 The Proto-Southwestern (PSW) consonants / 9

The basis of CD for Pos. 2-3, in addition to that given in A1-2 for Ca zero, applies to A2 and A6 as well and is as follows. In Cat. and Occ., no voiced obstruents occur word-finally. That the voiceless /p t k/ in correspondence with Sp/Po voiced /b d g/ are, in fact, morphophonemically (underlyingly) [+voice] is evidenced in verbal paradigms: the consonant in question is voiced in nonfinal position in such forms as the infinitive (Ca /pudé/, Oc /pudé/ 'pouvoir/poder').[7]

We therefore reconstruct */d/'s for all three positions and conflate into a single class of voiced alveodental stops.

A5	Position	(1)	(2)			(3)		(4)	(5)
	CEx	70	144	368	75	42	409	none	none
	Sp	k-	-k-	-k-	-k-	-k-	-k-		
	Po	k-	-k-	-k-	-k-	-k-	-k-		
	Ca	k-	-k-	-k	-∅	-k-	-k		
	Oc	k-	-k-	-k	-k	-k-	-k		
	PSW	*k-	*-k-			*-k-			

Basis of CD for Pos. 2 in Cat.: same as A1 and A3.

We reconstruct */k/'s for all three positions and conflate into a single class of voiceless velar stops functioning as onset but not as coda.

A6	Position	(1)	(2)	(3)		(4)	(5)
	CEx	59	240	428	174	none	none
	Sp	g-	-g-	-g-	-g-		
	Po	g-	-g-	-g-	-g-		
	Ca	g-	-g-	-g-	-k		
	Oc	g-	-g-	-g-	-k		
	PSW	*g-	*-g-	*-g-			

For the basis of CD in Pos. 3, see A4.

We reconstruct */g/'s for all three positions and conflate into a single class of voiced velar stops functioning as onset but not as coda.

A7	Position	(1)	(2)	(3)	(4)	(5)
	CEx	190	145	2	none	none
	Sp	f-	-f-	-f-		
	Po	f-	-f-	-f-		
	Ca	f-	-f-	-f-		
	Oc	f-	-f-	-f-		
	PSW	*f-	*-f-	*-f-		

10 / 1 Reconstruction of Proto-Southwestern Romance

We immediately reconstruct */f/'s for all three positions, as a single class of voiceless labiodental fricatives functioning as onset but not as coda.

A8	Position	(1)	(2)	(3)		(4)	(5)
	CEx	450	23	67		468	none	none
	Sp	b-	-b-	-b-		-b-		
	Po	v-	-v-	-v-		-v-		
	Ca	b-	-b-	-b-		-w		
	Oc	b-	-b-	-b-		-w		
	PSW	*v-	*-v-		*-v-			

What is the basis of CD in Pos. 3?

We reconstruct */v/'s in all three positions, as a single class of voiced labiodental fricatives functioning as onset but not as coda. Our chief motivation for the reconstruction of */v/ as well as */b/ is the complete separation of the labiodental from the bilabial in Port., patterning with the voiceless pair */p/ vs. */f/.[8]

A9	Position	(1)	(2)		(3)		(4)	(5)
	CEx	400	86	166	334	234	280	287
	Sp	s-	-s-	-s-	-s-	-x-	-s	-s-
	Po	s-	-s-	-s-	-s-	-š-	-s	-s-
	Ca	s-	-s-	-s	-s-	-š-	-s	-s-
	Oc	s-	-s-	-s	-s-	-s-	-s	-s-
	PSW	*s-	*-s-		*-s-		*-s	*-s-

The basis for CD in Pos. 3 is analogous to that for the same position in A3: although Sp /s/ and /x/ are separate phonemes, as are Po/Ca /s/ and /š/, the velar or palatal fricative occurs wherever the preceding nuclear correspondence is followed by /∅-y-∅-y/, not yet identified as a coda set, but see A17.

We therefore reconstruct */s/'s in all five positions, as a single class of voiceless alveodental sibilants functioning as either onset or coda.

A10	Position	(1)	(2)		(3)		(4)	(5)
	CEx	77	62	270	58	232	327	none
	Sp	θ-	-θ-	-θ-	-θ-	-θ-	-θ	
	Po	s-	-s-	-s-	-s-	-s-	-s	
	Ca	s-	-s-	-s	-s-	-s	-w	
	Oc	s-	-s-	-s	-s-	-s	-c	
	PSW	*c-	*-c-	*-c-	*-c-	*-c-	*-c	

1.1 The Proto-Southwestern (PSW) consonants / 11

These correspondences differ from those in A9 principally in Span., which consistently shows its phoneme /θ/ in contrast with /s/ in all positions. Pos. 4 shows further differences in both Cat. and Occ. Were it not for this latter evidence we should have to reconstruct this phoneme as */θ/ (why?). If we did so provisionally, only to conflate Pos. 1-3 with Pos. 4 by virtue of their noncontrastive distribution, we would in any case do well to select the protosymbol */c/, as still reflected in Occ. (the Cat. reflex is irrelevant here) and as representative of a hypothetical affricate [tˢ] or [ˡs] rather than a fricative and thus more likely to reflect the older phonetic shape.

In any case we shall reconstruct */c/'s in all four positions, as a single class of voiceless alveodental affricates functioning as onset but not as coda.

A11 Position	(1)	(2)	(3)			(4)	(5)
CEx	none	none	262	29	96	none	none
Sp			-s-	-s-	-s-		
Po			-z-	-ž-	-z-		
Ca			-z-	-z-	-s		
Oc			-z-	-z-	-s		
PSW			*-z-	-z-	-z-		

The bases for CD are analogous to two already appealed to in this position:

• In Cat. and Occ. no voiced obstruents occur word-finally;

• Although Po /z/ and /ž/ are separate phonemes, the palatal fricative occurs when the preceding nuclear correspondence is any one followed by the set /∅-y-∅-y/ (see A17).

We therefore reconstruct */z/ as a voiced alveodental affricate functioning as a postnuclear onset only, but clearly in contrast with */s/ in that one position.

A12 Position	(1)	(2)	(3)		(4)	(5)
CEx	none	316	472	116	none	none
Sp		-θ-	-θ-	-θ-		
Po		-z-	-z-	-z-		
Ca		-z-	-∅-	-w		
Oc		-z-	-z-	-c		
PSW		*-ẓ-	*-ẓ-			

What are the bases of CD in Pos. 3, for Cat. and for Occ.?

12 / 1 Reconstruction of Proto-Southwestern Romance

On the basis of patterning we may reconstruct */ẓ/'s for both positions, conflating to a single class of voiced alveodental affricates functioning as noninitial onset only, but clearly in contrast with */c/ in Pos. 3. We adopt the symbol in view although it is an actual phoneme only in Occ. and does not figure in these correspondences, because it patterns more neatly with the existing /z/ wherever a contrast between the two fails to occur, as well as with the /z/ which alternates morphophonemically with /c/ in Occ. paradigms, e.g. CEx 473 /buc/, plural /buzes/, or 116 /koc/, gerund /kuzént/. Spanish having no voiced fricatives, the sets for both */c/ and */ẓ/ show Sp /θ/. Cat. and Occ., for their part, have /w/ and /c/ respectively, not only for */c/ in final position but also for */ẓ/ where it is final in them and therefore cannot be voiced. Port. shows the voiced/voiceless contrast everywhere except finally, where it cannot have any voiced obstruent; underlyingly, however, it is /z/, as shown, e.g. in /mezes/ as the plural of 280 /mes/, and /vɔzes/ as the plural of 473 /vɔs/. Even so, we cannot reconstruct voiced */ẓ/ in Pos. 4 with no one of the languages showing a voiced phoneme there.

We continue with the reconstruction of the PSW resonants, for which the input data are displayed next.

A13 Position	(1)	(2)		(3)		(4)	(5)	
CEx	264	193	132	11	108	none	440	53
Sp	m-	-m-	-m-	-m-	-m-		-m-	-m-
Po	m-	-m-	-m-	-m-	-m-		-∅-	-∅-
Ca	m-	-m-	-m	-m-	-m		-m-	-∅-
Oc	m-	-m-	-m	-m-	-m		-m-	-m-
PSW	*m-	*-m-		*-m-			*-m-	

Port. has no nasal codas, but where the other languages have them the corresponding zero is always preceded by a nasalized nucleus. Note that Cat. likewise does not fill the coda position in subsets like CEx 53 because, with the nonoccurrence of final stops after nasals, the nasal itself is converted from coda to final onset; cf. also CEx 38 in A14.

We reconstruct */m/'s for all four available positions, and conflate them as a single class of bilabial nasals functioning as both onset and coda.

A14 Position	(1)	(2)		(3)						(4)		(5)	
CEx	295	209	52	165	454	195	261	281	466	41	37	70	341	38
Sp	n-	-n-	-n-	-n-	-n-	-n-	-n-	-n-	-n-	-n-	-n	-n-	-n	-n-
Po	n-	-n-	-n-	-ñ-	-y-	-y-	-w	-∅-	-ñ-	-∅	-∅	-w	-∅-	-∅-
Ca	n-	-n-	-∅	-n-	-n-	-∅	-∅	-n-	-∅	-∅	-∅	-∅	-n-	-∅-
Oc	n-	-n-	-∅	-n-	-n-	-∅	-∅	-n-	-∅	-∅	-∅	-∅	-n-	-n-

1.1 The Proto-Southwestern (PSW) consonants / 13

A14 Position	(1)	(2)	(3)			(4)	(5)
CEx			465		361		
Sp			-ñ-		-ñ-		
Po			-ñ-		-ñ-		
Ca			-ñ-		-ñ		
Oc			-ñ-		-n		
CEx			45		13		
Sp			-ñ-		-ñ-		
Po			-n-		-n-		
Ca			-ñ-		-ñ		
Oc			-n-		-n		
PSW	*n-	*-n-	*-n- ≠	*-ñ- ≠	*-N-	*-n	*-n-

We note at once that the three-way contrast in view here occurs only in Pos. 3. In the other positions, with Cat. and Occ. showing no final nasal in Pos. 2 or 4,[9] and with Port. having no final or coda nasals at all (see A13), the reconstruction of */n/ as a class of alveodental nasals functioning as both onset and coda is preponderantly indicated.

As for the critical Pos. 3, the evidence points as follows: the */n/ is clearly enough indicated where Span. has /n/ throughout; Cat. and Occ. have it consistently except, again, for final zero; Port. has zero except for /ñ/ after /i/, for /y/ after /e/, and for /w/ after /ã/. The reconstruction of */ñ/ as a palatal nasal is equally indicated where the palatal phoneme appears consistently except for Oc /n/ in final position, where this language does not permit its /ñ/ to occur. A nasal somehow different phonemically from either of these two is then indicated where Span. and Cat. show /ñ/ as against their /n/, and Port. and Occ. vice versa. We must posit that whether palatal or nonpalatal, this protonasal differs from either of the other two (or from both) by some unidentifiable feature; hence we adopt the neutral symbol */N/.

A15 Position	(1)	(2)	(3)			(4)	(5)
CEx	242	none	437	288	73	278	216
Sp	l-		-l-	-l-	-l-	-l	-l-
Po	l-		-y-	-∅-	-w	-l	-l-
Ca	ʎ-		-l-	-l-	-l	-l	-l-
Oc	l-		-l-	-l-	-l	-l	-l-
CEx			318	463			
Sp			-x-	-x-			
Po			-ʎ-	-ʎ-			
Ca			-ʎ-	-ʎ			
Oc			-ʎ̇-	-l			
CEx			203	60			
Sp			-ʎ-	-ʎ-			

14 / 1 Reconstruction of Proto-Southwestern Romance

A15	Position	(1)	(2)	(3)			(4)	(5)
	Po			-l-		-l-		
	Ca			-ʎ-		-ʎ		
	Oc			-l-		-l		
	PSW	*l-		*-l- ≠ *-ʎ- ≠ *-L-			*-l	*-l-

There emerge striking parallels between the three-way contrast evidenced here and that existing among the nasals. First, the contrast occurs in Pos. 3 only. Further, for all the other positions the reconstruction of */l/ as a class of alveodental laterals functioning as both onset and coda is eminently indicated, the sole etic variant being the Cat. palatal in Pos. 1. As regards the critical position, the evidence points as follows: the */l/ is indicated where all show it but Port., which has /y ~ ∅ ~ w/ (cf. A14); the */ʎ/ is equally indicated where the palatal phoneme, though matched by the nonpalatal and indeed nonlateral /x/ of Span., elsewhere appears consistently except for Oc /l/ in final position, where this language does not permit /ʎ/ to occur. A lateral somehow different phonemically from either of these two is then indicated where Span. and Cat. show /ʎ/ as against their /l/, and Port. and Occ. vice versa. Supported by these various parallels with the nasal situation, we may again posit that whether palatal or nonpalatal, this reconstructible lateral differs from either of the others (or from both) by some unidentifiable feature; hence we adopt the noncommittal symbol */L/.

A16	Position	(1)	(2)	(3)			(4)		(5)
	CEx		none	269	66	428	273	407	268
	Sp			-r-	-r-	-r-	-r	-r	-r-
	Po			-r-	-r-	-r-	-r	-r	-r-
	Ca			-r-	-r	-∅	-r	-∅	-r-
	Oc			-r-	-r	-∅	-r	-∅	-r-
	CEx		398	56	100				
	Sp		R-	-R-	-R-				
	Po		R-	-R-	-R-				
	Ca		R-	-R-	-R-				
	Oc		R-	-R-	-r				
			*R-	*-r- ≠ *-R-			*-r		*-r-

The basis of CD for Pos. 3-4 in Cat. and Occ.: the final /r/ is present when the word contains but one preceding syllable, but absent if it contains more than one.

Here it is to be noted that the contrasts occur in Pos. 3 only,[10] which is the case with the nasals and laterals reconstructed above. As to the other positions, however, whereas both */n/ and */l/ fill Pos. 1 and 4-5 alike, here the */r/ and the */R/ stand in noncontrastive distribution: the former in Pos. 4-5 but the latter in Pos. 1.[11]

We of course reconstruct two separate phonemes: */r/ as a class of flap vibrants functioning as both onset and coda, and */R/ as a class of trill vibrants functioning as onset only, but contrasting with the flap in Pos. 3 and differentiated from it by a tense/lax feature.

A17 Position	(1)	(2)	(3)			(4)	(5)			
CEx	121	none	4	102	260	394	115	8	159	197
Sp	y-		-y-	-∅-	-y-	-y	-∅-	-∅-	-∅-	-∅-
Po	ž-		-ž-	-y-	-y-	-y	-y-	-y-	-y-	-∅-
Ca	ž-		-ž-	-ž-	-č	-y	-y-	-∅-	-∅-	-y-
Oc	ǧ-		-ǧ-	-ǧ-	-y	-y	-∅-	-y-	-∅-	-∅-
PSW	*y-		*-y-			*-y	*-y-			

Evidence for the reconstruction of this consonant is tenuous at best, the eight items supporting it for Pos. 1 and 3 (see also CEx 202, 204, 227, 388) being offset by four in which the Span. phoneme is not /y/ but rather /x/ (CEx 205, 225-6, 229), with no observable basis for CD. In Pos. 3, Po /ž/ precedes a stressed nucleus while /y/ follows one; in Cat. it is final /č/ rather than the expected /š/ that regularly alternates morphophonemically with nonfinal /ž/, as in /Rač/$_{388}$, plural /Ražus/, or the adjective /Roč/ 'rouge/rojo', fem. sg. /Roža/. In Pos. 4-5, the evidence is clearer, with the /y/ in CD with zero relative to the preceding nuclear correspondence or, in Occ., a following /č/.

Thus, despite the preponderance of palatal obstruents in Pos. 1 and 3, we shall do well to posit a protoresonant; evidence is lacking for a voiceless correlate of yet another obstruent. We therefore may fairly reconstruct a */y/ (rather than a */ž/ or a */ǧ/) as a class of palatal resonants functioning as initial or postnuclear onset, and as coda.

In our corpus the consonant phoneme /w/ turns up only in certain onset clusters, and as a coda in a few Port. and Occ. items where it is matched by zero in Span. and Cat. In view of these rather severe constraints on its distribution, the few correspondences involving the /w/ need not be treated separately but rather as elements of consonantal and vocalic clusters; see A22, B7, and B12.

We deal next, then, with consonant clusters composed of obstruent plus liquid or glide—clusters which occur only in Pos. 1-3.

1 Reconstruction of Proto-Southwestern Romance

A18 Position	(1)	(2)	(3)	(1)	(2)	(3)
CEx	371	440	19	44	none	69
Sp	pr-	-pr-	-pr-	br-		-br-
Po	pr-	-pr-	-pr-	br-		-br-
Ca	pr-	-pr-	-pr-	br-		-br-
Oc	pr-	-pr-	-pr-	br-		-br-
PSW	*pr-	*-pr-	*-pr-	*br-		*-br-

We reconstruct the pair of bilabial-stop-plus-vibrant onset clusters */pr/ and */br/, contrasting as to voice in the obstruent component.

A19 Position	(1)	(2)	(3)	(1)	(2)	(3)
CEx	444	88	379	none	none	347
Sp	tr-	-tr-	-tr-			-dr-
Po	tr-	-tr-	-tr-			-dr-
Ca	tr-	-tr-	-tr-			-dr-
Oc	tr-	-tr-	-tr-			-yr-
PSW	*tr-	*-tr-	*-tr-			*-dr-

We need not hesitate to reconstruct the pair of alveodental-stop-plus-vibrant onset clusters */tr/ and */dr/, contrasting as to voice in the obstruent component, even with the voiced examples lacking in Pos. 1-2 and with Oc showing coda /y/ instead of the stop component in Pos. 3.

A20 Position	(1)	(2)	(3)	(1)	(2)	(3)
CEx	111	143	none	210	none	303
Sp	kr-	-kr-		gr-		-gr-
Po	kr-	-kr-		gr-		-gr-
Ca	kr-	-kr-		gr-		-gr-
Oc	kr-	-kr-		gr-		-gr-
PSW	*kr-	*-kr-		*gr-		*-gr-

We reconstruct the pair of velar-stop-plus-vibrant onset clusters */kr/ and */gr/, contrasting as to voice in the obstruent component.

A21 Position	(1)	(2)	(3)
CEx	195	none	none
Sp	fr-		
Po	fr-		
Ca	fr-		

1.1 The Proto-Southwestern (PSW) consonants / 17

A21	Position	(1)	(2)	(3)
	Oc	fr-		
	PSW	*fr-		

We are able to reconstruct the voiceless labiodental-fricative-plus-vibrant onset cluster */fr/, but the corpus furnishes no evidence for a voiced correlate.

A22	Position	(1)	(2)	(3)	(1)	(2)	(3)
	CEx	380	none	none	201	238	none
	Sp	kw-			gw-	-gw-	
	Po	kw-			gw-	-gw-	
	Ca	kw-			gw-	-gw-	
	Oc	k-			g-	-g-	
	PSW	*kw-			*gw-	*-gw-	

There is no problem in reconstructing the pair of velar-stop-plus-back-glide onset clusters */kw/ and */gw/, contrasting as to voice in the obstruent component, even though Occ. consistently lacks the glide element.

It should now be noted that clusters of obstruent-plus-lateral are not reconstructible for PSW, despite the regular occurrence of /pl bl kl gl fl/ in the Cat. and Occ. cognate items of, e.g., CEx 12, 38, 78, 146, 184, 206, 266, 315 or 348. The reason for the impossibility is that Span. and Port. do not show enough uniformity to enable us to set up viable correspondences. Thus:

● Where Cat. and Occ. have /pl/, Span. in Pos. 1 shows now /pl/ and now /ʎ/ before the same vowel (e.g. CEx 348, 349), and in Pos. 2 /č/ (CEx 12);

● Where Cat. and Occ. have /kl/, Span. shows /kl/ in one item (CEx 78) but again /ʎ/ elsewhere;

● Where Cat. and Occ. have /fl/, Span. in Pos. 1 shows /fl/ in one item (CEx 184) and /ʎ/ in one (CEx 183); in Pos. 2, again /č/ (CEx 146);

● In the lone item where Cat. and Occ. have /bl/ (CEx 38), Span. also has it, but in the two items where they have /gl/ (CEx 206, 315), Span. has something else.

Port., showing no obstruent-plus-lateral clusters at all—although it has them in its phonemic inventory—is just as inconsistent and agrees only in part with Span.

18 / 1 Reconstruction of Proto-Southwestern Romance

1.2 The Proto-Southwestern vowels. For clarity and simplicity of method, we shall do well to reconstruct the stressed vowels and the unstressed vowels separately, although of course ultimately it will be feasible to conflate the two, since they are merely in CD relative to the presence/absence of the word-stress prosodeme.

We begin with the stressed vowels: first the units, then certain diphthongs which, like the unit phonemes, function as syllabic nuclei. In all correspondence sets the stressed vowel is either penultimate, i.e. the nucleus of the next-to-last syllable of the word, or ultimate, i.e. standing in the final (or only) syllable of the word. In many a subset, actually, the stressed vowel is penultimate in Spanish and/or Port., but ultimate in Cat. and/or Occ. In any case, this particular complementation offers no etic variations. Of some interest, on the other hand, is the CD between so-called 'open' and 'closed' syllables—open syllables being defined as containing no coda consonant before the following (major or minor) syllable. Thus, for example, the /á/ in Sp /está/ or /estado/ or /estar/ stands in an open syllable, while in /estando/ it is in a syllable closed by the coda /n/. We present the data in terms of open (1) vs. closed (2) syllable position.

B1	Position	(1)			(2)		(1)	(2)
	CEx	74	65	182	476	75	259	none
	Sp	-i-	-i-	-i-	-i-	-i-	-u-	
	Po	-i-	-i-	-ĩ	-i-	-ĩ-	-u-	
	Ca	-i-	-i	-i	-i-	-i-	-u-	
	Oc	-i-	-i	-i	-i-	-i-	-ü-	
	PSW	*-i-			*-i-		*-u-	

The only CD in the etic sets is that of the Port. oral and nasal vowels. Not only in these, but indeed in all sets for stressed unit vowels, Port. shows phonemically nasalized vowels according to the following distribution chart. Representing the 'norm' is the nonnasalized Port. vowel which appears regularly in the prevalent, unconditioned subsets; the nasalized vowels vary according to four environments which are most efficiently characterized in terms of their manifestation in Span. A blank signifies that the vowel in view does not vary from the norm, while a parenthesis means that the set representing that vowel does not occur at all in the particular environment.

	Norm:		i	u	e	ɛ	ɔ	o	a
		Nasal coda	ĩ	ũ	ẽ	ẽ	õ	õ	ã
Envt.		Final /-n(e)/	ĩ	ũ	( )	ẽ	( )	ã	ã
in Sp:		Final /-no/		ũ		( )	õ	( )	ã
		Final /-na/				( )	( )		ã

1.2 The Proto-Southwestern vowels

From the foregoing sets we easily reconstruct PSW */i/ and */ú/, a pair of high vowels contrasting as to the feature of backness.

B2 Position	(1)				(2)		
CEx	385	48	40	276	194	338	445
Sp	-e	-e-	-e-	-e-	-e-	-e-	-e-
Po	-e	-e-	-e-	-ɛ-	-e-	-ɛ-	-ẽ-
Ca	-ɛ	-ɛ-	-e-	-ɛ-	-ɛ-	-ɛ-	-ɛ-
Oc	-e	-e-	-e-	-e-	-e-	-e-	-e-
PSW	*-e-				*-e-		

The prevalent, unconditioned subset for the reconstruction of */é/ is that of CEx 48 or 385. Spanish and Occitan consistently show /é/ as against Sp /yé/, Oc /ɛ́/, but Catalan exhibits the expected /é/ only in the limited environment of a following palatal, as in CEx 40 or 252. As for Portuguese, it has its lower /ɛ/ in verbs, unless the stressed stem-vowel is nasalized under the conditions set forth in B1. In so-called '-er verbs' this (nonnasal) /ɛ/ alternates in vowel harmony with the expected /é/—cf. (for CEx 276) the forms /metu/, /meta/ (Sp /meto/, /meta/) as against /mɛte/; in '-ar verbs' there is no such alternation—cf. (for CEx 338) /pɛsku/, pɛske/ (Sp /pesko/, /peske/) as well as /pɛska/.

B3 Position	(1)				(2)	
CEx	256	407	388	96	287	395
Sp	-o-	-o-	-o-	-o-	-o-	-o-
Po	-o-	-o-	-ã-	-ɔ-	-o-	-õ-
Ca	-o-	-o	-o	-o-	-o-	-o-
Oc	-u-	-u	-u	-u-	-u-	-u-
PSW	*-o-				*-o-	

The prevalent, unconditioned subset for PSW */ó/ is that of CEx 256, with Catalan in this case of the back vowel conforming with, rather than deviating from, Span. and Port., and with Occ. showing /ú/ in contrast to its nonback /ǘ/ as in the correspondence for PSW */ú/. Here again, Port. has its lower /ɔ/ in verbs where the stressed stem vowel is not nasalized; in '-er verbs' this /ɔ/ alternates with the expected /ó/—cf. (for CEx 96) /kózu/, /kóza/ (Sp /kóso/, /kósa/) as against /kɔze/; in '-ar verbs' there is no alternation.

Thus in B2-3 we have the evidence for the reconstruction of PSW */é/ and */ó/, a pair of higher-mid vowels contrasting with respect to backness.

20 / 1 Reconstruction of Proto-Southwestern Romance

B4 Position	(1)						(2)	
CEx	230	413	73	37	463	347	342	47
Sp	ye-	-i-	-ye-	-ye-	-ye-	-ye-	-ye-	-ye-
Po	ɛ-	-ɛ-	-ɛ-	-ẽ	-ɛ-	-ɛ-	-ɛ-	-ẽ-
Ca	e-	-e-	-ɛ-	-e	-e-	-e-	-ɛ-	-e-
Oc	ɛ-	-ɛ-	-ɛ-	-e	-yɛ-	-ɛy-	-ɛ-	-e-
PSW	*-ɛ-						*-ɛ-	

The prevalent, unconditioned subset for the reconstruction of */ɛ/ is that of CEx 230 or 301, with each language manifesting a contrast with its reflex of the higher-mid, nonback vowel. All four languages nevertheless deviate from the norm in one or another etic subset, thus:

• Spanish shows simple /i/ uniquely before its onset /ʎ/, while both Span. and Port. have /é/ before the coda correspondence /∅-y-∅-∅/ of A17;

• Catalan has its lower-mid /ɛ/ before a following liquid other than /ʎ/, or other than coda /r/ plus nonlabial onset—environments in which /é/ does not occur (CEx 73, 342), and /i/ before the A17 coda correspondence.

• Occitan has its higher-mid /é/ final before the onset correspondence /n-∅-∅-∅/ and the coda correspondence /n-∅-n-n/ of A14; it has the on-glide diphthong /yɛ́/ before /l/ in the onset correspondence /x-ʎ-ʎ-l/ of A15, as well as before the A17 coda correspondence.

B5 Position	(1)					(2)	
CEx	116	298	41	175	223	94	367
Sp	-we-	-we-	-we-	-o-	-o-	-we-	-we-
Po	-ɔ-	-o-	-õ-	-ɔ-	-o-	-ɔ-	-õ-
Ca	-ɔ-	-ɔ-	-ɔ-	-u-	-u-	-ɔ-	-ɔ-
Oc	-o-	-o-	-u-	-ɛ-	-ɛ-	-o-	-u-
PSW	*-ɔ-					*-ɔ-	

The prevalent, unconditioned subset for PSW */ɔ́/ is that of CEx 116, with again each language manifesting a contrast with its reflex of the higher-mid back vowel. But again, too, all four languages deviate from the norm in one or another etic subset, thus:

• Span. shows /ó/ before its onset /x/ and before the A17 coda correspondence;

1.2 The Proto-Southwestern vowels / 21

• Port. has its higher /ó/ in many nouns and adjectives with final /-u/, where however it stands in morphophonemic alternation with the expected /ɔ́/ in the plural and/or feminine forms—cf. (for CEx 310, 319) the noun plurals /ɔsus/, /ɔvus/, and the remaining forms of the adjective CEx 298: /nɔvus/, /nɔva/, /nɔvas/; also before the A17 coda correspondence;

• Cat. has the high vowel /ú/ before its /ʎ/ in the onset correspondence /x-ʎ-ʎ-ʎ/, and before the A17 coda correspondence;

• Occ. has its high vowel /ú/ final before the onset correspondence /n-∅-∅-∅/ and the coda correspondence /n-∅-n-n/ of A14; it has its nonback vowel /ɛ/ before a palatal onset.

Thus in B4-5 we have the evidence for the reconstruction of PSW */ɛ́/ and /ɔ́/, a pair of lower-mid vowels contrasting with respect to backness.

B6 Position		(1)			(2)	
CEx	158	69	233	53	378	8
Sp	-a	-a-	-a-	-a-	-a-	-e-
Po	-a	-a-	-ã	-a-	-ã-	-e-
Ca	-a	-a-	-a-	-a-	-a-	-e-
Oc	-a	-a-	-a-	-a-	-a-	-a-
PSW	*-a	*-a-		*-a-		

From the foregoing subsets there is no problem whatsoever in reconstructing PSW */á/, a low central vowel. We need only note that although all but Occ. have /é/ before the A17 coda correspondence, this subset contrasts with those for all the other vowels in that same environment.

There remains the reconstruction of one stressed diphthong, which occurs in an open syllable only, with the glide /w/ occupying the coda position. The relevant correspondences:

B7 CEx	317	71
Sp	o-	-o-
Po	ow-	-ow-
Ca	ɔ-	-ɔ-
Oc	aw-	-aw-
PSW	*aw	

We reconstruct this diphthong with a low syllabic vowel despite the nonlow, back vowels appearing in all the languages except Occ. It is precisely Occ. that shows its /á/ in the nucleus-plus-coda sequence /e-ey-e-ay/, and the patterning here is decidedly relevant. The sequence in view *could* be reconstructed as a diphthong, namely */áy/, although to do so would entail reconstructing also the contrasting diphthongs */éy/, */ɛ́y/, */ɔ́y/ and */úy/, an uneconomical solution since /y/ as a unit phoneme is available for the coda as well as the onset function; on the other hand, /w/ appears after no other vowel correspondence and no economy is involved in making */w/ a coda rather than */áw/ a diphthong.

We come now to the reconstruction of the PSW unstressed nuclei: five vowel units and a marginal diphthong. In all correspondences the unstressed vowel is either (1) pretonic in open syllable, (2) pretonic in closed syllable, or (3) posttonic and final. The data are presented in terms of these three subset positions.

B8	Position	(1)	(2)	(3)	(1)	(2)	(3)
	CEx	none	76	none	35	none	none
	Sp		-i-		-u-		
	Po		-ĩ-		-u-		
	Ca		-i-		-u-		
	Oc		-i-		-u-		
	PSW		*-i-		*-u-		

Scanty though the evidence is, we may safely reconstruct the pair */i/ and */u/, contrasting as to backness and occurring pretonic only.

B9	Position	(1)			(2)		(3)				
	CEx	3	410	151	147	123	316	441	33	421	163
	Sp	e-	-e-	e-	e-	-e-	-e	-e	-e	-∅	-e
	Po	i-	-e-	e-	ẽ-	-e-	-e	-e	-e	-e	-y
	Ca	ə-	-ə-	ə-	ə-	-ə-	-ə	-ə	-∅	-∅	-∅
	Oc	e-	-e-	e-	e-	-e-	-e	-∅	-∅	-∅	-∅
	PSW	*e-	*-e-	*e-	*-e-				*-e			

The unconditioned subset for the reconstruction of any unstressed vowel is found regularly in Pos. 1-2. Thus, here, it is that of CEx 410 or 123, the Catalan deviation being due to the fact that this language has but three unstressed vowel phonemes, namely, /i u ə/. In Pos. 1 Port. has /i/ word-initially (CEx 3). In Pos. 3:

• Cat. and Occ. show no final vowel after an onset which can itself occur word-final, i.e. as a minor syllable (and note the adjusted onset of Occ. in CEx 441);

• Span. shows no final vowel uniquely after /d/;

1.2 The Proto-Southwestern vowels / 23

• Port. reflects the final vowel throughout, though as the glide consonant /y/ wherever that language has a zero in the preceding onset correspondence (CEx 163).

We have thus reconstructed the mid, nonback unstressed PSW vowel */e/.

B10	Position	(1)	(2)			(3)			
	CEx	101	193	86	379	172	64	265
	Sp	-o-	o-	-o-	-o	-o	-o	-o
	Po	-o-	-o-	-õ-	-u	-u	-u	-w
	Ca	-u-	-u-	-u-	-ə	-u	-∅	-∅
	Oc	-u-	-u-	-u-	-e	-e	-∅	-∅
	PSW	*-o-	*-o-			*-o			

The unconditioned subset here is that of CEx 101 or 193. Again in Pos. 3:

• Cat. and Occ. show no final vowel after an onset which can occur word-final, and thus fail to contrast with the similar subsets for PSW */e/;

• Span. and Port. reflect the final vowel throughout, though Port. has it as the glide /w/ where that language has zero in the preceding onset correspondence (CEx 265).

The assignment of these etic subsets to PSW unstressed */o/ rather than */u/ is justified by three pieces of evidence:

• The */o/ is a mid vowel like its counterpart */e/, in patterned contrast with the latter as regards backness;

• Pretonically, Span. and Port. permit both /o/ and /u/ in their systems, while Cat. and Occ. do not permit /o/;

• Posttonically, Span. permits both /o/ and /u/ (though there are no items such as *tribu* in the corpus), while Port. and Cat. do not permit /o/ and Occ. manifests its /o/ in a different emic set, namely, that for unstressed */a/; thus all but Span. are indeterminate in affecting the assignment, and the Span. high/mid contrast tips the balance in favor of */o/.

B11	Position	(1)		(2)			(3)		(3)
	CEx	21	402	61	54	236	180	340	318
	Sp	a-	-a-	-a-	-a-	-e-	-a	-a	o-
	Po	a-	-a-	-a-	-ã-	-ey-	-a	-∅	o-

B11 Position	(1)		(2)			(3)		(3)
Ca	ə-	-ə-	-ə-	-ə-	-ə-	-ə	-ə	u-
Oc	a-	-a-	-a-	-a-	-a-	-o	-o	aw-
PSW	*a-	*-a-		*-a-		*-a-		*aw-

The unconditioned subset for the reconstruction of unstressed */a/ is that of CEx 21 or 61, with Occ. showing /o/ instead of the expected /a/ in Pos. 3, where in fact /a/ does not occur in the system of the language. Cat. regularly shows the same /ə/ as in the set for */e/, for the reason given in B9. Span. and Port. have /e/ before the coda correspondence of A17. Port. has zero in Pos. 3 wherever the stressed vowel is also low and there is zero in the preceding onset correspondence.

As for the diphthong reconstructible as */aw/, there is but one item in the corpus, but despite the lack of /w/ in Port., it is supported by the correspondence for the stressed diphthong */áw/ of B7.

1.3 Recapitulation of Proto-Southwestern phonology.

- Inventory of the reconstructed unit phonemes, in phonological space.

	F	C	B		Lb	Al	PV	?
H	i		u	Oc	p/b	t/d	k/g	
HM	e		o	Af		c/ẓ		
LM	ε		ɔ	Fc	f/v	s/z		
L		a		Na	m	n	ñ	N
				Lt		l	ʎ	L
				Vi		r		R
				SC			y	

KEY. H: high, HM: higher mid, LM: lower mid, L: low, F: front, C: center, B: back, Oc: occlusive, Af: affricate, Fc: fricative, N: nasal, Lt: lateral, Vi: vibrant, SC: semiconsonant, Lb: labial, Al: alveodental, PV: palatovelar.

- Inventory of the unit phonemes, diphthongs, and clusters according to function in syllable structure.

Nuclei: i e ε a ɔ o u   aw
Onsets: p b t d c ẓ k g f v s z m n ñ N l ʎ L r R y   pr br tr dr kr gr fr
                                                       kw gw

Codas: s m n l r

1.4 Reconstruction of the corpus in Proto-Southwestern / 25

Among the codas, the nasals /m/ and /n/ are not in contrast, but for the mere sake of visual familiarity we may continue to write, redundantly, /m/ before labial onsets and /n/ elsewhere.

1.4 Reconstruction of the corpus in Proto-Southwestern. The foregoing stock of protophonemes furnishes us the input data for taking the next steps and reconstructing also the full PSW forms of most, though by no means all, of the items in the corpus. The right-most column on the even-numbered pages of the corpus provides blank spaces in which the reconstructed words may be entered on the record. Many of these blanks are blocked with an interrogation mark (?) (e.g. CEx 9); some are preceded by an asterisk (*) (e.g. CEx 30), others by a dagger (†) (e.g., CEx 49), others by the sign plus/minus (±) (e.g. CEx 115); still other blanks are duplicated for double entries (e.g. CEx 16). Blanks not singled out in any of these several ways stand ready to be filled in, for the items so marked manifest only those regular correspondences which were taken account of in our reconstruction of the protophonemes. Thus for CEx 1 we may enter (and have, in fact, done so) the proper Proto-SWR form */kompra/.

First step. You may now proceed to fill in the untagged blanks.

The variously tagged blanks identify, then, the RESIDUE of items which fail to manifest, within each, one or more of the regular correspondences which constituted our reconstructive input.[12] This residue breaks down into several CATEGORIES, the identification of which will put us in a position to fill in all but the questioned blanks.

1.4.1 Residual categories. Category 1. This first residual category comprises those asterisked items in which one (or, marginally, two) of the languages simply has no cognate word in its lexicon. Thus, for instance, although Cat. lacks a cognate for CEx 30, the partial sets of vocalic and consonantal correspondences in all positions in all syllables point unequivocally toward a protoform */eskova/; likewise, although Occ. lacks the cognate for CEx 228, all else points obviously enough to */dia/.

Second step. You may proceed to fill in PSW forms for the asterisked items constituting Category 1, viz. CExs 31, 254, 258, 365, 381, 383, 386, 396, 435, 459.

Category 2. This second residual category comprises those items in which one (but not more than one) of the consonantal or vocalic correspondences is anomalous—i.e., it fails to match any of the full sets we have established as regular and hence constituting proper input to our reconstructions, because one (but not more than one) of the languages exhibits a deviation that belongs to no other established correspondence. Thus, for instance, in CEx 54, where all but Span. conform to the prevalent subset for the stressed vowel */ó/, Span. shows the diphthong /yó/, a nucleus which has no counterpart in the other languages and therefore fits no one of our established correspondences. In such a case we may safely reconstruct according to the majority, thus arriving at */kancon/ and relegating Sp *canción* to a separate 'on-hold' list for future reference; the reconstruction of protolanguages higher up in the *Stammbaum* may or may not help us to account for the form which, in terms of the data in hand, is simply aberrant.

Third step. You may now proceed to fill in PSW forms for the daggered items making up Category 2, viz. CExs 49, 54, 56, 310, 408, 467.[13]

Category 3. This third residual category comprises numerous items in which the vowel correspondences are regular, but with respect to any one of the consonant correspondence sets which they manifest, there is an irregular split between two emic sets—a split evidenced by three languages against one, or by two against two. Thus, for instance, in Pos. 4 of CEx 139, a 3/1 split has all but Port. showing the lateral for PSW */l/, while Po /l/ reflects rather PSW */L/. Since there is no ground for assigning priority, or dominance, to one partial set against the other, we can only posit alternative reconstructions of competing forms, or doublets as they are often termed, i.e. */eskala/ and */eskaLa/, entering both forms in the double blank provided. Similarly, in Pos. 4 of CEx 150, a 2/2 split finds Span. and Port. showing the /d-d/ for */d/, while Cat. and Occ. have the /z-z/ of the set for */z/; again we must posit competing doublets and record both */espada/ and */espaza/.[14]

Fourth step. You may now go on to reconstruct PSW doublets for the following CExs equipped with double blanks: 16, 39, 129, 140, 214, 289, 339, 360, 375, 404, 447,[15] 453.

Category 4. This fourth residual category is merely the obverse of Category 3: it comprises those items in which the consonant correspondences are regular, but with respect to any one of the vowel correspondence sets which they manifest, there is an irregular 3/1 or 2/2 split between two emic sets. Thus, for instance, in the stressed position of CEx 25, a 3/1 split has all but Occ. showing the lower-mid vowel for PSW */ɛ/, while Occ. /é/ reflects rather PSW */é/; thus we must posit doublets and enter both */cɛgo/ and */cego/. Similarly, in the pretonic vowel position of CEx 321, a 2/2 split finds Span. and Port. showing the /a-a/ of the set for */a/, while Cat. and Occ. have the /u-u/ of the set associated with */o/; hence we enter both */abɛrto/ and */obɛrto/.

Fifth step. You may now reconstruct the PSW doublets for the following CExs, also equipped with double spaces: 76, 103, 106, 111, 128, 142, 148, 153, 155, 186, 196, 202, 207, 213, 219, 238, 239, 304, 311, 322, 377, 390, 411, 415, 424, 426, 439, 470, 472.

Category 5. This fifth residual category is essentially like Categories 3 and 4. It involves items in which the split is between a set of consonants and null, or between a set of vowels and null—i.e., a plus-or-minus configuration. For example, in CEx 7, the Occ. coda /y/ is a plus, while the Sp/Po/Ca zero coda is a minus; here we may reconstruct with the protophoneme in question parenthesized, meaning 'read it with or without, i.e. plus or minus', e.g. */a(y)ma/. A very sizeable number of such cases entail a Pos. 1 zero in Span. vs. the /f-f-f/ associated with */f/ in the other three, e.g. CEx 176 */(f)ava/.

Sixth step. You may proceed to enter a single form embodying a parenthesized protophoneme in the blanks marked plus/minus (±), that is to say CExs 115, 164, 165, 168, 171, 172, 175, 177, 179, 180, 181, 191, 192, 193, 199, 221, 249, 253, 257, 272, 306, 313, 314, 475.

Category 6. The items in this sixth residual category contain two correspondence splits each, interdependent or not, as the case may be. For example, in CEx 24, a 2/2 split has Span. and Port. showing the stressed-vowel partial set /ó-ów/ followed by coda zero, as against the partial /á-á/ with coda /1-1/ in Cat. and Occ.; we may reconstruct the doublets */awtro/ and */altro/. Again, CEx 187 has the plus-or-minus split recorded as */(f)/, as well as the nasal correspondence for */n/ in Span, Cat., and Occ. as against the Port. /ɲ/ reflecting */N/: we thus enter */(f)eno/ and */(f)eNo/. Since such multiple splits are difficult at first to disentangle, all the competing forms in Category 6 have already been entered in the corpus for you.

Category 7. This final residual category is marked off by blanks already containing a (?) as their only practicable entry at the present stage of our operation. The majority of these items contain more than two split correspondences, one member of which may not belong to any established set. In a few cases (such as CEx 63, 80, 93, 346, 422), there may be only one split correspondence but one of the partials being manifested is unidentifiable and hence unassignable to any protoform—e.g. in CEx 63 it is impossible to tell whether the form competing with */kalvo/, as reflected by Occ., should be reconstructed as */kalveto/, or */kalvete/, or */kalvedo/, or */kalvede/.

There is nothing whatever to be done toward reconstructing the PSW forms for the questioned items. It is only the reconstruction of higher protolanguages—such as Proto-Western or Proto-Italo-Western, or Proto-Romance itself—that will enable us to effect what is called 'inverse reconstruction' and capture many of the elusive PSW items by executing, as it were, a pincers movement upon them through bringing to bear the evidence not alone of the four input languages, ineffectual by itself, but also that of the cognate languages French, Italian, Roumanian, and Sardinian. You will see in due course how this is to be achieved, as a by-product of further upward reconstruction.

Notes for Chapter 1

1. Neither Catalan nor Occitan, of course, is an official national language, but each has a standard dialect from which our samples are drawn: the Catalan of Barcelona and the Occitan of Montpellier and vicinity.

2. For nouns this means simply the 'singular' form, for adjectives the 'masculine singular', and for verbs the 'imperative singular'. (If the particular verb lacks imperative forms, or if the imperative singular is 'irregular', what is given is the 'present indicative' with no person/number suffix, e.g. Sp *puede* of *poder, viene* (rather than *ven*) of *venir.*)

3. For example, Sp /kasa/ and It /kasa/ as bare stems are comparable, but Sp /kasas/ and It /kase/ as plurals are not; the process of pluralization in Romance is reconstructible only with certain information not furnished by the correspondences.

4. As an extremely simple illustration of this requirement: the stressed-vowel correspondence /wé-ɔ́-ɔ́-ó/ can only be handled with the knowledge that, while Port. and Cat. have both an /ɔ/ and an /o/, neither Span. nor Occ. has an /ɔ/ in its stock of phonemes.

5. We recall that a word-final consonant is classed as the onset of a minor syllable with zero nucleus, rather than as a coda—which occurs therefore in a nonfinal syllable only. Where Span. and Port. show Pos. 3 and Cat./Occ. Pos. 4, we assign this straddling correspondence to Pos. 3 because the word-final nucleus is reconstructible for PSW just as when all four languages manifest one.

6. Also in Occ., the standard dialect admits equally /č/ or /(y)t/ in these correspondences (e.g. 251 /lyεč/ ~ /lyεyt/). See Set A17.

7. Cf. also two-gender paradigms with feminines: 256 Ca /ʎop : ʎobə/, Oc /lup : lubo/; 291 Ca /mut : mudə/, Oc /müt : müdo/; 240 Ca /ʎark : ʎargə/, Oc /lark : largo/.

8. The distinction is supported by the fact that Span. has no voiced fricative phonemes at all—[β δ γ] being mere allophones of the 'stops' /b d g/—while Cat. and Occ. have no /v/ although both facilitate the internal reconstruction of a phoneme other than */b/ by showing two separate morphophonemic alternations in paradigms involving their /b/—namely, /b/ ~ /p/ precisely where Port. shows /b/, e.g. Ca /ʎobə/ and Oc /lubo/ as against /ʎop/ and /lup/ (see A4 and note 7), in contrast to /v/, e.g. the fem. adjective /bibə/ in Cat. and /bibo/ in Occ., as against the masc. /biw/ in both.

9. Final /n/ does occur in Cat. and Occ., but in other correspondences. Where the nasal is coda /n/ in Span./Port. and in the reconstruction, /n/ may be final in Cat. and/or Occ.; in correspondences indicating other protonasals, i.e. */ñ/ or */N/, Occ. also shows final /n/. Wherever, on the evidence of Span. and Port., /n/ reconstructs as onset before any vowel other than /a/ or before no vowel (i.e. absolute-final in a minor syllable), Cat./Occ. show zero. In nominal or adjectival paradigms, however, an /n/ does indeed appear before a plural or a fem. suffix, thus manifesting a /∅ ~ n/ alternation as in, for example, Ca/Oc /pa/, plu. /pans/, or /sa/, masc. plu. /sans/ and fem. sing. /sanə/ in Cat., /sano/ in Occ.

10. Note that even in this position the /R/ does not occur word-finally in Cat. or Occ., as might be expected in CEx 100; it is either supported by a final vowel (Cat.) or replaced by /r/ (Occ.).

11. There are words in all four languages which have /R/ and /l/ as well as /n/ (see A14) in Pos. 2, but not in items available for comparison.

12. In terms of comparative theory, then, they contribute to modifying the basic principle of the immutability of the laws of sound change.

13. The list of 'on-hold' items referred to above will be accounted for one by one in Part Two.

14. In some instances the reflex in one or another language conforms to *either* of the two emic sets manifested, as in CEx 39, where Po /b/ in Pos. 3 clearly reflects */b/, while Ca/Oc /w-w/ reflect */v/, but Sp /b/ typifies either PSW consonant; in any case, we must posit doublets.

15. Even though this item is missing from Occ., it reconstructs plausibly with the two competing onsets of Pos. 1.

Chapter 2
The reconstruction of Proto-Romance: A guided exercise

2.0 Introduction. The foregoing reconstruction of Proto-Southwestern Romance was undertaken with two aims in view:

- to provide a pedagogical demonstration of the comparative method,

- to furnish a portion of the input data in order that you may apply the method on your own initiative, aiming at a reconstruction of Proto-Romance (PRom), the protolanguage which matches the common source of the various other intermediate languages in addition to Southwestern Romance; look over the *Stammbaum* (Appendix 2). If the requisite data were at hand, you could, of course, reconstruct Proto-Northwestern (PNW) by utilizing selected representatives of Gallo-Rhaetian, including French; or you could move a step higher and reconstruct Proto-Western out of PSW, PNW, and some Pyrenean language, or Proto-Italo-Romance out of Italian plus Dalmatian and (say) Venetian; then still higher and reconstruct Proto-Italo-Western on the basis of Proto-Western and Proto-Italo-Dalmatian. And

30 / 2 The reconstruction of Proto-Romance

although it would be more thorough and more symmetrical finally to reconstruct PRom on the basis of Proto-Italo-Western, Proto-Eastern, and Proto-Southern, there is no constraint on the comparative method such as to disallow the use of any convenient combination of protolanguages and existing languages. Thus you are free to exploit our available PSW plus French and Italian in lieu of Proto-Italo-Western, along with Daco-Roumanian in lieu of Proto-Eastern, and Logudorese Sardinian instead of Proto-Southern, all as input to the reconstruction of PRom. And this being so, the apparatus for conducting this exercise is available in the corpus: the odd-numbered pages of Appendix 1 list the Old French,[1] the standard Italian, the standard Roumanian, and the Logudorese Sard cognates of the 475 lexical items, together with blanks for the insertion of the respective PRom forms.

2.1 Reconstruction of the Proto-Romance (PRom) phonemes. First step. Leaving out of account for the present all data showing PSW doublets (including the plus-or-minus type) of Categories 3-6, or the untreatable residue of Category 7, work through the procedures analogous to those demonstrated in 1.1-3 of Chapter 1. You will, of course, need to know the phonemic inventory of each input language; and we therefore give you here, for convenient reference, an overview of the PSW, Old French, Italian, Roumanian, and Sardinian systems, arranged like that in 1.0.

```
C  U   PSW p b t d c ʒ       k g f v s z      m n ñ l ʎ r ʀ y w
O  N   OFr p b t d c ʒ č ǧ k g f v s z      m n ñ l ʎ r ʀ y w h
N  I   It   p b t d c ʒ č ǧ k g f v s   š   m n ñ l ʎ r     y w
S  T   Ro   p b t d c   č ǧ k g f v s z š ž m n   l   r     y w h
O      Sa   p b t d c ʒ č ǧ k g f   s   š   m n ñ l ʎ r     y
N

A  C   PSW  pr br tr dr kr gr fr                              kw gw
N  L   OFr  pr br tr dr kr gr fr vr pl bl kl gl fl
T  U   It   pr br tr dr kr gr fr vr pl bl kl gl fl            kw gw
S  S   Ro   pr br tr dr kr gr fr vr pl bl kl gl fl vl kv gv hr hl
       Sa   pr br tr dr kr gr fr


V  U   PSW i   e   ɛ   a   ɔ   o   u
O  N   OFr i   e   ɛ   a       o   u   ö   ü       ə
W  I   It  i   e   ɛ   a   ɔ   o   u
E  T   Ro  i   e       a       o   u           ɨ   ə
L      Sa  i   e       a       o   u
S
```

2.1 Reconstruction of the Proto-Romance (PRom) phonemes / 31

```
c  PSW                        aw
L  OFr    yɛ          yö      aw
U  It     yɛ                  wɔ
s  Ro  ye    ya  ęa   wa
   Sa
```

Wherever the blank for a PRom word is unencumbered by any asterisk, dagger, etc. betraying the item as somehow residual, the listed cognates may be accepted as embodying correspondences which are fully valid as regards consonants in any of four distributional positions,[2] as regards stressed vowels in either open or closed syllables, and as regards unstressed vowels either pretonic or posttonic.[3] You will note that many of these items exhibit only four viable entries, inasmuch as the PSW entry is a '?', or because one of the other input languages is simply missing. In this latter situation the Roumanian or the Sardinian item, as the case may be, has been deliberately omitted wherever it is irregular with regard to any segment; this is done in order to avoid loading the lists with tentative residue obscuring the picture unnecessarily. In some cases one or the other of these two languages totally lacks the cognate: thus Roumanian has none for CEx 7, or Sardinian for CEx 4, just as Old French has none for CEx 25.[4]

You will wish to profit also by the following helpful hints:

(1) Four correspondence sets embody the voiceless velar stop /k/ in one or more of the languages. Of these four sets, two occur before front-vowel correspondences and two before nonfront-vowel correspondences, as shown:

/__ −FV: Set A /k/k ~ č/k/k/k/   Set B /kw/k/kw/k/k/
/__ +FV: Set C /c/c/č/č/k/   Set D /k/k/k/č/k/.

Thus Set A is in emic contrast with Set B, as is Set C with Set D. Therefore if Set A is to be reconstructed as the unit */k/, and Set B as the cluster */kw/, then Set C can also be assigned to */k/ and Set D to */kw/, even though the latter contains no overt instance of /kw/ in the input.

Likewise, four separate sets involve the voiced correlate /g/ in one or more languages—two before front-vowel correspondences and two before non-front, thus:

/__ −FV: Set A' /g/g ~ ǧ/g/g/g/   Set B' /gw/g/gw/b/b/
/__ +FV: Set C' /y/ǧ/ǧ/ǧ/g/   Set D' /g/g/gw/−/−/.

Thus Set A' exactly parallels Set A and is reconstructible as */g/; while Set B' matches Set B sufficiently well to be assigned to */gw/. Set C' partially

32 / 2 The reconstruction of Proto-Romance

parallels Set C and is also reconstructible as the unit, while Set D' even contains a /gw/ to confirm assignment to the cluster. There is a further correspondence set partially overlapping Set C' and in contrast therewith as occurring only before front vowel, namely, /y-ǧ-ǧ-ž-y/, assignable to some consonant outside the velar obstruent series—presumably the palatal resonant */y/, by the same reasoning as given in A17 for the reconstruction of */y/ in PSW.[5]

(2) There are two ways of isolating the crucial consonant correspondences in items such as CEx 13, where PSW, OFr, and Roum show a single onset consonant in Pos. 3, while Ital and Sard show a 'geminate' consonant consisting of a Pos. 2 onset preceded by a phonemically identical coda:

• Pos. 2 /N-n-n-n-n/ preceded by coda /∅-∅-n-∅-n/, assigning the two It/Sa /n/'s differently;

• Pos. 3 /N-n-nn-n-nn/, arbitrarily taking the It/Sa geminate cluster as though it were an onset, even though this analysis runs counter to the syllable structure on which the determination of positions is based in the first place. Actually, this is merely a tactical question, inasmuch as the reconstructed geminate (*/nn/ or whatever) resulting from this procedure could ultimately be reanalyzed as a coda-plus-onset segment in terms of PRom syllable structure. The latter solution is recommended, for more efficient processing of the data.

(3) In items patterned like CEx 235, PSW and Old French show coda /y-y/, Italian and Sardinian a geminating coda, and Roumanian an obstruent coda. In order to identify the essential features and thus arrive at the optimal symbol for this particular protocoda, you will do well to compare the set in view—with a careful eye to patterning—with the contrasting /∅-∅-t-p-t/ coda set of (say) CEx 415 and also with the contrasting /∅-∅-t-∅-t/ (alternately Pos. 3 /t-t-tt-t-tt/ as suggested by (2)) of (say) CEx 208.

(4) Among the numerous etic sets of stressed-vowel correspondences, the widest variation occurs in Roumanian, with the basis of CD so complex as to be almost undecipherable without such guidelines as the following:

• In the sets regularly represented by PSW /ɛ/, Sa /é/, and OFr/It /ɛ ~ yɛ/ (the latter variation depending on what, by the way?), Ro shows high front /i/ before a nasal, whether onset or coda, as in CEx 37, 122;[6] elsewhere, /yé ~ yá/ in VOWEL HARMONY, i.e., in a feature correlation with one versus another emic set of posttonic vowels, as in CEx 172, 177, 347; the on-glide is absent, however, after a nonlabial onset, as in CEx 73, 381, 413.

• In either of the emically different sets represented on the one hand by PSW /é/, It/Sa /é/, OFr /ɛ ~ é/,⁷ and on the other hand by PSW /é/, It /é/, OFr /ɛ ~ é/,⁷ and Sa /i/, Ro shows high /i ~ ɨ/ in vowel harmony before /n/ (onset or coda), as in CEx 195, 455; elsewhere, /é ~ ęá/ in vowel harmony, as in CEx 40, 109, 245; the on-glide is absent, however, after a labial or palatal onset, as in CEx 77, 362.⁸

• In the sets represented by PSW/It/Sa /á/ and OFr /á ~ é/ (depending on what?), Ro shows central /ɨ/ before a nasal, whether onset or coda (except in /N-n-nn-n-nn/, cf. CEx 13), as in CEx 53, 55, 233, with a glide coda /y/ inserted before /n/ plus a posttonic front vowel, as in CEx 70, 325.

• In either of the emically different sets represented on the one hand by PSW /ɔ́/, OFr /ɔ́ ~ ő/ (depending on what?), It /ɔ́ ~ wɔ́/ (ditto), Sa /ó/, and on the other hand by PSW/It/Sa /ó/ and OFr /ú ~ ő/ (ditto), Ro shows high back /ú/ before a nasal, whether onset or coda, as in CEx 41, 196, 305; elsewhere, /ó ~ wá/ in vowel harmony,⁹ as in CEx 92, 93, 96.

2.2 Reconstruction of the corpus in Proto-Romance. Second step. Fill all the single, untagged blanks in the PRom column. (Again, the variously tagged blanks signal the categories of residual items to be supplied subsequently.) A ground rule: wherever, as in CEx 7, PSW offers doublets *one of which fits an established correspondence*, you may ignore the other and relegate whatever input item led to setting it up in the first place, to a special list for later reference. Thus, for example, while PSW */ama/ fits with OFr/It/Sa in pointing to PRom */ama/, PSW */ayma/ does not fit and hence Oc *aima* is to be set aside.¹⁰ Similarly, in CEx 39, the PSW doublets lead us to relegate Po *bebe*. The same procedure will apply to doublets of the '±' subtype; thus, in CEx 176, PSW */fava/ fits with OFr/It/Sa /f-f-f/ while */ava/ does not, causing us to set aside Sp *haba*, the contributor of the zero initial onset.

Since items in which one of the five languages is missing need not be taken as residue, Category 1 will this time comprise items in which *two* of the languages lack the requisite cognate.

Third step. Now fill all the asterisked blanks in the PRom column. In these items, the three available cognates conform fully to correspondences established in the second step.

Category 2 will again consist of items in which one (but not more than one) of the correspondences fails to match any established set because one of the languages exhibits a deviation belonging to no other correspondence. Thus, for example, in CEx 37, where all but Italian conform to the prevalent subset for the stressed vowel */ɛ́/ *in an open (i.e. coda-less) syllable*, Italian shows /é/ instead of the expected diphthong /yɛ́/; PRom */bɛne/ may be safely reconstructed according to the majority, and It *bene* (instead of **biene* to match *viene* of CEx 456) put 'on hold'. Exactly analogous to the back-vowel correspondences is CEx 297, reconstructible as */nɔve/ but with It *nove* put on hold as against *nuovo* of CEx 298.

Fourth step. Go on to fill in the daggered blanks which identify this residual category.

Categories 3 and 4 entail those items which manifest irregular splits in the consonant sets (Category 3) or in the vowel sets (Category 4). Thus, for instance, in Pos. 1 of CEx 59, a 3/1 split has PSW/It/Sa showing the /g-g-g/ for PRom */g/, while OFr has the /č/ which reflects PRom */k/; you may therefore posit the doublets */gattʊ/ and */kattʊ/. Similarly, in the posttonic vowel position of CEx 261, a 4/1 split has PSW/OFr/It/Sa pointing to one vowel and Ro to another.

Fifth step. Fill in the double spaces with assumed PRom doublets.

Category 5, like Categories 3-4, involves items in which the split is between a set of consonants, or a set of vowels, and null—the 'plus-or-minus' configuration. For example, in CEx 139 the PSW/OFr/Sa unstressed initial vowel is a plus, the It/Ro zero is a minus, and the reconstruction is with parentheses, i.e. */(ɪ)skala/; note that there are many items of just this sort, involving an initial onset-less syllable closed by coda */s/.

Sixth step. Enter a single form embodying a parenthesized protophoneme in each of the blanks marked '±'.

Category 6 comprises so few items that they are simply dumped into Category 7, the unreconstructibles marked by '?' and comprised not only of items with more than one split correspondence, but also of items with two languages (or, in marginal cases, just the crucial Sard) missing and the others showing one or more splits.

Notes for Chapter 2

1. The Old French cognates seem preferable because they afford a much more productive and convenient input than would their Modern French counterparts, for two reasons: (1) several of the original items have fallen into disuse and have been replaced by noncognates in the present-day language, e.g. CEx 3, for which Modern French offers only *âge*; (2) many of the Modern French items show considerably reduced phonemic shapes—e.g., CEx 17 *août* has come down from the earlier /əust/ to just /u/—a fact which makes for many a less tidy and somehow less reliable set of correspondences. The more full-bodied and hence more satisfactory forms which are provided, in both their graphic and their phonemic shapes, are actually those of a stage of the early French language more accurately designated as 'Franco-Orléanais', of the 11th-12th centuries, as disting-

uished from the later 'Francian' of the 13th-14th centuries and the still later 'French' proper of the 15th century on (see Agard 1980). It is to be noted that French orthography has remained generally faithful to medieval spelling practices, thus lagging considerably behind the phonological evolution. The items ending with a hyphen represent verbs—other than ə-stems—which always occur with one or another inflectional suffix independent of the correspondence sets at issue.

Stressed vowels are nowhere marked in the Old French entries, because stress is not phonemic in this language; phonetic stress is fully predictable as occurring on the last vowel in the word except where that vowel is /ə/, in which case stress is on the preceding vowel. For the other three languages, including PSW, the incidence of phonemic stress is readable by exactly the same rules as for the languages used in reconstructing PSW.

2. Pos. 4 is eliminated this time around, there being no instances of onset consonants occurring final in all five languages: although PSW, Old French, and Roumanian do have final consonants, Italian and Sardinian have none in the corpus (and only marginally in their entire lexica).

3. This time there are, however, two posttonic positions: final and nonfinal. They should be tracked separately.

4. Many of the items have been replaced in the Roumanian lexicon by non-Romance loan-words, chiefly of Slavic origin; or in the Sardinian lexicon by borrowings from standard Italian.

5. The foregoing sets are all found in Pos. 1-2. Pos. 3 sets severally matching them to a greater or lesser degree can be assigned without too much difficulty, as in CEx 10, 127, 198.

6. The high vowel is central /ɨ/ instead, between a labial onset and a nasal coda, as in CEx 457.

7. Again, depending on what? While this Old French alternation is further characterized by the incidence of a coda /y/ after the /é/, this coda clearly has no counterpart in the other languages and thus all such items will reconstruct with no coda.

8. The unit vowel is central /ə́/ instead, after a labial onset, as in CEx 360, 470.

9. Observe that the feature correlations here are not quite the same as those noted previously à propos of the front vowels.

10. The fact that Oc /ayma/ is reminiscent of OFr /ɛymə/ is doubtless not without significance, but it points to the possibility that the misfit represents a borrowing.

Chapter 3
The confrontation of Proto-Romance with attested Latin

3.1 The corpus in Latin. You are now to look up the Classical Latin (CLat) cognates of the corpus items in a bilingual (French-Latin, Spanish-Latin, or English-Latin) dictionary and transfer them to the blanks provided in the right-most column. Wherever the space is blocked by an asterisk (e.g. CEx 2), this means that there exists no corresponding item in the lexicon of CLat; there is therefore no entry to be made.

Since the PRom forms as reconstructed are all bare stems—i.e. devoid of any inflectional morphemes signaling nominal case/number, adjectival agreement, verbal tense/mood, person/number, or whatever—for proper comparison the CLat entries must likewise be base forms unadorned by grammatical suffixes. Since dictionary entries invariably include certain endings, your task will be to eliminate that excess baggage according to the following guidelines:

• Nouns come in two forms: the nominative singular and the genitive singular, in variations of shape which identify DECLENSION classes thus:
CEx 32: 1st Decl. BARBA, BARBAE; enter the stem BARBA
CEx 13: 2nd Decl. masc. ANNUS, ANNĪ; enter the stem ANNU
CEx 73: 2nd Decl. neut. CAELUM, CAELĪ; enter the stem CAELU
CEx 3: 3rd Decl. with truncated nominative AETĀS, AETĀTIS; enter the stem AETĀTE[1]
CEx 70: 3rd Decl. with identical nominative and genitive CANIS, CANIS; enter the stem CANE
CEx 197: 4th Decl. masc. FRUCTUS, FRUCTŪS; enter the stem as FRUCTŪ
CEx 90: 4th Decl. neut. CORNŪ, CORNŪS; enter the stem CORNŪ
CEx 186: 5th Decl. FIDES, FIDEI; enter the stem as FIDĒ[2]

• Adjectives come in up to three agreement forms; the masc., fem., and neut. of the nominative singular, thus:
CEx 5: 1st-2nd Decl. ACŪTUS, ACŪTA, ACŪTUM; enter the stem as ACŪTU
CEx 134: 3rd Decl. DULCIS, DULCE; enter the stem as DULCE[3]

• Most verbs come in four forms, varying by CONJUGATION classes: the first-person sing. of the present tense, the infinitive, the first-person sing. of

3.2 The phonemes of Latin / 37

the present perfect tense, and the neut. sing. form of the past participle, thus:
 CEx 7: 1st Conj. AMŌ, AMĀRE, AMĀVĪ, AMĀTUM; enter the stem as AMĀ
 CEx 124: 2nd Conj. DĒBEŌ, DĒBĒRE, DĒBUĪ, DĒBITUM; enter the stem as DĒBĒ
 CEx 39: 3rd Conj. BIBŌ, BIBERE, BIBĪ, BIBITUM; enter the stem as BIBE[4]
 CEx 322: 4th Conj. APERIŌ, APERĪRE, APERUĪ, APERTUM; enter the stem as APERĪ

A few CLat verbs are classed as DEPONENT, i.e. they have only passive-voice forms and are listed accordingly, e.g. CEx 294: NASCOR, NASCĪ, —, NĀTUM or CEx 338 PISCOR, PISCĀRĪ, —, PISCĀTUM. Enter the several stems as follows: for CEx 289 (4th Conj.) MORI, for CEx 294 (3rd Conj.) NASCE, and for CEx 338 (1st Conj.) PISCĀ; these stems are simply extrapolated according to the conjugation to which the deponent belongs.

3.2 The phonemes of Latin. Also in order to compare the PRom forms meaningfully with the CLat forms, the latter must of course be duly phonemicized—a very simple matter, since the letters with which CLat is nowadays conventionally written stand in very nearly one-to-one correlation (i.e. in a nearly perfect FIT) with the phonemes of the language, as illustrated in the following display:

```
C  U  Grapheme:  P  B  T  D  C  G  F  V  S  H  M  N  L  R  I
O  N  Phoneme:   p  b  t     d  k  g  f  w  s  h  m  n  l  r  y
N  I
S  T
O
N  C  Grapheme:  PR BR TR DR CR GR FR PL BL CL GL FL QU GU
A  L  Phoneme:   pr br tr dr kr gr fr pl bl kl gl fl kw gw
N  U
T  S
S

V  U  Grapheme:  I  E  A  O  U     Ī  Ē  Ā  Ō  Ū
O  N  Phoneme:   i  e  a  o  u     ī  ē  ā  ō  ū
W  I
E  T
L
S  C  Grapheme:  AE  AU
   L  Phoneme:   ay  aw
   U
   S
```

Additionally, graphic PH TH CH = phonemic /p t k/, PHR THR CHR = /pr tr kr/, PHL CHL = /pl kl/, in certain words borrowed from Greek, e.g. CEx 447; also graphic OE = phonemic /ē/, as in CEx 339, and graphic Y = phonemic /ī/, as in CEx 74.

Stress is a predictable function of the distribution of long and short nuclei within a lexical item and therefore is never marked, either graphically or phonemically. In disyllabic words, stress is automatically penultimate, as in CEx 13; in words of three or more syllables, stress falls on a penultimate vowel that is long, as in CEx 4; but on the antepenultimate if the penultimate is short, as in CEx 9.

Our next step is to compare the PRom and CLat forms of all items for which both are available. While the majority of such pairings yield perfectly regular correspondences, there is also a sizeable number of irregularities, or misfits with regard to one or more phonemes, each of which has its own individual explanation. These mismatched items are flagged with the symbol '≠' between the PRom and the CLat forms.[5] Disregarding these items, which will be explained in due course, you may proceed to search out and tabulate in systematic fashion the subcorpus of regularly matched PRom/CLat items.

In carrying out this exercise you will note that certain of the PRom phonemic entities have more than one counterpart in Latin, but not vice versa; e.g. PRom /a/ is matched by Lat /a/ or /ā/. We shall soon uncover the significance of this discrepancy. First, however, some considerations of a purely theoretical nature.

3.3 Reconstruction and reality. Proto-Romance, like any protolanguage arrived at by a linguist operating with the comparative method, is but a hypothetical construct and as such lays no claim to having been, in and of itself, a linguistic system in use by flesh-and-blood speakers of the real world. At the same time, the very act of reconstruction is pointless without the assumption that there did in fact exist, in space and time, an actual language which the protosystem approximates in all essential details—phonological, grammatical, and lexical—a language which was, precisely, the common ancestor of the present-day languages utilized as input to the reconstruction.

Was, then, the real language which we may posit as the common ancestor of the Romance tongues the very Latin language as we know it (what we label 'Classical Latin'), or was it indeed some other language evolved out of Latin, such as we might call 'Common Romance'? Or, another way of putting this question would be: was the real ancestor merely one dialect (call it 'Vulgar' or 'Popular') while CLat was another dialect, of one and the same Latin language? We need to find answers to these questions before we can proceed on solid ground to equate our PRom with one real speech system as against another.

Notes for Chapter 3

1. The -E- appears in certain other case-forms, in CD with the -I- relative to the subsequent phoneme.

2. Special cases: (1) CEx 139 and 272 come as the nom/gen *plurals* SCĀLAE, SCĀLĀRUM and MINĀCIAE, MINĀCIĀRUM; enter the stems simply as SCĂLA, MINĂCIA; (2) CEx 36 has a short nominative SOCER, SOCERĪ; disregard the truncation and enter the stem as SOCERU.

3. In the 3rd Decl. the masc. and fem. forms are identical, hence only two are listed. Special 1st-2nd Decl. instances are two items with R-final masc. forms: CEx 24 ALTER, ALTERA, ALTERUM and CEx 303 NIGER, NIGRA, NIGRUM; enter the stems as ALTERU and NIGRU, respectively.

4. A special case: CEx 370 POSSUM, POSSE, POTUI, —, is so irregular as to conceal its conjugation, which is 3rd; the stem may therefore be entered as POTE.

5. Where there are doublets in either column (e.g. CEx 6 or 35), one of the two forms will fit with its opposite number.

Part Two
From Latin down:
Phonological changes

0. Introduction: Orientation to the diachronic view

0.1 The differentiation of language and dialect.[1] The unity of what we call 'Latin' and what we call 'French' can be defended on the ground that the two are linked by an unbroken chain of speakers; but by this reasoning Latin and Spanish are also one language, or Latin and Italian, and so on. Yet no one will claim that French, Spanish, and Italian are now all one language. To call these clearly different languages 'dialects' of Latin in an historical context is likewise to beg the question. We seem forced to the conclusion that one language, namely Latin, has somehow in the course of time become more than one language; or else that it first became just *one* other language, and only later became several languages. In any case, how do we set about identifying and describing the process of becoming?

Crucial to our descriptive method are, first and foremost, acceptable working definitions of both language and dialect. And by 'acceptable' in this frame of reference is meant, of course, something much more precise and rigorous than the traditional definitions based on extrasystemic, sociopolitical, or merely behavioral criteria. We need definitions based, rather, on intrasystemic (in a word, structural) criteria. There are those who pronounce it impossible to redefine such age-old notions on any new basis, and would favor coining new terms instead. But one may disagree with this oblique approach and claim that linguists can, and should, continue to avail themselves of the consecrated terms 'language' and 'dialect', though distinguishing the one from the other in a different way from the layman.

The differentiation of language and dialect is an empirical issue to be resolved on the basis of shared linguistic structure. We need not trouble to ask whether, say, French and Vietnamese are dialects of the same language or separate languages. But the uniformity which underlies the surface diversity among observably similar systems—such as Occitan and Catalan—can be characterized in terms of CONGRUENT (not necessarily identical) phonological and grammatical representations. If one system provides the representation from which the representations of other systems can be derived by generative-type 'mapping rules', then the representations in question are congruent. Systems with congruent representations are then to be defined as dialects of one and the same language.

The level of representation accessible to native speakers is that of dialect, already a somewhat abstract level in that it subsumes a finite number of idiolects (i.e. of individual language competencies—the only true, basic psychological reality, after all) essentially identical in both deep and surface structure. A language is then a more abstract union and intersection of features shared by congruent dialects; and above languages there is a still more abstract level of relatedness among languages, i.e. a language complex or diasystem. A language—and much less so a diasystem—cannot be said to have psychological reality nor psycholinguistic implications. Setting aside the meaning of 'a language' traditionally given to this term by the sociolinguist, historian, or layman, the descriptive linguist will find it useful only as a taxonomic term, but, as such, indispensable in accounting for linguistic change, the topic which concerns us here.

Dialects undergo change over time. Through the addition, loss, or modification of their generative rules, their grammars are being restructured constantly. Each speaker creates his own grammar as a child, basing it on the speech to which he is exposed, and in this way dialects are passed from one generation to another uninterruptedly, as, for example, from a given generation of Latin speakers to a given generation of French speakers. Thus it is that the real agents of linguistic change are the flesh-and-blood speakers of a dialect, though clearly enough such speakers exercise no control over the higher-level language to which the dialect belongs. Dialects are actually changed by their users (though unconsciously); but the language is changed only by the linguist in his capacity as recorder, as classifier, as historian. The changes he introduces into his structural representation of a language are his to determine. Confronted with objective changes in the dialects, he himself changes the language that subsumes them. He is in this sense free to select his own criteria, and so to interpret on theoretical grounds the empirical data before him. We may accordingly adopt the methodological position detailed

0.2 Phonological criteria for language change and split / 43

in the paragraphs which follow. The criteria set forth first, in the present introduction, are valid in the domain of phonology alone. The relation of diachronic grammar to these criteria is intended to be implicit in the 'diachronic recapitulations' which appear at the conclusion of each stage in Part Three.[2]

0.2 Phonological criteria for language change and split. The phonological criteria for change and/or split relate to dialectal modifications in the underlying structure of lexical items, and are therefore independent of morphophonemic processes (of derivation, inflection, or external sandhi), which we shall leave out of consideration. The criteria entail, as we shall see, the loss or gain of a phonemic contrast. Loss of contrast flows from a single type of internal process: merger, known also as coalescence and taken to include the elimination of a phoneme, i.e. its 'merger with zero'. The underlying representations which we view as subject to merger include not only the irreducible unit phonemes that make up the basic inventory of the dialect, but also any and all clusters that function in parallel with the basic units in any of the three syntagmatic positions: syllable nucleus, syllable onset, syllable coda. Within this framework, total or unconditioned merger is defined as the elimination of a given contrast in a given position; partial or conditioned merger is seen as a mere redistribution of given syntagmatic environments. As for shifts, fissions, and fusions,[3] they bring about no alteration in the network of contrasts in a given position, even though a cluster has replaced a unit or vice versa. Neither loss nor gain is involved.

Gain of a phonemic contrast flows from two sources: one internal, one external. The internal source is the cleavage of a phoneme as the consequence of a merger—that is to say, a certain merger in a certain position may of itself remove whatever conditioning factor was keeping two allophones in another position from being separate phonemes. The external source of gain is simply the event known as borrowing—either from another language or from another dialect of the same language. The result, namely, the occurrence of two phonemes where there was but one before, may in a sense be seen as a type of cleavage and, as such, may figure in the same way as other cleavages in our criteria.

We may now proceed to enumerate the specific processes of loss or gain which serve as criteria to establish our parameter for language split, namely, the factor of congruence. For simplicity's sake we shall refer to various dialects as 'Set A' and 'Set B', each being a set of one or more dialects, and also to 'Set C' where a third is relevant. The symbols X, Y ... are understood to subsume underlying phonological entities, be they units or clusters, in any one of the three syntagmatic positions mentioned above. The four criteria are represented in summary form in Table 0.1, each one being

Table 0.1 The four criteria for congruence, specified positively or negatively for language change and for language split.

		Process as criterion	1	2	3	4
D	V	Set A	X⟶Y, Y↗		Z↗Z, Z↘Z'	X↘Y, Y↗ Z—Z
I	A					
A	R					
L	I					
E	A			X↘Y (& Z↗Z, Z↘Z')	X↘Y & Y↗	
C	T					
T	I					
A	O		(X↘X),		(W↗W, W↘W')	X↘Z, Z↗ Y—Y
L	N	Set B	(Y↗)			
O	U	Language change	−	+	+	+
T	T					
C	C					
O	O					
M	M	Language split	(−)	−	+	+
E	E					

Note. Parenthesized models are to be read as either concurrent or nonoccurrent without relevance to the outcome.

specified as positive or negative in relation to the determination of language change and language split. Illustrations of the four criteria applied to items from imaginary systems are displayed in Table 0.2 for further clarification.

Criterion 1. When Set A has been restructured through the loss of a phoneme /X/—e.g. /X, Y/ > /Y/ (even where /Y/ = zero)—but Set B has not lost /X/, then /X/ is to be retained at the language level. Thus not only is the language unchanged, but the two sets remain congruent; the merger in view being statable at the language level by a synchronic rule applicable to the restructured Set A. It makes no difference, here, whether Set B has lost some other phoneme which Set A has not lost—e.g. even /Y/, through a merger which is the reverse of that in Set A. It does not matter either, clearly, whether there is also a Set C which has undergone no loss at all.

Criterion 2. When *all* sets have lost /X/ through one and the same merger with /Y/, then /X/is to be removed from the language. The language will thus be changed, but it will not be split provided (a) there are no other restructurings consequent upon the merger, or (b) any consequent restructurings are shared by all the sets.

0.2 Phonological criteria for language change and split / 45

Table 0.2 Illustrations of the four criteria applied.

Criterion	Set A	Set B	Language	Synchronic rule
1	mada = mada	mada = mada	**mada**	none required
	mata > mada	mata = mata	**mata**	t → /d/ in A
	(mada = mada	mada > mata	**mada**	d → /t/ in B)
2	mate = mate	mate = mate	**mate**	none required
	mati [mači] > mače	mati [mači] > mače	**mače**	none required
3	mate = mate	mate = mate	**mate**	none required
	mati [mači] > mače	mati > mate	?	none allowable
	(mati [mači] > mače	mati [maθi] > maθe	?	none allowable)
4	man = man	man = man	**man**	none required
	min = min	min = min	**min**	none required
	men > min	men > man	?	none possible

Criterion 3. As with Criterion 2, the language will be changed when all sets have lost /X/ through identical merger with /Y/. It will also be split if consequent restructurings occur in one set but not in the other, or if the two sets undergo divergent restructurings. In either of the latter conditions, congruence could be maintained only at the cost of synchronic rules running counter to historical truth; and we may hold that to ignore this constraint could well open the way to unnatural, strained, or awkward ad hoc rule formulations.[4]

Criterion 4. When Set A has merged /X/ with /Y/, while Set B has merged that same /X/ with /Z/, so that both sets have lost /X/ though by separate routes, then /X/ is to be removed from the language. Thus the language is not only changed, but it is also split; for without /X/ the two sets can no longer be congruent, i.e. no rule can be devised to account for those items which show /Y/ in one set and /Z/ in the other, as against other items with /Y/ in both sets and still others with /Z/ in both sets.[5]

In summary, then, a language is to be changed whenever it loses or gains a phonological entity in one or another phonotactic position, and is to be split whenever it loses the factor of congruence whereby all its dialects can be accounted for by a single underlying representation plus synchronic mapping rules.

Dialects themselves, on the other hand, do more than simply lose or gain phonological entities: they also either shift (often by fusion or fission) a given entity, thus changing its distinctive-feature specification; or they redistribute existing entities within the structure of lexical items; or they merely add low-level phonetic rules with no phonological effect whatever. None of these latter dialectal modifications constitute grounds for changing the language, because the language will continue to account for them through mapping-rules. Nevertheless—and this is crucial to our method—advantage must be taken of a language change (whether also a split or not) to relexify any descendent language fully—i.e. to reflect in its recast morpheme structure not only the losses or gains which motivated the change, but also the shifts, redistributions etc. shared by all its dialects, in order to avoid the chaotic heaping of mapping-rule upon mapping-rule in an accumulation carried down through a theoretically infinite succession of languages. Thus we may argue that it is far more efficient taxonomy to 'rewrite' (i.e. restructure, relexify) languages at discrete intervals only, rather than in the virtual continuum of change that characterizes the recurrent restructuring of dialects.

We shall now endeavor to recapture and illuminate certain 'moments of truth' as we work our way downward in time from Republican Latin,[6] establishing every node and illustratively tracing the restructurings down one branching—arbitrarily, the one that leads to Spanish/Portuguese. The basic assumption is that each new descendent language in its turn develops dialects, each dialect having an ever-growing number of ordered synchronic phonological rules, many of them shared, of course, by two or more of the dialects, reflecting phonetic changes that have succeeded one another until the last one triggers the language change and/or split. The restructurings of the antecedent dialects as descendent languages may then be formulated in diachronic phonological rules—i.e. phonemic changes, also ordered at least partially, specifying mergers, cleavages, shifts, and the rest.

Chapters 1–10 deal, then, with phonological data exclusively; it is the phonological criteria for language change and split that determine and define for us the successive branchings in the *Stammbaum* (Appendix 2). Subsequently, in corresponding chapters of Part Three, the down-tracing process will be worked through again in purely grammatical terms, assuming the same changes and splits as already established rather than as newly determined by other—i.e. grammatical as opposed to phonological—criteria.

Notes for Introduction

1. The present discussion closely follows appropriate sections (many passages being taken verbatim) of Agard 1975, 1976, and 1980. They are reproduced here with the permission of the respective publishers. Acknowledgment of other scholars' input to the theoretical stance is included in the several articles, but is not repeated here.

2. Change and split must, it seems, be contingent on the phonological or on the grammatical factor, but not on both. If it were made dependent on both, the cost would be too heavy; that is to say, one criterion might be met

and still be rendered powerless, having vacuous and futile application so long as its counterpart in the other domain were not met.

3. In shift, one or more of the distinctive features change but the phoneme remains in contrast with all the other phonemes: e.g. a (voiceless) palatal fricative /š/ changing from [−back] to [+back] to become a (voiceless) velar fricative /x/. In fission a simple vowel becomes a diphthong, or a simple consonant a cluster: e.g. /e > ey/ or /k > ky/. In fusion, a diphthong becomes a monophthong, or a cluster a simple consonant: e.g. /ay > ɛ/ or /ty > č/.

4. A synchronic rule which mirrors a true diachronic fact obviously cannot do violence to naturalness, since the theory of naturalness has itself been developed from empirical observations of phonetic change. Conversely, however, a rule stating the reverse of an historical process would not necessarily violate naturalness; for example, a synchronic rule č → /t/ for Set A, involving simply a switch of the distinctive feature [Delayed Release] from plus to minus, is no less natural (though seemingly more marked) than a rule t → /č/. Consequently, it appears that historical truth must dominate naturalness as our primary constraint.

5. There is an important constraint here, however: if there exists also a Set C which has undergone no merger at all, so that in fact /X/ must remain in the language, then there is neither change nor split, and all three sets remain congruent through rules applicable to Set A and to Set B.

6. This is an alternative label for 'Gracchan Latin', which Hall (1974) dates from the middle of the second century B.C., restructured following the rhotacism of **s** and the loss of the diphthongs **ei, ou** (also **oi**?). 'Classical' Latin is to be seen as a standardized literary dialect of the Latin in view, but soon to become petrified in its total structure. From the moment the *sermo urbanus* surrendered its status as a 'living' dialect, subject to constant change as all speech is, it can no longer figure as a dialect of 'the language', i.e. of the complex of 'vulgar' dialects that constitute the living stream of a Latin about to change.

Chapter 1
The Latin language becomes the Common Romance language[1]

1.0 The phonological inventory of Latin. All the sound-changes to be taken into account, in this and following chapters, are confirmed by attested or reconstructive evidence and are duly noted in the Comparative Romance literature;[2] hence we need not be at pains to document their factual occurrence. We are concerned here only with their effects upon systems.

The inventory of Latin phonological representations is essentially that which we have already established in connection with our confrontation between the Latin system and corpus as attested and the PRom system and corpus as reconstructed. The Latin inventory is repeated here, arranged in terms of function in the structure of the syllable, i.e. in accordance with the model we shall adopt for displaying the systematic inventory of each successive language from Latin down to Spanish and Portuguese.

Nuclei: ī ū ē ō ā i u e o a
                                  ay
                                  aw

Onsets: p b t d k g f s m n l r y w h
         pr br tr dr kr gr fr
         pl bl   kl gl fl
                  kw gw

Codas: p b t d k g s m n l r =
         mp   nk

Among the codas: **m** and **n** are neutralized by feature assimilation to obstruent onsets, though it will be convenient to write *m* before labials, as well as necessary to write *m* in **m+n**. The symbol = will represent the first consonant in the coda-plus-onset sequence conventionally known as a geminate cluster. All remaining features of this coda are fully predictable from the following onset; all single onsets except **w** and **h** occur thus geminated; all the onset clusters may likewise be preceded by = assimilated to their first element.

1.1 Modification of stress rules. Stress is reassigned from a short antepenultimate nucleus in hiatus to the (also short) penultimate nucleus, e.g. [lin'te-o-lu-]$_{249}$ > [lin-te'o-lu-], or [mu'li-e-re-]$_{170}$ > [mu-li'e-re-].[3] Although no dialectal restructuring is entailed (since stress remains predictable, albeit by different rules), the change in view will be seen to have an input to, or 'feed', Change 1.2.

1.2 Syncope involving certain vowels. Variably to be sure, numerous words are syncopated through deletion of the (short) vocoid of either a noninitial pretonic or a nonfinal posttonic syllable, provided the resulting forms do not run counter to existing patterns of syllabic structure. Thus, for example, the short nuclei in question tend to be suppressed when the resulting codas or onsets are not new to their respective positions, e.g. ['o-ku-

1.2 Syncope involving certain vowels / 49

lu-]$_{309}$ > ['o-klu-] or ['ok-lu-], ['wi-ri-de-]$_{460}$ > ['wir-de-].[4] A special case of syncope involves that of short vocoids which, being in the requisite position, are at the same time in hiatus. Preliminarily, the mid vocoids in this position have been raised, i.e. [e o] > [i u]/_ V, which has already entailed a redistribution as accounted for by a diachronic rule at the dialectal level (a 'D-rule'):

(D-1)   /i u/————/i u/
        /e o/————/e o/.[5]

The broken line specifies the particular environmental condition which can (and in a fully detailed description, should be) spelled out; we refrain from doing so here, for fear of overloading the graphic presentation. By Rule D-1 /palea/$_{324}$ is restructured as /palia/, /linteolu/$_{249}$ as /lintiolu/, /koāgulu/ as /kuāgulu/ 'caillé/cuajada'. The synchronic mapping-rule at the language level (the 'M-rule') is, for all dialects:

(M-1)   **e o** → /i u/_ V.

Subsequently, when syncope begins to operate, the vocoids in question instead of dropping become nonsyllabic (i.e. nonnuclear), nonetheless reinforcing the simplification of syllable patterns in the same manner as noted just previously, i.e. [... xx′xx] > [... x′xx] or [... ′xxx] > [... ′xx]. There is a further phonological result in the dialects, their sequential redundancy rules being altered through a redistribution which takes one of two forms: (1) shunting of the onset back to the unfilled coda position, and substitution of glide for vowel as new onset, as in /palia/$_{324}$ ['pa-li-a] > ['pal-ya] /palya/; or (2) when the coda slot is already filled, shift of onset-plus-vowel to a new consonant-plus-glide onset cluster, as in /martiu/$_{270}$ ['mar-ti-u] > /'mar-tyu] /martyu/. The corresponding D-rule:

(D-2)   /i u/————/i u/
              ———/y w/
              ———Ø
        /e o/————/e o/.

In this way /palia/ is again restructured as /palya/, /lintiolu/ as /lintyolu/, /kwāgulu/ as /kwāglu/, /wiride/ as /wirde/, etc. The M-rule is a modification of (M-1) so as to account for syncope as a whole:

(M-2) $\begin{cases} \mathbf{i\ e} \to /y/ \\ \mathbf{u\ o} \to /w/ \end{cases}$ _V ~ (variably) Ø /_CV.

50 / 1 Latin becomes the Common Romance language

1.3 Monophthongization of diphthong /ay/ (AE). The sound-change [ai̯] > [ɛː] is a fusion through mutual assimilation (raising and fronting of the low vocoid, and lowering of the high) yielding a long mid front vocoid. The phonological result at the dialectal level is a diachronic shift, whereby /aytāte/$_3$ is restructured as /ētāte/, or /kaylu/$_{73}$ as /kēlu/ by the rule

(D-3)   /ay/———/ɛ̄/,

with the rewritten phoneme remaining in contrast with all other nuclei and so not perturbing the system. At the language level:

(M-3)   **ay** → /ɛ̄/.

1.4 Phonetic laxing of the short vowels. This sound-change, which is presumed to have begun before spoken Latin spread to Europe and Africa, affects all the nonlows and is accompanied by lowering, the more prevalently in the mid range. Although at the initial stage the laxing is not functional and entails no dialectal restructuring, nevertheless its input to the highly significant change which follows is unequivocal.

1.5 Modification of vowel length. Globally, as the speech of Rome is diffused throughout Italia and beyond by colonists and learned by new populations, phonetic vocoid length is either lost or redistributed. It is in the more central dialects (chiefly in, and north of, Italia) that the redistribution occurs, according to the following pattern. Long vocoids remain long in tonic open (codaless) syllables and become short elsewhere, while short vocoids become long in tonic open syllables and remain short elsewhere. Since longs and shorts are then in complementary distribution, the burden of contrast is shifted to the differences in laxness or height, just as much as it is where length is fully eliminated. (The rearranged phonetic length differences have no phonological effect for the present, though ultimately they will directly affect vowel development in descendent languages; see 5.3.) To the extent that Change 1.4 (laxing and lowering) has operated, then, the consequent phonological shift is accounted for by the following diachronic rules:

(D-4.1)   /i u e o/———/i̯ u̯ ę ǫ/

(D-4.2)   /ī ū ē ō/———/i u e o/.

We note that the two rules must apply in the order indicated, which in fact mirrors the chronological order of the corresponding phonetic changes and thus preserves the lax/nonlax contrast. By these rules /herī/$_{220}$ is restructured as /heri/ (or /ęri/, see 1.6), /fidē/$_{186}$ as /fi̯de/, /yoku/$_{225}$ as /yǫku̯/, /lupu/$_{256}$ as /lu̯pu̯/, etc., in addition to /fīlu/$_{179}$ as /filu̯/, /kūlu/$_{119}$ as /kulu̯/, /rēge/$_{394}$ as /regę/, sōle/$_{422}$ as /solę/, and so on. Somewhat different, lesser restructurings take place wherever, in peripheral southern or eastern dialects, Change 1.4 has failed to occur in the mid and/or high vocoids.[6] However, there are no corresponding mapping rules because by virtue of Change 1.4's failure to affect the low vocoids, nowhere do the pair /a : ā/ escape coalescence, and this merger meets our Criterion 2 for changing, though not splitting, the language. Although all dialects remain congruent, the phoneme **ā** is to be removed from the language along with the diphthong **ay** which, as /ɛ̄/, also merges in all dialects with /e/. The relevant D-rules:

(D-5) 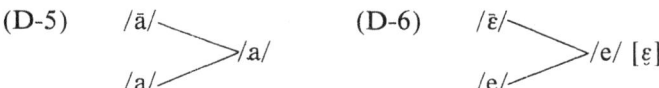 (D-6) /ɛ̄/⟩/e/ [ɛ]
/e/

Thus, for example, /kāsyu/₃₈₃ is restructured as /kasyu̩/, /kēlu/₇₃ as /ke̩lu̩/, /ɛ̄tāte/₃ as /e̩tate̩/.

1.6 Loss of the consonant /h/ (H). Unrelated to the foregoing mergers in the vocalism, whereby Latin becomes a new language, Common Romance (CRom), is the global loss of the contoid [h] through its merger with zero. Roughly between the time of Cicero (106-43 B.C.) and the beginning of the Empire (A.D. 27), all normal spontaneous dialects of Latin underwent this total, unconditioned loss. The sound-change in view restructures all dialects because it alters their inventory: there is global loss of a phonological unit as accounted for by

(D-7)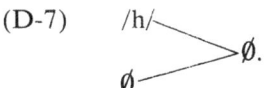

Thus, for example, herī/₂₂₀ is restructured as /erī/ (or /e̩ri/, see 1.5), hōra/₂₁₉ as /ora/, etc.[7] Furthermore, this systematic loss of a phoneme in all dialects again meets Criterion 2 for changing the language. However, since we cannot document the relative chronology of the two unrelated losses—that of **ā**, **ay**, on the one hand, and that of **h**, on the other—we may content ourselves with conflating the two and changing the language just once; this seems methodologically justified so long as between the two changes no other change can be shown to intervene.

1.7 Other dialectal changes. While Changes 1-5 are indeed subject to ordering relative to each other but are independent of Change 1.6, so also are certain other changes independent both of one another and of the two changes which induce the actual language change: such changes, for example, as

52 / 1 Latin becomes the Common Romance language

• the redistribution of word-final consonants, as in /dekem/$_{127}$ > /dękę/ or /kwid/$_{385}$ /kwi̯/.

• the loss of the nasal coda [n] before a fricative onset, as in /mēnse/$_{280}$ > /mesę/, etc.

• the variable assimilation of the coda [r] by the fricative onset [s], as in /ursu/$_{320}$ > /u̯ssu̯/ ~ /u̯rsu̯/, etc.

We can make no claim as to the actual chronological order in which the various unrelated changes took place, nor can we affirm that they occurred in the same order in all dialects. In fact, the probability is that they did not, and that in one or another dialect they were not all completed before the crucial 1.5 and/or 1.6. Where not, the speakers in question were using archaizing forms of Latin—surely a situation generalizable to language diachrony as a whole. For bookkeeping purposes, however, we shall do well to posit completion of all changes that *can* have been completed, and incorporate them into the representation of the new language.

1.8 Summary of the changes, and inventory of Common Romance. In summary, the phonological subsystem shaken up in the transition from Latin to CRom is that of the long vowels—the nonlows involved in shifts, and the low lost through coalescence. The language change is motivated by Criterion 2; there is no dialectal incongruence and therefore no language split. The diachronic statements attesting to the language change may be formulated as follows:

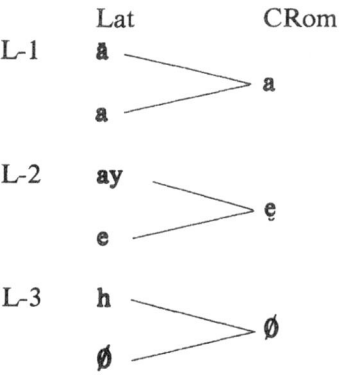

The full phonological inventory of the new language, Common Romance, thus becomes the following:

Nuclei: i   u   e   o   a   i̯   u̯   ę   ǫ
                         aw

Onsets: p b t d k g f s m n l r y w
pr br tr dr kr gr fr
pl bl   kl gl fl
         ty dy ky gy   sy
                  kw gw

Codas: p b t d k g s m n l r =
mp   nk

1.9 Equating Proto-Romance with Common Romance

1.9.1 Extrapolating the unreconstructible items of the corpus. The diachronic changes which took place as Latin became CRom are all reflected in the differences which we observed and tabulated between Cols. 9 and 10 of the corpus. You are therefore now in a position to extrapolate the CRom forms of the unreconstructible items—those marked '?' in Col. 9—by putting the Latin forms through whichever of the Latin-to-CRom changes apply to them. So, for example, in CEx 3, although the PRom form is unavailable, Lat AETĀTE > CRom **ętatę** by Changes D-3, D-5, and D-6 (subsumed in Changes L-1 and L-2); again in CEx 8, Lat ĀREA > CRom **arya** by Changes D-1, D-2, and D-5 (cf. Change L-1 plus restructuring). Accordingly, proceed now to extrapolate the missing CRom items and enter them (in parentheses or a different color) between the '?' and the Latin form. Do not, however, switch to the phonemic notation arrived at by the comparative method in Part One and used in Col. 9. So, for example, you will retain the resonant onset **w** in an item like CEx 474, and all coda-plus-y sequences; use of the coda = is your option, but be consistent.

In cases, on the other hand, where the PRom form *is* available but no corresponding entry appears in Col. 10, it may, of course, be posited that the item existed in CRom, and—since we now equate PRom and CRom phonologically, *albeit in different notation*—in the same phonemic shape. Wherever Low Latin or Late Latin textual attestations exist, they will be cited in further support of the basic assumption.

1.9.2 Residual discrepancies between Latin and Common Romance. With these principles in mind, we shall now single out for individual comment (a) the numerous residual, discrepant cases marked '≠' in which the PRom/CRom form fails to match the Latin form, and (b) the few cases where the Latin form is missing from the Classical lexicon but ultimately attested. The very few cases where the item is missing from both Latin and PRom, with its existence in CRom therefore in question, will be dealt with under later headings.

CEx 2. For items of this sort, etymological sources customarily cite a 'Vulgar Latin starred form', as in this instance **affila(re)*, whose absence

54 / 1 Latin becomes the Common Romance language

from both Roumanian and Sardinian leads to the hypothesis that it had a derivational origin later than CRom; see Italo-Western at 2.4.3.

CEx 17. The pretonic /a/ instead of the expected /aw/ may have been dialectal in CRom, for we note that the Sard reflex could come from either. In any case this presumed dissimilation, in the environment of a following /ú/, ultimately prevailed (see It-W).

CEx 20. Cited as 'VLat *arcione'; but with both Roum and Sard missing it may have developed by later derivation (see It-W).

CEx 23. Latin did have both the adjective and the neuter noun ALBU 'blanc/blanco'; the CRom feminine noun **alba** bespeaks absorption of the neuter-plural marker -**a** into the stem, forming a new 1st-decl. noun with semantic narrowing—a very frequent morphological shift at this stage.

CEx 27. The alveolar resonant coda /l/ plus another alveolar resonant onset (e.g. /n/) was an unusual sequence almost certainly subject to regressive assimilation in popular dialects of Latin, after which the restructured CRom **banyu̯** (from an intermediate /bannyu̯/?) as a result of Change D-2 is quite normal.

CEx 35. The doublet with pretonic /o/ being normal, the one with /u̯/ may be eliminated as a CRom variant, for it is manifested by PSW alone and can hence be regarded as having first developed dialectally as late as SW (see 6.6).

CEx 38. See It-W (2.4.3).

CEx 40. The variant with /-a/ shows again the amalgamation of the neuter-plural marker in a 1st-decl. singular, here also a noncount noun with collective reference to sticks of wood, or logs, as opposed to the substance itself.

CEx 58. Since Latin had CAPTĀ-, as a frequentative of CAPE(RE) meaning '(chercher à) saisir', our PRom form supposedly equates with a CRom **kaptya** (already in popular Latin?) alongside the surviving **kapta** (cf. Sp/Po *catar*).

CEx 59. CRom **ka=tu̯ ~ ga=tu̯** is said to have driven out Lat FĒLE- (which has no survivors) upon the domestication of cats in Rome. Gaulish or even African in origin, it is attested as *cattus* in Low Latin of the 5th cent.

CEx 62. Corresponding to our PRom */kalca/, of course, would be CRom **?kaltya**, a by-form which would have had no raison d'être, even in popular Latin, alongside **kalkya**. It is to be noted, though, that the pivotal input language pointing to medial /c/ rather than /č/ is Italian; apropos of which, a study of the individual history of this item will in fact lead us to discard PRom */kalca/ in favor of */kalča/; see Italo-Romance (3.5).

CEx 64. In this 3rd-decl. imparisyllabic neuter the nom/acc form **kapu̯t** prevailed over the basic stem in CRom (but cf. in Roumanian the plural of *cap* as well as the by-form *capăt*, at 2.3.2).

CEx 65. Latin did have a noun CAMĪNU- meaning 'cheminée/hogar'—which in fact survives in some of our languages, e.g. It *camino*, Rou *cămin*—but we

1.9 Equating Proto-Romance with Common Romance / 55

are dealing here rather with a word of allegedly Gallic origin cited as 'VL *camminus.*'

CEx 71. See It-W (2.4.3).

CEx 76. The initial dissimilation of the cluster /kw/ to simple /k/ in anticipation of a second /kw/ is confirmed by CEx 75, unreconstructible because of the final vowels yet unmistakably indicative of an initial plain */k/. As for the loss of the segment /gi/ from the formative -ĀGINTĀ, reducing it to the more manageable disyllabic **-anta**, it can well have originated in popular dialects of Latin; see also West-Ibero Romance at 6.4.3.

CEx 83. Cited as 'VLat *cominitia(re)*', this verb was derived in popular Latin or in CRom from Lat INITIĀ- with the prefix COM-, and the prevalent CRom form must have been **kominca** after early syncope.

CEx 87. Loss of the unstressed medial syllable /-pu-/ is a normal aspect of CRom syncope, the onset /p/ being thus squeezed out between the nasal coda and the following stop onset.

CEx 88. Note that all but the SW forms can reflect either */ó/ or */ɔ́/ before a nasal coda. However, since this item frequently occurred in the unfocused position of a preposition, or in the unstressed position of a prefix, we may be dealing with a hesitation between /ọ/ and /ɔ̌/; cf. the attested 13th cent. Castilian form *cuentra*, as well as the form *encuentra* of the verb 'rencontrer/encontrar'.

CEx 91. Italian has *corvo* as well as *corbo*, the former reflecting the classical CORVU- and the latter a popular by-form with /-rb-/.

CEx 93. In this 3rd-decl. neuter noun of the CEx 64 type, the nom/acc form **korpus** prevailed over the basic stem in CRom.

CEx 96. The switched conjugation-class from an expected *e*-stem to an *i*-stem in PRom is only partially valid; this verb in CRom must have been either an *e*-stem or an *i*-stem in dialectal (or free?) variation.

CEx 107. The switched conjugation-class from an expected *i*-stem to an *e*-stem (just the opposite of CEx 96) is also discussed in connection with CEx 96.

CEx 138. Cited as 'VLat *excappa(re)*', meaning something like 'slip out of one's cape even as a pursuer seizes it', this denominal verb was evidently in CRom along with the base noun **ka=pa**, attested in 7th cent. Low Latin. See also CEx 139.

CEx 139. The prosthetic /i̯-/ in this and many more items of similar initial shape was evidently variable in CRom, as an overt nucleus expanding the original minor-syllable /s-/, and perhaps already in Latin itself—the specific nucleus being selected by analogy to the reflex /i̯s-/ of the Latin prefix /e(k)s-/, as in CEx 138 (which also became variable).

CEx 140. With French alone pointing to a geminate as against a single lateral, we may discard */(I)skɔlla/ and posit only **(i)skola** for CRom (see 5.4, and also CEx 474).

CEx 141. For the initial /a-/ instead of the expected /aw-/, see CEx 17.

The CRom variable switch to /i̯-/ is doubtless analogical to items like CEx 138 or 139.

CEx 144. With Italian alone pointing unequivocally to medial */d/ as against */t/, we may, for reasons set forth at 3.5, discard */(ı)skudʊ/ and posit only **(i̯)skutu̯/** for CRom.

CEx 150. For the same reason as given in CEx 144, we may discard the variant */(ı)spada/ in favor of only **(i̯)spata** for CRom.

CEx 160. Cited as 'VLat *facia,' this is one of a few 5th-decl. nouns which switched to join the copious first declension as CRom **fakya**.

CEx 162. Although the shorter doublet is cited as 'VLat *fa(re),' there is no evidence of its existence prior to It-W (see 2.3.3); it may therefore be discarded as a CRom variant.

CEx 168. Another instance of conversion of a 2nd-decl. neuter plural noun to a 1st-decl. feminine in CRom, which appeared in inscriptions referring to the goddess of fate.

CEx 173. Here it was the fem. sing. form of an adjective, as occurring in the 'VLat' locution *festa dies, becoming a fem. noun in CRom.

CEx 175. A case identical to that of e.g. CEx 40.

CEx 177. The single /l/ in place of the geminate is a blend of the Lat nom/ acc form FEL and the stem FELLE-, the phonological structure of CRom not permitting final consonants as minor syllables.

CEx 189. Here we have the neuter-plural concord form of the Lat adjective FORTE (CEx 190), namely, FORTIA, as the CRom 1st-decl. fem. **fo̯rtya** with abstract meaning.

CEx 194. This is one of numerous words of Common Germanic origin which were borrowed into CRom through contacts dating from imperial times, centuries before the barbarian invasions. Unattested itself, the Gmc form is reconstructed as */fri̯sk/ (cf. German *frisch*, Eng *fresh*).

CEx 198. The PRom stem-final */-ı/ instead of the expected */-ε/ results from a switch in conjugation class from *e*-stem to *i*-stem in CRom.

CEx 201. See below at It-W.

CEx 202. With Italian alone pointing unequivocally to stressed /é/ as against /έ/, we may discard */gela/ and posit only **ge̯la** for CRom (see 3.5).

CEx 204. The doublet in final /-e/, reflected only in Roumanian, betrays a persistence of the apocopated nom.-sing. Lat form GENER alongside the general stem GENERU-.

CEx 213, 215. See below at It-W.

CEx 221. The coda /n/ in the initial syllable seems to have been introduced in It-W by analogy to the common prefix **i̯n-**, perhaps as in CEx 145 specifically; it may be rejected for CRom.

CEx 228. The switch of this particular 5th-declension noun to the 1st declension (cf. CEx 160) does not appear to antedate SW and therefore may be discarded from CRom. The apocopated form **di**, however, may be taken

1.9 Equating Proto-Romance with Common Romance / 57

as a doublet of **di̯ę** already in CRom, with absorption of the /e/ after the stressed vowel had become tense in hiatus; cf. also CEx 469.

CEx 231, 236. With Italian alone pointing to medial */g/ as against */k/, we may safely discard the spurious doublets */lagʊ/ and */laktuga/ from CRom (see 3.5).

CEx 238. The doublet with stressed */í/ as against */ì/ is believed to reflect a CRom dialectal variant with the vowel raised in anticipation of the glide [u̯] contained in the following onset; the Sard or Rou, of course, reflects either vowel.

CEx 245. With SW alone pointing to stressed */i/ instead of the expected */í/, we may discard the doublet */liga/ from CRom.

CEx 254. With Italian alone pointing unequivocally to stressed /ú/ as against /ɔ́/, we may safely discard the doublet */lungʊ/ for CRom.

CEx 256. The doublet with stressed /ú/ as against /ʊ́/ is thought to reflect a Lat dialectal (rustic?) variant with long -ū-; the Sard and Rou can, of course, reflect either vowel.

CEx 261. With Rou alone pointing to final /-a/ as against /-ʊ/, we may safely discard the doublet */mana/ from CRom.

CEx 271. Cited as 'VLat *martellus*', this diminutive (attested for Late Latin) evidently replaced the Lat diminutive MARCULU- (or MARTULU-?) in CRom.

CEx 278. A case identical to that of CEx 177.

CEx 279. With SW alone pointing to a single as against a geminate lateral, we may safely discard the doublet */mile/ from CRom.

CEx 282. We note that all but the SW forms can reflect either */ó/ or */ɔ́/ before a nasal coda. With SW alone pointing to */monte/ as against CEx 367 */pɔnte/, we may be dealing with a late modification reflecting a leveling with the unstressed /o/ of the formally and semantically related /montaña/ 'montagne/montaña'.

CEx 288. The Late Latin *molinum*, derived from CLat MOLA, is attested for the 6th cent. and was originally an adjective in such a phrase as *saxum molinum* 'meule/muela'.

CEx 296. Although SW alone points to a stressed /ɛ/ as against /i/, the two vowels are thought to have been dialectal variants in CRom, the doublet with the low vowel perhaps being influenced by CRom **nę́wu̯la** (< CLat NEBULA- 'brume/bruma') as though it were somehow a diminutive of **nę́wę**.

CEx 305. The shorter doublet reflects a continuation of the apocopated nom/acc sing. form NŌMEN, with regular loss of a minor-syllable nasal; the Sard form points to the full stem NŌMINE- with, however, a CRom leveling of the posttonic vowel to /e/ under pressure from the short form. (See also CEx 404.)

CEx 310. The fully reconstructible stressed */ɔ́/ instead of the expected */ó/ reflects a strong tendency in popular Latin speech to shorten this mid back-vowel before a labial onset. Hence we posit **ǫwu̯** for CRom.

CEx 311. The lack of syncope as reflected in Sard and Italian clearly reveals the influence of educated CRom speakers aware of the Latin model.

CEx 319. The nom/acc sing. form of this 3rd-decl. imparisyllabic neuter was os, abandoned by CRom in favor of the full stem but with a rare switch of declension; cf. the plural form ossa, which would have been that of *o̜=su̜m as well.

CEx 331. The PRom is indeterminate as between */parete/ and */parɪte/ without the Sard input, but in any case there is no evidence for the regular development of Lat -IE- to CRom /ye/ (Change D-2). Apparently, either the /i/ or the /e/ was absorbed in this unusually shaped item.

CEx 334. Cited as 'VLat *passa(re)', this denominal verb was supposedly built on CEx 333 in CRom.

CEx 335. Again, with Italian alone pointing to medial */g/ as opposed to */k/, we may discard the doublet */paga/ from CRom.

CEx 337. The fully reconstructible stressed */é/ instead of the expected */ɛ́/ seems due to the Latinizing influence of the clergy with their frequent occasion to speak this word.

CEx 341. This and CEx 343 obviously have the same Lat etymon. Of the semantic gaps left by the defection of Lat PUTĀ-, the one related to thinking was filled by cultivated CRom speakers splitting PĒNSĀ- in both form and meaning, thus differentiating two separate lexical items by restoring the coda (for they knew the Lat form) to the one as against the other.

CEx 345. Cited as 'VLat *pettia' but unattested, this item figures among the smallish number of words of Celtic origin which were borrowed into CRom.

CEx 356. Cited as 'VLat *plove(re)' but attested as early as the first cent. A.D., the basic stem appears to have acquired its /w/ by analogy with the preterite stem, with the noun PLUVIA (CEx 359) and with the adjective PLUVIU- while the stressed vowel dissimilated to [-hi].

CEx 359. Although *plovia is not attested as is the corresponding verb with /ɔ/, all the input languages except SW point straight to it.

CEx 362. Yet another conversion of a 2nd-declension neuter plural noun to a 1st-declension feminine in CRom, mediated semantically by transition from collective to individual reference to (a) fruit.

CEx 364. In this 3rd-declension neuter noun of the CEx 64 or 93 type, the nom/acc form PECTUS prevailed over the basic stem in CRom.

CEx 385. Final /-d/ was lost without a trace before the split of CRom.

CEx 394. Although Rou alone points to the codaless variant modeled on the irregular preterite and participial stem RUP- (cf. CEx 396), without the Sard input we cannot say whether or not the doublet in question was already in CRom.

CEx 404. The shorter doublet reflects a continuation of the apocopated nom/acc form SANGUEN of the old neuter variant, with regular loss of a minor-syllable nasal; the Sard form points to the full stem SANGUINE- with, however, a CRom leveling of the posttonic vowel to /e/ under pressure from the short form (see also CEx 305).

CEx 408. With Rou alone pointing to final /-ʊ/ as against /-e/, we may safely discard the doublet */sapoɴʊ/ from CRom (see Rou at 2.4.2).

CEx 416. The shorter doublet is based on the nom. sing. form SERPĒNS, which by regular sound-change became /sẹrpes/ in CRom and subsequently lost its case-marker -s to produce a mere variant of the stem-based original.

CEx 420. This represents the Lat SAETA, with rustic variant SĒTA, which originally denoted only a (hog's) bristle but is attested with its present, extended meaning in Low Latin.

CEx 421. The doublet in /-ɪs/, with a normal reflex in Sard, continues the nom. sing. form of this 3rd-decl. noun of the subclass known as *i*-stems (relics of a separate declension in OLat); the basic stem in CRom could thus have been either **sitị** or **sitẹ**.

CEx 429. Cited as 'VLat *talia(re)*', this CRom verb was derived from the Lat noun TĀLEA 'bouture/talla'.

CEx 431. In this 3rd-decl. neuter of the CEx 64, 93 or 364 type, the nom/acc form TEMPUS prevailed over the basic stem in CRom.

CEx 435. This is a reflex of the Lat noun TESTA 'pot (de terre)', one popular use of which was in jocular reference to a person's head.

CEx 444. Cited as VLat *tractia(re)*', this CRom verb was derived from the Lat noun TRACTU- 'trait/trecho'. It furnishes the only example in the corpus of the phonemic sequence /kty/, which already before the split of CRom must have assimilated (at least variably) to /ky/ (cf. Italian), even though /ty/ would have produced the same result in any of the other languages.

CEx 456. With Sard alone pointing to a PRom stem-final */-ɛ/ instead of the expected */-ɪ/ of a Lat *i*-stem, we may posit the CRom stem as **wẹnị** rather than **wẹnẹ**; in fact, it was only in southern dialects leading to SoRom that the switch in conjugation class occurred, and only in a few verbs.

CEx 463. The 5th-cent. *Appendix Probi*, in its most oft-cited example, prescribes '*vetulus*, non *veclus*'. The original diminutive, formed on the nom. form VETUS (rather than on the basic stem VETERE-), popularly underwent early syncope; and since /t/ was not a frequent coda, nor */tl/ an onset cluster, either syllabification necessitated the substitution of /k/ for /t/ to produce CRom **wẹklụ**.

CEx 469. The doublet with /i/ instead of the expected /ɪ/ reflects a variable tensing, in CRom, of the high stressed vowel in hiatus before /a/; cf. the similar behavior, not even variable, before /e/ in CEx 228.

CEx 472. The pretonic /ɪ/ instead of the expected /i/ is due to a

60 / 1 Latin becomes the Common Romance language

dissimilative shortening of the first of two identical long vowels. Although the Sard reflex can be that of either, Rou points to the change as having occurred already in CRom. But see Portuguese at 10.4.

CEx 475. The stressed /ɔ/ instead of the expected /ɛ/ is due to analogical leveling with the stressed vowel of CEx 306, within the possessive adjective paradigm.

Notes for Chapter 1

1. As applied to what had become by present criteria a new language, this new label quite properly supersedes not only the imprecise and much-abused term 'Vulgar Latin', but also Hall's preferred term 'Popular Latin' and, indeed, Agard's (1976) 'Imperial Latin'. The Latin language of the first century A.D. was, like any language, a composite of regional and social dialects stemming from the *sermo cotidianus* or *usualis*, from the *sermo plebeius* or *vulgaris*, and from the *sermo rusticus*—all three levels, and it was these that constituted, properly speaking, Popular Latin. As for the term 'Proto-Romance', which must be kept fully distinct from Common Romance, it refers simply to the common source of all existing Romance languages *as reconstructed by the comparative method*, and therefore should be reserved for use in a different frame of reference. The fact remains that all the grammatical features for which the comparative method does *not* show evidence—e.g. the phoneme **h** or a six-case nominal system—need not be ascribed to Common Romance as we define it. Proto-Romance and Common Romance are, in this sense, the two faces of one and the same coin.

2. The attested or direct evidence, random rather than systematic, consists mainly (as summarized in Elcock 1960:21) of traces of colloquial usage in the work of Latin writers; observations by Latin grammarians; spellings in inscriptions; and the pronunciation of loan-words from other languages.

3. The subscript number following an illustrative item identifies it in the corpus. Absence of a number, and an accompanying gloss instead, simply means that the item is not included in the corpus.

4. There is, of course, the well-known case of the diminutive of VETUS VETERE, namély, VETULU-$_{463}$, in which the pressure to syncopate side-stepped the nonoccurrent */-tl-/ by substituting the high-frequency /-kl-/ (*'vetulus' non 'veclus'*, admonishes the *Appendix Probi*).

5. The nonredundant distinctive-feature specification for the segments in view would be:

/i/ $\begin{bmatrix} +\text{syl} \\ +\text{high} \\ -\text{back} \end{bmatrix}$
/u/ $\begin{bmatrix} +\text{syl} \\ +\text{high} \\ +\text{back} \end{bmatrix}$
/e/ $\begin{bmatrix} +\text{syl} \\ -\text{high} \\ -\text{back} \\ -\text{low} \end{bmatrix}$
/o/ $\begin{bmatrix} +\text{syl} \\ -\text{high} \\ +\text{back} \\ -\text{low} \end{bmatrix}$

Of course, every one of our diachronic statements and synchronic mapping rules could, and doubtless theoretically should, be couched in distinctive-feature terms. There seems little advantage, however, in cluttering the present pages with so cumbersome a form of representation.

6. While certain Lucanian and Sicilian dialects give evidence of the lax/nonlax opposition in the mid but not the high vowels, Sardinian dialects indicate no lax/nonlax opposition having developed in any vowel at all. And while other Lucanian dialects show the opposition to have appeared in both the high and the mid front-vowels but only the mid back-vowel, Roumanian shows it in both front vowels but neither back vowel.

7. The further conversion of contiguous, identical vowels into a single long (or nonlax) vowel (as in /kohorte/$_{99}$ > /koorte/ = /kōrte/ (or /kortẹ/) may be considered simultaneous with Rule D-7, as specified by on-going redundancy rules.

Chapter 2
Common Romance splits into Southern, Eastern, and Italo-Western Romance

2.0 Introduction. Common Romance splits three ways into Southern, Eastern, and Italo-Western Romance. Southern comprises those dialects of lower Italia (mostly in Lucania) which ultimately prevailed in Sicilia, Sardinia, Corsica, and North Africa; Eastern comprises those dialects which eventually spread to Dacia and Moesia; Italo-Western comprises the inner core of the Roman Empire: Italia (minus Lucania), Dalmatia, Pannonia, Noricum, Gallia, Iberia.

2.1 Preliminary changes. We first take account of certain sound-changes—accompanied or not by dialectal restructurings—which are (a) not themselves productive of language change by our criteria, and are (b) independent of, yet evidently completed by the time of, the crucial development which will lead us to split CRom into three descendent languages. Such preliminary changes are:

2.1.1 Phonetic laxing of postvocalic consonants. Strictly on the phonetic level at this stage: the tendency through much of the Romania toward the lenition (i.e. laxing) of postvocalic contoids, whether onset or coda. Some of Sardinia and Corsica, most of Italia including Sicilia, and the entire West (with the possible exception of the Pyrenean hinterland) seem to have been affected.

2.1.2 Fusion of nonlabial consonants with a following yod. In a very widespread restructuring at the dialect level: the fusion of the nonlabials /t d k g s n l/ with a following yod as palatal obstruents. Where the original segment instead of being one of the item-medial clusters /ty dy ky gy/ was itself coda-plus-onset, the result is normally a geminate sequence. Thus, for example, /martyu̯/$_{270}$ is restructured as /marcu̯/, /ǫrdyu̯/ 'orge' as /ǫrẓu̯/, /lankya/$_{237}$ as /lanča/; but /pu̯tyu̯/$_{375}$ as /pu̯ccu̯/, /medyu̯/$_{277}$ as /meẓẓu̯/, /lakyu̯/$_{232}$ as /laččų/, /korrigya/$_{102}$ as /korriyya/[1], /basya/$_{28}$ as /baša/[2], /palya/$_{324}$ as /paʎʎa/, /winya/$_{465}$ as /wiñña/.

2.1.3 Dialectal merger of /č/ with /c/. In southern and eastern dialects, though not in Italo-western ones, there is a subsequent merger of /c/ and /č/ as /c/, yielding e.g. /braccu̯/$_{44}$ like /pu̯ccu̯/$_{375}$.

2.1.4 Dialectal merger of /kw/ with /k/. In southern, eastern, and Dalmatian dialects /kw/ merges with /k/ before any vowel (e.g. /kwando/$_{376}$ > /kando/), while in the bulk of Italo-western ones the loss of the glide is limited to word-initial /kw/ before a front vowel, as in /kwi̯/$_{385}$ > /ki̯/, or /kwere̯/$_{381}$ > /kere̯/. In Italo-western dialects the phonological result is no merger, however, because in the crucial environment /k/ already had developed the palatal allophone [č], which therefore merges instead with the palatal reflex of earlier /ky/ as occurring before nonfront vowels; thus in these dialects /kelu̯/$_{73}$ is restructured as /čelu̯/, though in the *language* it is still **kelu̯** because southern dialects have not palatalized the velar at all; nor have Dalmatian ones before /e/; and eastern ones—though they will eventually palatalize it *after* the merger of /kw/ with /k/—will not even then restructure it because they no longer have a /č/ for the eventual [č] to merge with.

• In parallel with its voiceless correlate, the /g/ in Italo-western dialects also had before a front vowel the palatal allophone [ǧ], which now, however, merges phonologically with yod itself, variably as [ǧ] or [ž] or [y], thus restructuring e.g. /gela/$_{202}$ as /yela/, though in the language it remains **gela** for reasons analogous to those given earlier with respect to the voiceless velar.

2.2 The crucial change: Lowering of the lax high vowels and consequent dialectal mergers. Subsequently, it is a question of the unconditioned lowering of the lax high vocoids—wherever one or both of them exist in any dialect—to higher-mid position. The lax/nonlax contrast of an assumed [e o] with existing [ẹ ọ] at the same height is quickly erased, as is also that of the

2.3 Summary of the split, and inventory of Italo-Western Romance

unstressed [ɛ ɔ] and [e o], and the phonological outcome is a merger as expressed by the diachronic rule

(D-8) /i̯ u̯/
/e o/ ⟶ /e o/.
/ę̆ ǫ̆/

By this rule /si̯te̯/$_{421}$ is restructured as /sete/, /bu̯=ka/$_{42}$ as /bo=ka/, /lu̯pu̯/$_{256}$ as /lopo/, /pędę/$_{346}$ as /pede/, etc. This is the trigger for the change and split, according to Criterion 4, because after this merger there remains a lax/nonlax contrast in the domain of tonic mid vowels alone, as far as any Romance dialect whatever is concerned. As a result of three partially intersecting mergers—Lat /i u/ with /ī ū/ (Rule D-5 extended, and see note 6) in southern dialects; Lat /u/ with /ū/ but CRom /i̯/ with /e/ in eastern dialects; and CRom /i̯ u̯/ with /e o/ (D-8) in Italo-western dialects[3]—no dialect any longer has high lax (originally short) vowels in its inventory, and therefore these units are to be removed from the language. Without them, however, an incongruence arises between each set of dialects as shown herewith:

CEx	Common Romance	Southern dialects	Eastern dialects	Italo-western dialects	Congruence
179	**filu̯**	filu	firu	filu	+
360	**pi̯lu̯**	pilu	peru	pelu	−
77	**kera**	kera	kera	kera	+
119	**kulu̯**	kulu	kuru	kulu	+
214	**gu̯la**	gula	gura	gola	−
422	**solę**	sole	sore	sole	+

That is to say, incongruence between Southern and Eastern is at CEx 360, incongruence between Eastern and Italo-Western is at CEx 214, and incongruence between Southern and Italo-Western is at both 360 and 214. As a result of this three-way incongruence, each of the three sets of dialects comes to constitute, by our criteria, a separate new language.

2.3 Summary of the split, and inventory of Italo-Western Romance. In summary, the phonological subsystem shaken up in the transition from Common Romance to Southern, Eastern, and Italo-Western Romance is that of the lax vowels, the highs being lost through coalescence, and therefore the mids alone continuing to be specified for the feature [lax]. The language change and split are dictated by Criterion 4. The relevant diachronic statements at the language level:

64 / 2 Common Romance splits into Southern, Eastern, and Italo-Western

The phonological inventory of the new language that interests us further in the present treatment, namely, Italo-Western Romance (It-W), is then the following:

Nuclei: i u e o ɛ ɔ⁴ a
                        aw

Onsets: p b t d c ʒ č k g f s š m n ñ l ʎ r y
        pr br tr dr   kr gr fr
        pl bl   kl gl fl
                            kw gw

Codas: p b t d k g s m n l r =
         nk

2.4 Residual discrepancies. The diachronic changes which took place as CRom split to become Southern, Eastern, and Italo-Western Romance are all reflected in Cols. 8, 7, and 6/5 of the corpus, although, of course, the respective input languages are end products embodying many subsequent developments as well. We pause at this point to comment on certain Sard, Rou, and Ital entries as representative of the first three descendants of CRom.

2.4.1 In Southern Romance as reflected by Sardinian. The majority of the gaps in Col. 8 mask either irregular changes such as CEx 1 /kómpora/ instead of the expected */kómpara/, or recent borrowings from standard Italian such as CEx 5 *acutu*, of which there are a great many. We single out only the following items of more than passing interest.

CEx 24. Sard /átteru/, with the lateral coda seemingly assimilated, nevertheless shows lack of syncope for Southern in this item.

CEx 80. The basic stem CORDE- has no reflex in any descendent; its survival in CRom is questionable, since by the split it had evidently given way to the nom/acc sing. form /kɔr/ (< COR), as evidenced by the Sard form in which the vowel filling out the final syllable typically echoes the stressed vowel.

CEx 125. The Sard form bespeaks a continuation of the nom. sing. with inflectional **-s** alongside the basic stem; cf. also the West Ibero evidence.

CEx 126. Southern lost this verb in favor of **nara**, a reflex of Lat NARRĀ 'conter/contar', which itself failed to survive in Eastern and It-W.

CEx 128. Some Southern dialects lost this noun and compensatorily generalized the meaning of /póddige/ 'pouce/pulgar' from Lat POLLICE-.

CEx 211. Southern alone retained Lat MAGNU- in this general meaning, as reflected in Sard /mannu/, although it survived in a phrase-bound form to surface in West Ibero-Romance as the noun /tamaño/.

CEx 262. The Lat etymon designated a mere hut or cabin; the less marked word denoting a dwelling or abode was DOMU-, which survived in Southern alone as Sard /domu/.

CEx 377. The Sard form is /baranta/, with initial /b/ instead of the expected /k/; also, '4' (CEx 379) is /báttoro/, '14' (CEx S81) is /battórdigi/, and '15' (CEx 384) is /bíndigi/. This labial onset, single or geminate, appears as the regular reflex of Lat medial /kw/ and /gw/ also in CEx 75, 76, 230, 238, 404, and in /abba/ 'eau/agua', though not regularly in initial position because the outcome is mere reduction, without labialization, in the verb /kere/ (CEx 381) and in the entire lexical subset of interrogative/relative words (e.g. CEx 82, 376, 380). It is not impossible that the bilabial onsets reflect ancient dialectal variations within Lat, traceable to the influence of other Italic languages such as Osco-Umbrian or Illyrian.

2.4.2 In Eastern Romance as reflected by Roumanian.

The gaps in Col. 7 indicate (a) unexpected phonemic changes, (b) 19th-cent. neologisms borrowed into Standard Roumanian from within Latin/Romance, or (c) earlier borrowings into Eastern (or an intermediate descendent) from outside Romance, mainly one or another Slavic language, (d) a few inherited but noncognate items with semantic equivalence. We single out the following items as being of potential interest.

CEx 7. The verb *iubește*, of Slavic origin, typifies the replacement of most Romance items denoting intimate interpersonal relationships.

CEx 9. The stressed /i/ rather than /ɨ/ here is the normal reflex of */ă/ before the posttonic high front /i/ (cf. the morphophonemic alternation in *vinzi* 'tu vends/vendes' as against *vînd* 'je vends/vendo'). This word now means 'coeur/corazón' (hence the gap at CEx 80), while 'âme/alma' is matched semantically by a derivative of the inherited Lat verb SUFFLĀ- 'souffler/soplar'.

CEx 10. Rou *amic*, though identical phonemically to what must have been the Eastern form, is nevertheless a Latinism which has had no tendency to dislodge the ancient Slavic replacement *prieten*.

CEx 12. Rou *amplu* instead of the expected **implu* is a Latinism.

CEx 17. Like Rou *August* /áwgust/, the names of the months are all Latinisms mediated by 16th-cent. borrowing from Greek/Slavic in the context of the Eastern Church.

CEx 22. Rou *argilă* is a Gallicism.

CEx 24. Rou *alt* rather than the expected **altru* may possibly reflect the Lat nom. sing. masc. ALTER with loss of final /-r/, reanalyzed as the fem. pl.

concord form /alt+e/ to produce the new masc. sing. (and basic stem) /alt/.

CEx 25. Rou has instead *orb*, the reflex of ORBU- which in Lat referred to deprivation not limited to eyesight.

CEx 27. The Rou form *baie* /baye/ continues the nom/acc plural form BALNEA. Eastern unstressed /a/ was raised to /ə/ in most positions, but as the neuter-plural marker **-a** it fell together morphophonemically with the 1st-decl. fem.-pl. marker **-e** from Lat -AE.

CEx 38. The Rou word here is the inherited adjective *alb* (< Lat ALBU-), replaced in It-W (and later also in Sard) by a Germanic loanword (see It-W at 2.4.3).

CEx 42. The Rou cognate has shifted semantically to 'joue/mejilla', with the present meaning filled by $gură_{214}$, itself shifted from 'gueule/gola' and replaced in that range by a word of uncertain origin.

CEx 43. Rou here uses the verb *fierbe*, regular reflex of Lat FERVĒ- and cognate of It/Po *ferve*, Sp *hierve* (not in corpus).

CEx 46. Rou has *pătrat*, for which see CEx 379.

CEx 54. Rou has *cîntec* /kɨntek/, a direct reflex of Lat CANTICU-, which meant 'chanson' while CANTIŌNE- meant 'incantation'.

CEx 58. The older Lat verb with this precise meaning was VĒNĀ-, which survives in Rou as the root in *vinează* (for the formative suffix see CEx 200).

CEx 60. Rou *castel* instead of the expected *căstiel is a 17th-cent. Latin loan via German.

CEx 62. The Rou verb is *incalţă* /ɨnkalcə/, showing the prefix *in-* which became highly productive in deriving verbs from other parts of speech.

CEx 64. The plural of Rou *cap* in its primary meaning of 'tête/cabeza' is *capete* /kápete/, which alone preserves the basic stem CAPITE-; see also CEx 27. The language also has the noun *capăt* /kápət/, by back-formation from the plural, with the associated meaning 'bout/cabo'.

CEx 68. Rou here uses the same word as CEx 360.

CEx 76. The equivalent *cinzeci* illustrates the Rou system of compounding the decade series after a Slavic model: *doi, trei, patru, cinci* ... plus the plural of nominalized $zece_{127}$.

CEx 81. Rou has *porumb*, patently a cross between Lat COLUMBA and PALUMBE-, the latter turning up also in West Ibero (see 6.4.3).

CEx 82. Rou has *cît*, with the nasal coda lost in a blending of Lat QUANTU- and QUOT(U-).

Cex 83. The Rou word here is the inherited verb *incepe* (< Lat INCIPE-), replaced in It-W (and perhaps later in Sard?).

CEx 88. The Rou form *contra* instead of the expected *cuntră is a Latinism no longer much in use except as a prefix, and losing ground to an older Slavicism.

2.4 Residual discrepancies / 67

CEx 99. Rou has *curte* instead of the expected **corte*, going back to dialectal variation in CRom.

CEx 100. The Rou verb *curge* instead of the expected **cure* is based on the participle *curs* (< Lat CURSU-), by analogy with e.g. *merge* 'aller/ir', participle *mers*—all this perhaps to avoid the embarrassing homophony of the 1st-pers. sing. form **cur* with CEx 119.

CEx 101. Rou has the doublets *cunună* 'guirlande' and *coroană* 'couronne', the latter partly Latinized.

CEx 102. Rou has *curea* /kureá/ instead of the expected */kureye/, as though from a hypothetical CRom */korr(y)ella/, influenced by /kɔryʊ/$_{115}$.

CEx 103. Rou has *scurt*, with prothetic /s-/ from Lat EX- by contamination with a hypothetical Eastern verb */ekskurta/.

CEx 105. Rou *costă* instead of the expected **coastă* is an Italianism.

CEx 106. The Rou participle is regularized as *coperit*.

CEx 113. Rou here uses the same word as CEx 112.

CEx 115. Rou now uses the same word as CEx 336.

CEx 121. Rou *deja* /dežá/, with its prefixed *de-*, is calqued on French. Much commoner is the function word *și* 'et/y', which acquires the present meaning by syntactic position.

CEx 129. The Rou form could be a reflex of the Lat (neuter) plural DAMNA switched to a 1st-decl. fem., but it is thought to be a neologism modeled phonologically on CEx 31.

CEx 133. The Rou equivalent *durere* is an example of deverbal noun derivation by means of the suffix *-re* (here added to the infinitive form /dureá/ of CEx 163), historically the infinitive marker and still sometimes misnamed, descriptively, the 'long infinitive'.

CEx 135. The equivalent *doisprezece* illustrates the Rou system of compounding the teens, also modeled on Slavic: *unu, doi, trei* ... plus the atonic preposition *spre* (< Lat SUPER, CRom /supre/ 'sur/sobre') plus *zece*$_{127}$.

CEx 140. The Rou form is *școală*, with Slavicizing palatalization of the initial (minor) syllable.

CEx 143. Rou *scris* instead of **script* illustrates the reformation of many past participles by generalizing the suffix *-s* added to the verb's root.

CEx 146. Rou *infern* rather than **infiern* is Italianizing.

CEx 148. Rou *intră*, which has the dialectal variant *întră*, may result from generalizing the /i/ which would be regular in certain forms of the verb, by virtue of vowel harmony.

CEx 149. While losing this item, Rou alone has preserved the semantically close Lat adjective DĒNSU- as *des*.

CEx 150. Rou *spadă* instead of the expected **spată* is an Italianism.

CEx 151, 152. Rou alone continues the 2nd-decl. masc. forms; the meaning was apparently synonymous in CEx 151, more specific in CEx 152.

68 / 2 Common Romance splits into Southern, Eastern, and Italo-Western

CEx 154. Rou *speră* instead of *speară is a neologism.

CEx 159. Rou *strîmt* continues the CRom dialectal variant /strịnktụ/, with the nasal coda intruding by analogy from the Lat verb STRINGE-, of which this was originally the past participle.

CEx 161. Rou *foame* instead of *fame shows the same aberration as Portuguese *fome*, Rhaetian and Lombard *fom*. In some dialects of CRom it may have been contaminated by reflexes of Lat FŌMITE- (with nom. FŌMES), originally 'tinder' with extended meanings of 'bait' or 'temptation'.

CEx 165. Rou *făină*, with the medial onset /r/ missing, may go back to an Eastern assimilative variant */fanina/ (cf. CEx 101), with the new /n/ palatalizing before /i/ and subsequently lost like the /ñ/ in (say) CEx 27.

CEx 166. Rou *fals*, alongside the neologism *fals*, is influenced by German *falsch*.

CEx 169. Rou *femeie*, which looks at least a partial cognate, is actually a direct reflex of Lat FAMILIA 'famille' with a very late semantic shift, the word for 'family' having been replaced by the Latinism *familie* /familie/.

CEx 178. Rou *febră* instead of *fiebre is a Latinizing and/or Italianizing neologism, entering the lexicon as a ə-stem like many new feminine stems.

CEx 180. The Rou cognate, obsolete, has given way to the diminutive *fiică* /fikə/ formed with the stressless suffix *-ică*.

CEx 182. Rou *fine* exists, but as a neologism; the usual item is Slavic.

CEx 183. Rou *flacără* is a blend of Lat FLAMMA and FACULA, the latter a diminutive of FACE- 'torche'.

CEx 188. Rou *fîntînă* has the Sard cognate *funtana* as well as the Fr *fontaine*, already the usual item in OFr rather than the specialized *funt*. The ultimate source of this lexical alternant is the fem. sing. form of the Lat adjective FONTĀNU-.

CEx 189. Rou *forță* instead of *foarță (cf. CEx 190) is a Gallicism/Italianism.

CEx 193. Rou *furnică* instead of *furmică traces back, dialectally, to CRom.

CEx 197. The Rou cognate, obsolescent, is giving way to the Latinizing *fruct*.

CEx 200. The Rou stem *fumează* illustrates verb-derivation by means of the formative suffix *-ează*, cognate with Ital *-eggia*, Sp *-ea*, Po *-eia*, and a reflex of Lat -IDIĀ-, once highly productive in Roumanian.

CEx 202. Rou has *înghiață*, derived by typical prefixation from the noun *ghiață* 'glace/hielo', regular reflex of CRom **glakya** (< Lat GLACIĒ-).

CEx 205. The Rou cognate has become specialized to mean 'race/raza', with the present range covered by *lume* (itself shifted; cf. CEx 257).

CEx 206. The Rou form shows a dialectal switch of this feminine from 3rd to 1st decl. as early as CRom; Ital shows it also for It-W.

CEx 216, 217. The Rou derivational prefix is typical for the verb, and is extended analogically to the adjective itself for differentiation from alt_{24}.

2.4 Residual discrepancies / 69

CEx 219. The Rou cognate has shifted semantically to mean 'fois/vez', with the range of 'heure/hora' now shared with an early Slavicism by the neologism *oră*.

CEx 221. Rou has the fem. *iarnă*, which can come from the Lat neuter-plural substantive HIBERNA 'winter quarters', or from an *a*-final concord-form of the adjective which became a 2nd-decl. masc. replacing HIEME- already in CRom.

CEx 222. The Rou cognate is a direct reflex of the nom. sing. form HOMO, which competed with the basic stem from CRom on down; Ital shows it also for It-W. The plural remained built on the basic stem, however: Rou has *oameni* /wámeny/, Ital *uomini* /wómini/.

CEx 224. Rou *insulă* with its nasal coda is strictly a Latinism.

CEx 234. Rou *lasă* rather than the expected **lapsă* may reflect dialectal loss of the CRom coda /k/ already in Eastern, perhaps at first in forms where the root was unstressed.

CEx 237. Rou *lance* rather than **lînță* is an Italianism entering via Slavic or Hungarian.

CEx 243. Rou *literă* /literə/ could be a direct reflex of the Lat doublet LĪTERA, but is actually a late neologism.

CEx 249. Rou has *lințoliu* /lincóliu/, said to be an Italianism.

CEx 250. Rou has *leu*, a 17th-cent. Latinism based on the nom. sing. form LEO; whereas all the other cognates come directly from the basic stem with /-n-/.

CEx 257, 258. The Rou cognate of 257 has shifted to mean both 'gens/gente' and 'monde/mundo', with the semantic range of both the present items given over to *lumină*, from the Lat plural form LŪMINA, and to *luminare* (< the Lat derivative LŪMINARE- 'fenêtre/ventana' as a source of light).

CEx 261. Rou *mînă* with final /-ə/ reflects a switch of this unusual 4th-declension feminine to the *ă*-stem class precisely because of its gender.

CEx 264, 265. Rou has *rău*, a reflex of Lat REU- shifted from a noun meaning 'accusé/reo' to the adjective meaning 'mauvais/malo', also in nominal and adverbial use.

CEx 266. The Rou cognate has become a noun with the highly specialized meaning of 'cerdo castrado' (Eng. 'barrow'); its place here is taken by *bărbătesc*, a derivative of *bărbat* (< Lat BARBĀTU- 'barbu/barbado').

CEx 269. Rou has the verb *mărită* 'épouser/casarse' (said of a woman), but for the noun in view it alone has kept (as *soț*) the CLat SOCIU-, signifying a partner or associate in one or another relationship including marriage.

CEx 272. Rou has *amenință*, with the variably added prefix (< CLat AD-) going back to CRom (cf. SW representing It-W) but with the coda /n/ unexplained.

CEx 276. In this meaning Rou has only $pune_{366}$.

CEx 280. Although Common Roumanian still had *mese*, Daco-Roumanian has lost it in favor of extended $lună_{259}$, which also keeps its original meaning of 'lune/luna'.

CEx 281. Instead of the expected *muneată, Rou has both the Italianism monetă and the Venetianism monedă (via Greek).

CEx 283. Rou has mursecă /múrsekə/, a direct reflex of the CRom derivative **morsika-**, as well as muşcă, a probable blend.

CEx 288. The related Rou moară is a true reflex of CLat MOLA 'meule/ muela', which the other languages share in the original meaning (not in corpus).

CEx 292. CRom /muru̯/ survived in Eastern, though Rou mur is a Latinism alongside a Slavic loan.

CEx 293. Rou matur instead of *mătur is neologizing.

CEx 295. Rou navă instead of *naie is Latinizing/Italianizing, adapting as an ă-stem like many neologistic feminines.

CEx 304. Rou nucă instead of *nuce reflects a shift of stem-class—nuci being a regular plural for either—under the influence of a lexico-semantic subsystem whereby the word for a fruit is a feminine ă-stem while that for the tree bearing it is a masculine consonant-stem; cf. therefore also nuc 'noyer/ nogal'.

CEx 307. Rou nud is actually an Italianism.

CEx 316. For Rou unsprezece see CEx 135.

CEx 321, 322. Rou uses the root -chide (< CLat -CLŪDE-, stem alternant of CLAUDE-) with contrasting prefixes: deschide for 'ouvrir/abrir', închide for 'fermer/cerrar'.

CEx 328. The Rou cognate has become highly specialized, while the semantically equivalent palat is a Grecianism.

CEx 334. Threatened by homophony with CEx 343 in the East, this verb was ultimately replaced in Rou by trece, lone survivor of Lat TRĂICE-, originally meaning 'traverser/atravesar'.

CEx 337. Rou has păcătuieşte, formed on the noun păcat (< CLat PECCĀTU- in turn derived from PECCĀ-), illustrating derivation by the suffix -eşte from the Latin inchoative -SCE- which, recut as /-éšte/, became even more productive in Roumanian than elsewhere.

CEx 338. Rou has pescuieşte, derived from peşte$_{363}$ with the same formative as mentioned in the preceding CEx.

CEx 344. Rou has lost the cognate in favor of puţin, seemingly an Eastern diminutive, dialectal in CRom, of CLat PUTU-, which as an adjective meant 'pur/puro' and as a noun 'garçon/muchacho' (the latter surviving in Venetian and, though with geminate /tt/ and a different semantic shift, in Italian).

CEx 346. Rou has picior, denoting foot and/or leg undifferentiated, seemingly from Eastern */pekyolu/, a dialectal reduction of CRom */pedi̯kyo̯lu̯/, a diminutive formed on CLat PEDICA, in turn a derivative of PEDE-; but the semantics are less than satisfactory.

CEx 348. Rou piaţă instead of *plaţă is an Italianism entering via Greek, also embracing the meaning of CEx 268.

2.4 Residual discrepancies / 71

CEx 352. The Rou *plins* instead of *plint* is a nominalization of the participle (in *-s*, cf. CEx 143) of the verb *plinge*$_{351}$.

CEx 354. Standard Rou uses the neologism *plantă*, though the inherited *plintă* also occurs dialectally.

CEx 355. Rou has *plin* rather than the expected **pliu* (cf. CEx 195, 210), doubtless by leveling with the other forms in the agreement paradigm: /n/ normal in all three (cf. CEx 454), and /i/ normal in the plurals where the final vowel is front (as well as in the derived verb *împlineşte*).

CEx 358. The Rou cognate means 'partir', in direct semantic opposition to 'arriver/llegar' in West-Ibero—both originally associated with the notion of (un)folding sails.

CEx 377. For Rou *patruzeci* see CEx 76.

CEx 379. The Rou form is *patru*, with initial /p/ instead of the expected /k/, as also in CEx 46. A bilabial onset, voiceless or voiced accordingly, appears as the regular reflex of Lat medial /kw/ or /gw/ before a nonfront vowel only (thus unlike Sard), also in CEx 230, 238, and in *apă* 'eau/agua', though not regularly in initial position because the outcome is mere reduction, without labialization, before a front vowel and in the entire lexical subset of interrogative/relative words (e.g. CEx 82, 376, 385). A possible explanation for this phenomenon in Eastern as well as in Southern Romance is suggested in 2.4.1 (Sard CEx 377).

CEx 384. For Rou *cinsprezece* see CEx 135.

CEx 386. The Rou cognate, together with the Sard and the French, go back to a CRom diminutive **radikina**, attested for Low Latin, and in competition with the simplex which was lost only in Eastern.

CEx 388. The Rou form, now a fem. *ă*-stem, reflects the Lat (neuter) plural RADIA.

CEx 400. Since **sîn* would have collided with CEx 411, Rou uses a reflex of the CRom derivative **sanatosu**, namely, *sănătos*.

CEx 403. In the sense of 'santé' Rou uses *sănătate*, with slightly peculiar vocalism but essentially cognate with the various reflexes of the CLat derivative SĀNITĀTE- (not in corpus).

CEx 401. The Rou *sfînt* instead of **sînt* is crossed with the Slavic equivalent with initial /sf-/.

CEx 406. Rou has *salvă* as a Latinism.

Cex 408. Rou has *săpun* instead of **săpune* under Slavic influence.

CEx 410. As the corresponding title of respect, Rou uses *domn*, a reflex of CLat DOMINU- and cognate with Ital *donno*, Sp *dueño*, Po *dono* (not in corpus).

CEx 411. Rou has *sîn* rather than **sîu*, perhaps back-formed on the plural *sîni* (earlier *sîne*).

CEx 417. Rou uses *serveşte*, with the formative mentioned earlier at CEx 337, even though in this instance there is no question of derivation.

72 / 2 Common Romance splits into Southern, Eastern, and Italo-Western

CEx 418. Rou has lost this item in favor of *singur* /singur/, retained as the lone reflex in Romance of CLat SINGULU-.

CEx 419. Rou has *şase* instead of **şaps(e)*, adding an unexpected final /-e/ to match that of *şapte* '7' in rhythm, yet losing the coda the better to differentiate the two numbers.

CEx 432. The Rou cognate has taken over the meaning 'jeune/joven', rendering obsolete the original *juve* from CLat IUVENE-, cf. Ital *giovine* or *giovane* etc. (not in corpus).

CEx 436. Rou has *ţese* instead of **ţepse*, with coda loss comparable to that noted earlier for CEx 234.

CEx 440. Rou uses the lexified locution *(in)totdeauna*.

CEx 445, 446. For Rou *treisprezece* and *treizeci*, see CExs 135, 76.

CEx 448. Rou has *trei* instead of **tres*, the /-i/ (like that of *doi* '2') being a redundantly analogized plural-agreement marker.

CEx 451. This item has been lost and its meaning taken over by $cîştigă_{61}$, which has also been extended to cover 'gagner/ganar' but replaced as 'punir' by a loan from Greek.

CEx 461. This item has been replaced by *imbracă*, reflex of the CRom verb **imbraka** derived from the Latin noun of Celtic origin BRĀCAE 'chausses/calzas'.

CEx 462. The Rou cognate is specialized to denote a head of livestock, with the gap filled by *viaţă* as derived from the adjective viu_{464} by means of *-eaţă*, reflex of the CLat nominal suffix -ITIA.

CEx 463. Rou *vechi* instead of **viechi* is phonological, due merely to dissimulatory loss of the first yod in Common Rou */vyekyu/.

CEx 467. For Rou *douăzeci* see CEx 76.

CEx 473. Rou has *voce* as a neologism competing with a Slavic loan.

CEx 474. Rou has *zboară* instead of the expected **voară*, the minor-syllable /z-/ representing a variably added prefix going back to CLat EX-, voiced here before a voiced onset.

2.4.3 In Italo-Western Romance as reflected by Italian. We now proceed to comment on certain items (or gaps) in Col. 6 as indicative of developments in Italo-Western.

CEx 2. Cited as 'VLat **affila(re)*' but unattested, this verb can have been derived from $FĪLU-_{179}$ in It-W only.

CEx 20. Cited as 'VLat **arcione*' as a diminutive of CLat ARCU- 'arc/arco', this item was evidently first formed in It-W for reference to any small bow and was eventually specialized.

CEx 38. Except for its crystallization as a noun (see CEx 23), the CLat adjective ALBU- gave way in It-W to one of several early loans from Common Germanic (CGmc). The present one originally denoted general brightness or lightness rather than specific whiteness.

CEx 71. CLat CAUSA, originally 'cause/causa', came to supplant RĒ- in It-W, but both died out in Southern and in Eastern, with Sard eventually borrowing the Italian word and Rou generalizing CLat LUCRU- 'profit/provecho' as *lucru*.

CEx 162. The Italian basic stem *fa* instead of the expected **face* (although the latter does remain as a stem allomorph) points to a variable reduction of this verb to join the inherited short stems da_{131}, *(e)sta* 'estar' and *va* 'aller/ir'; the change might also have been influenced by the continuing viability of the CRom imperative form /fa/, a direct reflex of the CLat monosyllabic FAC.

CEx 201. This is another of the CGmc loans which entered It-W prior to the major invasions; the initial /w-/ of the etymon differed from the labiodental phone [v] already representing It-W /w/, and in most dialects it was assigned to the voiced onset cluster /gw/ occurring theretofore only medially after a nasal coda (as in /lengwa/$_{238}$); thus the It-W form is reconstructible as */gwarda/.

CEx 206. Italian as well as Rou reflects a switch of declension which was variable at most in It-W (cf. French and SW).

CEx 213, 215. These are two more of the CGmc loans entering It-W with initial /gw/; see CEx 201.

CEx 230. The It-W form remains unchanged from CRom as /ɛkwa/, reflected subsequently in SW.

Notes for Chapter 2

1. The CRom voiced velar had no laxed postnuclear occurrence such as to yield */ǧ/, for it had already semivocalized to yod as coda before /y/, and as onset before a front vowel, e.g. not only /korrįgya/ > /korrįyya/ but also regę/$_{394}$ > /reyę/. There was some tendency also to parallel merger of /d+y/ as in /radyu̧/$_{387}$ > /rayyu̧/ alongside /mędyu̧/.

2. Both /š/ and /šš/ occur postvocalically: the single is the shift of a postnuclear onset cluster /sy/ (appearing instead of the expected /s+y/--e.g. /basya/ > /baša/), while the geminate is the shift of coda-plus-onset /s+sy/—e.g. /bassya/ 'baisser/bajar' > /bašša/.

3. Lax /u̧/ variably becomes /u/ instead of /o/ (a) in unstressed position, particularly final, in some dialects; (b) in stressed position mainly before velars and palatals (i.e. [-anterior]), cf. the hesitation leading to *poing*$_{361}$ as expected in French but to *puño* not **poño* in Spanish.

4. The contrast between the mid vowels (α back) is now better characterized as one of height rather than of laxness, with the old ę ǫ rewritten as ɛ ɔ and specified as [−hi +mid] as against the [+hi +mid] e o, the two heights being neutralized in unstressed position. As for the incidence of stress in the word, it needs to be marked only when antepenultimate (displaced), as, for example, in **ánema**$_9$ (< CRom **ánima**).

Chapter 3
Italo-Western splits into Italo-Dalmatian and Western Romance

3.0 Introduction. Italo-Western Romance splits binarily into Italo-Dalmatian and Western Romance. The former language comprises dialects of northeastern, central, and some of southern Italia, also of (mainly coastal?) areas of Dalmatia, and Pannonia; the latter language comprises dialects of northwestern Italia, Noricum, Gallia, and Iberia.

3.1 Preliminary changes. The lack of congruence will result from completion of the loss of the velar codas, a loss already begun with the assimilation, in some southern and Italo-Western dialects of CRom, of the laxed allophones of /g/ and /k/ to following nonvelar onsets. In those dialects, for example, /lakte/$_{235}$ had already been restructured as /latte/, /laksa/$_{234}$ as /lassa/, /lignu/$_{40}$ as /linnu/, /frigdu/ 'froid/frio' as /friddu/. Completion of the loss is described in Change 3.2; first, the preliminary changes.

3.1.1 Dialectal fusion of geminates into single, tense consonants. Dialectally, in all of the Romania except central and southern Italia and the southern islands, coda-plus-onset geminates become fused into single, nonlax onsets, as, for example, in It-W **pa=sa**$_{334}$ /passa/ > /pasa/, or **sɛ=te**$_{415}$ /sɛte/ > /sɛte/. The phonological effect of this generalized fusion is to throw the new, nonlax single onsets into functional contrast with the lax single-contoid onsets which had already developed phonetically in many dialects of CRom (see 2.1): so, for example, **kasa**$_{262}$ /kasa/ > /kaṣa/, or **sete**$_{421}$ /sete/ > /seṭe/.[1] Item-initial and postcoda (and post-**aw**) onsets remain nonlax, hence the opposition is medial postvocalic only.

There is no evidence that the voiced affricates **ʒ** and **ǧ** had lax correlates, because as fused reflexes of the CRom onsets **dy** and **gy** they had no postvocalic occurrence. The voiceless onset **ty** seemingly had sporadic occurrences in competition with the expected coda-plus-onset **t+y**, as in **ratyone**$_{388}$ > It-W **racone** /racone/ instead of the expected */raccone/.

3.1.2 Dialectal merger of postvocalic /w/ with /b̯/. By a redistribution, onset **w** no longer occurs postvocalically, the /w/ having merged (in all dialects) with /b̯/ as [β] in that environment—e.g. /nɔwe/$_{297}$, /lawa/$_{242}$ restructured as /nɔb̯e/, /lab̯a/.

3.2 The crucial change: Semivocalization of the coda /k/ / 75

3.1.3 Semivocalization of the coda /g/. Wherever the allophones of coda /g/—i.e. fricative [γ] before onset [d], and nasal [ŋ] before onset [n]—had escaped dialectal assimilation, they now semivocalize to [i̯] (or marginally [u̯][2]). The phonological result for western dialects is a shift entailing the replacement of /g/ by /y/ among the codas:

(D-9)   Coda /g/ —— /y/,

e.g. /legnu/ > /leynu/, /fregdu/ > /freydu/. Synchronically:

(M-4)   g → /y/_C.

3.2 The crucial change: Semivocalization of the coda /k/. Wherever in the West (including northern Italia) the fricative allophone [x] of coda /k/ before onsets /t/ and /s/ still remains (having escaped assimilation in some dialects of CRom), it now becomes semivocalized as yod, or more probably voiceless yod, though direct evidence for the latter is lacking. The phonological outcome is a merger with /y/, which by virtue of Change 3.3 now occurred as coda:

(D-10)   Coda /k/
                    $\Big\rangle$ /y/.
              /y/

Examples: /ɔkto/$_{223}$ > /ɔyto/, /lakte/ > /layte/, /akse/$_{155}$ > /ayse/, /laksa/ > /laysa/. There is no corresponding M-rule, because in the remaining dialects (of Italia and Dalmatia) this coda was largely non-occurrent by virtue of its assimilation in CRom.[3] As a result of the differential treatments in view, velar codas[4] are to be removed from the inventory of the language. And according to Criterion 4, without these entities the language can no longer properly account for both Italo-Dalmatian and western dialects, which have become incongruent as shown:

CEx	Italo-Western Romance	Italo-Dalmatian dialects	Western dialects	Congruence
40	**legnu**	leyno	leynu	+
334	**pa=sa**	pa(s)sa	pasa	+
234	**laksa**	la(s)sa	laysa	−
235	**lakte**	la(t)te	layte	−
415	**sɛ=te**	sɛ(t)te	sɛte	+

Technically, the two incongruent correspondences could be mapped by positing coda **y** for the language, with a synchronic rule for Italo-Dalmatian dialects assimilating the yod to following /t/ or /s/. But what principle would this violate?

3.3 Summary of the split, and inventory of Western Romance. In summary, the phonological subsystem shaken up in the transition from Italo-Western to Italo-Dalmatian and Western Romance is that of the velar codas, lost via differential coalescences; the language change and split are mandated by Criterion 4. The relevant diachronic statements:

$$\text{It-W / Coda} \begin{cases} k \longleftarrow = \text{/It-D} \\ y \longrightarrow y \text{ /W} \end{cases}$$

The phonological inventory of the new language that interests us further in the present treatment, namely, Western Romance (W), is then the following:

Nuclei: i u e o ɛ ɔ a

Onsets: p b t d c ʒ č ǧ k g f s š m n ñ l ʎ r y w
        pr br tr dr   kr gr fr
        pl bl   kl gl fl
                                 kw gw

        p̣ ḅ ṭ ḍ c̣   č̣   ḳ ġ f̣ ṣ ṣ̌ ṃ ṇ ḷ   ṛ ỵ
        pr br tr dr   ḳr ġr f̣r
        pl bl   ḳl ġl f̣l
                              ḳw

Codas: p b t d s m n ñ l r y w

Remarks. (1) The diphthong **aw** no longer need figure among the nuclei, for the back semivowel **w** is now assignable to the codas as a correlate of the new semivowel coda **y**; the two are to undergo closely linked developments later.

(2) Coda **ñ** is a spin-off of Change 3.4, involving the mutual assimilation of the antecedent coda cluster **nk** as in Lat SANCTU-$_{401}$ or PUNCTU- 'point/punto' (> We **sañtu poñtu ~ puñtu**).

3.4 Residual discrepancies in Italo-Dalmatian Romance as reflected by Italian. The diachronic changes which took place as Italo-Western split to become Italo-Dalmatian and Western Romance are all reflected in Cols. 1–7 of the corpus, although the input languages Italian, Old French, and the rest are end-products embodying numerous later developments as well. We pause at this point to comment on certain Italian entries as representative of the

3.4 Residual discrepancies in Italo-Dalmatian Romance / 77

non-Western branch of It-W, from Italo-Dalmatian down to Modern Italian.

CEx 3. All nouns ending in It-W /-tate/, chiefly those in which the final sequence was a nominal suffix (cf. CLat CĀRITĀTE-, VĒRITĀTE-... from the adjectives CĀRU-, VĒRU-...) have been truncated to /-tá/ in modern Italian.

CEx 36. Italian alone reflects the unsyncopated It-W variant /sɔ́keru/, perhaps under learnèd influence. It also exemplifies the phonemic redistribution whereby /k/ before front vowel, phonetically [č] from early on except in Dalmatian dialects before /e/, is restructured as /č/ after Dalmatian and Italo-Romance have split.

CEx 37. Italian *bene* instead of the expected **biene* is thought due to the analogy of even the stressed lower-mid vowels' normal failure to diphthongize in syntactically weak position before an adjective or the like as head of its phrase. However, the diphthongization of It-Dal /ɛ/ and /ɔ/ in open syllables was confined to Tuscany and there are some cases of this sort which are best explained simply as prevailing from non-Tuscan dialects of Northern or Central Italian.

CEx 72. Italian has *cavolo* /kávolo/, a reflex of the CRom variant /kawlu̯/ (attested in Late Latin) with also a Tuscanization of the South Italian disyllabic /a+u/ from /aw/. As for Italian *caule*, it is strictly a Latinism in form and meaning.

CEx 83. Italian *comincia* instead of the expected **comenza* is due to a mix-up falsely equating a North Italian /c/ with the Tuscan /č/ of *lancia* instead of the /c/ of *lenza*. The high stressed vowel is of course then a regular development before a palatal onset.

CEx 96. Italian *cuce* instead of **cose* results from a similar mix-up falsely equating a North Italian /š/ with the Tuscan /č/ of *bacio* (the Italian single /š/ not occurring medially) instead of the /s/ of *naso*. Again, the high stressed vowel is then a regular development.

CEx 118. The Italian *coscia* as against **cossa* reflects the Western development of It-W /k+s/ as /y+s/ rather than as /s+s/; the influence was perhaps Gallo-Italian in origin. It is further to be noted, however, that It-W /s+k/ before front vowel (as in /kreske/$_{110}$) regularly became Italo /š+š/ via [s+č > š+č], while in neighboring Western dialects it had metathesized to /k+s/ in this environment and thus participated in the development through /y+s/ to /š+š/. Thus the number of items ending up with /šš/ in both descendants was sizeable, and to find the present /kɔšša/ among them is not surprising; cf. also CEx 234.

CEx 125. The high stressed vowel of Italian is phonologically normal in this type of hiatus.

CEx 127. The Italian final /-i/ instead of /-e/ is doubtless influenced by the stem alternant /-diči/ of the teen-words, in which the medial unstressed /i/ is regular and the second assimilated to it in height.

CEx 128. The variable weakening and/or loss of the /g/ between the two identical front vowels, possibly already in popular dialects of Latin, led to divergent results in CRom and in It-W, among them telescoping of /i+i/ as /ī/ prior to loss of length, thus yielding the CRom variant /ditu̯/ as reflected in Italian *dito* and in Campidanese Sard *didu*.

CEx 144, 150, 151. The Italian medial /d/ or /g/ instead of /t/ or /k/ in these (but not all) items betrays northern influence upon the mainly Tuscanizing process of standardization. After the split of It-W, the voicing of lax obstruents that characterized most Western lects was not only present in neighboring Gallo-Italian dialects of Northwestern Romance (see 3.1) but also had penetrated northern varieties of Italo-Romance (e.g. Emilian, Venetian) as far down as the 'La Spezia-Rimini Line'; see 4.2.

CEx 170. The Italian *moglie* instead of *mogliere shows that It-W, as well as some dialects of CRom, had a doublet continuing the Lat short nom. sing. MULIER, with stress on the first syllable and loss of final consonant.

CEx 197. The Ital form shows that by It-W a competing fem. *a*-stem was in existence even though there had been no Lat neuter-plural model in -*a* for this 4th-decl. noun.

CEx 202. The Ital stressed /é/ instead of /yé/ in this item is unexplained; but cf. 1.9 at CEx 296: where there is regular /neve/ there is irregular /ǧelo/, and where there is regular /ǧɛlo/ there is irregular /nɛve/.

CEx 230. Ital has lost this item in favor of the derived feminine *cavalla* (see CEx 67).

CEx 231, 236, 246. For the Ital medial /g/ instead of /k/ in these items, see above, CEx 151.

CEx 234. For the Ital *lascia* and the more southern dialect variant *lassa*, see above at CEx 118 and note also the coexistence from Lat on down of the archaizing Ital *lassa* and Fr *lasse* 'fatiguer/cansar' (< CLat LASSĀ-).

CEx 239. The Ital *coniglio* instead of the expected *conicchio betrays the Western development of CRom/It-W medial /kl/ and is therefore attributable to northern influence; compare the doublets *specchio* and *speglio* 'miroir/espejo'.

CEx 244, 301. The Ital stressed /ɛ/ instead of /yɛ/ represents a mere leveling to the unstressed stem alternant as in the infinitive *levare*, etc. In many verbs the leveling has gone the other way, with the diphthong throughout the paradigm as in *chiede(re)*$_{381}$.

CEx 247. As regards the Ital stressed /ɛ/ instead of /yɛ/ in this noun, there are some cases of this sort which are best explained as prevailing from non-Tuscan dialects of Northern or Central Italian.

CEx 249. The Ital pretonic /e/ instead of /i/ is believed to result from a blend with *lenza*, from the fem. sing. form of the CLat LINTEU-, derived from LĪNU-$_{248}$.

3.4 Residual discrepancies in Italo-Dalmatian Romance / 79

CEx 254. The Ital *lungo* instead of **longo* is said to be from a Florentine subdialect of Tuscan, though for what reason is not clear.

CEx 297. The Ital *nove* instead of **nuove* seemingly reflects the standardization of a non-Tuscan (nondiphthonged) variant for the convenient differentiation of this number-word from any form of the adjective $nuovo_{298}$, particularly, of course, the fem. plu. *nuove*.

CEx 303. Ital *nero* instead of **negro*, together with Fr *noir* as against **noire* as base, reflect the existence of a dialectal /neru/ alongside the regular /negru/ already in It-W.

CEx 311. Ital *opera* instead of **uopera* or **uopra* probably betrays Latinizing rather than specifically non-Tuscan influence, in view also of the absence of syncope.

CEx 335, 358. For the Ital medial /g/ instead of /k/, see above at CEx 151.

CEx 365. Ital *pepe* instead of **pepre* or **pepere* shows, like CEx 170, that It-W, as well as some dialects of CRom, had a doublet continuing the Lat short nom/acc sing. PIPER, with stress on the first syllable and regular loss of final consonant.

CEx 370. The Ital short form *può* instead of the full **puote* is a generalized apocopation originally occurring in syntactically unstressed position before a following verbal in the infinitive.

CEx 381. Ital *chiede* instead of **chiere* is thought to result from dissimilation, originally in the forms containing a second /r/, e.g. infinitive *chiedere*, future tense *chiederà*, etc.

CEx 387. Ital *ragione* instead of **ra(z)zone* results from the mistaken equating of North Italian /ʒ/ with the Tuscan /ǧ/ of $maggio_{260}$ instead of the /ʒ/ of $mezzo_{277}$.

CEx 393. Ital *rio* instead of the expected **rivo* betrays a possible loss of medial /w/ before final /-u̯/ as far back as CRom—a regular loss, provided the /w/ of **wiwu**$_{464}$ is preserved by association with the CRom verb **wiwe**$_{468}$. It is to be noted that the relevant Sard and Rou forms can stem from either /-iwu̯/ or /-iu̯/.

CEx 394. Ital *re* instead of **rege* shows that It-W, as well as some dialects of CRom, had a doublet continuing the CLat monosyllabic nom. sing. REX, with regular loss of final /-ks/ in Ital; cf. also CEx 419.

CEx 414. The Ital form with single /m/ as contrasted with the geminate in $femmina_{170}$, is doubtless analogous to those stem alternants in which the vowels on either side are unstressed, e.g. *seminare, seminato*...

CEx 443. The Ital form with geminate /tt/ reflects a (perhaps more emphatic?) popular variant current in CRom, as evidenced also by the Sard for Southern; the Rou can come from either a single or a geminate. As for the unexpected stressed vowel, it is not satisfactorily explained but could go back to an even more expressive CRom variant with both vowels high (by assimilation): */tuttu̯/ or */tu̯ttu̯/.

CEx 446, 467. For Ital *trenta, venti* as against Sard *trinta, vinti*, cf. CEx 128. In the present items, some (but not all) It-W dialects went to /é/ via a CRom assimilation and telescoping: /i-i̯ > i̯-i̯ > i̯/.

CEx 474. Ital *vola* instead of **vuola* is another case of paradigmatic leveling, cf. *volare* etc., also achieving differentiation from the verb *vuole* 'vouloir/querer'.

Notes for Chapter 3

1. Where laxing had *not* taken place, e.g. in Dalmatian dialects of It-W as well as in dialects of Eastern Romance, the result of degemination was, of course, mere merger with postvocalic singles.

2. Although central Italian dialects later fuse /y+n/ into /ñ/ just as western dialects do, this diachronic change cannot be stated at this point for It-W, because some southern Italian dialects preserve the coda-plus-onset string, as /y+n/ or as /w+n/.

3. Actually, not in all Italian dialects had [k] been assimilated to [s]. Where it variably remains to become lax instead, and then to fricativize, the resultant string [x̠-s] later fuses as [šš], and the final outcome is a considerable hesitation between older /ss/ and newer /šš/; cf. standard It *coscia*$_{118}$, *lascia* as against *asse*$_{155}$ or *sasso* 'roche/roca'.

4. This includes the velar elements in the infrequent coda cluster **nk**, as in **sanktu**$_{401}$ > /sanytu/ or sayntu/ (?). Cf. also CRom **magis** 'plus/más', reduced very early (as attested by both It and Rou *mai*) to /mays/ as well as /mas/.

Chapter 4
Western splits into Unshifted Western and Shifted Western Romance

4.0 Introduction. Western Romance splits binarily into Unshifted Western and Shifted Western Romance. The lack of congruence will result from developments affecting the lax obstruents as onsets—that is, precisely in the position where laxness is a phonologically distinctive feature.

4.1 The crucial changes

4.1.1 Dialectal merger of the lax with the tense obstruents.
In dialects on both slopes of the Pyrenees, and stretching well southward into central Iberia—in other words, in dialects which will ultimately emerge as Gascon, Aragonese, and Mozarabic—the lax obstruents become tense:[1] [p̬] > [p] and so on throughout the list of lax obstruents. The phonological result is the loss of the feature [lax] through full merger with the nonlax correlates, as expressed in the following rule:

(D-11) /P̬/ ⟩/P/,
         /P/

in which /P/ subsumes all the consonants involved in the diachronic change; e.g. /kap̬ra/$_{69}$ > /kapra/.

4.1.2 Dialectal merger of the lax voiceless with the tense voiced obstruents.
In the remaining dialects of the West—including those of Italia as far down as the 'La Spezia-Rimini Line' separating northern from central Italian dialect areas—the lax voiceless obstruents become voiced, and the stops among them tense: [p̬] > [b], [t̬] > [d], [c̬] > [ẓ], and so on. The phonological restructurings which this entails are considerable, and varied. In the case of the stops, there is a series of mergers with their voiced nonlax correlates, as follows:

(D-12) /p̬ t̬ c̬ č̬ k̬/ ⟩/b d ẓ ǧ g/,
         /b d ẓ ǧ g/

e.g. /kap̬ra/$_{69}$ > /kabra/, /set̬e/$_{421}$ > /sede/, etc. These mergers bring the voiced stops /b d/ into phonemic contrast, postvocalically, with a parallel pair of new voiced fricatives /v δ/, by virtue of the shifts

(D-13) /b d/ —— /v δ/,

harking back to phonetic changes already accomplished in CRom or It-W. Examples are /nɔb̬e/$_{247}$ > /nɔve/, /pɛde/$_{346}$ > /pɛδe/. In addition, the fricative shifts

(D-14) /f̬ s̬ š̬/ —— /v z ž/

supply two new voiced sibilants, as in /kas̬a/ > /kaza/, /kaš̬u/$_{383}$ > /kažu/.[2]

4 Western splits into Unshifted and Shifted Western Romance

There are no new synchronic rules corresponding to D-11 through D-14, because as a result of the differential treatments described, lax obstruents are to be removed from the inventory of the language. Again according to Criterion 4, without these entities the language can no longer properly account for both unshifted and shifted western dialects, which have become incongruent, as shown:

CEx	Western Romance	Unshifted dialects	Shifted dialects	Congruence
415	sɛte	sɛte	sɛte	+
421	seṭe	sete	sede	−
376	kwando	kwando	kwando	+
346	peḍe	pɛde	pɛðe	−
44	braču	braču	braču	+
327	paçe	pače	paġe	−
351	planġe	planġe	planġe	+
334	pasa	pasa	pasa	+
262	kaṣa	kasa	kaza	−

Technically, such correspondences as /sete/ vs. /sede/ and /pɛde/ vs. /pɛðe/ could be accounted for by positing d and δ, respectively, for the language and appealing to complementation between postvocalic and postcoda environments; but why would this be inadmissible by our principles?

4.2 Summary of the split, and inventory of Shifted Western Romance.

In summary, the phonological subsystem shaken up in the transition from Western to Unshifted and Shifted Western Romance is that of the lax obstruents, all lost through differential coalescences or through shifts; the language change and split are motivated by Criterion 4 as applied to the coalescences. The relevant diachronic statements at the language level:

$$\text{W/ } \begin{matrix} \text{p t c č k} \\ \underline{\text{p t ç č k}} \\ \text{b d ʒ ǧ g} \end{matrix} \begin{matrix} \longrightarrow \text{p t c č k /Unsh-W} \\ \\ \longrightarrow \text{b d ʒ ǧ g /Sh-W} \end{matrix}$$

The phonological inventory of the new language that interests us further, namely, Shifted Western Romance, is then as follows:

Nuclei: i u e o ɛ ɔ a

Onsets: p t c č k f s š m n ñ l r y
        pr tr   kr fr
        pl   kl fl
                  kw

b d ẓ ǧ g   v ð z ž m̦ n̦   ḷ ṛ
br dr   gr vr
bl   gl
          gw

Codas: p d v s m n ñ l r y w

Notes for Chapter 4

1. There is, of course, the possibility that in these dialects the original laxing of obstruents simply never took place; but of this we have no evidence, while we do have clear indications that they were phonetically laxed as codas, as were the resonants in all positions.
2. After all this, the complementary distribution of the phonetically long and short stressed vocoids is more complex but still viable.

Chapter 5
Shifted Western splits into Northwestern and Southwestern Romance

5.0 Introduction. Shifted Western Romance splits binarily into Northwestern and Southwestern Romance. The former language covers areas of northwestern Italia, of the northern half of Gallia, and of Rhaetia; the latter covers areas of the southern half of Gallia, of northeastern and northwestern Iberia. The lack of congruence will result from the loss of the lax resonants and the attendant elimination of the feature [lax] altogether from the consonant systems.

5.1 Preliminary changes

5.1.1 Dialectal merger of /č/ with /c/. Except in some northwestern dialects (mainly of Rhaetia), the voiceless palatal affricate [č] fronted to become the alveodental affricate [c] in all positions, the phonological result being a total merger as expressed in the diachronic rule

(D-15)   /č/ ⟶
              ⟩ /c/,
         /c/ ⟶

as in /čɛntu/$_{47}$ > /cɛntu/, or /braču/$_{44}$ > /bracu/. As for the voiced correlate, its phonetic shape had floated dialectally since Italo-Western, remaining [ǧ] or deaffricating within the [ž] ~ [y̌] ~ [y] range, ultimately merging phonologically with the existing **y** as the retained /ǧ/ in some dialects of Sh-W, and as the retained /y/ instead in others.

Just how early the merger of /č/ with /c/ took place is difficult to say. It may well have occurred already in Western Romance, prior to the real shift. For *if* (say) W **pače**$_{327}$ had *everywhere* gone on to *paǧe by virtue of that shift (as it did in some northwestern dialects), its subsequent evolution to SW **paʒe** and not *paye would be surprising in view of the merger of Sh-W **ǧ** with **y** in other positions to produce, e.g., SW **yɛnte**$_{205}$ or **planye**$_{351}$, like **ya**$_{121}$ or **mayo**$_{260}$.

5.1.2 Dialectal merger of /ž/ with /z/. Also except in Rhaetian dialects, diphthongal nuclei developed before /ž/, thus bringing this palatal sibilant into CD with its nonpalatal counterpart /z/ and causing it to merge phonologically therewith, though phonetically it continued to vary between [ž] and [z]; thus, for example, /baža/$_{28}$ > /bayza/, or /kažu/$_{383}$ /kayzu/. The voiceless correlate /š/, though not found in any item of the corpus, remained in tenuous opposition with /s/; cf. /baša/ 'baisser/bajar' as against /pasa/$_{334}$.

5.2 The crucial change: Dialectal merger of the lax with the tense resonants and subsequent gain of vowel length. The loss of laxness in the resonants proceeds unevenly by dialect areas: in northern and southern Gallia, and in parts of Rhaetia, [m̞ n̞ l̞] all three become tense and only [r̞] does not, at least not in the sense of a multiple trill associated with [R] from old [r+r]. In some of northern Italia [m̞ l̞] become tense but [n̞] does not, while nonlax [r] becomes lax. In Iberia, both eastern and western, [m̞] alone loses laxness. Phonologically, the results of the changes that do take place are mergers as expressed in the diachronic rule

(D-15)   /m̞ n̞ l̞ r̞/
         /m n l r/ ⟩ /m n l r/.

The only one of these changes to pervade the entire Western Romance territory is the loss of lax [m̞], but this lone merger is sufficient to meet our Criterion 2 for changing the language, and we must therefore inquire whether or not the merger eliminates a conditioning factor that permits two allophones of one phoneme to cleave into two phonemes. We discern that it does indeed eliminate the basis of complementation for phonetically short and long stressed vocoids, wherever this difference exists; refer back to Change 1.5 in Lat. As we note again, length after being lost phonemically was at first conditioned phonetically by syllable structure. Later, when geminate

5.3 Summary of the split / 85

contoids were reduced from coda-plus-onset to onset alone, the basis shifted: the vocoids were short in closed syllables, but either short or long in open syllables in correlation with the laxness of the following onset: short before nonlax onsets, long before lax ones. Still later, in Shifted Western with the distribution of [lax] rearranged, vocoids were short before voiceless obstruents, long before voiced ones. But before resonant onsets the basis was still the feature [lax] until the loss of laxness resulted in a difference of length before one and the same resonant onset. By this mechanism all the northwestern dialects with vocoid length are restructured phonologically with vowel length: e.g. /klama/$_{18}$ is restructured as /klāma/, beside /flama/$_{183}$ unchanged. Thus, by Criterion 3 congruence between northwestern dialects with length and southwestern dialects without length is negative, and language split is imposed, as shown:

CEx	Shifted Western	Northwestern dialects	Southwestern dialects	Congruence
183	**flama**	flama	flama	+
18	**klāma**	klāma	klama	−

Query: Why could we not set up **klāma** for the language, with a mapping rule ā → /a/ for southwestern dialects?

5.3 Summary of the split, and inventory of Southwestern Romance. In summary, the phonological subsystem shaken up in the transition from Unshifted Western to Northwestern and Southwestern Romance is that of the lax resonants, with at least the /m̥/ lost globally by coalescence; the language change and split are dictated by Criterion 3. The relevant diachronic statement at the language level:

ShW / i u e o ɛ ɔ a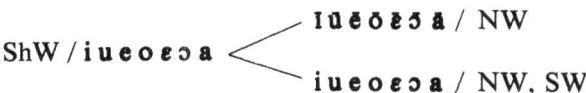

The phonological inventory of the new language that interests us further, namely, Southwestern Romance (SW), is then the following:

Nuclei: i u e o ɛ ɔ a

Onsets: p t c k f   s š   m n ñ l ʎ r y
         pr tr   kr fr
         pl   kl fl
         py   kw

86 / 5 Shifted Western splits into Northwestern and Southwestern

b d ẓ g v ð z   ṇ ḷ ṛ
br dr   gr vr
bl   gl
        gw vy   my

Codas: d s m n ñ l r y w

Remarks. (1) A major redistributional restructuring: no longer occurrent is the word-initial minor-syllable **s-** as in Lat SPISSU$_{149}$. Some, but not all, dialects of each descendent language down through Shifted Western manifested a prothetic /i̯/, later of course /e/, in place of the zero nucleus— e.g. W **espesu**. Since all southwestern dialects of ShW had shown this nucleus, the new language is restructured with **e** replacing zero in pretonic, though not posttonic, syllables (not, for example, in CEx 448 or the like).

(2) The newly added labial-plus-yod subset reflects nothing more than a reanalysis of the coda-plus-onset strings **p+y**, **v+y**, etc. as onset clusters, now that syllable structure no longer has a relation to vowel length (as it still had in northwestern dialects of Shifted Western).

5.4 Residual discrepancies in Northwestern Romance as reflected by Old French.
The diachronic changes which took place as Western Romance split to become Unshifted and Shifted Western, and later as Shifted Western (ShW) split into Northwestern and Southwestern Romance, are all reflected in Cols. 1–5 of the corpus, although the input languages Old French (OFr) and the rest are end products embodying numerous later developments as well. We pause at this point to draw attention to certain OFr entries which represent the Northwestern branch of ShW.

CEx 5. OFr /agü/ instead of the expected */əü/ (a form which did come down as the past participle of the verb 'avoir/haber') seems to bespeak an irregular treatment of ShW postvocalic /g/ (< W /k̬/) analogous to that of /gr/ (< W /k̬r/) in CLat ĀCRE- > ShW and NW /agre/ > OFr /ɛygrə/.

CEx 25. OFr already had /avöglə/, a reflex of Late (medical) Latin *ab oculo* (see CEx 309) borrowed in the Merovingian period (6th-7th cent.) to replace what would have been reduced phonologically to /ci/ (hence homophonous with the demonstrative adverb *ci* 'ici/aquí') from ShW and NW /cɛgo/.

CEx 30. The OFr replacement of NW /skova/ is a medieval borrowing from Breton, a Celtic language.

CEx 31. The OFr replacement of NW /skamnu/ is of Germanic origin.

CEx 35. Instead of the present item, which originally referred to blood relationship, OFr kept /süyrə/ from the CLat adjective SORŌRIU-, a derivative of SORŌRE- 'soeur/hermana' and extended to denote the male as well as the female relative by marriage.

5.4 Residual discrepancies in Northwestern Romance / 87

CEx 50. The OFr form is said to stem from 'VLat *certanu-*' as a derivative of the original CLat adjective.

CEx 93. The OFr form shows that the doublets with and without final /-s/ survived all the way down into NW (cf. also CEx 431).

CEx 100. The basic stem of this verb in OFr was **kur-**, retaining the reflex of NW medial /R/.

CEx 108. Although some Gallo-Rhaetian dialects of NW had kept this item, OFr had /kryɛm/, said to be a continuation of 'VLat *creme(re)*', a crossing of (It-)W /trɛme/ 'trembler/temblar' and a Gaulish /kr/-initial root.

CEx 120. This noun acquired the inherited prefix /də-/ (< CLat DĒ-) in OFr, possibly in avoidance of homophony with the noun /gre/ 'gré/voluntad', reflex of the CLat adjective GRĀTU- 'agréable/grato' (not in corpus).

CEx 128. The OFr form reflects NW /dedu/, from It-W /detu/ rather than /ditu/ (cf. the Ital form at 3.4).

CEx 130. Although some Gallo-Rhaetian dialects of NW kept this monosyllabic verbal root, OFr had discarded it altogether in favor of CEx 131.

CEx 136. The syncope going back to CRom—as reflected in both Eastern and It-W (Ital has the by-form *dritto*)—is unusual in that it occurs here in an initial syllable.

CEx 140. The OFr /ɛskolə/ instead of /ɛskölə/ was the result of cultivated Latinizing influence.

CEx 145. The OFr form shows that the CLat prefixal variant IN-, with long vowel before fricative onset as against short vowel elsewhere, hesitated already in CRom between /in-/ and /i̯n-/.

CEx 156. The OFr /ɛsteylə/ instead of /ɛstɛlə/ is said to stem from a 'VLat' variant with long stressed vowel and single /l/, i.e. a CRom */stela/ alongside the inherited /stɛlla/.

CEx 199. Although Rhaetian dialects preserved NW /fumu/, OFr replaced it with a deverbal derivative from the feminine form of the past participle of CEx 200.

CEx 216, 217. OFr alone acquired the initial /h-/, a newly borrowed phoneme, by contamination with the Frankish lexical equivalent of the root item in view.

CEx 226. The OFr /ǧuə/ instead of */ǧöə/ represents a leveling to the unstressed stem alternant, as in the infinitive /ǧuer/ etc.

CEx 240. The OFr form reflects a leveling of NW /largu/ (> */larg/ > */lark/) to the fem. sing. form of this adjective, with final /-a/.

CEx 257, 258. OFr continues the plural form of CLat LŪMINARE- as a fem. sing. (cf. also Rou at 2.4.2). NW had kept /lume/ but apparently not /luǧe/.

CEx 265. OFr already had /mawvɛys/, a direct reflex of 'VLat *malifatius*' attested in Late Latin with the meaning 'ill-fated'. Except for one or two fossilized uses as an adjective, /mal/ survived only as the noun/adverb of CEx 264.

CEx 268. The OFr pretonic /a/ instead of the expected /ɛ/ reflects a very early NW tendency toward variable lowering, especially before a liquid coda or onset; the Late Latin variant *marcatus* is itself attested for Northern Gaul, doubtless echoing a current pronunciation of the vernacular word.

CEx 312. OFr had /ɔñuŋ/, a reflex of CLat UNIŌNE- 'perle/perla' with semantic shift attested for the 1st cent. A.D.

CEx 321, 322. The OFr root /övr-/ (stressed) and its atonic alternants with /u-/ is clearly enough a continuation of CLat OPERĪ- 'couvrir/cubrir' instead of APERĪ-, the two having become semantic competitors in CRom once the derivative with prefixed /ko-/ fully displaced the /o/-initial simplex in its original meaning.

CEx 328. OFr /palɛyc/ instead of */palac/ (cf. CEx 44) reflects a ShW /palaẓu/, with voiced sibilant, from a CRom dialectal variant /palacu̯/, in which the original -TI- failed to produce a geminate /cc/.

CEx 373. OFr /pric/ instead of */prɛc/ reflects a ShW /prɛẓu/ from the CRom variant /prɛcu̯/; see CEx 328 just above.

CEx 375. The OFr /püyc/ instead of */poyc/ may represent a Latin dialectal (rustic?) variant with long -ū-; the Sard and Rou can, of course, reflect either vowel (cf. CEx 256 at 1.9).

CEx 383. OFr had /fɔrmaǧə/ (cf. also Ital *formaggio* as preferred to the more specialized *cacio*), reflecting 'VLat *formaticum*,' a derivative of the CLat FŌRMA which referred originally to any mold and was later narrowed.

CEx 393. OFr had /ʀivyɛrə/, said to be from 'VLat *riparia*', nominalization of the neuter plural form of the CRom adjective /riparyu̯/, derived from the CLat root in view here.

CEx 398. The Ofr /ʀuə/ instead of */ʀöə/ is thought due to the analogy of the unstressed alternants of the root in derivatives and/or the verb /ʀuə/ from CLat ROTĀ- 'rouer/rodar'.

CEx 422. OFr /solɛʎ/ instead of the expected */söl/ is a by-form stemming directly from 'VLat *soliculus*' (< CRom /soli̯klu̯/), merely a diminutive derived from SŌLE by means of the CLat suffix -ICULU-.

CEx 431. The OFr form shows that the doublets with and without final /-s/ survived all the way down into NW (cf. also CEx 93).

CEx 443. For OFr /tut/ rather than */tö/, see Italian above (3.4).

CEx 447. The OFr initial /tr-/ instead of /t-/ is thought possibly due to analogy with the prefix /trez-/ (< CLat TRĀNS-), thus leaving the final segment identifiable semantically with 'or/oro' (CEx 317).

CEx 467. The OFr stressed /i/ instead of /á/ (cf. /trantə/$_{446}$) is phonologically regular, reflecting a NW raising of a stressed vowel to [+hi] before word-final /-i/.

CEx 470. The final /-ə/ in this OFr feminine reflects the ending of the CLat plural form VĒLA.

5.5 The confrontation of Southwestern with Proto-Southwestern / 89

CEx 474. OFr /volə/ instead of */völə/ seems to have been leveled to the unstressed root alternant, as, for example, in the gerund /volant/. The pretonic /o/ of NW had variably become either /u/ or /o/ in OFr—there are numerous cases of both in the corpus—and the present verb seems to have opted for the nonhigh vowel (doubtless still [o] phonetically) as against the high vowel in /vol-/$_{S109}$. The leveling in /volə/ then further served to avoid homophony in the stressed alternants /völ-/ of both verbs, as e.g. in /völənt/.

5.5 The confrontation of Southwestern with reconstructed Proto-Southwestern Romance. It is now time for a major digression, namely, the confrontation of SW as reached in the downtracking, with *Proto*-SW as reconstructed in Part One. There is somewhat more discrepancy between the two phonological inventories than in the case of CRom vs. PRom, seemingly because irregular developments on the way down from CRom to SW have generated considerable amounts of residue from the standpoint of comparative reconstruction. Thus we shall see that of the two phonemes included in the inventory of SW but missing from that of PSW, one is contained in items that were unreconstructible. Let us account for each.

• SW δ, inherited from ShW, was not reconstructible because no viable correspondences were forthcoming. The following items tagged '?' for PSW may now be extrapolated for SW as follows, with account taken of changes effected in It-W, in W, in ShW, as well as the changes under immediate view:

CEx	CRom	SW	CEx	CRom	SW
109	kredę	kreδe	307	nudu̦	nuδo
112	krudu̦	kruδo	346	pędę	peδe
113	krudelę	kruδele	382	koda	koδa
120	gradu̦	graδo	386	radikę	raδiẓe
135	dódękị	dóδeẓe	391	ridę	riδe
186	fịde	feδe	427	sudorę	suδoŗe
255	lawda	lawδa	428	kadę	kaδe
274	merkedę	merceδe	445	trédękị	tréδeẓe
300	nidu̦	niδo	471	wịde	veδe
302	nodu̦	noδo			

• SW š, also inherited, was unreconstructible for lack of input data, while its voiced correlate ž was reconstructed as */z/ on the basis of an etic set occurring after the reconstructed coda */y/. However, subsequent developments in the individual languages are more neatly accounted for if this pair of palatal sibilants is assumed as retained in SW. Accordingly, CEx 28, 29,

383 may be rewritten as SW **bayža, bayžo, kayžo** rather than with /z/ as reconstructed.

• The SW obstruent-plus-lateral onset clusters /pl bl kl gl fl/, likewise inherited from ShW, were not reconstructible because of conflicting testimony by Span. and Port., despite good supporting evidence from Cat. and Occ. The following further items tagged '?' for PSW may now be extrapolated for SW as follows, with account taken of other intermediate changes:

CEx	CRom	SW	CEx	CRom	SW
12	amplu̱	amplo	350	planu̱	plaṇo
18	klama	klama	351	plange	planye
38	blanku̱[1]	blanko	352	planktu̱	plañto
78	klaṛu̱	klaṛo	353	plake	plaẓe
146	i̱nfla	enfla	354	planta	planta
183	flamma	flama	355	plenu̱	pleṇo
266	masklu̱	masklo	356	plo̱we	plɔve
315	u̱ngla	ongla	358	pleka	plega
348	platya	placa	359	plo̱ya	plɔya

• The remaining PSW items marked '?' in the corpus may now also be extrapolated for SW by working down from CRom without further problems, bearing in mind that the symbols for the lax resonants /n̪ l̪ r̪/, as inherited from Western, should be used for SW rather than the /n l r/ as reconstructed, while their nonlax correlates should be notated with /n l r/ rather than the reconstructed /N L R/; so, for example, CEx 22, CRom **argi=la** > SW **aryila** (not *****aryiLa**), or CEx 393, CRom **riwu̱** > SW **rio** (not *****Rio**), etc.

Note for Chapter 5

1. Item CEx 38 is, of course, of It-W origin (see 2.4.3).

Chapter 6
Southwestern splits into South Gallo-, East Ibero-, and West Ibero-Romance

6.0 Introduction. Southwestern Romance splits trinarily into South Gallo-, East Ibero-, and West Ibero-Romance. The lack of congruence will result from changes in the voiced fricative [ð], which lacks a voiced correlate. Thus isolated, it undergoes divergent treatments as detailed in 6.2.

6.1 Preliminary change: Dialectal raising of /a/ before codas /y/ and /w/. In Iberian (but not Gallic) dialects of SW, the vocoid [a] is fronted and raised to [ɛ] before the front coda [y], and backed and raised to [ɔ] before the back coda [w], the partial mergers with /ɛ/ and /ɔ/ thus producing the phonological sequences /ɛy ɔw/ in lieu of /ay aw/. Later, in western Iberian dialects only, [ɛy ɔw] are further raised to [ey ow], the former sequence thus merging with existing /ey/; e.g. SW **ayra**$_8$, **lɛyto**$_{251}$, **awro**$_{317}$ > /eyra/, /leyto/, /owro/.

6.2 The crucial changes

6.2.1 Dialectal merger of /ð/ with /z/. In dialects of southern Gallia leading to Occitan, Provençal etc., [ð] stridentizes to [z], the phonological outcome being a merger:

(D-16)   /ð/ ⟩
         /z/ ⟩ /z/ (as against /z̞/).

Example: /suðore/$_{427}$ > /suzor/.

6.2.2 Dialectal merger of /ð/ with /z̞/. In dialects of eastern Iberia leading to Catalan, the [ð] also stridentizes, but toward a more apical [z̞], and merges phonologically with the voiced output of an earlier shift whereby the affricates [c z̞] were fricativized to apical [s̞ z̞] while remaining in contrast with the dorsal [s z] of /s z/. Phonologically:

(D-17)   /ð/ ⟩
         /z̞/ ⟩ /z̞/ (as against /z/).

Example: /suðore/$_{427}$ > /suz̞or/, like /raz̞one/$_{387}$ > /raz̞on/.

6.2.3 Dialectal loss of /δ/. Finally, in dialects of western Iberia leading to Castilian, Asturo-Leonese, and Galician, [δ] is lost and merges phonologically with zero:

(D-18) /δ/⟶ ∅.
         ∅ ⟶

Example: /suδore/$_{427}$ > /suor/.

In consequence of the foregoing three divergent dialectal restructurings, by Criterion 4 congruence among the three sets is lacking and a language split is indicated as shown:

CEx	Southwestern Romance	So. Gallic dialects	Ea. Iberian dialects	We. Iberian dialects	Congruence
153	**espozo**	espoz̧	espoz̧	espozo	+
327	**paże**	paz̧	paz̧	paże	+
S102	**trae**	tra-	tra-	trae	+
438	**kaδe**	kaz̧-	kaz̧-	kae	−

That is to say, at Item 438 each set is incongruent with either of the other two, and each therefore comes to represent, by our criteria, a separate new language.

6.3 Summary of the split, and inventory of West Ibero-Romance. In summary, the phonological entity affected in the transition from Southwestern to South Gallo-, East Ibero-, and West Ibero-Romance is that member of the continuant obstruent onsets which failed to pattern with the rest by virtue of having no voiceless correlate. The language change and split are motivated by Criterion 4. The relevant diachronic statement at the language level:

SW /δ, z/ ⟶ z̧ /SGa   SW /δ, z/ ⟶ z̧ /EIb   SW /δ, ∅/ ⟶ ∅ /WIb

The phonological inventory of the language that interests us further, namely, West Ibero-Romance, is then as follows:

Nuclei: i u e o ɛ ɔ a

Onsets: p t c k f s š m n ñ l ʎ r y
         pr tr   kr fr

```
           pl    kl  fl
           py    kw
           b  d  ẓ  g  v  z  ž       ṇ     ḷ      ṛ
           br dr    gr vr
           bl
                    gw vy     my
```

Codas: d s m n ñ l r y w

6.4 Residual discrepancies. The diachronic changes which took place as SW split to become South Gallo-, East Ibero-, and West Ibero-Romance are all reflected in Cols. 1–4 of the corpus, although, of course, the respective input languages are end-products embodying numerous subsequent developments as well. Note that all regular changes are implicit in the reconstruction, and apply also where the SW has been extrapolated from CRom. We now pause to comment on certain Oc, Cat, and Sp/Po entries which fit neither the reconstruction nor the extrapolation and are therefore to be accounted residual.

6.4.1 In South Gallo-Romance as reflected by Occitan. Note: The deviations at CExs 119, 185, 206, 224, 267, 307, 386 are omitted as obscure or uninteresting, or both.

CEx 7. Oc *aima* instead of *ama is clearly a medieval borrowing of OFr *aime*.

CEx 9. Oc *arma* bespeaks dissimilation of the first nasal, put into coda position by syncope to */anma/ but not tolerated before a nasal onset, through loss of the feature [nas].

CEx 25. Oc *cec* instead of *cèc is what underlies the reconstructed SW doublet; it could conceivably be a direct reflex of a Lat dialectal variant /kēku-/, unattested, to be sure, but cf. the dialectal variation elsewhere in CEx 187 or 312.

CEx 31. The Oc replacement of SW **eskano**, namely, *banc*, is the same Germanic word as in OFr, from which it was most probably borrowed.

CEx 49. Oc *cèrvi* instead of *cèrp—which would be homophonous with *sèrp*$_{416}$—involves the addition of final /-i/ (perhaps under the influence of the derived though unattested adjective *cerbin (< CLat CERVĪNU-), in order to avoid the lexical collision threatening after the original loss of final vowels.

CEx 56. Oc *carri* instead of *car—which would be homophonous with *car*$_{66}$—shows the same addition of final /-i/, to avoid lexical collision, as just noted for CEx 49.

CEx 63. Oc *calvet* instead of *calp involves the addition of the well-attested diminutive suffix *-et*, reflex of CRom -i̯=tu̯.

CEx 85. Oc *coneis* instead of the expected *conois reflects two irregular developments. (1) In It-W there had occurred a variable metathesis of medial /-sk-/ to /-ks-/, leading to e.g. /krekse/ as a doublet of /kreske/$_{110}$, or /pekse/ as doublet of /peske/$_{363}$, and giving rise to W /-ys-/ alongside /-sč-/; the dual development continued through ShW into both NW and SW, where dialects leading to OFr and to Oc/Cat kept only the /-ys-/. (2) At the same time most SW dialects, including those leading to Oc, switched the stressed back vowel (cf. OFr /konoys/) analogically to that of the verbal suffix /-eys/ ~ -is/, seemingly apprehended as a separate word-building element since Latin; cf. OFr /pareys/ 'paraître/parecer', from Late Latin PĀRĒSCE- as derived from PĀRĒ-.

CEx 93. Oc *còs*, like OFr /kors/, reflects the CLat CORPUS (with /-s/ as part of the stem in the short nom/acc form), rather than the It-W doublet /kɔrpo/ with the /-s/ analogized out as though sensed as the plural suffix. As for the lost coda /r/, shared with Cat, it is not satisfactorily explained.

CEx 104. Oc *cotèl*, with the expected coda /l/ lacking, appears dialectally in Old Oc both with and without it, and points to the possible influence of OFr /kutɛl/, which had regularly vocalized coda /l/ in the transition from Central Oïl.

CEx 107. Oc *cuèrp* directly reflects the SGa bare stem *kɔbri, with back-vowel umlaut—i.e. fronting of the stressed /ɔ/ to /ö/ before a high stem vowel, the /-i/ dialectally replacing the regular /-e/ in verbs with *i*-stem morphophonemic patterning. The front rounded phoneme /ö/ later unrounded to /ɛ/ in standard Oc. Independently, this very same development can be seen as regular in items like CEx 118, where the conditioning factor for the umlaut is any immediately following palatal onset.

CEx 110. Oc *creis* rather than *cretz does not reflect the avoidance of homophony with *cretz*$_{109}$, but rather the It-W metathesis detailed above at CEx 85.

CEx 112. Oc *cru* rather than *crus may reflect a very early loss—perhaps in many dialects of SW—of /δ/ between identical vowels where not supported by morphophonemic alternants as in verbs; cf. CExs 186, 274, 346.

CEx 125. Oc *dièu* regularly reflects SGa **dɛu** with front-vowel umlaut—i.e. diphthonging of the stressed /ɛ/ to /yɛ/ before a high stem vowel, the /-u/ dialectally replacing the regular /-o/ in hiatus and later semivocalizing instead of dropping.

CEx 129. Oc *dam* rather than *dan (which, however, occurs dialectally in Oc) reflects a preservation of CRom coda-plus-onset /m+n/ which in It-W assimilated in most dialects to geminate /n+n/. In only OFr and Oc are reflexes of /m+n/ preserved; see also CEx 169 and 423.

CEx 134. Oc *doç*, with the expected coda /l/ lacking, appears dialectally in Old Occitan both with and without it, as well as with the semivocalized coda /w/, again suggesting the influence of OFr /duc/.

6.4 Residual discrepancies / 95

CEx 136. This item shows the unusual initial-syllable syncope going back to CRom, as already mentioned for OFr (5.4).

CEx 141. For Oc *escota*, again with the expected coda /1/ absent, see CEx 104 and 134.

CEx 148. For Oc *intra* and not *entra* (dialectally both exist), see CEx 145 at 5.4.

CEx 156. Oc *facia* seems to be a semilearnèd restructuring of the expected **faça* or **faç*, blending the CRom doublet **fakya** and the CLat etymon.

CEx 162. For the shorter doublet of both Oc and Cat, see Italian at 3.4.

CEx 220. Oc *ièr* normally reflects SGa **eri** with front-vowel umlaut; cf. CEx 125.

CEx 228. Oc has *jorn* /ǧurn/, which competes with the present item as do Cat *jorn* /žorn/ and OFr /ǧurn/ as well as Ital *giorno* /ǧorno/. Nominalized as early as It-W, it stems from the CLat adjective DIURNU-, derived from the original DIĒ-.

CEx 234. The initial /d-/ instead of /l-/, clearly reconstructible for SW, betrays a hesitation, in a few items, between these two onset consonants—separated only by the feature [lateral]—going as far back perhaps as Old (preclassical) Latin. Evidence that the CRom doublets **laksa** and **daksa** coexisted is available from two of the three descendants: Southern, with one or the other onset in dialects of Sardinia, Sicily, and Southern Italy; and It-W, with only the lateral coming down into NW but both into SW: only the nonlateral for EIb, but both for SGa (/d-/ in Gascon and Languedocian, /l-/ elsewhere) and WIb (/layša/ attested in earliest Old Spanish).

CEx 321, 322. For the rounded initial vowel of both Oc and Cat, see OFr (5.4).

CEx 382. Oc *coa* instead of **cosa* may be a borrowing from OFr (or Catalan?) in avoidance of near-homophony with Old Oc /koza/, a dialectal variant of CEx 71.

CEx 383. Oc and Cat have both replaced this item with *formatge* as borrowed from OFr (see 5.4).

CEx 388. Oc *raia* instead of **rai* reflects the Latin (neuter) plural RADIA; cf. Rou at 2.4.2.

CEx 397. Oc *redond* instead of **rodond* (with the pretonic vowel of SW as reflected in Cat) betrays a fronting shift of that vowel dialectally by analogy with the high-frequency prefix /re-/.

CEx 398. Oc *semena*, instead of the form with initial stress, reflects a normalization of the displaced stress, effected in some dialects of SW prior to syncope; cf. Po, which goes with Oc as against Sp/Ca.

CEx 417. Oc *servis* exemplifies numerous *i*-stem verbs which, from CRom on down, augmented their bare present-tense forms with the inchoative suffix which was -SCE- in CLat—cf. Rou *serveşte* instead of *ṣerve, Ital *finisce* and not **fine*, OFr *finis* and not **fin* (the latter two from CLat FINI- 'finir/acabar' (not in corpus), Cat *bulleix*$_{43}$ and not **boll*.

CEx 422. Oc *solelh* represents a medieval borrowing of /solεʎ/ from OFr, although /sol/ also existed in Old Oc.

CEx 431. For Oc *temps* with final /-s/, see CEx 93.

CEx 443. Oc *tot* could come from It-W /totu/ or /tottu/ (via SW /todo/ or /toto/); but the morphophonemics give it away: the fem. sing. form is *tota*, not **toda*.

CEx 447. For the Oc and Cat initial /tr-/ instead of /t-/, see OFr (5.4), probable source of the deviation.

CEx 461. For Oc *vestis*, also with the formative suffix /-is/, see CEx 417 above.

6.4.2 In East Ibero-Romance as reflected by Catalan. Note: The deviations at CExs 30, 153, 185, 186, 207, 219, 220, 223, 224, 241, 272, 302, 305, 308, 386, 390, 411, 415, 424, 439 are omitted as obscure or uninteresting, or both.

CEx 9. The failure of this item to syncopate in Cat, as well as the unstressed /i/ instead of /ə/, is indicative of Latinizing influence, very probably clerical.

CEx 31. The Cat replacement of SW **eskano**, namely *banc*, is the same Germanic word as in Oc and OFr, doubtless diffused from North to South.

CEx 43. For the Cat form cf. CEx 417 in 6.4.1.

CEx 49. Cat *cervo* instead of **cerb*—which would be homophonous with *serp*$_{416}$—involves the addition of final /-u/ to avoid lexical collision threatening with the original loss of final vowels in dialects of SW.

CEx 56. Cat *carro* instead of **car*—which would be homophonous with *car*$_{66}$—displays the same addition of final /-u/ just noted in CEx 49.

CEx 85. The explanation for Cat *coneix* rather than **conoix* is identical to that given for the Oc item; see 6.4.1.

CEx 89. For Cat *cos*, see Oc *còs* in 6.4.1.

CEx 103. Cat *curt* instead of the expected **cort* is thought attributable to a Lat dialectal variant with long -ū-, unless it is merely a Latinizing doublet which won out after loss of final vowels rendered the inherited form homophonous with *cort*$_{99}$ (but see Portuguese residue in 10.4).

CEx 111. This item is actually not residual; it reflects the phonologically normal unrounding of SW /ó/ after EIb /ʒ/ had merged with /v/ as /w/ in Cat; cf. also CEx 473.

CEx 128. Cat *dit* stems directly from the CRom doublet /ditu̯/; cf. Ital at 2.4.3.

CEx 136. See the Oc form in 6.4.1.

CEx 146. For Cat *infla* rather than *enfla*, see CEx 145 in 5.4 above.

CEx 150. The Cat form with /-z-/ is generally thought to be a medieval borrowing from Occ.

CEx 156. The medial onset /tr/ in this item must have been introduced dialectally in SW, since it is shared with WIb; see 6.4.3.

CEx 172. Cat *ferro* instead of **fer* shows still another addition of a final vowel, perhaps merely to preserve the /R/ from merger with /r/. While the corresponding Oc form *ferre* could as well be a direct continuation of SW /fɛro/, the Cat form with final /-u/ could not, for SW final /-o/ and /-e/ merged to become /-ə/ in EIb-Cat in environments where it was not permitted to merge with zero.

CEx 254. Cat has lost this item and uses *llarg*$_{240}$ in the requisite meaning, while *ample*$_{12}$ serves to denote 'large/ancho'; cf. Spanish at 9.5.

CEx 258. Cat, like OFr, has lost this item and uses only its reflex of CEx 257.

CEx 283. Cat has replaced this item (cf. the homophony with CEx 284–5) with *mossega* /musɛgə/, a reflex of 'VLat *morsica(re)*' with the variable /r+s/ > /s+s/ of CRom (see CEx 320). It also appears in Oc as the favored competitor *mossega* /musego/.

CEx 320. For Cat *os* rather than *ors*, see Spanish at 9.5.

CEx 328, 373, 375. For Cat *palau, preu,* and *pou* instead of the expected **palaç, *preç,* and **poç,* see OFr at 5.4.

CEx 349. Cat has lost this item, merely extending the noun *ferida* 'blessure/herida' over a slightly wider range.

CEx 381. Cat has simply lost this verb, replacing it with *busca* in the meaning 'quérir (chercher)/buscar' borrowed from Spanish; cf., however, WIb (6.4.3).

CEx 396. Cat has merely regularized this participle to *romput*.

CEx 417. For Cat *serveix*, see Oc (6.4.1).

CEx 431. For Cat *tems*, see Oc *temps* (6.4.1).

CEx 436. This verb has switched to an *i*-stem and hence shows the typical formative of CEx 417.

CEx 443, 447. The observations made in 6.4.2 on the Oc items apply equally to Cat.

6.4.3 In West Ibero-Romance as reflected by Spanish and/or Portuguese.

CEx 9. WIb /alma/ results merely from denasalization of the coda /n/ before nasal onset, after syncope in SW.

CEx 24. WIb /owtro/ results from two changes: (1) variable semi-vocalization of the SW coda /l/, as exemplified also in CEx 167, thus yielding */awtro/; (2) phonologically regular raising of /a/ to /o/ before /w/, as detailed in 6.1.

CEx 76. WIb had /cinkwaenta/ (attested in early Castilian), reflecting a CRom variant with only the /g/ lost rather than the entire syllable.

CEx 80. The WIb form was /koracon/, apparently a redundant augmentative of an earlier dialectal */koraco/, itself derived from the common original /kɔre/ with an augmentative suffix tracing back to CLat -ĀCEU- (> CRom **-a=ču̯**).

CEx 81. WIb /palomba/ traces back to CLat PALUMBE- (denoting a bird very similar to a COLUMBU-), with a declension shift by analogy with the fem. COLUMBA.

CEx 111. WIb /kruc/ rather than */kroc/ illustrates the triumph of the clerical, Latinizing pronunciation over the popular in certain items of the religious vocabulary.

CEx 135. WIb had /dodẓe/ (attested in early documents), as did SW before it. The rare coda-plus-onset string (result of early syncope) had blocked the loss of final unstressed /-e/ after simple onsets, which had already begun in ShW. The dental coda went to zero by assimilation to the following dental-initial [dᶻ] or [ᵈz] of the /ẓ/.

CEx 156. WIb /estrela/, with medial onset /tr/ in place of the inherited /t/, may reflect a CRom doublet */strella/, blending the normal form with an older Lat STERULA and perhaps also influenced by the Hellenizing ASTRU-.

CEx 167. For WIb /fowce/ instead of */falce/, see above for CEx 24.

CEx 227. WIb had /ǧugo/ and not */ǧogo/, perhaps continuing a rustic variant with long vowel already in Latin itself.

CEx 241. WIb /lágrima/ again probably represents clerical speech, though the form with medial atonic /e/ is also attested for early Castilian.

CEx 246. The WIb item meant both 'lieu/lugar' and 'tout de suite/en seguida', the latter stemming from the ablative /(in) lǫko/ of CRom replacing CLat ILLICŌ ~ ĪLICŌ 'sur-le-champ'. Gradually, WIb /logal/, from the CRom derived adjective /lǫkalẹ/, came to compete with /lɔgo/ as 'lieu', and by medieval times the latter had narrowed down to the temporal adverbial meaning.

CEx 299. WIb had /naric/, reflex of the CRom plural variant /narikẹ/ of CLat NĀRĒS. Taken as a singular in WIb, it was repluralized in reference to the nostrils as the singular form remained to replace the lost */nazo/.

CEx 304. WIb /nɔc/ as against the expected */noc/ has no satisfactory explanation.

CEx 358. This verb, with its original meaning preserved in the other descendents of It-W, had already shifted semantically from 'ployer, plier/ doblar' to 'arriver/llegar' by the WIb stage. Note that the extended meaning (connected with the folding of sails) here is exactly the opposite of Rou *pleacă* 'partir' (2.4.2).

CEx 359. WIb /pluvya/ instead of */plɔvya/ has no satisfactory explanation.

CEx 377. For WIb /kwaraenta/, see above at CEx 76.

CEx 381. WIb /kɛre/ replaced the lost */vɔle/ (< CLat VOLE-, not in corpus) as the ordinary verb meaning 'vouloir/querer'.
CEx 445. For WIb /tredẓe/, see above at CEx 135.

Chapter 7
West Ibero-Romance splits into Castilian, Asturian, and Galician

7.0 Introduction. West-Ibero Romance splits three ways into Castilian, Asturian, and Galician. The lack of congruence will result from loss of the onset clusters /pl kl fl/.[1]

7.1 Preliminary changes

7.1.1 Dialectal loss of the lax resonants /l̪/ and /n̪/. In Galician dialects, the lax resonants [l̪] and [n̪] weaken phonetically to the point of merger with zero—the [l̪] between vowels, the [n̪] between vowels and final as well—the phonological result being full neutralization of the lax/nonlax contrast and consequent loss of /l̪ n̪/, as shown herewith:

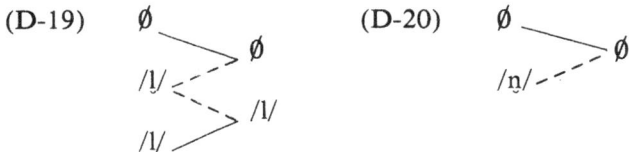

7.1.2 Dialectal nasalization of vowels. Meanwhile, prior to the loss in view, any nucleus preceding an [n̪] had become assimilatively nasalized, so that with the loss nasal vowels came into contrast with oral vowels. Examples: /fil̪o/$_{179}$ > /fĩo/, /cɛl̪o/$_{73}$ > /cɛo/, /tel̪a/$_{437}$ > /tea/, /sal̪ude/$_{403}$ > /saude/ (but cf. /mɛl̪/$_{278}$ > /mɛl/ as against /pɛle/$_{336}$ unchanged); /vin̪o/$_{466}$ > /vĩo/, /fin̪/$_{182}$ > /fĩ/, /bɛn̪/$_{37}$ > /bɛ̃/, /pan̪/$_{325}$ > /pã/, /lan̪a/$_{233}$ > /lãa/, /amen̪aca/$_{272}$ > /amẽaca/, /sen̪o/$_{411}$ > /sẽo/, /lun̪a/$_{259}$ > /lũa/. Likewise, following the phonetic nasalization of any nucleus occurring before it, the coda /n/ was lost through merger with zero and the nucleus therefore phonologized as a nasal vowel—e.g. /vɛnto/₄₅₇ > /vɛ̃to/, /kampo/₅₃ > /kãpo/, /lɔngo/₂₅₄ > /lɔ̃go/ (cf. /lɔgo/₂₄₆).

7.1.3 Dialectal merger of /ž/ with /z/. In eastern (i.e. Castilian[2] and Asturian) but not Galician dialects, the voiced palatal sibilant [ž], of postnuclear occurrence only, merges with its dorsal counterpart [z̩], the phonological result being

(D-21)   /ž/ ⟶ /z/.
         /z/ ⟶

Example: /beyžo/₂₉ > /beyzo/.

7.1.4 Dialectal shift of /ʎ/ to /ž/. In Castilian dialects only, subsequently to Change 7.1.3, the palatal [l] is delateralized and fricativized to [ž]—phonologically just a shift as in

(D-22)   /ʎ/ ——— /ž/.

Example: /fiʎo/₁₈₁ > /fižo/.

7.1.5 Dialectal loss of codas /y/ and /w/. In all Castilian and some (eastern) Asturian dialects, the semivocoid codas [y] and [w] weaken phonetically to the point of merger with zero, the phonological result being total loss of these two codas:

(D-23)   Coda /y/ ⟶ ∅   (D-24)   Coda /w/ ⟶ ∅.
         ∅ ⟶   ∅ ⟶

Examples: /keyzo/₃₈₃ > /kezo/, /koyšo/ > /košo/ 'boiteux/cojo', /kɔyro/₁₁₅ > /kɔro/, /powko/₃₄₄ > /poko/.

7.1.6 Dialectal cleavage of /t/ into /t/ and /č/. As a direct result of Change 7.1.5, the palatal allophone [ṭ] of the dental onset /t/ which had followed the coda /y/ is upgraded to phonemic status, since both [t] and [ṭ] now contrast after a nucleus in Castilian dialects—e.g. [ˈle-ṭe]₂₃₅ (<[ˈlei̯-ṭe]) vs. [ˈme-te]₂₇₆. The new phoneme may be written /č/, with the symbol for the palatal affricate which it will become. Phonologically, we are dealing with a cleavage:

(D-25)   /t/ ⟶ /t/
              ⟶ /č/.

Examples: /peyto/$_{364}$ > /pečo/, /ɔyto/$_{223}$ > /ɔčo/, /muyto/$_{34}$ > /mučo/.[3] An M-rule is still viable for Castilian dialects; how would you formulate it?

7.1.7 Dialectal raising of /ɔ/ before palatal onset.
In Castilian dialects only, the lower-mid vocoid [ɔ] is raised to higher-mid [o] before a palatal onset—phonologically a partial merger as in

(D-26) /ɔ/ ——— /ɔ/
        /o/ ——— /o/.

Examples: /ɔžo/$_{309}$ > /ožo/, /pɔyo/ 'banc/poyo' > /poyo/, /ɔčo/$_{223}$ > /očo/, /nɔče/$_{308}$ > /noče/.

7.1.8 Dialectal diphthongization of /ɛ/ and /ɔ/.
In all Castilian and some (eastern) Asturian dialects, the lower-mid vocoids [ɛ ɔ] 'break' to become the respective on-glide diphthongs [i̯e u̯e], via intermediate phonetic stages which certainly include [u̯ɔ] (attested) and probably [u̯ʌ] for the [+back] member. Phonologically we have merely a shift, as in

(D-27) /ɛ ɔ/ ——— /ye we/.

Examples abound in the corpus, e.g. /tɛne/$_{433}$ > /tyene/, /pɛ/$_{346}$ > /pye/, /pɔde/$_{370}$ > /pwede/.[4]

7.1.9 Dialectal merger of /l/ with /ʎ/ postvocalically.
In both Castilian and Asturian dialects, the nonlax lateral [l] is palatalized to [l̯] in postnuclear position. The phonological results are divergent: a partial coalescence in Asturian dialects:

(D-24) /l/ ——— /l/
        /ʎ/ ——— /ʎ/,

but a mere phonetic shift with no phonological effect in Castilian dialects because the latter have previously shifted their /ʎ/ by Rule D-22 and the new [l̯] is merely the postvocalic allophone of /l/. Thus, /galo/$_{89}$ > /gaʎo/ in Asturian dialects, but remains /galo/['ga-l̯o] in Castilian ones. What are the corresponding M-rules?

7.2 The crucial change: Partial dialectal mergers of the onset clusters /pl kl fl/.
Meanwhile, in all dialects of WIb the lateral component in the onsets /pl kl fl/ has been phonetically palatalized to yield [pl̯ kl̯ fl̯].[5] In postcoda position (after nasal or [s]) the three clusters are then mutually assimilated and fused into one and the same palatal affricate [tš], perhaps via the stage

102 / 7 West Ibero-Romance splits into Castilian, Asturian, and Galician

[tˡ]. In postnuclear or initial position, on the other hand, only Galician dialects show this change, while in the rest there is instead a mere reduction to [l] through loss of the obstruent component. The phonological outcomes which trigger the split of the language are the following. On the Asturian side:

(D-25)   /ʎ/
                    ⟩ /ʎ/,
        /pl kl fl/

on the Castilian side:

(D-26)   /l/ ⟵——— /l/
                    ↘
        /pl kl fl/ ---↘ /ʎ/
                    ↘
              /č/ ——— /č/,

and on the Galician side merely:

(D-27)   /pl kl fl/ ——— /č/.

There are no synchronic mapping-rules, for the differential treatment of the crucial clusters meets Criterion 4 and renders the three sets of dialects incongruent, as shown herewith:

CEx	West Ibero-Romance	Castilian dialects	Asturian dialects	Galician dialects	Congruence
223	ɔyto	očo	ɔyto	ɔyto	+
12	amplo	ančo	anʎo	ančo	+
266	masklo	masčo	masʎo	masčo	+
324	paʎa	paža	paʎa	paʎa	−
S1	afla	aʎa	aʎa	ača	−
89	galo	gaʎo	gaʎo	galo	+
349	plaga	ʎaga	ʎaga	čaga	−
18	klama	ʎama	ʎama	čama	−
183	flama	ʎama	ʎama	čama	−

At no item is the incongruence actually three-way, but Galician dialects are incongruent with the rest at four of the items, while Castilian dialects are incongruent with the rest at Item 324.

7.3 Summary of the split, and inventory of Castilian. In summary, the phonological subsystem shaken up in the transition from West Ibero-

7.3 Summary of the split, and inventory of Castilian / 103

Romance to Castilian, Asturian, and Galician is that of the obstruent-plus-lateral clusters, all lost through merger or shift; the language change and split are motivated by Criterion 4. The relevant diachronic statement at the language level:

$$\text{WIb} / \left\{ \begin{array}{c} \text{pl kl fl} \\ \diagdown \\ \text{ʎ} \end{array} \right\} \text{ʎ /Ast}$$

$$\text{WIb} / \quad \text{pl kl fl} < \begin{array}{c} \text{ʎ} \\ \text{č} \end{array} \Biggr\} \text{/Cas}$$

$$\text{WIb} / \quad \text{pl kl fl} \text{ —— č/Gal}$$

The phonological inventories of the new languages which interest us further, namely, Galician (Gal) and Castilian, are then the following:

GAL(ICIAN)

Nuclei: i u e o ɛ ɔ a ĩ ũ ẽ õ ɛ̃ ɔ̃ ã

Onsets: p t c č k f s š m n ñ l ʎ r ʀ y
        pr tr   kr fr
                 kw
        b d ʒ ǧ g v z ž
        br dr   gr vr
                 gw

Codas: b d s l r y w

Remark. The onset clusters **py vy my** have disappeared as the result of a switch of the yod component from the cluster to the preceding vowel (phonetically a metathesis), as in **apyo** 'céleri/apio' > **aypo**, **pluvya**$_{359}$ > **čuyva**, **vendimya** 'vendange/vendimia' > **vendima**. (The yod is absorbed by the high front **i** as in the third example.)

CAST(ILIAN)

Nuclei: i   u   e   o   a
           yu ye yo ya
               we wo wa

7 West Ibero-Romance splits into Castilian, Asturian, and Galician

```
Onsets:  p   t    c  č   k  f  s  š  m  n  ñ  l  ʎ  r  ʀ
         pr  tr           kr fr
         b   d    ʒ       g  v  z  ž
         br  dr           gr vr
                             vl

Codas:   b   d    s    n    l    r    y
```

Remarks. (1) The on-glide diphthongs **yu yo ya** are restructurings of onset **y** plus vowel, resulting from the new partial identity shared by old **yerno**$_{204}$ with the new **yerba**$_{218}$ (< WIb **ɛrba**), necessitating reassignment to a diphthong analogous to **ye** in **ya**$_{121}$, **yugo**$_{227}$, or **yo** 'je/yo'.

(2) The on-glide diphthongs **wo wa** are likewise restructurings of onset **kw** or **gw** plus vowel, resulting from the need to analyze e.g. the new **kweʎo**$_{95}$ as having **k+we**, and hence also to resegment the **kw+a** of **kwatro**$_{379}$ as **k+wa**, the **gw+o** of **antigwo**$_{16}$ as **g+wo**, etc.

(3) The onset clusters **py vy my** as well as **kw gw** have disappeared through reassignment of the glide element to the succeeding nucleus, as just explained.

(4) The nasal codas **m n ñ** are reduced to just one—with allophones [m n ɲ ŋ] in complementation with the following onset—after the merger of /ñ/ with /n/ as in, say, WIb **sañto**$_{401}$ > Cas **santo** ~ **sančo**.[6]

Note. The diachronic changes which took place as WIb split to become Cast, Ast, and Gal are reflected in Cols. 1-2 of the corpus, although, of course, the respective input languages—Spanish and Portuguese—are end-products embodying many subsequent changes as well. We first digress to sketch in the subsequent history of Spanish, and then further pause to comment on various Col. 1 items which are to be accounted as residual either (a) already in Cas, or (b) later in Span. Thereafter, still before proceeding to the split of Galician, we will comment also on Col. 2 entries to be viewed as residual already in Galician.

Notes for Chapter 7

1. This split runs counter to Agard's (1976) binary split of WIb into Galician and 'Cantabrian', the latter label applied unconventionally to the common source of both Castilian and Asturo-Leonese. The subsequently posited split of Cantabrian into Asturo-Leonese and Castilian was based primarily on the cleavage of /f/ into an /f : h/ contrast as a result of borrowings into Castilian, where Asturo-Leonese had just /f/ (incongruence by Criterion 3). This gain, together with the borrowing also of new obstruent-plus-lateral onsets as against /ʎ/, and of [ǧ] or [ž] as against /y/, is here ascribed to a split of Castilian into Burgalés (the language of Burgos, the

earlier capital city in Castilla la Vieja) and Toledano (the language of Toledo, the later capital city in Castilla la Nueva). Toledano eventually dies out as Burgalés not only comes to overlay both Castillas but also goes on to spread fanwise through the center and south of Iberia, pinching off Asturo-Leonese to its west and Aragonese to its east, absorbing much of them and all of Mozarabic (the latter transmitting innumerable lexical items of Arabic origin), and eventually splitting into North Castilian and South Castilian, the direct product in Agard (1976) of Castilian itself. The present adjustment to the *Stammbaum* is based on a piece of the evidence adduced in Chapter 8 which was overlooked in formulating the earlier version. In any case, once North Castilian and South Castilian are established as separate languages, the further evolution is clear: the Sephardic dialects of South Castilian directly perpetuate that language, while Andalucian/American dialects of South Castilian develop in such a way as to become again, and more tightly, congruent with North Castilian than with Sephardic and thus switch their affiliation to the former. This switch comes to constitute a new language, call it Spanish, with dialects North Spanish and South Spanish—or Castilian Spanish and Andalucian/American Spanish—or, in terms of two regional standards: Madrid Standard and American Standard.

2. More accurately 'Pre-Castilian', as located in the region east of the Asturias between the Cantabrian Mountains and the sea, but not yet the entire area which was to become Castilla la Vieja.

3. Prior to this development, coda [1] had shown a variable tendency to semivocalize in all WIb dialects—a trend begun even before the split of SW at least after /a/, because it 'fed' the backing/raising (in western Iberian dialects) of the vowel /a/ to /ɔ/ and then /o/ before coda /w/ (see 6.1), as in **altro**$_{24}$ > /awtro/ > **owtro**, or **falce**$_{167}$ > /fawce/ > **fowce**. But we note, on the other hand, the unvocalized coda in **alto**$_{217}$, **salva**$_{406}$, etc. When the coda had semivocalized—to /y/ rather than /w/—after the vowel /o/, that nucleus was (immediately?) raised to merge with /u/, doubtless because /o/ did not occur before coda /y/, as in **eskolta**$_{141}$ > **eskuyta, koltɛlo**$_{104}$ > **kuytɛlo**.

4. Asturian dialects having been exempt from Changes 7.1.4 and 7.1.7, they generate by 7.1.8 such forms as /nweče/ for CEx 308, /weyo/ for CEx 309, or /wey/ for 'aujourd'hui/hoy'.

5. The voiced-initial correlates of these clusters have a different history as follows. In initial position, /bl/ and /gl/ (there is, of course, no initial */vl/) simply lose their occlusive element and merge with /l/ in all dialects before any palatalization sets in—e.g. /blástema/ 'dommage/lástima' > /lástema/, /glánd(en)e/$_{206}$ > /land(n)e/. In postcoda position, where /n+gl/ alone is found, palatalization and fusion lead ultimately to a simple /ñ/ via an intermediate /ñ+ʎ/ in all dialects—e.g. /ongla/$_{315}$ > */uñʎa/ > /uña/. In postnuclear position, /bl/ and /vl/ (there is no */gl/ because this cluster had merged with /ʎ/ as far back as ShW) remain for the most part unchanged—e.g. /doble/ 'double/doble' or /favla/ 'parler/hablar'.

6. As to this alternate form (the proper noun *Sancho*), once the [č] becomes a phoneme by the same mechanism as detailed in 7.5, mutatis mutandis, the palatal coda [ɲ] ceases to be phonemic.

Chapter 8
Castilian splits into Toledan and Burgalese

8.0 Introduction. Castilian splits binarily into Toledan and Burgalese. The lack of congruence will result from the cleavage of the labiodental fricative onset f into f and h. The development proceeds in two steps.

8.1 Preliminary change: Backing of [f] to [h]. In dialects along the coasts and on the slopes near the inner curve of the Bay of Biscay—an area of indigenous Basque-speaking populations—the CRom fricative [f] of the onsets /f fr fl/ became a bilabial [Φ] early enough to have phonological results in particular descendants of both South-Gallo (Gascon) and West-Ibero (Castilian). By the end of the first millennium the allophone [Φ] had delabialized and backed to [h]—in all positions in Gascon dialects but only before simple vocoids in dialects of Castilla la Vieja centered around Burgos. For in all the latter dialects, where /ɛ ɔ/ had already diphthongized and shifted to /yé wé/, the on-glide seemingly inhibited the passage from [Φ] to [h], as did the liquid release in [Φr]; ([Φl] evidently no longer occurred; see 7.2).

8.2 The crucial change: Dialectal borrowing of new [f] and consequent gain of /h/. Later, in the 12th-13th centuries after the establishment of the Castilian capital at Toledo in Castilla la Nueva, the prescriptive pressures of scholarly and refined diction seemingly restored the pristine labiodental [f] before simple nuclei, before [yé] though not /wé/ (keeping the [Φ] in that position), in /fr/, and (naturally) in reshaped items containing /fl/ (see Remark below, to inventory of Burgalese). When restoration of [f] subsequently spread into Burgalese-type dialects *in some but not all lexical items with* [h]—e.g. in *fiebre*$_{178}$ or *fe*$_{186}$ (a church word) but not in *hiel*$_{177}$ (cf. *fiel* 'fidèle/fiel') or *heno*$_{187}$—the phonological outcome was clearly enough the upgrading of the old [h] to phonemic status, and the resultant occurrence of two phonemes where one had been before represents a type of CLEAVAGE which, according to our Criterion 3, determines a change in the language.

Since Toledan dialects have no [h]≠[f] contrast they cannot now add an /h/, and in this way incongruence is established.

8.3 Inventory of Burgalese Castilian. The phonological inventory of the new language that interests us further, namely Burgalese, is then the following:

Nuclei: i u e o a
          yu ye yo ya
          we wo wa

Onsets: p t c č   k f s š h m n ñ l ʎ r ʀ
        pr tr   kr fr
        pl   kl fl
        b d   ʒ   g v z ž
        br dr   gr vr
        bl   gl vl

Codas: b d s n l r y

Remark. The added clusters **pl kl fl** and **bl gl**, which had been lost in the break-up of WIb, were reintroduced in some but not all lexical items of both the Toledan and the Burgalese dialects of Castilian by cultivated speakers and writers on the model of Latin and/or neighboring languages—e.g. Aragonese, Catalan, Provençal, or Occitan—all of which preserved the onset clusters in view. Conceivably first Toledan and later Burgalese should each be regarded as having become a new language by virtue of these additions to its phonemic inventory (Criterion 3 again); but the exact timing of the loans is uncertain and we may therefore conflate these changes with the one which clearly motivates the split of Castilian. Examples are **klaro**$_{78}$, **placa**$_{348}$, **plañe**$_{351}$, **plaʒe**$_{353}$, **plomo**$_{357}$, **flor**$_{184}$, **blanko**$_{38}$, **syeglo** 'siècle/siglo'.

Chapter 9
Burgalese Castilian splits into North Castilian and South Castilian

9.0 Introduction. Burgalese Castilian splits binarily into North Castilian and South Castilian. The lack of congruence will result from the loss of a strident obstruent.

9.1 Preliminary change: Shift of /c ẓ/ to /ṣ ẓ/. After Burgalese Castilian has spread fanwise through the center and south of the peninsula, first overlaying Toledan Castilian, then pinching off Asturo-Leonese to the West and Aragonese to the East, absorbing much of them and all of Mozarabic, changes begin among the strident obstruents. Everywhere, first, affricate [c ẓ] fricativize to apicodental [ṣ ẓ]. Phonologically, this is simply a shift:

(D-28)   /c ẓ/ ——— /ṣ ẓ/,

which is accounted for by a synchronic rule and causes no change in the language.

9.2 The crucial change: Partially intersecting dialectal mergers of /ẓ/. Subsequently, in the south, apical and dorsal sibilants become identical, with attendant phonological merger:

(D-29)   /ṣ ẓ/
          /s z/ $\Big>$ /s z/.

Later, in the north, the voiced trio [z ẓ ž] become voiceless [s ṣ š] and this results in a different restructuring through a different merger:

(D-30)   /z ẓ ž/
          /s ṣ š/ $\Big>$ /s ṣ š/.[1]

In consequence of these two partially intersecting mergers, the northern and southern dialects of the language become incongruent by Criterion 4, as demonstrated herewith:

9.4 The amalgamation of North Castilian and South Castilian / 109

CEx	Burgalese Castilian	Southern dialects	Northern dialects	Congruence
334	**pasa**	pasa	pasa	+
262	**kaza**	kaza	kasa	+
348	**placa**	plasa	plaṣa	+
353	**plaʒe**	plaze	plaṣe	−

As a result of these restructurings, the two divergent sets of dialects become by our criteria new languages.

9.3 Summary of the split, and inventories of North Castilian and South Castilian. In summary, the phonological subsystem shaken up in the transition to North Castilian and South Castilian is that of the sibilant obstruents; the language change and split are motivated by Criterion 4 as applied to the differential coalescences of the voiced apical strident /ẓ/. The phonological inventories of the two descendent languages are reduced as follows: North Castilian has lost the voiced sibilants **ʒ z ž**, the voiced fricative **v**, and the corresponding clusters **vr vl** through merger of /v vr vl/ with /b br bl/;[2] South Castilian has lost only the apical affricates **c ʒ**.

9.4 The amalgamation of North Castilian and South Castilian as Spanish and the inventory of this language. At the end of the 15th century SCas, indigenous to Andalucía and Extremadura, was carried to the New World by the Spanish conquistadores and to eastern Europe by the expatriated Spanish Jews. Despite the complete cessation of interaction between the two groups, their dialects have remained congruent to this day by virtue of a rather elaborate set of M-rules. In other terms there never was a split of SCas involving only American Spanish varieties on one side. More to the point, however, is the fact that in Andalucian and American dialects there was a merger of the voiced sibilants /z ž/ with their voiceless correlates /s š/, paralleling the very NCas development that had helped determine the split of Cas (see 9.1). The curious phonological result of this restructuring is that the dialects of southern Spain and of Spanish America become *again* congruent with the NCas dialects of Madrid and northern Spain, while at the same time remaining congruent with the SCas dialects of the Sephardim. Confronted with this apparent anomaly we can say either that Andalucian/American Spanish belongs simultaneously to two languages, or that it has switched its language affiliation from SCas to NCas in such a way as to constitute a new language, Spanish, with dialects North Spanish and South Spanish—or Castilian Spanish and Andalucian/American Spanish—or, in terms of two regional standards: Madrid standard and American standard. The latter claim may seem preferable for three reasons. First, it may be methodologically, not to say theoretically, undesirable ever to allow any

9 Burgalese Castilian splits into North and South Castilian

dialect double allegiance at all. Second, the switch can be justified in a synchronic context by assigning the straddler to the language from whose underlying representation it can be derived with the simplest and/or fewest M-rules—in which case NCas is clearly the winner. Third, the switch is supported by external history: whereas the Jews left Spain, severing contact with all other speakers of either SCas or NCas, the remaining Spaniards speaking SCas maintained and increased their interaction with those speaking NCas, both in the homeland and overseas, all through the vast imperial adventure.

The phonological inventory of the new language, Spanish, is then the following:

Nuclei: i   u   e   o   a
             yu ye yo ya
         wi   we wo wa

Onsets: p   t   č   k   f   θ   s   x   h   m   n   ñ   l   ʎ   r   R
         pr tr   kr fr
         pl   kl fl
         b   d   g
         br dr   gr
         bl   gl

Codas: p   t   k   f   θ   s   n   l   r   y   w

Remarks. (1) The disappearance of **c** and the appearance of **θ** reflects a completion of the phonetic shift which began with [c > ṣ] and led to a nonstrident interdental fricative [θ] by around 1600.

(2) The disappearance of **š** and the appearance of **x** reflects a palatal-to-velar backing of the onset in view—a shift generalized by 1700 or so, although the original [š] persists in sporadic rural dialects. (In numerous dialects of both southern Spain and America, the [x] has develarized to an aspirate [h] and has merged phonologically with the on-going /h/ where the latter had not already gone to zero (see just below), as in e.g. /hiho/ for CEx 181.

(3) The **h** is still present in the phonological inventory of the language because it persists in popular dialects of both hemispheres. Since 1600 or so, the aspirate has been lost through merger with zero in most dialects including the literary, official, and regional standards, which therefore all require the M-rule **h** → /∅/.

(4) The addition of the on-glide **wi** results from a fairly recent switch in syllabicity from [ui̯] (for /u+y/ to [u̯i], as, for example, in **kuyda** 'soigne/cuida' > **kwida**).

9.5 Residual discrepancies in Castilian and/or Spanish / 111

(5) The expanded list of codas is due to the large-scale borrowing, reaching its peak in the 16th-17th centuries, of lexical items from Classical Latin and/or Greek (e.g. **apto, Ritmo, tékniko, digno, difterya, causa**). The addition of θ, however, results from a redistribution: the coda [d] of the new Latinisms comes into contrast with the [δ] of North Cas **žudga** or **-adgo**, forcing a reassignment of the latter to /θ/—which at this point has, like /s/, voiced allophones before voiced onsets (Sp /xuθga/ as ['xuδ-γa], cf. /desde/ as ['dez-δe]). The vast gain of codas provides at the same time a motive for changing the North Castilian language (generally known to philologists as 'Old Spanish') in accordance with our criteria. There seems to be no valid reason for not conflating the two acquisitions in view—the SCas graft and the classicizing lexicon—into a single language change.

9.5 Residual discrepancies in Castilian and/or Spanish as reflected by Spanish. We may now return to the corpus to examine Castilian and/or Spanish residue.

CEx 22. The medial /θ/ is not in fact residual; it is our only example of the regular development of WIb **y** which in Castilian dialects had merged with /ž/ after coda /r/; cf. also /esparθe/ < CLat SPARGE- 'répandre/esparcir' (not in corpus).

CEx 38. For the stressed nucleus /ú/, see below at CEx 107.

CEx 54. Spanish *canción*, with the stressed diphthongal nucleus /yó/ instead of the expected simple /ó/, is a Latinism of recent date. Cas having favored the synonym *cantar*, it is not known how early WIb */kankon/ fell away.

CEx 83. The stressed diphthong /yé/ instead of the simple /é/ expected from the SW form is believed attributable to the analogy of the more popular and current synonym *empieza*.

CEx 105. Sp /kwesta/ instead of the expected */kosta/ may well betray a doublet harking back very far—cf. Ital /kɔsta/, seemingly reflecting the same low back nucleus.

CEx 107. Cas had already spread the /u/—which first developed where the original unstressed /o/ was followed by a yod-initial suffix (e.g. in /kubriéndo/ or /kubrió/)—to the stem-stressed forms, while retaining the /o/ elsewhere. Spanish later generalized the high vowel throughout the entire paradigm of this and certain other *i*-stem verbs; note also CEx 38, and the analogous front-vowel cases of CExs 417, 461.

CEx 112. In a certain number of items, the lost WIb δ seems to have been restored to Cas as **d**, in a backlash of the following sort. Even the postvocalic /d/, reflex of Western **t** (as in, say, CEx 291), was becoming a fricative [δ] and tending to approach zero already in Cas popular speech, particularly in the high-frequency sequences *-ado*, *-ido*, *-udo* (or *-ada*, *-ida*, *-uda*). The resulting vulgarisms in /-ao, -io, -uo/ etc., constantly subjected already then

112 / 9 Burgalese Castilian splits into North and South Castilian

to cultivated pressures, could have from a very early date (i.e. even before the split of Cas) gathered up */kruo/$_{112}$, */grao/$_{120}$, */nio/$_{300}$, */noo/$_{302}$, */nuo/$_{307}$, */suor/$_{427}$, as well as various other items long innocent of any [δ], as candidates for the blanket correction that happened to render *crudo, grado* etc. more elegantly Latinate than, say, *mudo* or *prado*. For a fuller discussion of this particular problem, see Agard (1973).

CEx 118. WIb */kɔša/ may have been driven out of the Cas lexicon by the adjective */kɔšo/ 'boiteux, cojo' (not in corpus), by reason of semantic incompatibility, in favor of the semilearned reflex *muslo* of Lat MUSCULU-, although this assumption is weakened by the persistence of both the noun and the adjective in Galician.

CEx 125. Cas had /dios/ (as well as /dio/, based on the accusative case), in which the stressed /i/ was the normal reflex of a WIb mid-front vowel in hiatus before /o/ or /a/; cf. CEx 469, or /mio/ < CLat MEU- (not in corpus). The stress-shift/diphthongization occurred only in Sp itself (cf. Seph /dio/ as reflecting the SCas form).

CEx 134. Cas *dulce* is not considered to be a straight Latinism, but rather an educated embellishment of /duc(e)/ (also attested), itself a reflex of SW /dolce/ developing from the changes outlined in 7.1.6, note 3, with the semivocalized coda /y/ eliminated before the affricate in patterning with (say) /muyto/$_{34}$ > /mučo/.

CEx 161. CLat FAME- had a popular variant with stem *FAMINE-, which survived dialectally all the way down into Cas dialects of WIb in which the second medial onset, following early syncope, was dissimilatively denasalized to yield */famre/, then assimilatively clustered to produce */fambre/. It is to be noted that there are several other instances of Cas preference for ShW nouns in '-(e)ne wherever this longer stem variant was available to be generalized and handed down; cf. CEx 222 and others.

CEx 169. The Cas development of */fembra/ from SW */fém(e)na/ exactly parallels that of CEx 161 and other nouns ending variably in '-(e)ne. Cf. also CEx 414.

CEx 184. See CExs 160ff. above, on the Burgalese borrowing of /fl-/ subsequently to its change to /ʎ-/ in the split of WIb.

CEx 196. Cas had the inherited *fruente*, but Spanish reduced the stressed nucleus to simple /é/ after the cluster.

CEx 204. Spanish resolved the unacceptable Cas sequence /n+r/ resulting from syncope—as in ShW */ǧeṇ(e)ṛu/ and */téṇ(e)ṛu/$_{432}$—by transposing coda and onset.

CEx 205. Western Romance had merged the onsets /ǧ-/ and /y-/, prevalently as /ǧ/ but in north central Iberian dialects as /y/ instead (CEx 121, 202, 204, 227, 351). In Toledan and Burgalese Castilian, elegant class speech reintroduced a phone [ǧ], again on the model of Latin (as liturgically pronounced) or neighboring languages, in some but not all lexical items. (See also CEx 225–6; also *joven*$_{S-48}$ or *ángel* (not in corpus). The shape *yente* is

9.5 Residual discrepancies in Castilian and/or Spanish / 113

documented, but most such are not.) The new [ǧ] found itself at once in complementation with the postnuclear [ž] which had developed out of WIb [ʎ] and it therefore became a member of the phoneme /ž/, which thence had fricative and affricate allophones just as are reflected in Sephardic to this day.

CEx 206. For the merger of WIb initial /gl-/ with /l-/, see above at 7.2, note 5. Typically, the Sp form reflects a 'VLat' (i.e. CRom) stem variant */glandi̯ne̯/, with denasalization of the onset /n/ following syncope, partially analogous to the process detailed at CEx 161.

CEx 207. Cas had the inherited *gosto*; the modern Sp *gusto* is strictly a learned substitution.

CEx 213. Cas /geRa/ instead of the expected */gyeRa/ is thought to reflect an old variant with a stressed nucleus closer to the original short [e] (not [ɛ]) of the Gmc etymon.

CEx 220. The deictic prefix *a-* (as on *aqui* etc.) seems to have been added variably in SW; Cat also has it here.

CEx 222. Cas had both *omne* and *uemne*, Sp at first both *(h)ombre* and *(h)uembre*. (The modern orthographic *h* was added to words which had the long-lost aspirate phoneme in their Latin etyma, of course after phonological loss of the /h/ (also written *h*) from WIb /f/.) Although the diphthonged variant was the normal development, the early use of this particular noun as an indefinite [−human] subject equivalent to Fr *on* or Cat *hom*, hence unfocused in the sentence and reduced in stress, may have checked the diphthongization and thus generated a variant which entered competition with the original form in all syntactic positions and eventually triumphed altogether.

CEx 225–6 and 229. For the initial /x-/ (< Cas /ž/) as against the expected /y-/ in these three items, see above at CEx 205. In *junio* the final syllable /-nyo/ instead of /-ño/ bespeaks extra Latinizing influence.

CEx 240. This adjective still had its general Romance meaning in Cas; Sp alone has shifted it to supplant *luengo* in everyday usage, while leaving $ancho_{12}$ to encompass *largo*'s former range.

CEx 244. The regular *lieva* is well documented for Cas; the unique redistribution of initial onset and stressed nucleus, plus generalization of the resultant /ʎ-/ to the full paradigm, was brought about in Spanish.

CEx 257. Cas *lumne* > Sp *lumbre* typically descends from the Lat general stem LŪMINE- (see CEx 161).

CEx 274. Although the item superficially resembles those discussed at CEx 112, the environment is not that for restitution of the /d/ and we are more probably dealing here with a straight church Latinism.

CEx 277. This obvious Latinism perforce replaced the inherited reflex */meo/ as the latter collided with stem-stressed forms of the semitaboo verb *mear* 'uriner/orinar'.

CEx 300, 307. See above at CEx 112.

CEx 305. Cas *nomne* > Sp *nombre* characteristically reflects the Lat general stem NŌMINE- (see CEx 161).

CEx 311. Cas had *uebra* as expected; Sp reduced the stressed nucleus analogically, together with that of the verb *obrar*.

CEx 320. Sp *oso* traces all the way back to the CRom doublet */ṵssṵ/, which betrays a change of the coda-onset cluster /r+s/ to geminate /s+s/ already variable in (popular) Latin. Note that Cat *os* also reflects this origin.

CEx 328. The final syllable in /-yo/ easily reveals the item to be a Latinism.

CEx 336. Cas had the expected *pielle*. Sp depalatalized the /ʎ/ by dissimilation from the yod in the preceding syllable, then recut *piele+s* to *piel+es*, with the lateral as final onset on the model of CEx 177 or 278.

CEx 351, 353, 357. For the onset /pl-/ instead of /ʎ-/ in these items, see above at CEx 160ff.

CEx 363. Cas had both /pec/ and /peše/, as Sp still keeps both *pez* and *peje* with the former far more prevalent now. The doublets stem, respectively, from It-W */peske/ and the variable metathesis to */pekse/ which led to W */peyse/ and which alone survived in NW, though both continued to compete in SW and its descendents.

CEx 373. Cas /precyo/ instead of */pryeco/ betrays itself as fully Latinizing.

CEx 382. WIb evidently had the doublets */koa/ and */kola/. The variant with /l/ occurs in a few Italo-Romance dialects and is probably as old as CRom or even popular Latin, through blending with CEx 119, with which its semantic affinity is unmistakable.

CEx 404. Cas *sangne* > Sp *sangre* typically reflects the Lat general stem SANGUINE-.

CEx 408. Cas had /šabon/, with the palatalized onset perhaps borrowed from the cognate Mozarabic language (a descendent of UnshW with phonological as well as lexical borrowings from Arabic) in the course of the reconquest of the peninsula from the Moorish overlords. A few similar cases exist, e.g. Sp *jibia* (< Cas /šibya/ < CLat SĒPIA 'seiche'), or *jugo* (< Cas /šugo/ < Lat SŪCU- 'jus, suc').

CEx 417. Cas had already spread the /i/—which first developed where the original unstressed /e/ was followed by a yod-initial suffix (e.g. in /sirv+yendo/ or /sirv+yó/—to the stem-stressed forms, while retaining the /e/ elsewhere. Cf. the like treatment in $vestir_{461}$ or *seguir* 'suivre', and note the slight difference in treatment from CEx 107.

CEx 427. For the medial /d/, see above at CEx 112.

CEx 435. This noun designating the human head, which replaced CEx 64 in that meaning in some dialects of Italo-Western, seemingly ran into opposition from the derived item */kabeca/ in WIb, where it was further restricted to reference to the forehead and subsequently lost altogether from Castilian, in favor of CEx 196.

CEx 446. Cas had /treinta/, with stress on the /i/, reflecting a CRom variant */triginta/ or (later) */treginta/, with subsequent loss of the /g/ (cf. 1.9.2, CEx 76). Sp of course shifted the stress to produce the modern form.

CEx 459. Cas already had *gusano*, a word of uncertain and perhaps pre-Romance origin; there is no trace of WIb */vɛrme/ despite its persistence in Portuguese.

CEx 461. For the stressed nucleus /i/, see above at CEx 417.

CEx 467. Cas had /veinte/, with stress on the /i/, reflecting a CRom variant */wiginti/ or (later) */veginti/, with subsequent loss of the /g/. For all this, cf. CEx 446 above.

Notes for Chapter 9

1. The affricate allophone [ǧ] of the palatal /ž/ had already merged with the postnuclear fricative [ž] and therefore did not coalesce with the voiceless [č] of the phoneme /č/.

2. Examples are **vaka**$_{450}$ > **baka, livre**$_{S-51}$ > **libre, havla** > **abla** 'parler/hablar'. The phonetic change which led to the loss of /v/ (and its associated clusters) through merger with /b/ may originally have coincided with the evolution of its voiceless correlate /f/—i.e. from a labiodental to a bilabial fricative—[v] > [β] as paralleling [f] > [Φ]—in the same sets of WIb and SGal dialects. (Gascon dialects of SGal also lost the /v/.) Rather than delabializing and backing to some kind of voiced aspirate, however, the new [β] would have fallen together with the identical postnuclear fricative allophone of /b/—a partial coalescence then followed by that of the new [β] with occlusive [b] in initial and postcoda position, thus completing the phonological merger of /v/ with /b/. Centuries later, the cultivated Toledan dialect would have restored the pristine labiodental /v/, orthographically and probably also phonemically, except in sporadic unrecognized cases such as /boda/ 'mariage/boda' from the (neuter) plural of CLat vōtu-. Although the orthographic *v* stuck, the restored /b/≠/v/ contrast failed to penetrate Burgalese Castilian.

Chapter 10
Galician splits into Gallegan and Portuguese

10.0 Introduction. Galician splits binarily into Gallegan and Portuguese. The lack of congruence will result from the loss of a strident obstruent.

10.1 Preliminary changes

10.1.1 Fusion of final vowel strings. In all dialects, final strings of two back vowels or of two low vowels fuse into single vowels, nasal if the first is nasal—e.g. /soo/$_{418}$ > /sɔ/,[1] /paa/$_{340}$ > /pa/, /bɔ̃o/$_{41}$ > /bɔ̃/, /ũo/$_{449}$ > /ũ/.

10.1.2 Denasalization in nasal-plus-oral vowel strings. Subsequently, all strings of nasal plus oral vowel—except [ã+o], which remains in contrast with oral [a+o] (e.g. /mão/$_{261}$ vs. /mao/$_{265}$—denasalize their first element, e.g. /sẽo/$_{411}$ > /seo/, /korõa/$_{101}$ > /koroa/, /mõeda/$_{281}$ > /moeda/. Prior to the denasalization, however, uniquely in the environment /ĩ_V/, a transitory [ɲ], having developed between the two vowels, then merges with existing /ñ/, e.g. /vĩo/$_{466}$ > [vĩɲo] > /viño/. (Before any of the nasal onsets /m n ñ/, any nucleus is lightly nasalized but in this position there is no contrast with oral vowels and the nasalization is therefore subphonemic.)

10.1.3 Shift of /c ɟ/ to /ṣ ẓ/. Everywhere, the affricates [c ɟ] fricativize to apicodental [ṣ ẓ], but remain in contrast with dorsal [s z]. Phonologically, this is simply a shift:

(D-31) /c ɟ/ ——— /ṣ ẓ/,

which is accounted for by a synchronic rule at the language level and causes no change in the language. Then in Portugal, apical and dorsal sibilants lose their strident/nonstrident contrast and become identical, with attendant phonological mergers:

(D-32)   /ṣ ẓ/
                       >/s z/.
         /s z/

10.2 The crucial change: Partially intersecting dialectal mergers of /z̧/.
Subsequently, in Galicia, the voiced trio [z̧ z ž] become voiceless [s̩ s š] and this change results in a different restructuring through a different merger:

(D-33) /z̧ z ž/ ⟶
        /s̩ s š/ ⟶ /s̩ s š/.

In consequence of these two partly intersecting mergers, Gallegan and Portuguese dialects become incongruent by Criterion 4, as demonstrated herewith:

CEx	Galician language	Gallegan dialects	Portuguese dialects	Congruence
334	**pasa**	pasa	pasa	+
262	**kaza**	kasa	kaza	+
348	**praca**	praṣa	prasa	+
353	**praz̧e**	praṣe	praze	−

As a result of these restructurings the two divergent sets of dialects become new languages.

10.3. Summary of the split, and inventory of Portuguese. The phonological subsystem shaken up in the transition is that of the sibilant obstruents, with the change and split motivated by Criterion 4 as applied to the differential coalescences of the voiced apical strident /z̧/—coalescences directly analogous to those which had, earlier, split Castilian into North and South Castilian. The voiced-voiceless merger (Rule D-33) was one which evidently had radiated out from its focal area of innovation in Castilla, whence it spread to its sister languages, thereby causing the split of Galician. This is an arresting aspect of languages in contact: the case of a sound-change originating in Language A and overlaying a dialect of Language B and, by so doing, causing Language B to split.

The strident-nonstrident merger in Portuguese (i.e. southerly) dialects (Rule D-32) was a change shared by southern dialects of Castilian, and also by Catalan, the lone descendent of East Ibero-Romance. In all South Gallic (Oc) descendents of SW, as well as all North Gallic (Oïl) and some Italo-Gallic descendents of NW, a one-stage merger of **c z̧** with **s z** directly through mere loss of affrication may—assuming that it radiated southward then eastward along the Mediterranean coast—have spurred the relevant mergers in Iberia.

10 Galician splits into Gallegan and Portuguese

The corresponding diachronic statements at the language level are:

$$\text{Gal/} \begin{cases} \underset{\sim}{z}\ z\ \check{z} \\ \underset{\sim}{s}\ s\ \check{s} \end{cases} > \underset{\sim}{\S}\ s\ \check{s} \ /\text{Glg} \qquad \text{Gal/} \begin{cases} \underset{\sim}{\S}\ \underset{\sim}{z} \\ \underset{\sim}{s}\ z \end{cases} > s\ z\ /\text{Port}$$

The phonological inventory of the Portuguese language is the following:

Nuclei: i u e o ɛ ɔ a ĩ ũ ẽ õ ã

Onsets: p b t d k g f v s z š ž m n ñ l ʎ r ʀ y
        pr br tr dr kr gr fr vr
        pl bl   kl gl fl
                  kw gw

Codas: p b t d k g f s n l r y w

Remarks. (1) The disappearance of the affricate onsets č ǧ is due to their respective coalescence, in Portuguese though not in Gallegan, with the fricative onsets š ž as in **čama**$_{18}$ > **šama**, **ačo**$_{12}$ > **ašu**, **mačo**$_{266}$ > **mašu**, **ǧɔga**$_{226}$ > **žɔga**. In Gallegan (as in WIb) the distribution of š ž had been very limited, occurring only postvocalically.

(2) The disappearance of the lower-mid nasal nuclei ɛ̃ ɔ̃ is due to their respective coalescence, in Portuguese though not in Gallegan, with the higher-mid nasal nuclei ẽ õ as in **vɛ̃**$_{456}$ > **vẽ**, **vɛ̃to**$_{457}$ > **vẽtu**, **bɔ̃**$_{41}$ > **bõ**, **pɔ̃te**$_{367}$ > **põte**. The front ẽ is realized as a phonetically diphthongal [ẽĩ] in final position, but this is noncontrastive and there is no value in phonologizing it as a diphthong.

(3) The new diphthong **oy** results from the raising of /ɛy ɔy/ to /ey oy/ (the front diphthong merely merging with existing /ey/), as in **lɛyto**$_{251}$ > **leytu**, or **ɔyto**$_{223}$ > **oytu**, prior to the development noted in Remark (2).

(4) A final mid vowel in hiatus after any nonidentical (oral or nasal) vowel was first raised to high and then semivocalized to the corresponding glide, thus in effect becoming a minor-syllable onset. Examples are **meo** 'mien/mío' > **mew**,[2] **cɛo**$_{73}$ > **sɛw**, **põe**$_{366}$ > **põy**, **mao**$_{265}$ > **maw**, **mão**$_{261}$ > **mãw**.

(5) The onset clusters **pl bl kl gl fl**, lost in the transition from WIb (see 7.9), reappear here in consequence of a lexical expansion already begun in medieval times, namely, the borrowing—by both Portuguese and Gallegan dialects of Galician—of items from related languages (e.g. Castilian, Oc, or Classical Latin), for example, *planta, bloco, claro, glória, flor*.[3]

(6) The expanded list of codas is due to the subsequent borrowing, on a much larger scale, reaching its peak in the 16th-17th centuries, of lexical items from Classical Latin and/or Greek—e.g. *apto, objeto, ritmo, admira, técnico, digno, diftéria* . . .

10.4 Residual discrepancies in Galician and/or Portuguese, as reflected by Portuguese.

We now return to the corpus for one last time, to look at Galician and/or Portuguese residual items.

CEx 15. Gal had the regular /ɛlo/ (from earlier */aɛlo/), but this rather vague shape was discarded by Port in favor of the French, Occitan, or Provençal form /anɛl/.

CEx 38. For *branco* and not **blanco*, see below at CEx 348.

CEx 72. The normal loss of final /-e/ from ShW */kawle/ seems to have been variable at best in the environment of the coda-plus-onset segment /-wl-/. Gal dialects of WIb */kowl(e)/ in which the /-e/ remained in place then lost the /l/ as though between vowels and produced a form */kowe/ in which the hiatus was subsequently filled by an intrusive /v/. This is well supported by CEx 255: ShW and SW /lawδa/ > WIb */lowa/, leading naturally to Cas /loa/ but to Gal /lowva/; cf. also SW /awδe/ 'ouïr/oir', ending up as Gal /owve/.

CEx 85. Gal alone reflects the original CRom /ŋ+n/, which in this item generally dropped the velar coda instead of evolving to /ññ/ (later /ñ/) as was the general rule. Variable also was the SW dialectal switch of the stressed vowel from the inherited /ó/ to the /é/ of the frequent derivational suffix /-esce/ which set in dialectally by analogy. Of all these still competing base shapes in WIb, Cas was free to select /kono-/ or /kone-/ but not /koño-/, while Gal was faced with either /koño-/ or /koñe-/ as alternative to a lost intervocalic /n/ (as in, say, CEx 239).

CEx 103. Gal /kurto/ instead of the expected */korto/ seems to confirm the first explanation offered for the Catalan cognate *curt* in 6.4.2.

CEx 105. Port /kusta/ instead of the expected form with mid-back vowel may be due to paradigmatic leveling after pretonic /o/ was regularly raised to /u/ (see 10.3, note 2).

CEx 135. It is perhaps not too improbable to view Gal *doce* as a blend of the earlier-attested *duce* (evolved in WIb together with Cas *duce* from SW /dolce/) and a hypothetical */dowce/, the doublets resulting from variable [±back] semivocalization of the lateral coda before the onset /c/ (cf. SW **falce**$_{167}$ > WIb **fowce**.

CEx 136. The pretonic nucleus of the Gal form, if not Latinizing, alone reflects the long -ī- of Classical Latin, while the popular short-vowel variant prevailed everywhere else.

CEx 139. Rather than the expected */eská/, Gal has /eskada/, a normal reflex of Low Latin *scalata*. Port has kept the form with /-d-/ in addition to borrowing (in specialized sense at first) *escala* from Italian.

CEx 140. Gal /eskɔla/ instead of the expected */eskoa/ is a Latinism. Though the original WIb lax /l̯/ had been lost, the new /l/ stemming from WIb nonlax /l/ facilitated borrowing of the lateral intervocalically with no effect on phonemic distribution.

CEx 141. Gal /eskuta/ instead of the expected */eskuyta/ results from generalizing the phonologically regular simple vowel of the unstressed stem-alternant throughout the verbal paradigm.

CEx 142. In Gal /eskrɛve/ instead of the expected */eskrive/, the lowered root vowel betrays primarily a dissimilation from the stem vowel wherever stressed, i.e. /eskriví-/ > /eskreví-/. Secondarily, in Port, the verb switched from an *i*-stem to an *e*-stem and in so doing generalized the lower root vowel throughout the paradigm.

CEx 160. Gal had /fac/; Port added the final /-e/ under Gallicizing and/or Latinizing influence, conceivably to escape homophony with the truncated stem /fas/ of the verb **faze**$_{162}$.

CEx 155. Gal /eyšo/ as against /eyše/ may possibly trace as far back as a CRom popular variant */aksu̯/.

CEx 161. In Gal, /fome/ and /fame/ were competing doublets; Port standardized the former despite dialectal persistence of /fame/. Although the doublet with /o/ traces far back (cf. Rou in 2.4.2), it may have been reinforced in Port by the *klang* with the form /kome/ of the verb *comer* 'manger/comer'.

CEx 184. Attested for Gal are both *chor* and *frol*, the latter showing metathesis within the borrowed form which prevailed in Port (as it did also in Sp) under *culto* influences. For more on this item and CEx 185, see below at CEx 348.

CEx 187. Gal had /fẽo/, but Port restored the /n/, possibly to avoid homophony with the adjective *feio* 'laid/feo'. Although the inherited /n̦/ had been lost, the new /n/ stemming from WIb nonlax /n/ facilitated borrowing of this nasal intervocalically with no effect on phonemic distribution.

CEx 198. With the Port merger of pretonic /o/ with /u/, *i*-stem verbs with [+back] root vowel coalesced into one and the same pattern of alternation, viz. unstressed /u/ and stressed /ú ~ ɔ́/, depending on what follows, thus: /fužír/, /fúžu/ but /fɔ́že/ like /durmír/, /dúrmu/ but /dɔ́rme/. Cf. also /sɔ́be/ of the verb *subir* 'monter/subir'.

CEx 204. Gal resolved the unacceptable WIb sequence /n+r/ resulting from syncope—as in ShW */ǧen̦(e)ru/ and */tén̦(e)ru/$_{432}$—by tensing the liquid onset to /R/ in postcoda position.

CEx 214. Gal /gɔla/ instead of the expected */goa/ is thought to represent a dialectal blend of WIb /gol̦a/ and /kɔlo/$_{95}$ (which originally had a neuter plural form with final /-a/), thus accounting for both the stressed vowel and the medial onset.

CEx 219. Gal /ɔra/ instead of the expected */ora/ has no satisfactory explanation.

CEx 220. Gal lost the WIb item /(a)ɛr/, replacing it with /õte/ or /õtẽ/, a reflex of */an̦ɔyte/; cf. the semantic opposite /amañã/ 'demain/mañana', also with the demonstrative prefix tracing back, partially at least, to the

10.4 Residual discrepancies in Galician and/or Portuguese / 121

ablative case-form CLat HĀC of the deictic determiner as in 'cette nuit/ anoche'.

CEx 222. Gal and Port /ɔmẽ/ reflects an unsyncopated WIb variant which underlies the Cat and Oc cognates as well, namely, */ɔmen(e)/, as against the shape */ɔmne/ reflected in Cas, which must have been syncopated back in SW, prior to the loss of final atonic /-e/.

CEx 224. Gal /isʎa/ and Port /iʎa/ may reflect the normal development of medial /s+l/ (the only example available) and therefore may not be residual.

CEx 238. For Gal and Port /lingwa/ as against /lengwa/, see CRom, 1.9.

CEx 249. Gal /lēcɔl/ instead of the expected */lēcɔ́/ is said to result from truncation of the final stem vowel prior to intervocalic loss of /l̯/, but this is hardly an explanation; a better hypothesis would be that of a reshaping under foreign (Oc or Cat) influence.

CEx 255. For the extraneous medial /v/, see above at CEx 72.

CEx 263. The stressed /ɔ́/ instead of /ó/ in this and the other three irregular comparative adjectives *menor, melhor,* and *pior* has no satisfactory explanation.

CEx 289. Gal /mɔRe/ instead of the expected */mɔre/ is thought due to an early dialectal switch of this verb from an *i*-stem to an *e*-stem, and a subsequent syncopation of the infinitive */mɔ́rere/ and the future */moreréy/, in which /r+r/ would automatically yield /R/. Extension of this /R/ throughout the paradigm would then account for the rest, though the explanation is dubious because there are no parallel examples and /kɛ́re+re/$_{381}$ did not syncopate in like manner. It is conceivable, nevertheless, as a strategy to avoid homophony with certain forms of the verb *morar*, more frequent than its Spanish cognate in the meaning 'habiter/habitar'.

CEx 306. Gal had /nɔstro/, but the attestation of Cas *nueso* alongside *nuestro* bespeaks a reduced shape */nɔso/ already in WIb. This latter was no doubt the prenominal, unfocused possessive determiner—cf. the dual treatment of the same item in French, yielding prenominal *notre* (pl. *nos*) as against *nôtre(s)*. After a period of competition in all positions, Port discarded */nɔstru/ in favor of /nɔsu/, while the full form was winning out in Spanish.

CEx 320. Gal had both the regular /oso/ and a dialectal /uso/, but Port restored the coda /r/ to the more Latinate of the doublets under *culto* influence, possibly in avoidance of homophony with /osu/$_{319}$ (< Gal /ɔso/).

CEx 339. Gal had /pēa/, but Port restored the /n/, as was done in a few other instances (cf. CEx 187).

CEx 348. Gal acquired the onset clusters /pl kl fl/ and /bl/ under essentially the same cultivated and/or erudite circumstances as did Toledo

Castilian. Gallegan dialects went on to merge each and every one of these laterally released clusters with its familiar /r/-final counterpart, but Port dialects did this only variably, so that both sets remained in the language as it kept *claro, flor, plange*... (CExs 78, 184, 351...) but changed to *branco, froco, pranto*... (CExs 38, 185, 352...).

CEx 359. The Port form betrays the considerable hesitation between /u/ and /uy/ in items where the presence of the semivowel coda was phonologically normal; Gal had /šuyva/, and cf. Port /mūytu/$_{34}$ and /ʀuyvu/$_{S-86}$ (cognate of Fr *rouge* and Sp *rubio*), as against /eskuta/$_{141}$ or /kutɛlu/$_{104}$.

CEx 360. Gal /pelo/ instead of the expected /*peo/ is thought to represent a dialectal blend of WIb /pel̯o/ and the semantically neighboring /kabelo/$_{68}$, thus accounting for the medial lateral.

CEx 373. The Port form, with medial /s/ instead of /z/, is apparently a Latinism like its counterpart in Spanish; cf. the Port verb /prɛza/ 'priser/ preciar'.

CEx 382. Gal had /koa/, which could stem from either of the WIb doublets */koa/ or */kol̯a/. Port /kawda/ is clearly a Latinism.

CEx 389. Gal had /ʀeīa/, but Port changed the pretonic /e/ to /a/ by way of avoiding a reduction of the hiatus which would have yielded */ʀiña/.

CEx 414. Gal /semēa/ and Port /semeya/ show the inherited stress of WIb */sɛm(e)na/ regularized as in all verbs, as opposed to e.g. the noun /fémia/$_{169}$.

CEx 426. Gal had the regular /sordo/, and some Port dialects still have it. The standard Port form, rather than Latinizing, is seen as perhaps attracted by the high vowel of CEx 291 in such a phrase as *surdo e mudo*.

CEx 435. This noun signifies 'front/frente' rather than 'tête/cabeza' in Port; see 9.3.

CEx 453. Rather than be let to lose its /l/ and collapse with the stem /vae/ of the common verb *ir* 'aller/ir', the medial lateral was reinforced within the paradigm by its alternation with /ʎ/ (cf. /vaʎ+o/ 'je vaux/valgo' and the subjunctive form /vaʎ+a/.

CEx 472. The pretonic /i/ as against /e/ in the other languages seems to reflect a retention of the original long -ī- in competition with the widely dissimilated short vowel.

CEx 473. The /ɔ/ instead of /o/ could bespeak Port avoidance of collision with the pronoun /vos/ 'vous/vosotros'.

CEx 475. See above at CEx 306, mutatis mutandis.

Notes for Chapter 10

1. Except in verb stems (e.g. /kre/$_{109}$) and in the pronoun /ke/$_{385}$, final stressed higher-mid nuclei become lower-mid, e.g. /fɛ/$_{186}$ (cf. /pɛ/$_{346}$) or /nɔ/$_{302}$.

2. When not in hiatus, final /-o/ was raised to /-u/ in all dialects (e.g. /gato/$_{59}$ > /gatu/), as was pretonic /o/ (e.g. /koracãw/$_{80}$ > /kuracãw/); atonic /e/ went up to /i/ just in dialects leading to Brazilian standard, mainly in final position (e.g. /sɛte/$_{415}$ > /sɛti/). In the special case of **-eo**, the insertion of a front glide (perhaps by analogy with regular **-ea** > **-eya**) variably blocked the process in view, as in **seo**$_{411}$ > **seyu**, like **vea**$_{454}$ > **veya**. For the highly frequent occurrence of the segments /ɛy ɔy ay/ and /õy ãy/ also in the morphophonemics of Portuguese noun and adjective inflection, see Volume 1, Appendix 1. Historically, in the presence of the plural suffix /-s/ a stem-final /-e/ did not drop, and thus intervocalic /l̬/ was regularly lost in plurals but not in bare stems: cf. /anɛl̬e/$_{15}$ > /anɛl/ as against /anɛl̬es/ > /anɛys/.

3. The earliest borrowings did not accept the obstruent-plus-laterals, replacing them with the existing clusters containing [r], e.g. **praca**$_{348}$, **kravu**$_{S-18}$, **frowšu** 'lâche/flojo'. Gallegan never did accept them, and therefore has *craro* 'clair/claro' etc.

Part Three
From Latin down: Grammatical changes

Stage 1: A grammar of Latin, together with diachronic changes in its popular dialects

0. Introduction. The structural sketch furnished herewith is primarily though not exclusively synchronic, for together with the theoretically unchanging morphosyntax of Classical Latin we shall detail also the pertinent diachronic changes known to have taken place in one or another popular dialect of the language. For the synchronic part of the description we adhere to the same grammatical model as was adopted in Volume 1 as a basis for comparing and contrasting, synchronically, five present-day Romance languages. For convenience of back-reference to the model and its organization, even the paragraph numbering will be held constant. All the changes taken into account, in this as well as in subsequent sections, are confirmed by attested or reconstructive evidence and are duly noted, along with phonological changes, in the Comparative Romance literature; hence we need not be at pains to document their factual occurrence.

Nominal structures

1. The common-noun phrase

1.0 Internal structure of the common-noun phrase (CNP). The formula for the underlying structure of the Latin CNP is

CNP → Case Number (Determiner) Head (Modifier)

The finite system of cases contains five terms, traditionally identified as the nominative (nom), genitive (gen), dative (dat), accusative (acc), and ablative (abl) cases.[1] As will be amply demonstrated in subsequent sections, cases are markers of the functions of nominals within larger constructions such as clauses. The number system comprises precisely two terms: singular and plural. The two obligatory attributes of case and number appear in the surface structure in one and the same suffix on the head noun, which we examine first.

1.1 Common nouns as heads. The surface formula for the common noun (CN) as a grammatical word is

CN → Stem + Case/Number suffix.

The suffix constitutes an obligatory inflectional ending combining two morphemes in one portmanteau morph, namely, a morpheme of case and a morpheme of number. The case morpheme is a function-marker which serves to identify the syntactic role of the CNP within a larger construction—e.g. the function of subject, object, or whatever in a clause. The number morpheme provides the semantic contrast singular vs. plural. The package of case and number takes the form of a suffix which hops not only to the head noun but also to such attributes as are constrained by their form class (e.g. adjectives) to add the suffix also and thus to agree with the head noun.

1.2 Gender and inflection of nouns

1.2.1 Gender. Every Latin noun (common or proper) belongs to one of three gender classes: feminine, masculine, neuter. Gender is a syntactic property of the noun, not a morphological one; there is but one inflectional characteristic among many in the paradigm of the noun that signals grammatical gender as such. There are, to be sure, certain derivational suffixes, such as -ĪCE- (cf. CULTŌRE- → CULTRĪCE-) which refer semantically to an individual (person or animal) of the female sex; this includes the final single vowel in pairs like FĪLIU-$_{181}$: FĪLIA-$_{180}$ or CLIENTE- : CLIENTA-. All the derived nouns built with these suffixes are in fact feminine, as are all simple-stem nouns denoting females—e.g. MĀTRE-$_{S-57}$ or VACCA-$_{450}$. Similarly, all stems designating males are masculine.

Many nouns which denote inanimate objects belong to the neuter gender, which in fact includes no nouns for living beings. Conversely, however, many nouns which denote inanimate objects, or abstractions, or living beings whose sex is not included among the noun's semantic features, are arbitrarily feminine or masculine—e.g. FORMICA-₁₉₃ is feminine, while VERME-₄₅₉ is masculine.

The primary morphological classification of Latin nouns is based on the final vowel phoneme of the stem (rather than of the case/number suffix), and only a partial correlation exists between this vowel and gender. Traditionally, there are said to be five DECLENSIONS, which correspond to our stem classes as follows:

First declension	A-stems	no neuters; mostly feminines
Second declension	O-stems	no feminines
Third declension	E-stems	all genders
Fourth declension	U-stems	all genders; mostly masculines
Fifth declension	Ē-stems	feminines only

1.2.2 Inflection. Multiplying five for the case dimension times two for the number dimension, we get a theoretical ten suffixes per noun paradigm.[2] In the inflection of neuter nouns, however, the case/number (C/N) morph is the same for nominative singular and accusative singular, as well as for nominative plural and accusative plural. Thus, in Table 1.1 neuter nouns are specified with the feature [+N], while feminines and masculines are designated [−N], since the feminine/masculine distinction is not correlated with the suffixal shapes; in other words, these two genders are exclusively syntactic, not paradigmatic, features.

The nominative singular (NmSg) suffix alternant of [−N] nouns is either -s (SIGMATIC, specified [+sig]) or ∅ (NONSIGMATIC, specified [−sig]). In addition, the NmSg suffix either has or has not the property of truncating the stem by deleting the stem vowel and thus giving the NmSg form one less syllable than the other forms; paradigms exhibiting this behavior are IMPARISYLLABIC and are here specified as [−par] as opposed to those which are PARISYLLABIC (specified as [+par]). With [+N] nouns there can be no question of the feature [sig], but some E-stems do show the (im)parisyllabic variation.[3]

Table 1.1 obviously does not include the genitive, dative, and ablative case forms of the sample nouns, for the principal reason that these members of the case/number paradigm have not survived into the Romance languages. We do not describe the actual morphophonemics of the reduced paradigms displayed, but the data on which to base such a description is all present in the illustrations. If you undertake such a project on your own, include as input also the following items from the corpus:

3	111	182	222	278	325	364	416	S-7
11	120	184	231	280	327	365	421	S-17
26	123	186	235	282	330	367	422	S-25
52	133	188	247	284	331	386	427	S-30
64	155	196	250	295	332	387	431	S-39

128 / Stage 1: A grammar of Latin

72	160	197	252	296	333	403	441	S-44
79	161	204	257	304	336	404	452	S-49
80	167	205	258	305	346	407	458	S-56
97	177	206	268	308	352	411	459	S-57
99	178	207	274	319	363	412	473	S-61
								S-106
								S-108

Dictionaries of Latin list nouns by their NmSg form, followed by the GnSg, and give the gender. The final shapes of the GnSg are uniformly as follows: 1st decl. -AE, 2nd decl. -I, 3rd decl. -IS, 4th decl. -ŪS, 5th decl., -EI ~ EI.[4]

Diachronic changes in popular Latin.

● Case. The set of terms in the case system is reduced as the abl. is lost while the gen. and the dat. become functionally one (the gen./dat.). The surface mechanisms triggering the losses are: (1) the abl. sing. merges phonologically and functionally with the acc. sing., (2) the dat. sing., the dat. plur. and the abl. plur. are replaced functionally by the gen. sing., the gen. plur. and the acc. plur. respectively.

● Gender. The neuter gender is lost as [+N] o-stems and u-stems come to behave like [−N] masculines when number is singular, and like [−N] feminines when number is plural, the NmAcPl suffix -A perhaps 'sounding' feminine because essentially all A-stems are of that gender; some [+N] E-stems become entirely masculine or entirely feminine, though not without long-lasting hesitation, as in the case of MARE$_{273}$ or LACTE$_{235}$.

There is no change in the surface formula for the common noun as a grammatical word, but with regard to inflectional processes (and morphophonemics) the interrelation of stem-class and [−N] gender as a basis for classification shifts in the following way:

Masculines: Nominative-vs-accusative distinction in both numbers
Feminines: No nominative-vs-accusative distinction in singular, because of phonological loss of the AcSg inflection -M; in A-stems only, distinction in plural
Ambigenes:[5] No nominative-vs-accusative distinction in plural.

1.3 Determiners in the CNP

1.3.1 Adjectival/adverbial words. These are a lexical set, subdivisible by semantic criteria into the limiters (definite and indefinite), the quantifiers (numeral, indefinite, comparative) and the specifiers, and the demonstratives.[6]

Table 1.1. Latin noun morphology.

			A-stems (1st Decl.)	**o**-stems (2nd Decl.)	**E**-stems (3rd Decl.)	**u**-stems (4th Decl.)	**ē**-stems (5th Decl.)
[-N]	[+sig] [+par]	NmSg AcSg NmPl AcPl	**casa^∅** → CASA **m** → CASAM **i** → CASAE **:s** → CASĀS	**anno^s** → ANNUS **m** → ANNUM **i** → ANNĪ **:s** → ANNŌS	**cane^s** → CANIS **m** → CANEM **:s** → CANĒS **:s** → CANĒS	**manu^s** → MANUS **m** → MANUM **:s** → MANŪS **:s** → MANŪS	**diē^s** → DIĒS **m** → DIEM **:s** → DIĒS **:s** → DIĒS
	[+sig] [−par]	NmSg AcSg NmPl AcPl			**dente^↓s** → DĒNS **m** → DENTEM **:s** → DENTĒS **:s** → DENTĒS		
	[−sig] [+par]	NmSg AcSg NmPl AcPl		**libro^↓** → LIBER **m** → LIBRUM **i** → LIBRĪ **:s** → LIBRŌS	**patre^∅** → PATER **m** → PATREM **:s** → PATRĒS **:s** → PATRĒS		
	[−sig] [−par]	NmSg AcSg NmPl AcPl		**socero^↓∅** → SOCER **m** → SOCERUM **i** → SOCERĪ **:s** → SOCERŌS	**mulier^↓∅** → MULIER **m** → MULIEREM **:s** → MULIERĒS **:s** → MULIERĒS		
[+N]	[+par]	NmAcSg NmAcPl		**ŏvo^m** → OVUM **a** → ŌVA	**mare^∅** → MARE **a** → MARIA	**cornu^:** → CORNŪ **a** → CORNUA	
	[−par]	NmAcSg NmAcPl			**corpore^↓∅** → CORPUS **a** → CORPORA		

● It is to be noted immediately that there are no articles—definite, indefinite, or partitive. In Latin both countable and noncountable nouns can occur with no determiner at all and with the semantic features of (in)definiteness communicable only at the discourse level through patterns of word-order or the like; thus, for example, in a clause like EDERE ŌVA, with no determiner present in the CNP, the noun basically equates with either *les oeufs/los huevos* or *des oeufs/huevos*, while VĪNUM in BIBE VĪNUM may mean either *le vin* or *du vin*.

There being no articles, it is obvious that the function class of determiners does not include two-adjective strings of the type described for Romance at 1.3.2 in Volume 1. The Romance specifiers restricted to cooccurrence with an article in these strings are reflexes of specifying determiners such as ALTER 'l'autre/el otro', in semantic contrast as to definiteness with ALIS 'un autre/otro'. Similarly, the ordinal PRIMUS alone equates with Fr *le premier*, Sp *el primero* etc.

● Only the demonstratives constitute a lexico-grammatical subsystem with precisely five terms:

Person-oriented	Speaker (D-1)	HĪC, HAEC, HŌC
	Addressee (D-2)	ISTE, ISTA, ISTUD
	Other (D-3)	ILLE, ILLA, ILLUD
	Anaphoric (ANA)	IS, EA, ID
	Intensive (INT)	IPSE, IPSA, IPSUM

Diachronically, the subsystem in view undergoes a shake-up which may be plotted as follows:

```
HĪC   (D-1) ─────────────────        ∅
ISTE  (D-2) ─────────  (D-1)         ISTE
IPSE  (INT)       ─── (D-2/ANA/INT)  IPSE
IS    (ANA) ─                        ∅
ILLE  (D-3) ──────── (D-3/ANA)       ILLE
```

Directly opposite the left entry is its formal continuation, while the connecting lines indicate the change of function within the subsystem. This is to say that HĪC and IS are lost from the lexicon (but see note 8), with ISTE shifting functionally from D-2 to fill the D-1 gap left by HĪC, with IPSE moving into the person-oriented set, and with either IPSE or ILLE (depending on dialect) playing also the anaphoric role and thus already moving toward becoming, eventually in later languages, mere definite articles.

1.3.2 CNPs functioning as quantifying determiner. Various nouns denoting units of quantity or measure occur as head within a dependent CNP which serves to quantify the head of a higher CNP. In all such cases, the quantifying phrase is linked to the higher head, in the surface structure, by the marker of the genitive case. Thus, for example:

Det. MAIOR PARS + Head TERRA → MAIOR PARS TERRAE 'la plupart de la terre'
Det. MĪLIA + Pl. + Head MĪLITE- → MĪLIA MĪLITUM 'des milliers de soldats'
Det. TANTUM[7] + SPATIU- → TANTUM SPATII 'tant d'espace'

Diachronically, the genitive case ceases functioning in this type of structure, giving way to the preposition-like functor DĒ, which originally generated the ablative case on any noun dependent upon it but, with the gradual demise of the ablative, comes to 'take' instead the accusative case; thus, in phrases such as the above, TERRAE is replaced by DĒ TERRAM, MĪLITUM by DĒ MĪLITĒS, SPATII by DĒ SPATIUM, and so on.

1.3.3 Determinative expressions of evaluation, result, comparison. These constructions are all discontinuous, consisting of a head such as the evaluative SATIS 'assez/bastante' or the resultative/comparative TANTUM, or the comparative PLŪS or MINUS, plus an adverbial or clausal attribute following the higher head. Of these types, only the comparative quantifier is of particular interest and will be discussed at 14.1 of Stage 1.

1.4 Modifiers in the CNP. Dependent constructions embeddable within the CNP in Latin are the same four as those listed for our Romance languages at 4.1.4 of Volume 1. Changes in these dependent constructions are noted below in the apposite paragraphs.

1.5 The CNP and discourse factors: Substitution and reduction. As regards the CNP and the discourse phenomena of substitution and reduction, both substitution by pronominalization and reduction by head deletion are found in Latin, with no particular constraints imposed by the class of determiner or by the presence/absence of a modifier. It is to be noted, however, that in Romance a very frequent environment for deletion is that of an article as determiner (see Volume 1, 1.5.1); but since Latin has no article, the only recourse is pronominalization of the head. Thus, for example, while Spanish can reduce *el hijo del senador* to *el del senador*, in the equivalent Latin phrase the undetermined FĪLIUS cannot be deleted and can therefore at most be pronominalized (as IS, ILLE or SO).

2. The proper-noun phrase

2.0 Internal structure of the proper-noun phrase (PNP). The formula for the underlying structure of the Latin PNP is

PNP → Case Head (Modifier).

The cases are the same five, reducing diachronically to the same three, as for the CNP. The PNP clearly differs from the CNP in having no attribute of plural number or determiner. Neither is appropriate, because every proper noun head is underlyingly singular or plural, and because semantic compatibility is lacking between proper nouns and determiners. Before going further we must distinguish two subtypes of proper noun: person names and place names.

2.1 Person names as heads. The referent of a person name being a unique individual, these nouns are inherently singular;[8] the inflectional morphs which they necessarily carry are those packaging case with singular number—e.g. nom. LŪCIUS, acc. LŪCIUM, etc.) Like common nouns with animate referents, they have the syntactic property of gender in one-to-one correlation with the sex of the named individual; thus, for example, GĀIUS names a male and is masculine, GĀIA names a female and is feminine.

A person name head may be compounded, comprising a person name (*praenomen* in Latin terminology) followed by two surnames: a clan name (*nomen*) and a family name (*cognomen*), in this case to be taken as classifiers/specifiers rather than as modifiers. Examples are MARCUS TULLIUS CICERO or PUBLIUS VERGILIUS MARO, in which the middle *nomen* copies the gender of the head *praenomen* but the *cognomen* does not.

2.2 Modifiers with person-name heads. Dependent constructions functioning as modifiers of a person name as head are:

(a) One or more adjectives designated *agnomen*, which further identify the particular individual by his activities, by other genealogical ties, or whatever—e.g. PUBLIUS CORNELIUS SCĪPIO + AFRICĀNUS + AEMILIĀNUS, or TULLIA + SECUNDA.

(b) A noun, which serves to identify and which agrees with the head noun in case, e.g. nom. SERVIUS RĒX, acc. SERVIUM RĒGEM. This modifier is limited to the appositive subtype of dependent CNP as mentioned further on in 4 (and especially in note 12).

Any further instances of common-noun-like syntactic behavior on the part of person names are probably attributable to actual common-nominalization in the lexicon, which alone seems able to account for such a phrase as, say, DUODECIM CAESARĒS.

2.3 Reduction of the PNP. Where the context allows for recovery, reduction of a PNP with person-name head may occur through deletion of a (usually) masculine *praenomen* and/or *nomen*, leaving just the *cognomen*, i.e. GĀIUS CLAUDIUS NERO → NERO, or LŪCIUS ANNAEUS SENECA → SENECA.

2.4 Place names as heads of PNPs. The referent of a place name being typically a single geographic or geopolitical entity, the majority are singular (e.g. ITALIA, RŌMA, TIBERIS) though some are inherently plural (e.g. GADĒS, now *Cádiz*), though never with a contrast of number in the same reference. Some place names are masculine (POMPĒII), some feminine (PERSIA), some neuter (HERCULĀNEUM).

2.5 Modifiers with place-name heads. Dependent constructions functioning as modifiers of a place name as head are identifying or characterizing adjectivals, as in MAGNA GRAECIA or GALLIA TRANSALPĪNA.

3. The pronoun phrase

3.0 Internal structure of the pronoun phrase (ProP). The formula for the underlying structure of the Latin ProP is

ProP → Case Head (Modifier).

Here, once again, there is no plural number or determiner attribute. Neither is appropriate, since every pronoun is underlyingly singular or underlyingly plural, and since determiners and pronouns are semantically incompatible.

3.1 Pronouns as heads. These are personal, limiting, and quantifying pronouns. The personal subset, subdivided into locals and substitutes, comprises subsystems as shown herewith:

Local	+1st−Pl	+2nd−Pl	+1st+Pl	+2nd+Pl
	EGO/MĒ[9]	TŪ/TĒ	NŌS	VŌS

Substitute		Masculine	Feminine	Neuter
D-1	−Pl	HĪC/HUNC	HAEC/HANC	HŌC
	+Pl	HĪS/HŌS	HAE/HĀS	HAEC
D-2	−Pl	ISTE/ISTUM	ISTA/ISTAM	ISTUD
	+Pl	ISTĪ/ISTŌS	ISTAE/ISTĀS	ISTA

D-3	−Pl	ILLE/ILLUM	ILLA/ILLAM	ILLUD
	+Pl	ILLĪ/ILLŌS	ILLAE/ILLĀS	ILLA
INT	−Pl	IPSE/IPSUM	IPSA/IPSAM	IPSUM
	+Pl	IPSĪ/IPSŌS	IPSAE/IPSĀS	IPSA
ANA	−Pl	IS/EUM	EA/EAM	ID
	+Pl	EĪ/EŌS	EAE/EĀS	EA
RFLX	±Pl	SĒ (all genders)		

Diachronic changes in popular Latin.

● Case. The reduction of the PNP case system is the same as that noted earlier for the CNP. In the inflectional morphology of the locals, and of the [−pl] substitutes surviving along with their determiner counterparts, the dative morph persists and ultimately displaces the genitive one, rather than the other way around. Retained therefore as gen./dat. forms are MIHI, TIBI, NŌBĪS, VŌBĪS, and EĪ, ISTĪ, ILLĪ, IPSĪ, SIBI.

● Gender. The substitute pronouns also undergo a shake-up analogous to that already noted within the demonstrative determiners, with, however, the following spin-off in the singular. As the neuter gender is lost, in pronouns as well as in nouns, there results a cleavage of each member into a substitute proper and an abstract pronoun, the former continuing to occur in two genders (masc. and fem.) and the latter becoming masculine but having semantic reference only to acts, states, or unidentified [−human] entities. With the final -D or -M of the original neuter forms lost phonologically, the contrast remains clear-cut in the final vowels of the nominative case forms: masculine substitutes in -E versus abstracts in -U, even though the accusative case forms remain homophonous in /-u/ (after loss of /-m/). The cleavage in view seemingly precedes loss of D-1 HĪC, for the neuter form HŌC survives in CRom as a nondemonstrative (i.e. merely anaphoric) abstract.[10]

3.2 Modifiers in the ProP. All personal or substitute pronoun heads are modifiable by either of the special limiting adjectives SŌLU- or IPSE-, the latter familiar as determiner in a CNP, but here indistinguishable functionally from a modifier—e.g. EGO SŌLUS, EA SŌLA, NŌS IPSĪ, ID IPSUM.

When in popular Latin IPSE- as determiner shifts from intensive to anaphoric in some dialects, and to D-2 in others, the feature [+INT] is transferred to certain newly derived determiner forms such as MET+IPSE- or (MET+)IPS+IMU- as replacements for the determiner IDEM 'le même/el mismo' (defunct along with IS, from which it derived).[11]

4. Dependent nominals functioning as modifiers in larger nominals

4.3 Genitive modifiers. In standard grammars of Latin, the subtypes of nominal modifier enumerated in Volume 1, 4.1-4 for Romance are subsumed mainly under genitives as expressing 'the relation of one noun to another' (i.e. of nominal modifier to nominal head in our terminology), and are subdivided into subjective, objective, and partitive genitives. All such modifiers occur 'in the genitive case',[12] i.e. having one of the two genitive portmanteau morphs ([±pl]) suffixed to the head (and copied by any adjectival material) as a marker of its function. However, alongside the genitive modifiers there exist some few introduced by prepositions such as EX, AB, DĒ, or even AD, with the nominal object in the ablative or accusative case as required.

In dialects of popular Latin this latter morphological distinction becomes blurred, with the ablative giving way to the accusative after any Prep; and along with this goes a tendency for DĒ-marked modifiers to displace even genitive ones, particularly among the subjective genitives of source, material, or measure/quality (e.g. CORIUM TAURĪ 'du cuir de taureau', DUO TALENTA AURĪ 'deux talents d'or', FOSSA TRIUM PEDUM 'une fosse de trois pieds'), as well as the partitive genitives leading to the delimiting modifiers of Romance (4.4, e.g. ŪNUS CŌNSULUM 'un des consuls').[13] On the other hand, the subjective genitives of possession, as well as the objective genitives— together comprising those which will lead to our Romance genitive modifiers proper (4.3)—resist the switch more vigorously, perhaps in part because the genitive case forms of determiners and of pronouns, surely quite frequent in expressions of possession, etc., are phonologically more distinctive than those of nouns (e.g. IS, ILLE ... +gen. → ĒIUS, ILLĪUS ...).

4.3.1 The replacement of possessive genitives. Any nominal modifier in Latin can be pronominalized. The genitive case forms of the personal pronouns are as illustrated, and in addition there corresponds to each a possessive adjective (cf. Pattern 'B' in Romance), as shown in the right column:

				Personal pronouns in genitive case	Possessive adjectives
Local	+1st	−Pl		MEĪ	MEUS
	+2nd	−Pl		TUĪ	TUUS
	+1st	+Pl		NOSTRĪ ~ -TRUM	NOSTER
	+2nd	+Pl		VESTRĪ ~ -TRUM	VESTER
Substitute	D-1	−Pl		HŬIUS	
		+Pl		HŎRUM (fem. HĀRUM)	
	D-2	−Pl		ISTĪUS	
		+Pl		ISTŌRUM (fem. ISTĀRUM)	
	D-3	−Pl		ILLĪUS	
		+Pl		ILLŌRUM (fem. ILLĀRUM)	SUUS[14]
	INT	−Pl		IPSĪUS	
		+Pl		IPSŌRUM (fem. IPSĀRUM)	
	ANA	−Pl		ĒIUS	
		+Pl		EŌRUM (fem. EĀRUM)	
	RFLX	±Pl		SUĪ	

The possessive adjectives copy suffixally the case/number of the phrase and the gender of the head noun. The substitute use of these adjs. is the norm in possessive genitives, and possible in objective genitives, but blocked in other genitive modifiers. This may help to account for the anomalous triumph of the dative over the genitive forms of the pronouns, as noted in 3.1.[15]

4.3.2 The reduction of genitive modifiers. In accordance with pragmatic aspects of the discourse this is achieved in Latin by merely moving the modifier—whether a NP, a ProP, or a substitute possessive adjective—leftward into the determiner position and thus ahead of the phrasal stress—e.g. GRÁTIA DĚĪ → DĚĪ GRÁTIA, or DÓMUS ĚIUS → ĚIUS DÓMUS, or PÁTER NŎSTER → NŎSTER PÁTER.

4.6 Coordinated nominals. Latin makes use of the device known as COORDINATION at the phrase level, at the clause level, and at the sentence level. The prime means of coordinating given structures, at whatever level, is the COORDINATING CONJUNCTION—or, as we have termed this minor part of speech in Volume 1, 4.6, simply the CONJUNCTION. Three all-purpose Latin conjunctions which function at any level are the copulative ET 'et/y' and NEC 'ni', and the alternative AUT 'ou/o'. These conjunctions serve to coordinate any type of nominal, in most cases regardless of the function of that nominal in a higher construction. Either copulative or alternative coordination may be reinforced/intensified by placing the same conjunction before both elements—e.g. ET TŪ ET EGO, or AUT HŌC AUT ILLUD.[16] Further references to coordination will be made as appropriate at the ends of subsequent sections.

Adjectival structures

5. The adjective phrase

5.0 Internal structure of the adjective phrase (AdjP). The formula for the underlying structure of the Latin AdjP is

AdjP → (Quantifier) Head (Complement)

5.1 Adjectives as heads. Unlike the common noun with its optional morpheme of plurality, the adj. has no morphemic paradigm. Underlyingly, it consists of stem only; its suffixal inflections, devoid of lexical meaning, are surface markers of agreement—with the noun it stands in construction with—in case, number and gender; that is to say, they copy the case and number of the higher phrase in which they stand, as well as the gender of the noun itself. The five cases, two numbers, and three genders to be distinguished add up to a theoretical thirty concord markings per adj., but there is much overlap and neutralization. Also not all adjs. reflect all three genders, a fact which affords a basis for division into two morphophonemic classes.

• One of these classes exhibits inflection with suffixal shapes matched to those of the A-stem and O-stem nouns of the 1st and 2nd declensions: A-stem endings for feminine agreement, O-stem endings for masculine and neuter agreement—thus, BONUS, BONA, BONUM$_{41}$ shows masculine forms like those of ANNUS$_{13}$, feminine forms like those of CASA$_{262}$, and neuter forms like those of ŌVUM$_{310}$.[17]

• The other class is inflected with allomorphs matched to those of the E-stem nouns of the 3rd declension. Inasmuch as such nouns have one and the same set of endings whether they are masc. or fem., the matching adjs. perforce fail to differentiate masc. from fem. concord—thus, e.g. FORTIS, FORTE$_{190}$ has [−N] forms like those of either CANIS$_{70}$ (m.) or TURRIS$_{441}$ (f.) and [+N] forms like those of MARE$_{273}$.[18]

The special adjs. which function as determiners have genitive and dative morphs at variance with those of ordinary adjs. The latter need not be noted, because they have not survived into Romance. Those of the determiners resemble those of some pronouns, and together some of these oddments *have* survived, as will be noted where relevant.

Of prime interest also are the so-called participial adjs. derived within the lexicon from verbs by suffixation. There are four of these deverbal adj. types, two of which may be designated as active and two as passive. The [−pas] pair are the present participle, formed with the 3rd-decl. suffix -NS, as in CANTĀNS 'chantant/cantante'; and the future participle, derived with the 1st/2nd-decl. suffix -TŪRUS, as in CANTĀTŪRUS.[19] The [+pas] pair are the gerundive, derived with the 1st/2nd-decl. suffix -NDUS as in CANTANDUS,[20] and the past participle (for which a better term would be perfective participle, cf. 8.3.3), formed with the 1st/2nd decl. suffix -TUS as in CANTĀTUS 'chanté/cantado'. Every Latin verb forms the [−pas] pair, but only transitive verbs yield the [+pas] items.

Diachronic change. What with the loss of the neuter gender in nouns, and of the dative and ablative cases, the number of portmanteau agreement suffixes in typical adjs. is reduced from 30 (5 case × 2 number × 3 gender) to 12 (3 case × 2 number × 2 gender), disregarding overlaps. In becoming nonfunctional, the [+N] plural concord suffix -A tends to get confused with the homophonous fem. sing. -A of 1st/2nd-decl. type adjs., and as a result penetrates the 3rd-decl. class to some extent, giving rise to FORTIA or DULCIA for fem. *sing.* concord as against FORTIS or DULCIS for masc. sing., and even, in some instances, causing a class switch, as with TRISTIS, TRISTE becoming TRISTUS, TRISTA.

5.2 Quantifiers in the AdjP. Among these constituents, the Latin words of quantity are the same lexical items as the quantifying determiners, except that the adverbs QUOT 'combien/cuánto', TOT 'tant/tanto', and PLŪS 'plus/más' have the respective variants QUAM, TAM, and MAGIS. There exist also two suffixal quantifiers: the comparative -IOR (∼ -IUS for neuter agreement) and the (absolute or relative) superlative -ISSIMUS.

Diachronic change. The superlative suffix is lost altogether[21]—in favor of MULTUM, FORTE, PRAE or PER in absolute meaning, and through merger with the comparative in relative meaning.[22] The comparative suffix had always given way to PLŪS or MAGIS before polysyllabic adjs., and in time it, too, is supplanted by one or the other of these items in all but a very few dialects,[23] except for its widespread survival attached to the suppletive alternants of four common adjs.:

$$\begin{bmatrix} \text{BONUS} \\ \text{MALUS} \\ \text{MAGNUS} \\ \text{PARVUS} \end{bmatrix} + \text{-IOR} \rightarrow \begin{bmatrix} \text{MELIOR} \\ \text{PĒIOR} \\ \text{MĀIOR} \\ \text{MINOR} \end{bmatrix}$$

After the loss of the neuter gender, the concord-forms MELIUS, PĒIUS, MĀIUS, MINUS remain in the language as adverbs, though MĀIUS is eventually absorbed by its phonetic and semantic rival MAGIS.

5.3 Complements in the AdjP. Dependent constructions embeddable within the AdjP in Latin are nominals, prepositional adverbials, and clauses. Some nominals as complements occur in the genitive case, others in the dative, still others in the ablative, while some few are introduced by Preps such as AB, AD, or IN, with the nominal object in the ablative or accusative case as required. Diachronically, as the case distinction became blurred, the dative complements are displaced by AD-marked ones and—by analogy with changes in dependent nominals in the genitive—the genitive complements are displaced by DĒ-marked ones—e.g. CUPIDUS VĪTAE → CUPIDUS DE VĪTAM (with loss of final /-m/) 'avide de (la) vie'.

6. Dependent adjectivals functioning as modifiers within NPs

6. The basic position for an adjectival modifier is following the noun head as in, say, CIVIS ROMĀNUS, or LECTIŌ DIFFICILIOR, or HOMINĒS BENEFICĪ ET BENIGNĪ. For purely pragmatic reasons, however, an adjectival modifier may precede the noun head or may even be discontinuous, i.e. split by the head. Adjectivals may be coordinated by a copulative or alternative conjunction, as in the third example just cited, as well as by a third type of conjunction, the adversative SED 'mais/pero', often set off by NŌN before the first coordinate. This particular item failed to survive into Romance, giving way ultimately to adaptive reflexes of the adverb MAGIS; see 14.2.

Adverbial structures

7. The adverb phrase

7.0 Internal structure of the adverb phrase (AdvP). The formula for the underlying structure of the Latin AdvP is

AdvP → (Quantifier) Head ±Complement.

7.1 Adverbs as heads. Unlike the noun, the adjective, or the verb, the Latin adverb has no morphological paradigm. Derivational rather than inflectional is the suffix added to adjectives to form adverbs of manner/

degree: -Ē for 1st/2nd-decl. stems (e.g. AMPLĒ from AMPLUS$_{12}$, PŪRĒ from PŪRUS), and -(T)ER for 3rd-decl. stems (e.g. FORTITER from FORTIS$_{190}$, DULCITER from DULCIS$_{134}$.[24] Diachronically, the allomorph -(T)ER is discarded in favor of -Ē across the board, shortened to -E as it always had been in BENE$_{37}$ and MALE$_{264}$. Since the alternant of this suffix thus becomes identical with the stem-final -E of FORTE or DULCE, the result is a new -E ~ ∅ alternation. The overt -E itself then begins to disappear, and thus the adverbialization of adjs. gradually becomes unmarked. The suffix survives but sporadically, as e.g. /bene, male, tarde, pūre, -iske/ (the latter from the suffix -ISCUS) mostly wind up as underived adverbs dissociated morphologically from their apposite adjectives.

As we have done in our contrastive analysis of the Romance languages, so also in the present descriptive highlights of Latin syntax we shall conflate the three traditionally distinct parts of speech adverb, preposition, and (subordinating) conjunction into the single form-class adv., subdivided thus:

Class 1: Traditional prepositions and subordinators characterized here as transitive adverbs after which an object is obligatory—e.g. AB, AD, CUM, DĒ, EX, IN, INTER, PER, PRŌ, SINE, SUB, TRĀNS; DUM, QUOD, UT;

Class 2: Words traditionally tagged as 'preposition and adverb', here called prep./adv.—i.e. transitive adverbs after which an object complement is optional—e.g. ANTE, CIRCĀ, CONTRĀ, EXTRĀ, INTRĀ, POST, SUPER, ULTRĀ;

Class 3: Adverbs proper, here intransitive—a long list further subdivisible into advs. of time, place, manner, and degree, including those with a demonstrative feature (e.g. NUNC, TUM, HĪC, IBI, ITA, SĪC) or an interrogative one (e.g. QUANDŌ, UBI, QUŌMODO).

7.2 Complements in the AdvP. Object complements of transitive adverbs are nominals or clauses.[25] The former are of interest because their function, like that of any nominal, is signaled by a case. After thirty-odd Class 1/2 advs. (the majority), the case is accusative; after ten or so (including AB, DĒ, EX, SINE), it is ablative; while after four (IN, SUB, SUBTER, and SUPER), it is accusative or ablative according to a semantic feature of [±locomotion] on the verbal in which the adverbial is functioning—e.g. IN URBEM to denote movement *into* the city, IN URBE for what takes place *within* the city.

Diachronically, when certain case markers are neutralized and the ablative disappears, all nominal complements of transitive adverbs (i.e. of preps.) come to be marked with the accusative—thus, for example, EX LIBRŌS for EX LIBRĪS, or IN TERRĀS but no longer IN TERRĪS.

7.3 Quantifiers in the AdvP. Quantifiers in the Latin AdvP are the same array of structures as enumerated for the AdjP in 5.2.[26]

Verbal structures

8. The verb phrase

8.0 Internal structure of the verb phrase (VP). The formula for the underlying structure of the Latin VP is

VP → (Negator) (Aspect) (Voice) Head

8.1 Verbs as heads. The surface formula for the verb as a grammatical word is verb → stem (suffix), the parentheses signifying that the bare stem may also occur. The suffixes are of five orders: (1) the perfective suffix; (2) tense/mood suffixes, which represent a basic constituent of the next-higher construction level, namely, modality in the clause rather than in the VP itself; (3) concord suffixes which, added to the second order, mark a particular relationship between subject and predicate at the clause level and are discussed, along with the second order, in that connection; (4) the infinitive suffix which, in complementation with the second and third orders, indicates certain syntactic relationships of the VP to surrounding material; (5) the passive suffix.

The primary classification of this complicated verb morphology is based on the final vowel phoneme of the stem. Traditionally, there are said to be four CONJUGATIONS, which correspond to five morphophonemic stem classes as follows:

First conjugation	Ā-stems
Second conjugation	Ē-stems
Third conjugation	E-stems and I-stems[27]
Fourth conjugation	Ī-stems

8.2 The attributes of aspect and voice. Since these constituents of the VP are manifested in the surface structure by suffixes on the verb head, we take them up next and postpone coverage of the negator to 8.3.

8.2.1 The perfective aspect. The function of this optional attribute is performed by a suffix which hops to the verb head immediately after the stem. The shape of this suffix varies considerably with the stem-class of the verb: in Ā-stems and Ī-stems it is basically -VI, as illustrated herewith in forms of AMĀ-7:

142 / Stage 1: A grammar of Latin

	−Perfective	+Perfective
Present:	AMAT/AMET	AMĀVIT/AMĀVERIT
Past:	AMĀBAT/AMĀRET	AMĀVERAT/AMĀVISSET
Future:	AMĀBIT	AMĀVERIT
Infinitive:	AMĀRE	AMĀVISSE

On most other stems the suffix is -UI- or -SI-, though on a few it is zero, with or without a stem alternant as in, e.g., FĒC- of FACE-$_{162}$ or CECID- of CADE-$_{438}$.

That the perfective aspect is independent of the tense/mood system is proven by the simple fact that it occurs as well with the separate infinitive form of the verb. One may also claim that the derived adjectives AMANDU- (gerundive) and AMĀTU- (past participle) are distinguished by the presence of the feature [+perf] in the latter.

8.2.2 The passive voice. The function of this optional attribute is performed by a suffix which hops to the verb head after either a concord suffix or the infinitive suffix has already been added. It has various allomorphs conditioned by what precedes it, the prevalent ones being -R ~ -UR, as illustrated in other forms of AMĀ-:

Present Tense	−Passive	+Passive
1st Sg.	AMŌ/AMEM	AMOR/AMER
2nd Sg.	AMĀS	AMĀRIS
3rd Sg.	AMAT	AMĀTUR
1st Pl.	AMĀMUS	AMĀMUR
2nd Pl.	AMĀTIS	AMĀMINĪ[28]
3rd Pl.	AMANT	AMANTUR
Infinitive	AMĀRE	AMĀRĪ

8.2.3 Cooccurrence of perfective and passive. Although the perfective aspect and the passive voice constituents can both occur in the same VP, in the environment of each other these attributes assume totally different forms. The perfective aspect is conveyed by the auxiliary verb ES- 'être/ser', and the passive voice by the past participle of the head verb, semantically specified as [+pas] (and redundantly as [+perf]). Being adjectival in its surface form, the participle agrees in case/number/gender with the nominal subject of the clause whose predicate the VP represents. The following synopsis of tense/ mood and infinitive forms of AMĀ- embodies the cooccurrence situation:

	−Perfective −Passive	−Perfective +Passive	+Perfective −Passive	+Perfective +Passive
Present	AMAT	AMĀTUR	AMĀVIT	AMĀTUS EST
Past	AMĀBAT	AMĀBĀTUR	AMĀVERAT	AMĀTUS ERAT
Future	AMĀBIT	AMĀBITUR	AMĀVERIT	AMĀTUS ERIT
Infinitive	AMĀRE	AMĀRĪ	AMĀVISSE	AMĀTUS ESSE

A number of Latin verbs labeled DEPONENT, although intransitive and therefore incapable of taking the passive voice attribute, nevertheless exhibit only passive forms in the surface output, e.g. PISCĀRĪ$_{338}$ instead of the expected *PISCĀRE, SEQUITUR instead of *SEQUIT '(il) suit/sigue', or NĀTUS SUM '(je) suis né/he nacido'.

Diachronic change. In popular dialects the passive suffix—both as the morpheme of the passive voice in the VP and as the empty morph attached to a deponent verb—is lost without a trace. For the deponents, analogous forms without the suffix emerge spontaneously on existing models, simple NASCIT replacing NASCITUR, SEQUERE replacing SEQUĪ, PISCĀVIT replacing PISCĀTUS EST, and so on. In the case of regular verbs, retention of the passive voice involves a series of changes resulting in its removal from the VP structure, as will be more readily understood if discussed later under an aspect of clause structure (see 10.3).

8.3 The negator. This is the sole attribute of the Latin VP that is not a suffix in the surface structure. It has the alternant forms NŌN and NĒ, which occur in complementary distribution relative to certain factors of clause structure (see 10.4). The position of the negator not only is first in the VP underlyingly, but also it must surface just before the head verb (as in, say, NŌN SCIŌ 'je ne sais/no sé') and is separable therefrom only by the enclitic interrogator -NE, an element of clause structure, as in NŌNNE SCĪS 'ne sais-tu pas?/¿no sabes?'

Diachronically, only the alternant NŌN survives in popular dialects and into Romance.

8.4 Coordinated verbals. VPs may be coordinated, though not adversatively, e.g. LEGERE ET SCRĪBERE. If the negator slot is filled underlyingly, the only viable conjunction is NEC (~ NEQUE), which effectively neutralizes copulative and alternative coordination. It is required before both elements, thus paralleling ET LEGERE ET SCRĪBERE or AUT LEGERE AUT SCRĪBERE, with the first occurrence replacing the regular negative particle: thus, for example underlying NŌN LEGERE + ET/AUT + NŌN SCRĪBERE becomes NEC LEGERE NEC SCRĪBERE.

Clausal structures

9. The clause: A general overview

9.0 Internal structure of the clause (C1). The formula for the underlying structure of the Latin clause is

Cl → (Interrogator)[29] ± Subject ± Complement(s) ± Modality (Modifier) + Predicate.

9.1 Verbals as predicates. The indispensable predicate slot in a clause is filled exclusively by a verbal, i.e. a verb or a VP. Thus, for example, the verb PLUIT 'il pleut/llueve' can be functioning as predicate in a clause which has no subject, no complement, and no modifier, and so can of itself constitute a clause. The other slots are filled severally by various nonverbal structures.

9.2 Subjects. The subject slot is filled primarily by any type of nominal, secondarily by an embedded clause (12.1-2). A nominal subject is invariably marked by the nominative case, as in CAESAR VĪVIT 'César vit', PĀX NŌN DŪRAT 'la paix ne dure pas', or TEMPUS FUGIT 'le temps passe vite'. For the position of the subject relative to the predicate, and for subject-predicate linkage by verb inflection, see later sections.

9.3 Complements. The complement function in a clause is filled primarily by a nominal, an adjectival, or an adverbial; secondarily by an embedded clause. Complements vary in both form and semantic function according to the lexical category of the verb in the predicate. There are three main categories of verb, two of which are subcategorized: transitive, linking, and intransitive. And, as determined severally by the verbal categories and subcategories, there are four distinct types of complement: object, dative, equivalent, and oblique. We may describe and illustrate the four under the several verbal headings.

9.3.1 Transitive verbs and their complements

9.3.1.1 Transitive-1 verbs. The goal, or object, of an action directed toward an entity is expressed by means of a complement traditionally called direct object and known here simply as OBJECT. The form of an object is typically nominal, though it can also be an embedded clause. A nominal object is always marked as such by being in the accusative case, as in DEŌS ADŌRĀRE 'adorer les dieux', NŌS SALVĀRE 'nous sauver', IŪLIAM ADMĪRĀRĪ 'admirer Julie'.[30] The examples just provided have the object preceding the predicate, for the simple reason that Latin is said to be an 'SOV' (i.e.

9.3 Complements / 145

Subject-Object-Verb) language; though at the same time it is characterized as having fairly 'free word-order', and in fact there may well be no basic position for either the subject or a complement vis-à-vis the predicate, the surface order being determined by factors in the discourse with the focus on the right-most, final constituent, be it predicate, as in CANIS AVEM VIDET, on the subject, as in AVEM VIDET CANIS, or indeed on the object, as in CANIS VIDET AVEM 'le chien voit l'oiseau'. Most trans-1 verbs—e.g. PREHENDERE$_{372}$ or TENĒRE$_{433}$—simply never occur without an object. There are, however, many trans-1s such as CANTĀRE$_{55}$ or BIBERE$_{39}$ which need not always be accompanied by an expressed object, even though one is always implied as 'understood'.

9.3.1.2 Transitive-2 verbs.
A number of transitive verbs denote a predication which entails not only an object but also a recipient or beneficiary. The someone to or for whom the action is performed is expressed by means of a complement traditionally called indirect object and known here as DATIVE (COMPLEMENT). The form of a dative is exclusively nominal, with [+animate] head, and it always carries the dative case suffix,[31] as in INFANTIBUS NŌMINA DARE 'donner des noms aux enfants' or NIHIL IŪDICĪ DĪCERE 'ne rien dire au juge'. Given the free word-order that we are assuming for Latin, there is no basic position for a dative vis-à-vis any other constituent. Discourse factors and focus may thus account for as many as 24 different orders in a clause with both an object and a dative, such as PATER FĪLIŌ PECŪNIAM DAT 'le père donne de l'argent au fils', no ambiguity being possible with subject, object, and dative all in the appropriate case.

Most trans-2 verbs—e.g. DARE$_{130}$ or MITTERE$_{276}$—simply never occur without their object overtly expressed, although their dative may be missing as in, say, NUNTIUM MITTERE 'envoyer un message', the unexpressed recipient being understood.

9.3.1.3 Transitive-3 verbs.
A third group of transitives denote a predication entailing not only an object (always expressed) but also the consequent location, situation, or activity in which the object finds itself. This last is expressed by means of a complement traditionally called simply complement and known here more precisely as an OBLIQUE (COMPLEMENT). The form of an oblique with a trans-3 is typically adverbial, as in LITTERĀS IBI PŌNERE 'mettre les lettres là', ALIQUEM AD CĒNAM INVĪTĀRE 'inviter quelqu'un au dîner'; though it can also be a nominal in the genitive or ablative case, e.g. ALIQUEM FURTĪ ARGUERE 'accuser quelqu'un d'un vol', EŌS METŪ LIBERĀRE 'les délivrer de la peur'.

9.3.1.4 Transitive-4 verbs.
Yet a fourth group of transitives denote an action of equating their object with some entity or characteristic. This equivalence is expressed by means of a complement traditionally called

objective complement, or secondary object, and known here as an EQUIVALENT (COMPLEMENT). The form of an equivalent is either a nominal (for an entity) in the accusative case, as in CAESAREM IMPERĀTŌREM CREĀRE 'faire César empereur', CŌNSULEM PRŌDITŌREM VOCĀRE 'appeler le consul un traître', or an adjectival (for a characteristic) agreeing with the object, as in CĪVĒS BEĀTŌS REDDERE 'rendre les citoyens heureux'. An equivalent necessarily comes after the object, for distinguishing the one from the other in this instance of two nominals in the accusative.

9.3.2 Linking verbs and their complements. A few verbs serve to link, i.e. equate, one entity with another or an entity with a characteristic. The first entity is expressed by the subject, and what the subject is (or becomes, or seems) is expressed in the type of complement traditionally called predicate nominative or predicate adjective, but known here as the same complement, namely, equivalent, already identified as occurring with trans-4 verbs. The form of an equivalent after a linking verb is typically a nominal or an adjectival, though it can also be an embedded clause. A nominal is marked by the nominative case to match the subject, as in MARCUS VICTOR EST 'Marc est (le) vainqueur', while an adjectival agrees with the subject, as in MARCUS FORTIS ERAT 'Marc était brave'. The linking verbs simply never occur without their complement overtly expressed. In certain limited contexts they may be followed by an optional dative, as in OMNIBUS OPUS ESSE 'être nécessaire à tous'.

9.3.3 Intransitive verbs and their complements

9.3.3.1 Intransitive-1 verbs. A sizeable number of verbs, unlike either transitives with their required object or linking verbs with their required equivalent, yet require an oblique—i.e. the type of complement already identified under trans-3. Likewise with these intrans-1s, the complement is typically adverbial in form, as in HŪC VENĪRE 'venir jusqu'ici' or IN PATRIĀ MANĒRE 'rester dans la patrie', though it can as well be a nominal in any one of four cases: accusative, ablative, genitive, or dative.[32] Commonest among the intrans-1s are verbs of moving (ĪRE 'aller/ir', EXĪRE 'sortir/salir', INTRĀRE$_{148}$ ...), of staying or standing (MANĒRE, STĀRE ...), and indeed of being (ESSE) in a nonlinking sense. Compare, for example, for the latter, the dative-case oblique in DOMUS MIHI NŌN EST 'la maison n'est pas à moi' (where ESSE shares a feature with, say, PERTINĒRE 'appartenir/pertenecer') with DOMUS MEA NŌN EST 'la maison n'est pas la mienne', equating the subject and a possessive adj. characterizing it.

9.3.3.2 Intransitive-2 verbs. A very considerable number of intransitive verbs require no complement at all—e.g. NĀSCĪ$_{294}$, MORĪ$_{289}$, DORMĪRE$_{132}$, EXISTERE, LABŌRĀRE ...

9.4 Modifiers in the clause. The form filling this slot is an adverbial denoting time, place, manner, degree, circumstances, etc., as in HODIĒ INCIPERE 'commencer aujourd'hui', ĒLEGANTER SCRĪBERE 'écrire élégamment', IN URBE STUDĒRE 'étudier en ville', CUM AMĪCĪS PRANDĒRE 'dîner avec des amis'; or a nominal in the accusative to denote a span of time or distance, as in QUĪNQUE ANNŌS PUGNĀRE 'combattre cinq ans' or MŪRUM DUŌS PEDĒS MOVĒRE 'mouvoir le mur deux pieds'; or a nominal in the ablative to denote a location.[33] The position of a modifier is basically free relative to that of subject or complement(s).

Diachronic change. Complements marked by cases other than the nominative or the accusative undergo changes as follows in popular dialects.

- Since the genitive and dative case-marking suffixes remain functionally distinct from one another in the [+def] determiners and the personal pronouns, but not in nouns, the elsewhere undifferentiated gen./dat. NP, while continuing as a genitive modifier in higher NPs (see 4.3), gives way increasingly to AD-plus-acc. PrepPs in the dative complement slot, e.g. /ad fīliu/ for FĪLIŌ in PATER FĪLIŌ PECŪNIAM DAT.

- Oblique complements in either trans-3 or intrans-3 clauses where genitive-marked are replaced by DĒ-plus-acc. phrases; where ablative-marked become marked by AB, EX or DĒ plus acc., as in /ab rōma/ or /ē rōma/ or /dē rōma/ for RŌMĀ in RŌMĀ ABESSE or whatever; where accusative- or dative-marked become marked by AD-plus-acc., as in /ad rōma/ for RŌMAM in RŌMAM REDĪRE, or /ad deu/ for DEŌ in DEŌ SERVĪRE or the like.

- Ablative-marked modifiers denoting 'place in which' invariably become PrepPs, including those few with the special locative suffix mentioned in note 33.

9.5 Modality. This slot in the clause, underlyingly ordered just ahead of the predicate position, is filled by a suffix of tense/mood which hops to the first verboid element to its right, be it the head of the predicate verbal or, if present, the perfective suffix or the passive Aux ESSE.

9.5.1 The tense/mood system. In the tense/mood system of Latin, both tense and mood are obligatory. There are three tenses: present, past, future; and two moods: indicative and subjunctive. A major constraint: both moods cooccur with the present and the past, but only the indicative with the future. Morphologically, it is difficult if not impossible to separate the tense segment from the mood segment, and it is therefore doubtless best to say that each suffixal shape represents a portmanteau morph packaging both tense and mood. In the following synopsis of the verb AMĀRE, the relevant suffixes are the segments occurring between the stem AMĀ-, plus-or-minus the perfective suffix -V(I)- to their left, and the person/number concord suffix -T to their right. (As we shall soon see, a concord suffix is obligatory whenever modality is present.)

	Present		Past		Future	
	−Perf	+Perf	−Perf	+Perf	−Perf	+Perf
Indicative:	AMAT	AMĀVIT	AMĀBAT	AMĀVERAT	AMĀBIT	AMĀVERIT
Subjunctive:	AMET	AMĀVERIT	AMĀRET	AMĀVISSET	...	...

The presence of passive voice in the predicate does not affect this morphology—e.g. AMAT/AMET becomes AMĀTUR/AMĒTUR and so on, while in the +perf +pass environment the modality suffix skips over the (adjectivalized) head proper and attaches to the passive Aux.

9.5.2 Semantics of the moods and tenses. The following statements are valid only for sentence-dominated (i.e. independent) clauses, and not for embedded (i.e. dependent) ones.

● The indicative mood, semantically unmarked, serves to convey straight assertions (or, of course, questions). In the presence of this mood, the three tenses severally denote present, past, and future time with respect to the moment of speaking. The present may also denote undifferentiated time in the case of durative (continuing) or iterative (recurrent) predications; the past is 'imperfective', i.e. it denotes an action in progress or recurrent at a stated or implied point of reference in the past. In the presence of perfective predicates, the tenses denote completion of the action *as of* some other stated or implied point of time-reference: the present moment, a moment in the past, or a moment in the future, as the case may be.

● The subjunctive mood, semantically marked, expresses such modifications as exhortation, command, wish, doubt (in questions), or assertion contingent on a given condition. Together with this mood the present tense denotes simply nonpast time (typically future); the past tense expresses obligations unfulfilled in the past, or wishes unfulfilled in the present.[34] In perfective predicates, the present tense refers strictly to future time, the past tense strictly to past time.

Diachronically, use of the subjunctive mood is greatly reduced in independent clauses, surviving for the most part only in hortative/optative expressions—e.g. VIDEĀMUS 'voyons/veamos' or VĪVAT RĒX 'vive le roi/ viva el rey'—and replaced in other contexts by various paraphrases such as the verbs DĒBĒRE₁₂₄ or VELLE_S-109 in the indicative and with an embedded clause as complement.

9.6 Subject-predicate linkage by person/number inflection. This system comprises a set of six surface markers, hence not morphemes in their own right, in the form of person/number (P/N) concord suffixes which copy the person and number of the subject of the clause onto the tense/mood segment of the modality, once the latter has itself hopped to the predicate verbal in the surface output. Although the consequent cooccurrence of up to three suffixes on a given Latin verb stem—one representing perfective aspect (or passive voice) of the predicate, another the tense/mood of the modality, and a third the P/N concord that must accompany the latter—makes for complicated morphophonemics, the more so because Latin has many irregular verbs, the P/N suffixes are for the most part easily segmentable as shown herewith:

Sg. P-1:   -O ~ -M   Pl. P-1   -MUS
    P-2:   -S   P-2   -TIS
    Other: -T   Other: -NT

10. Special types of clauses

10.1 Clauses with indefinite underlying subject. An underlying subject specified only as [+human −def] is expressed at the surface in the following ways:

● With transitive verbs and their objects, the object nominal switches function to become the surface subject, and the predicate is expanded by the reflexive pronoun SĒ in nonreflexive reference, as in e.g. VIRTUS SĒ NŌVIT 'la vertu se connaît'. This, of course, is not normally suitable in the environment of a [+human] object, where the nominal would be interpreted as the true agent and the SĒ as a real reflexive signal.

● With transitive verbs under the foregoing constraint, or when devoid of a surface object, or with intransitive verbs, a passive clause without agent is usual, as in AEGRĪ CŪRANTUR 'les malades sont soignés', BENE EDITUR 'on mange bien', HĪC INTRĀTUR 'on entre ici'.

● As alternative to either of the foregoing strategies, an unspecified subject can be expressed by attachment of the plural concord suffix to the verbal in contexts where there can be no question of a discourse-deleted plural nominal as subject, e.g. NĀVEM AEDIFICANT 'on bâtit un navire' or DĪCUNT . . . 'on dit/dicen'.

10.2 Clauses with null subject. These totally subjectless clauses have in their predicate a verb of the syntactic subclass traditionally known as impersonal, not because they carry no P/N concord suffix—they do take the singular suffix -T, and under certain conditions the plural -NT—but because there exists no subject whose P/N the modality can actually copy; there is indeed no underlying subject involved. Verbs belonging to this null-subject subset (−S) are, principally:

• Intrans-2s which, in themselves, denote actions of nature (weather and the like), e.g. PLUERE$_{356}$, NINGERE 'neiger/nevar';

• The copula ESSE when it denotes the mere existence (vs. nonexistence) of some entity, e.g. EST LŪX 'hay luz', SUNT MULTAE NŪBĒS 'hay muchas nubes', the latter showing the underlying object promoted to syntactic subject in the surface output, as indicated by the P/N concord.

10.3 Passive clauses. It was pointed out in 8.2.2-3 that in popular dialects of Latin the passive suffix is lost altogether. As a result of this diachronic change, the periphrastic form of the passive voice construction cooccurrent with perfective aspect shifts semantically in such a way as to fill the gap. That is to say, the participle discards its (redundant) [+perf] feature, and the AuxV ESSE goes from marking just [+perf] to marking the [−perf] ≠ [+perf] contrast in the prevalent way. The change, as tabulated synoptically (indicative modality only):

		−Passive	+Passive	
[−Perf]	Present:	AMAT	AMĀTUR	AMĀTUS EST
	Past:	AMĀBAT	AMĀBĀTUR	AMĀTUS ERAT
	Future:	AMĀBIT	AMĀBITUR	AMĀTUS ERIT
[+Perf]	Present:	AMĀVIT	AMĀTUS EST	AMĀTUS FUIT[35]
	Past:	AMĀVERAT	AMĀTUS ERAT	AMĀTUS FUERAT
	Future:	AMĀVERIT	AMĀTUS ERIT	AMĀTUS FUERIT

The foregoing applies mainly to transitive verbals. Intransitives passivized to express an unspecified underlying subject then tend to be reflexivized by analogy with transitives already using this alternative, e.g. DĪCITUR : SĒ DĪCIT (alongside DICTUS EST) :: INTRĀTUR : (new) SĒ INTRAT.[36]

10.4 Imperative clauses. These consist of (1) a P-2 local pronoun as subject, (2) a null modality, (3) a predicate ± complement(s). They never cooccur with perfective or passive predicates.

10.4.1 The subject in imperative clauses. The limited selection of TŪ or VŌS determines the choice of concord marker on the predicate verb: when the subject is TŪ, concord is marked by the mere absence of a suffix and the verb thus consists of bare stem only, e.g. AMĀ 'aime/ama', PŌNE 'mets/pon', VENĪ 'viens/ven', DĪC 'dis/di', FAC 'fais/haz' (the last two apocopated). With the subject VŌS, the concord suffix is -TE or (rarely) -TŌTE. The subject pronoun itself is normally deleted as obvious and redundant in the situational context.

10.4.2 Prohibitions. Imperative clauses with negated VP do not exist in Latin. Prohibitions are expressed through two strategies: (i) a clause with hortatory subjunctive modality and containing the negator NĒ, e.g. NĒ PLŌRĒS 'ne pleure pas/no llores', or (ii) an imperative clause with, as predicate, the VP NŌLĪ ~ NŌLĪTE (imperative forms of NOLLE 'ne pas vouloir/no querer'), followed by an embedded clause with its predicate VP in the infinitive, e.g. NŌLĪ PŪTĀRE 'ne pense pas/no pienses'.

Diachronically, the concord suffix -TE alone survives. Prohibitions addressed to TŪ come to be expressed either as in (i) above, with NĒ increasingly replaced by the unmarked negator NŌN (hence NŌN PLŌRĒS) or through a blend of (i) and (ii) producing NŌN PLŌRĀRE. Similarly, in prohibitions addressed to VŌS, NĒ PLŌRĒTIS > NŌN PLŌRĒTIS or alternatively, via simple negation of the imperative itself, NŌN PLŌRĀTE.

10.5 Negative clauses. By NEGATIVE CLAUSE is meant a clause whose predicate is constituted by a negated VP (cf. 8.3). In addition to the optional negator constituent of the VP, the Latin lexicon contains a sublist of items characterized by the feature [+neg]. These words, which cut across the part-of-speech classification, are basically the [+neg] limiting adjectives NULLU- and NEUTRU- 'aucun/ninguno', the [+neg +hum] limiting pronoun NĒMINE- 'personne/nadie', the [+neg −hum] limiting pronoun NIHIL 'rien/nada', the [+neg] adverbs NUMQUAM 'jamais/nunca' and NUSQUAM 'nulle part/ninguna parte', and the [+neg] conjunction NEC ~ NEQUE 'ni/ni'. With minor exceptions, if one of the negative words in view occurs in a negative clause as just defined, the effect is for the two negative features to cancel each other out and result in a nonnegative, i.e. affirmative, predication; thus, for example, NŌN SCIŌ NIHIL does not mean the same as Sp 'no sé nada' but rather is semantically tantamount to SCIŌ ALIQUID 'sé algo'. This arithmetic-like rule whereby 'two negatives make a positive' lost its applicability in popular speech, however, so that diachronically a 'double negative' clause like NŌN SCIŌ NIHIL came in fact to be a bonafide negative clause equivalent in meaning to the classical SCIŌ NIHIL or NIHIL SCIŌ.[37]

Clauses and discourse

11. Movement and reduction transformations

11.1 Extraposition of subjects and of complements. Since Latin primarily indicates the function and interrelation of constituents by means of inflection rather than by position, the order of elements within a clause is essentially free to vary in response to the context of discourse. Given the basic 'S(ubject) O(bject) V(erb)' order of, say, PUER PUELLAM AMAT, extraposition of subject and/or complement can generate as many as five transformed orders: 'SVO', 'OSV', 'OVS', 'VSO', and 'VOS'. (Test this out with the sample clause PUER (S) PUELLAM (O) AMAT (V)). Generally speaking, what stands first is the topic or theme (the rest being comment or rheme), while what comes last is being highlighted, under the peak of the intonation contour, as information wholly new to the discourse. The only syntactic constraint involved in all this is that any constituent containing a Q-word must stand first, e.g. as in QUEM (O) PUER (S) AMAT (V) but not, say, *PUER QUEM AMAT or *PUER AMAT QUEM.

11.2 Reduction of subjects. At the opposite extreme from highlighting a subject as new and essential information stands the discarding of a subject altogether as being fully established from the context and in no need of repetition. In this situation a Latin subject nominal may be fully deleted, as in such an exchange as QUEM GĀIUS VĪDIT?—IŪLIUM VĪDIT or VĪDIT IŪLIUM. As the example shows, however, the subject is not lost without a trace because of the P/N suffix on the verbal, which has been obligatorily added prior to the deletion and which supplies at least the person and number of the reduced subject.

11.3. Reduction of complements. Latin complements may be 'thrown away' for the same pragmatic motives as subjects. Some, such as [−def] objects, or equivalent or oblique complements, are fully deletable, but [+def] objects and datives are not. NPs may, of course, be replaced by substitute pronouns in these as in any functions; and there exists, just in the case of object/dative pronominals whether local or substitute, a special strategy for reduction—namely, deletion of their word-stress. Within a phonological phrase these unstressed pronouns are primarily intertonic as in, say, EGO TĒ AMŌ 'yo te amo'. In very short clauses they are, precisely because of their reduction, excluded from the initial position typically reserved for the topic—i.e. *TĒ AMŌ 'te amo' does not occur with EGO deleted and with TĒ destressed—but they are permitted in final position, *faute de mieux*, so to say, as in AMŌ TĒ or AMĀ MĒ 'aime-moi/ámame' (with deleted subject), where, however, the focus is on the verb and the reduced pronoun becomes

12.1-3 As subject or complement within a higher clause / 153

enclitic to the verb after the manner of, say, the interrogative particle NE in AMASNE 'aimes-tu?'

Diachronically, with the progressive loss of function-marking by means of case inflection, the burden of intelligibility is increasingly shifted to the order of constituents within the clause. As this goes on, the originally basic order 'SVO' gives way more and more to the extraposition 'SOV' (PUER AMAT PUELLAM), though in certain contexts 'OVS' (PUELLAM AMAT PUER) is also quite viable.

Dependent clauses

12. Dependent clauses with full modality

12.0 Introduction. The function of subject, of complement or of modifier may be filled transformationally by an embedded clause. In the present section we shall illustrate those environments in which an embedded clause is free to embody its own subject (in the nominative case) and to vary the tense—though never the mood—of its own modality; in 13 we shall observe how in a number of environments the subject of the lower clause is obligatorily deleted, or altered as to case, and its modality reduced.

12.1-3. As subject or complement within a higher clause. Whichever of these be the function of the embedded clause, its modality is constrained to be in either the indicative or the subjunctive mood; this overriding constraint is imposed by the binary semantic feature identified and defined in Volume 1, 13.0, as [±reservation], or [±res] for short—a feature involving a mental attitude of subjective questioning, doubt, or uncertainty as to the actual fulfillment of a past or present predication not vouched for, or of anticipation (without certainty) as to a future one. In Latin, if the predication in question is vouched for as factual, i.e. if the attitude projected in the relevant constituent of the higher clause is [−res], the mood in the lower modality is indicative; if the predication is not regarded as factual, i.e. if the attitude projected is [+res], the mood is subjunctive. The complementizer introducing an embedded clause is most frequently UT, although QUOD (in origin a relativizer, see 12.4.5) is also available in certain clearly [−res] cases, e.g. VIDĒTUR QUOD . . . , EST MAGNUM QUOD . . . , and this applies particularly to affective verbs taking a clause as object, such as GAUDĒRE 'se réjouir/ alegrarse' (e.g. GAUDEŌ QUOD . . .), all indicative. In so-called indirect questions as objects, wherever the interrogative feature [+Q] is embodied in an actual Q-word—fronted within its clause just as in any construction, regardless of its function therein—then the complementizer is zeroed out as in NESCIŌ QUOTA HŌRA SIT or ROGĀVIMUS QUIS VĒNISSET, with the subjunctive mood as though projected by the incidence of [+res] in the matrix verb of asking, (not) knowing, or whatever. Without an actual Q-word present, the underlying yes/no [+Q] is typically conveyed merely by the standard interrogative clitic -NE (with NUM predictably replacing NŌNNE), though occasionally also by the complementizer SĪ, which alternatively introduces conditional clauses (see next section), as in DĪC MIHI SĪ CĪVIS ROMĀNUS ES.

Diachronically, the complementizer QUOD increasingly displaces UT, in introducing subjunctive as well as indicative clauses, until the latter disappears altogether—resulting in, e.g. [+res] OPUS EST QUOD . . . or VOLO QUOD . . . , as well as [−res] GAUDEŌ QUOD . . . In indirect-question clauses, the mood remains indicative as it had been in older Latin, and the complementizer for yes/no questions is uniformly SĪ.

12.3.1 As protasis in a conditional clause. One type of embedded clause to function as modifier within a higher clause is the protasis (= the condition) in a conditional clause: i.e. the clause is introduced by the complementizer SĪ and stipulates the condition on which the truth value or fulfillment of the predication is contingent. The modality of protasis and apodasis (i.e. of condition and conclusion) are necessarily congruent with respect to both tense and mood, as illustrated herewith:

		Conclusion	Condition	
(a)	Present Indicative:	NŌS NŌN IOCĀMUS	SĪ PLUIT	[−res], i.e. implying no attitude toward fulfillment
(b)	Imperf. Indicative:	NŌS NŌN IOCĀBĀMUS	SĪ PLUĒBAT	
(c)	Future Indicative:	NŌS NŌN IOCĀBIMUS	SĪ PLUET	
(d)	Present Subjunctive:	NŌS NŌN IOCĒMUS	SĪ PLUAT	[+res], i.e. expressing attitude of doubt or denial of fulfillment
(e)	Imperf. Subjunctive:	NŌS NŌN IOCĀRĒMUS	SĪ PLUERET	
(f)	Pluperf. Subjunctive:	NŌS NŌN IOCĀVISSIMUS	SĪ PLUISSET	

Item (f), with perfective VP, denotes 'contrary-to-fact' in the past in opposition to 'contrary-to-fact' in the present as expressed in (e).

Diachronically, the item (f) pattern comes to express [+res] in hypothetical conditions present or future as well as past, thus encroaching on both (d) and (e), eventually crowding them out of use.

12.4-5 As modifier within a NP. In this case an embedded clause is of the type which serves to characterize the head of the phrase, i.e. the so-called Relative Clause. In the surface structure, a string consisting of the repeated head plus any other attribute is reduced transformationally to the Q-word QUIS. QUAE. QUID. agreeing with the head in gender/number and marked for case in accordance with the function of the head in the reduced clause, and with the nom. sing. form alternating to QUI and the neuter sing. to QUOD. The Q-word is always fronted, thus serving typically to introduce the relative clause in the manner of a complementizer; though when the Q-word is inside an object of preposition, it is the entire PrepP that is fronted, e.g. TERMINUS AD QUEM..., TERMINUS Ā QUŌ... Relative clause modifiers also occur within ProPs—for example, IS QUI..., HŌC QUOD..., NĒMO QUEM...

When the head noun or pronoun designates an entity characterized exclusively by the modifier and in all other respects unspecified and unidentified—i.e. someone or something anticipated or required that may or may not exist in reality—that head (pro)noun is [+res] and so requires the subjunctive mood in the modality of the relative clause.

Diachronically, the ablative forms of the relativizer of course disappear; gender/number agreement is abandoned, except possibly for the neuter plural QUAE as against the now interchangeable neuter sing. alternants QUID ~ QUOD; thus also the feminine forms drop out altogether, as well as the accusative plural QUŌS in favor of nom./acc. QUĪ.

12.6 As modifier within an AdvP. The Q-adverbs UBI and UNDE (place), QUANDŌ (time), QUAM and QUŌMODO (manner) also function as relativizers within an AdvP in which the head is a demonstrative adverb, e.g. TUM QUANDŌ..., SĪC QUŌMODO..., deletable at the surface so that the AdvP is introduced directly by the relativizer, which in itself may carry [+res] and thus determine the mood of the embedded clause.

12.7 As object within a PrepP. Such Latin words as CUM, DUM, NISI, ETSĪ, ANTEQUAM, POSTQUAM, PRIUSQUAM, QUIA, QUONIAM, QUAMQUAM, and various others are traditionally called subordinating conjunctions, but in the present analysis they may be classed as adverbs of the subclasses we have labeled preposition or prep./adv.[38] They contain, in themselves, the feature opposition [±res], whereby the mood of a clausal object is constrained.

Diachronically, most of these items go out of use (e.g. DUM, ETSĪ...) in favor of assorted competitors such as (PER HŌC) QUOD for QUIA or QUONIAM 'parce que/porque', or QUANDŌ for CUM, etc. Of the set listed here, only the temporal ANTE 'avant/antes' and POST 'après/después' survive.

13. Dependent clauses with reduced modality

13.0 Introduction. The reduction of modality in an embedded clause consists in deleting the tense/mood and attaching to the predicate VP the infinitive suffix or some other suffix as a marker of this reduction. There is then no complementizer.

13.1 The infinitive suffix -RE. The infinitive suffix -RE occurs in the following environments.

• When the embedded clause is functioning as subject in the higher clause, the subject within the lower clause surfaces in the accusative instead of the expected nominative case, as in APPĀRET EŌS NŌN SCĪRE, or TĒ HŌC FACERE (MIHI) GRĀTUM EST.[39] However, the lower subject is obligatorily deleted if it is coreferent with an object or dative in the matrix clause, as in CANTĀRE MĒ DĒLECTAT or RESPONDĒRE MIHI NŌN PLACET. To be noted also is the case where the lower subject is underlyingly [+human] yet lexically unspecified, as in ERRĀRE EST HUMĀNUM, or OBOEDĪRE OPORTET, or VIDĒRE EST CRĒDERE.[40]

• When the embedded clause is functioning as object in the higher clause as part of the pattern labeled indirect discourse (= *ōrātiō oblīqua*), again the subject within the lower clause is put in the accusative case, e.g. EGO EUM BENE SCRĪBERE SCIŌ, or CAESAR LĒGĀTŌS ABISSE DĪXIT.[41] Here a lower subject may never be deleted, and if it is coreferent with that of the matrix clause, it is reduced to a reflexive pronoun, as in IS NEGAT SĒ PRŪDĒNS ESSE. On the other hand, when the lower clause is object of a verb which does not introduce indirect discourse, such as POSSE, DĒBĒRE, SOLĒRE, VELLE, AUDĒRE, INCIPERE..., deletion of a coreferent subject is obligatory along with the reduction of modality, as in NŌS CURRERE NŌN POSSUMUS, MĪLITĒS PUGNĀRE VOLĒBANT, etc.[42]

Diachronically, *ōrātiō oblīqua* falls into disuse, with modality reduction to the infinitive viable exclusively in the absence of an expressed lower subject. Consequently, when the lower clause does contain an overt subject, after verbs of indirect discourse as well as elsewhere, modality is not reducible to the infinitive; even indirect discourse resorts to a QUOD-clause, with the mood indicative. A spin-off of the *ōrātiō oblīqua* nevertheless remains as a viable alternative to the QUOD-clause in the special case of the trans-1 FACERE, a verb of causation rather than of indirect discourse and therefore exceptional to begin with. In a clausal object of this verb, the lower subject may remain in the accusative case, as in EGO EUM OCCĪDERE FACIAM 'je le ferai tuer/yo lo haré matar'. And even as the glosses show, there is potential ambiguity when the lower subject is unspecified because indefinite and when the lower verb is itself transitive—thus, in the present example, EUM can refer to the killer (subject of OCCĪDERE) or to the victim (object of OCCĪDERE).

13.2 Other suffixes. Other suffixes available for marking predicates with reduced modality in the absence of a lower subject are the -NDU- of the gerund or gerundive, the -TU- of the past participle or the supine, the -NTE- of the present participle, or the -TŪRU- of the future participle. Nominalized or adjectivalized by these suffixes, the resulting verbal forms are inflectable for case-marking and hence function in various types of modifying clause—e.g. in PAX PETENDA EST 'la paix est à demander' or AD PĀCEM PETENDA EUNT or PĀCIS PETENDAE CAUSĀ EUNT (gerundive), PĀCEM PETĪTUM EUNT (supine), PĀCEM PETENTES EUNT (present participle), PĀCEM PETĪTŪRĪ EUNT (future participle).

Diachronically, use of these numerous reductions in embedded clauses is much curtailed. The supine continues to have limited viability, but the most vigorous survivor is the gerund/gerundive -NDŌ, adverbialized relic of an ablative-case modifier denoting the cause, circumstances, manner, or the like, of a predication. For any of the foregoing variations the popular form would be, evidently, EUNT PETENDŌ PĀCEM.

14. Dependent clauses in expressions of comparison

14.0 Introduction. The Latin comparative quantifiers (see 5.2) have as attributes the two types of comparative expression widely known as comparisons of inequality and comparisons of equality. Both of these attributive functions are performed by embedded clauses which, in the surface output, are drastically reduced through pragmatic deletions. The clausal attributes in question are equally indispensable whether the head word itself is functioning as quantifying determiner in a CNP (e.g. PLŪS TEMPORIS 'plus de temps/más tiempo'), as quantifier in an AdjP or AdvP (e.g. FORTIOR/FORTIUS 'plus fort/más fuerte' or TAM SAEPE 'aussi souvent/tan a menudo'), as pronoun (e.g. MAGIS SCĪRE 'savoir plus//saber más'), or as adverb (e.g. TANTUM AMĀRE 'aimer tant/amar tanto').

14.1 Comparisons of inequality. In these, the comparative quantifiers are PLŪS, MAGIS, MINUS, and the suffix -IOR/-IUS.[43] In what may be characterized as symmetrical comparisons (the commoner subtype), one item is said to exceed, or fall short of, another item with respect to some specified property or behavior. The first item is a constituent of the matrix clause, the second item is a constituent of the embedded clause, and the two perform identical functions within their respective clauses. These constituents may be subjects, complements of any type, modifiers, even predicates and modalities. The following examples embody the various underlying patterns, with the compared items underscored.

Function of compared items	Matrix clause:	Embedded clause:
Subject:	⎧ MARCUS LABŌRAT + MAGIS [ ] ⎨ MARCUS FORTIS EST + -IOR [ ] ⎩ MARCUS VIRTŪTEM HABET + PLŪS [ ]	IŪLIUS LABŌRAT IŪLIUS FORTIS EST IŪLIUS VIRTŪTEM HABET
Object:	MARCUM TIMĒMUS + MAGIS [ ]	IŪLIUM TIMĒMUS
Dative:	MARCŌ SCRĪBIMUS + MAGIS [ ]	IŪLIŌ SCRĪBIMUS
Modifier:	MARCUS HĪC SEDET + MAGIS [ ]	MARCUS ILLĪC SEDET
Predicate:	MARCUS DORMIT + MAGIS [ ]	MARCUS LEGIT
Modality:	MARCUS TĒ AMAT + MAGIS [ ]	MARCUS TĒ AMĀBAT

In the surface output the following transformations take place:

● The comparative quantifier, if determining a noun (VIRTŪTEM), or quantifying an adjective, moves to precede (or hop to) the item it quantifies, while the attributive complement remains in final position in the matrix clause.

● The complementizer QUAM (rarely AC or ATQUE) is inserted to introduce the attributive complement, although if the second item is a nominal subject or object, QUAM may be omitted and the nominal shifted from the expected nominative or accusative case to the ablative.

● All material except the second item itself is obligatorily deleted from the attributive clause.

Thus, the surface forms of the foregoing examples are, with various reorderings, also possible:

MARCUS MAGIS { QUAM IŪLIUS / IŪLIŌ } LABŌRAT

MARCUS PLŪS VIRTŪTIS HABET { QUAM IŪLIUS / IŪLIŌ }

MARCUS FORTIOR EST { QUAM IŪLIUS / IŪLIŌ }

MARCUM TIMĒMUS MAGIS { QUAM IŪLIUM / IŪLIŌ }

MARCŌ SCRĪBIMUS MAGIS QUAM IŪLIŌ
MARCUS HĪC SEDET MAGIS QUAM ILLĪC
MARCUS DORMIT MAGIS QUAM LEGIT
MARCUS TĒ AMAT MAGIS QUAM TĒ AMĀBAT

In what may be characterized as asymmetrical comparisons, the compared item in the matrix clause lacks any offsetting item and is merely said to exceed the extent expected or apparent. The compared item may be in any function:

Matrix clause: Embedded clause:

MARCUS FORTIS EST + -IOR [ ]   ←[SCĪS MARCUM FORTEM ESSE]
MARCUS SENEX EST + -IOR [ ]   ←[MARCUS SENEX VIDĒTUR]

The surface output entails the same sorts of transformation as with symmetrical comparisons, yielding (with possible reorderings):

MARCUS FORTIOR EST QUAM SCĪS
MARCUS SENIOR EST QUAM VIDĒTUR

14.2 Comparisons of equality. In these the comparative quantifiers are TAM, TANTUM, TOT. In symmetrical comparisons of this type, one item is said to measure up to another with respect to a specified property or behavior; in asymmetricals a single item is said to measure up to the extent expected or apparent. As regards constituency and function, the structuring of the compared items is the same as in comparisons of inequality; hence, displays of the underlying patterns could match exactly those given in 12.2, mutatis mutandis, and with the same three transformations to generate the surface output, thus:

MARCUS TANTUM QUANTUM IŪLIUS LABŌRAT
MARCUS TANTUM VIRTŪTIS QUANTUM IŪLIUS HABET
MARCUS TAM FORTIS EST QUAM IŪLIUS
MARCUM TIMĒMUS TANTUM QUANTUM IŪLIUM
MARCUS TOT LIBRŌS QUOT IŪLIUS POSSIDET

It is to be noted that the complementizers correlate formally with the quantifiers.

Diachronically, the popular decline of the comparative suffix -IOR in favor of PLŪS ~ MAGIS has already been noted in 5.2. The ablative-case marking of the second item in a (symmetrical) comparison of inequality is replaced by a DĒ-phrase, thus making DĒ an actual complementizer in competition with QUAM; at the same time, both begin to receive incipient competition from

QUID. In comparisons of equality TOT . . . QUOT all but vanishes, leaving just TAM . . . QUAM and TANTUM . . . QUANTUM, with, however, QUŌMODO (from an original SĪC . . . QUŌMODO) starting to vie with both QUAM and QUANTUM except in asymmetricals, where DĒ plus QUANTUM comes into variable use as well.

Sentential structures

15. The sentence

15.0 Internal structure of the sentence (S). The basic constituency for the Latin sentence, not subject to ordering and with both elements obligatory, is shown in the formula

$$S \rightarrow \left\{ \begin{array}{l} \text{segmental constituent} \\ \text{prosodic constituent} \end{array} \right\}$$

15.1 Clauses as segmental constituents. The segmental slot in a sentence is filled first and foremost by a clause, as in the sentence IACTA ĀLEA EST. In typical conversational exchanges, however, the clausal constituent is very often pragmatically reduced to a mere word or phrase, namely, that word or phrase which conveys the expected new information; all the old information, redundant as it would be in a dialogue situation, is discarded via deletion. The indispensable remainder of a clause reduced under such circumstances may be defined as a SENTENTIAL FRAGMENT; whenever it is accompanied by a contextually meaningful prosodic component, it in fact constitutes one part of a sentence. The fragment can be manifesting any one of the possible constituents of a clause, except, of course, a modality, including the words SĪC 'oui/si' and NŌN 'non/no' as reductions of segmentals such as SĪC FĒCĪ or NŌN FĒCĪ.

15.2 Intonation contours as prosodies. The prosodic function in a Latin sentence indubitably consists of a suprasegmental intonation contour formed on the basis of distinctive pitches at certain points along the linear segment, plus a terminal juncture. The material functioning morphologically in this way is phonological rather than grammatical in character, and consists of (1) phonemic differences of pitch, plus (2) fall, rise, or hold of the pitch whereon the voice fades before a pause. This much of a basic framework is essentially valid for all human languages going all the way back into prehistory. The concepts and terminology needed for contemporary descriptions of Latin intonation did not yet exist, despite elaborate information about poetic rhythm and versification. We therefore do not know how many distinctive pitches and terminal junctures the Latin prosodic system had, nor how many significant pitch points along the linear segment, nor how these correlated with the phonetic word-stresses. Proceeding, nevertheless, on the justified assumption that the Latin sentence did have a prosodic constituent, we may move to a consideration of the sentence as speech act, at the level of discourse.

16. The sentence as speech act

16.0 Introduction. In a conversational exchange a given speech act—or, more loosely termed, utterance—either (1) makes a statement requiring no speech act in response, (2) asks a question requiring another speech act in response, or (3) issues a request or order expecting compliance in word (speech act) or deed (other act). It is in correlation with these various pragmatic functions that the sentence as speech act possesses certain formal properties, as we may now proceed to observe. The traits to be looked for occur in one or in both constituents of the sentence: segmental and/or prosodic.

16.1 Declarations and exclamations. Speech acts that require no speech act in response subcategorize into those which are merely DECLARATIVE and those which are not only declarative but also EXCLAMATORY.

16.1.1 Purely declarative speech acts. Purely declarative speech acts have the feature [−Q] in the sense that the segmental clause contains no Q-word.[44] Prosodically, they are either UNMARKED or MARKED, as the case may be. Unmarked declaratives carry a mere filler intonation with no semantic overload; marked declaratives carry some other, nonneutral intonation which signals one or another nuance of subjective attitude such as approval, reservation, emotional involvement, or whatever.

16.1.2 Additionally exclamatory declarative speech acts. Additionally exclamatory declarative speech acts are [+Q] in that some constituent of the segmental clause is, or contains, a Q-word. Of the total stock of these specialized pronouns, adjectives, and adverbs, only the quantifiers QUANTUM (pro.), QUANTUS (adj.), QUAM/QUOT (advs.), the limiters QUĪ (QUAE, QUID) and QUĀLIS (adjs.), and the adverb of manner QUŌMODO are available. A phrase with the Q-word unconditionally in first position may fill any function within a clause (e.g. QUAM CELERITER CURRUNT!), but their commonest occurrence is in sentence fragments such as QUOT CALAMITĀTĒS! or QUAE VĪTA!

16.2 Questions. Speech acts that ask a question requiring another speech act in response fall into two major subgroups: (1) yes/no questions and (2) information questions.

16.2.1 Yes/no questions. Yes/no questions expect a response which is minimally sīc or nōn, itself a declarative speech act. Any further response constitutes an additional speech act of whatever sort.[45] Interrogatives of the yes/no type are [−Q] and are prosodically unmarked (though probably with a rising terminal), for they are segmentally marked by one or the other of the interrogative particles -NE and NUM.[46] The former is enclitic to the first word in the sentence, as in either GAIANE VENIT or VENITNE GĀIA, and expects either yes or no as an answer. When an affirmative answer is expected, the predicate is negativized, e.g. NŌNNE VENIT GĀIA; when a negative answer is expected, NUM is used instead of -NE, as in NUM VENIT GĀIA.

16.2.2 Information questions. Information questions require a declarative speech act other than a mere affirmation or negation. Interrogations of this type are [+Q] and are prosodically unmarked or marked, as the case may be. Unmarked information questions carry a mere filler intonation (most probably the same as over unmarked declaratives) with no semantic overload. On the other hand, prosodically marked questions of this subtype carry an interrogative intonation and constitute an *unrequired* response to a declaration. In this pragmatic situation the marked intonation, instead of being merely redundant in the presence of the Q-word, signals a desire on the respondent's part to have the preceding speech act either repeated (perhaps because of misunderstanding) or reaffirmed (perhaps because of disbelief).

As has been made clear thus far, any Q-word—or any phrase containing one—is fronted to a position preceding the predicate regardless of its function in the clause.

16.3 Commands/requests. Speech acts that issue a command, order, or request expecting compliance in word or deed are IMPERATIVE speech acts. They are [−Q] and, as a rule, unmarked prosodically, carrying merely the typical, semantically unloaded filler intonation. The clause which functions as their segmental constituent is, uniquely, the special type of clause identified already at the clause level as imperative. These speech acts are very often, though not necessarily, accompanied by a preceding or following fragment consisting of (i) a 'tactful softener' such as sī vīs 'si tu veux/si quieres', SĪ PLACET, or the like; or (ii) a stripped-down nominal identifying the individual(s) to whom the request or order is addressed;[47] or (iii) both a softener and an address form. Since the essential syntactic trait of an imperative clause is its very lack of modality, there is no way to distinguish imperative from declarative fragments if they contain no predicate. While imperative fragments are in fact rare, they do exist and are presumably recognizable by marked prosody, as, for example, in EXCELSIOR! or SILENTIUM!

Diachronically, in exclamations, the adverbial quantifiers QUOT and QUAM die out in favor of adjectival ones, QUOT giving way to QUANTUS (just as in information questions) and QUAM to QUANTUM or QUID (as in QUID RAPIDĒ! instead of QUAM RAPIDĒ!). In yes/no questions, the particles -NE and NUM disappear from use, thus shifting the entire burden of signaling interrogation onto the prosodic constituent and so changing it from unmarked to marked in, for example, GĀIA (NŌN) VENIT? or (NŌN) VENIT GĀIA?

Diachronic recapitulation. Herewith, now, a summary of the dialectal changes noted in the grammar of Latin which affect the underlying structural formulas and/or the constituent systems, and which therefore must be taken into account in our restructuring of the one new descendent language, Common Romance.

• In the structure of the NP (i.e. CNP, PNP, ProP): (a) reduction from five to three cases (nom., acc., gen./dat.); (b) loss of two terms from the demonstrative determiner subsystem, namely, D-1 HĪC, HAEC, HŌC and the anaphoric IS, EA, ID; (c) in the personal pronoun system, cleavage of the substitute subset into (personal) substitute and (nonpersonal) abstract pronouns.

• In the structure of the VP: loss of the constituent (Voice).

• In the structure of the clause: (a) loss of the constituent (Interrogator), (b) reordering of the constituents with reference to the position of the predicate ('SOV' to 'SVO'), (c) generalization of the [+perfective +passive] periphrasis to constitute the passive clause as such (a special type).

Notes for Stage 1

1. Traditionally, there is a sixth case, the so-called vocative, but it is not a case in the morphemic sense defined; it can as well be viewed as merely a syntactic variant of the nominative case (cf. note 47).
2. Not all ten occur with every noun, for the simple and familiar reason that noncountables (e.g. LACTE$_{235}$) cannot cooccur with plural number and hence carry only the singular inflection. Also, there are a few instances of homophony.
3. The missing stem vowel of [−par] neuters such as OS$_{319}$ is recoverable only from the genitive singular (OSSIS, short -E- being regularly raised before -s) and the ablative singular (OSSE).

4. Older Latin had I-stem nouns as distinct from E-stems, but by Classical Latin times these two paradigms are variably amalgamated so that the AcSg of e.g. TURRE-$_{441}$ is variably TURREM or TURRIM. Among the items of the corpus, only SITE-$_{421}$ need be taken as irregular, with its AcSg SITIM instead of the expected *SITEM.

5. We adapt the French term *ambigène*, used by grammarians to classify Roumanian nouns which still have this property.

6. The so-called possessive adjectives also occupy a surface place among the determiners; but in the present analysis they represent reductions of genitive nominals which function as modifiers and which are moved leftward into the determiner slot when so reduced.

7. The neuter noun TANTUM is derived from the adjective TANTU-, meaning 'si grand/tan grande'. There are other such nominalizations, e.g. PLŪS as in PLŪS PECŪNIAE 'plus d'argent/más dinero'.

8. There are marginal exceptions of the type HESPERIDĒS, a plural referring to the daughters of Hesperus.

9. Where two alternants are listed, they represent the nominative and accusative cases, respectively.

10. CRom */ok/ survived into Oïl as */o/ and SGal as */ok/; it also fused with other lexical items to yield Oïl /co/, Oc *aco*, It *ciò* and *però*, Sp *pero*, Cat *però*, while even vestiges of the lost substitute itself lived on in several fused items such as Fr *ici, ça, encore* (HANC HŌRAM), Sp *aquí, acá, anoche, ogaño*, It *qui, qua, ancora*, Cat *encara*.

11. IPSE as determiner can also form a marginal type of determiner phrase with the structure ISTE IPSE or ILLE IPSE, and these are also fused in CRom to yield such forms as are reflected, e.g., by It *stesso* 'même/mismo'.

12. While the identifying modifier in a nominal like OPPIDUM RŌMAE 'la ville de Rome' is in the genitive as expected, such modifiers when serving in purely nonrestrictive opposition appear instead in the same case as the head, that case being, of course, set by the function of the nominal in its clause—so, for example, CICERO ORATOR (nominative as subject) as against CICERŌNEM ŌRĀTŌREM (accusative as object).

13. Even in Classical Latin, cardinal quantifiers (and QUIDAM 'certain') tend in any case to be followed by an EX-plus-ablative phrase instead of a genitive.

14. The adjective SUU- is strictly reflexive in reference and is preferred in that context.

15. Seemingly reinforced by the survival of NŌBĪS and VŌBĪS, the homophonous ablatives retain their form instead of giving way to the accusative after EX, DĒ, etc.

16. Copulative ET has the stylistic variants AC ~ ATQUE and enclitic -QUE, the latter in the well-known phrase SENĀTUS POPULUSQUE RŌMĀNUS, coordinating the two noun heads so tightly as to require but the one modifying

adjective. Alternative AUT has the variant VEL, denoting choice rather than exclusion. However, none of these variants has survived into Romance.

17. Some of these are fully [–sig] like the o-stem noun SOCER$_{36}$ (e.g. TENER$_{432}$ ~ TENERA ~ TENERUM) or LIBER (e.g. NIGER$_{303}$ ~ NIGRA ~ NIGRUM).

18. By exception, there are a few which are [±sig] and by this device distinguish masc. vs. fem. concord in just the NmSg morphs, e.g. [–sig] masc. ĀCER or CELER, [+sig] fem. ĀCRIS or CELERIS; conversely, there are also a few [–par] items which fail to distinguish [+N] from [–N] agreement in just this same NmSg portmanteau, e.g. [+sig] ATRŌX, [–sig] PĀR or VETUS (with AcSg PĀR ~ PĀREM or VETUS ~ VETEREM).

19. The future participle has no Romance equivalent, but the clausal structure CANTĀTŪRUS ESSE (known to Latin grammarians as the First Periphrastic Conjugation) may be glossed as 'avoir à chanter/haber de cantar'.

20. The gerundive has no Romance equivalent (it is not to be confused with the nonadjectival gerund, which does), but the clausal CANTANDUS ESSE (known as the Second Periphrastic Conjugation) may be glossed as 'être à chanter/ser para cantar'.

21. It *-issimo*, Sp *-isimo* etc. are borrowed, not inherited, suffixes.

22. The attribute in a superlative quantifier phrase (cf. Volume 1, 5.2.4), typically a CNP in the genitive or a PrepP introduced by EX or INTER plus a CNP in the ablative, yields in popular dialects to DE plus a CNP in the accusative.

23. It turns up in early Old French and Old Provençal texts, as attested in *graignor* 'plus grand', *halzor* 'plus haut', *forzor* 'plus fort', etc.

24. Adjectives formed with the suffixed comparative quantifier -IOR (e.g. MELIOR, PĒIOR) merely use their neuter form adverbially (MELIUS, PĒIUS) with no suffix.

25. Class 3 adverbials as complements do not seem to occur in Latin as they do in Romance. It is perhaps the lexical loss of certain Class 3 adverbs such as HINC 'd'ici/de aquí', ILLINC 'de là/de allí', ILLŪC 'jusque-là/hasta allá', including also compounds like ABHINC, POSTHĀC, DEINDE, SUBINDE, that gives rise to phrasal replacements, some as early as CRom.

26. Adverbials may be coordinated copulatively (e.g. by ET) or alternatively (say by AUT); adverbialized adjectives may be coordinated adversatively as well, e.g. by (NŌN . . .) SED.

27. The two short-vowel stem classes are conventionally assigned to one and the same conjugation because the I-stems are few in number and there is much phonemic overlap. Both show /e/ in the infinitive (CADERE, CAPERE), in the imperative singular (CADE, CAPE), and both show /i/ in the majority of present-tense forms (CADIT, CAPIT etc.), although the -E- is elided and the -I- retained before a suffix-initial vowel (CADO vs. CAPIO, CADUNT vs. CAPIUNT, CADAT vs. CAPIAT, etc.).

28. The suffix -MINĪ is obviously enough a portmanteau morph combining the concord suffix and the passive suffix, and it may be preferable to take -RIS as a portmanteau also.

29. The interrogator will be held for illustration in connection with sentences at 16.2.1.

30. In the present context, it is sufficient to cite most of the verbs as infinitives, for modalities are irrelevant to the description in hand.

31. By exception, either the [−anim] object or the [+anim] recipient of a verb of asking or teaching becomes its object, and the two can cooccur—thus ILLUD ROGĀRE 'demander cela', or VŌS ROGĀRE 'vous demander', or even ILLUD VŌS ROGĀRE 'vous demander cela'.

32. The choice among these cases is governed by the lexico-semantic features of the predicate verb—e.g. accusative in RŌMAM REDĪRE 'retourner à Rome' vs. ablative in RŌMĀ ABESSE 'être absent de Rome'; also ablative with CARĒRE 'manquer (de)' or CŌNSTĀRE 'consister (de)'; genitive with RECORDĀRĪ 'se souvenir (de)' or MISERĒRE 'avoir pitié (de)'; dative with OBOEDĪRE 'obéir', CRĒDERE$_{109}$, SERVĪRE$_{417}$ PLACĒRE$_{353}$ . . .

33. A handful of common nouns and place-name nouns have a special LOCATIVE suffix (the vestige of an ancient locative case), overlapping in some of these nouns with the genitive or dative suffix but not to be taken as such—i.e. DOMĪ 'à la maison', HUMĪ 'par terre', RŪRĪ 'à la campagne', RŌMAE 'à Rome', ATHĒNĪS 'à Athènes', etc.

34. This is apart from conditional sentences, which will be dealt with separately under embedded clauses (12.3).

35. Morphemically, this AuxV, like many irregular verbs, has a suppletive stem packaging the perfective morpheme.

36. INTRĀTUS EST was seemingly never available for this purpose; see 8.2 of Stage 2 for its entirely different development.

37. Coordination of clauses is possible with any of the conjunctions mentioned thus far. At this particular level, however, in popular Latin the adversatives SED and AC die out in favor of a special (originally poetic) use of the quantifier MAGIS in the sense of 'plutôt/más bien'.

38. Some of these (CUM, DUM . . .) take only an embedded clause as object and hence equate with preps.; others carry the suffix -QUAM before a clausal object but not before a nominal object or no object (ANTE, POST . . .) and hence are prep./adv.

39. In this environment a QUOD-clause (see 12.1) is also viable optionally, as in GRĀTUM EST QUOD TŪ HŌC FACIS.

40. Here one of the lower clauses, presumably the latter, is functioning as equivalent complement.

41. Such reduction is therefore possible in the case of an indirect question as object of a verb of knowing or the like, in e.g. NESCIŌ QUID DĪCERE or SCĪSNE CUI CRĒDERE.

42. After verbs of this sort the *orātiō oblīqua* construction is in fact disallowed, and modality reduction can occur *only* when subjects are coreferent.

43. In addition, any of these may in turn be quantified by essentially any one of the indefinite quantifiers (e.g. MULTUM FORTIOR . . .).

44. This does not apply to the content of a dependent, embedded clause.

45. Alternative responses are VĒRUM 'vrai/verdad', or an echoing of the modality of the question, together with the lone verb which embodies it—negated if appropriate and adjusted for P/N agreement if necessary.

46. These particles are actually the fillers of the interrogator constituent in the internal structure of the clause (see 9.0 and note 29).

47. The address form typically occurs in the nominative case, although if it is a noun of the second declension with sigmatic nominative singular (e.g. PETRUS, AMĪCUS), the ending -US is replaced by the special vocative suffix -E (PETRE, AMĪCE). This morphological quirk has caused traditional grammar to identify a sixth Latin case, the so-called VOCATIVE, in which any address-form—regardless of its formal identity with the nominative—is said to occur. But it is clearly not a case in the essential sense of marking the function of a nominal within a higher construction, for it occurs only in a sentence fragment.

Stage 2:
The grammar of the Common Romance language, together with diachronic changes in its Southern, Eastern, and Italo-Western dialects

0. Introduction. From this point forward, our synchronic structural statement concerning the grammars of the successive languages Common Romance, Italo-Western, and (Shifted) Western are purposely limited to descriptions which either (i) entail a restructuring of the previous underlying phrase grammar and a consequent reformulation by the linguist, or (ii) undergo for the first time some diachronic change from any antecedent language within the *Stammbaum*. The section numbering will still be held constant, the gaps in it thus simply indicating that there has been no change either in the underlying formulae or in the systems of filler forms functioning as a given constituent at a given level.

Nominal structures

1. The common-noun phrase

1.2 Gender and inflection of nouns

1.2.1 Gender. Every CRom noun (common or proper) belongs to either the masculine or the feminine gender. Stems denoting males are masculine. Stems (including those derived with -a etc.) denoting females are feminine. And while many nouns denoting inanimate objects, or abstractions, or living beings of indeterminate sex, are arbitrarily masculine or feminine, there are also many semantically [−anim] items which are masculine in their singular form but feminine in their plural form, i.e. they are ambigenes—e.g. **braččụ** (m.), **bračč+a** (f.) The gender classes have just two syntactic properties: masculine agreement and feminine agreement, the ambigenes projecting masculine agreement when singular and feminine agreement when plural.

1.2.2 Inflection. There are three cases to be marked: the nominative, the accusative, and the genitive/dative, or OBLIQUE. Table 2.1 displays some

Table 2.1 Common Romance noun morphology.

	Stem	NmSg	AcSg	NmPl	AcPl
[MASC]	**kęlu-**	/kęlus/	/kęlu/	/kęli/	/kęlos/
	kanę-	/kanis/	/kanę/	/kani/[1]	/kanes/
	dęntę-	/dęntis/	/dęntę/	/dęnti/	/dęntes/
	ǫspitę-	/ǫspis/	/ǫspitę/[2]	/ǫspiti/	/ǫspites/
[FEM]	**kasa-**	/kasa/		/kasę/	/kasas/
	florę-	/florę/		/flores/	
	mulyęrę-	/mulyę(rę)/[3]		/mulyęres/	
	die-	/die/		/dies/	
[AMBI]	**ǫwu-**	/ǫwus/	/ǫwu/	/ǫwa/	
	ǫssu-	/ǫssus/	/ǫssu/	/ǫssa/	
	kǫrnu-	/kǫrnus/	/kǫrnu/	/kǫrna/	
	kǫrpǫrę-	/kǫrpus/[4]		/kǫrpǫra/	

sample nouns, again only in the nominative and accusative cases, and with several explanatory footnotes.

Diachronic changes in southern, eastern, and Italo-western dialects. With respect to gender: in southern dialects all ambigenes, and in Italo-western dialects all but a few ambigenes, become masculines. As regards case: all dialects undergo further losses as follows. In southern dialects, case distinction is eliminated as both the nominative and the oblique are lost through replacement by the accusative, now become a form unmarked for case. In eastern dialects, the NmSg and the AcSg forms merge as a result of phonological loss of word-final (minor-syllable) **-s**, while the NmPl replaces the (**s**-less) AcPl, leaving only the oblique forms marked for case. In Italo-western dialects the oblique is lost through replacement by the accusative, which remains in contrast with the nominative in a two-case system. The surface formulas for the CN as a grammatical word are then to be rewritten in the restructuring of the descendent languages.

(So)　CN → Stem (±Number suffix)
(Ea)　CN → Stem (Oblique case suffix) (±Number suffix)
(It-W)　CN → Stem + Case/Number suffix

The It-W formula is thus unchanged from that of CRom, although the actual C/N suffixes are reduced in number to four portmanteau morphs (two case × two number).

1.3 Determiners in the CNP

1.3.1 Adjectival/adverbial words. Within this lexical set, the demonstrative subsystem consists of D-1 iste, D-2 ipse, D-3 ille. Diachronically, this subset undergoes divergent developments in southern, eastern, and Italo-western dialects, including the cleavage of one or another member into ongoing, tonic demonstratives (many of them reinforced by a prefix) and a new, atonic definite article (DA) in each of the three, as shown here without inflectional suffixes:[5]

CRom		So	Ea	It-We
D-1	ist- ———	D-1 kuist-	D-1 (akkw)est-	D-1 (akkw)est- ~ (ku)est- ~ (eč)čest-
D-2 ANA INT	ips- ⟨	D-2 kuiss- DA (is)s-	INT eps-	D-2 (akkw)eps-[6] DA (ep)s-
D-3 ANA	ill- ⟨	D-3 kuill- DA -ll-[7]	D-3 (akkw)ell-	D-3 akkwell- ~ (ku)ell- ~ (eč)čell- DA (el)l-

As to the prefixal material, southern and Italo-western /ku-/ < CRom /ękku̯/ (variant of Lat ECCE 'voilà'); eastern and Italo-western /akkw-/ < Lat ATQUE 'et (même)'; Italo-western /(eč)č/ < CRom /ękky-/ (Lat ECCE- in hiatus).

The new subclass of articles is swelled through the cleavage of the numeral quantifier **un-** into the ongoing numeral quantifier and a new, atonic indefinite article in opposition to the definite, in all three descendents.

1.5 The CNP and discourse factors: Reduction. With the advent of a definite article, it becomes possible in all dialects to delete the head of a CNP in this environment, provided, of course, that the modifier slot is also filled. In the environment of a deleted head, the article is not as yet uniformly atonic, and therefore tends to appear in the corresponding demonstrative form though without demonstrative force.

3. The pronoun phrase

3.1 Pronouns as heads. As a result of the cleavage of the substitute personal pronouns consequent upon loss of the neuter gender in popular

Latin, the basic CRom inventory includes a set of ABSTRACT pronouns as well as the inherited personal, limiting, and quantifying pronouns. Diachronically, the personal and abstract subsets evolve into separate southern, eastern, and Italo-western subsystems, as shown in Table 2.2. It is to be noted that although the oblique case is lost from It-W noun morphology, it survives in the inflection of the singular local pronouns, the reflexive, and the substitute **ill-**, and therefore still belongs in the underlying formula for the It-W ProP. It is these same pronouns which, when pragmatically de-stressed in their function as complement in a clause, become reduced to clitics on the predicate verbal; this diachronic process will be demonstrated under Reduction of Complements in 11.3.

4. Dependent nominals functioning as modifiers in larger nominals

4.3.1-2 The replacement and reduction of possessive genitive modifiers. The CRom possessive adjectives substituting for nominals in genitive function—either case-marked or **de**-marked—continue the Latin set as **mę-, tų-, nǫstr-, wǫstr-** (< VESTR- by analogical leveling), and **sų-**, all with regular adjective morphology. When pragmatically de-stressed, these adjectives occur also in certain apocopated forms already current in spoken Latin, namely, **m-, t-, s-**, with the stem vowel lost in the hiatus (cf. syncope) and with the inflectional **-m** of the accusative singular retained in the masculine, but evidently not the feminine, forms;[11] also **noss-** and **woss-**, though perhaps only in popular speech. These shortened forms of the possessive adjectives survive as reduced variants in Italo-western dialects only. With the exception of some, but not all, Italo-western dialects, the substitute **s(ų)-** no longer replaces a plural nominal. This particular property is assigned instead to /issoru/ in southern dialects, and to /elloru/ in certain Italo-western ones (see Table 2.1 in Stage 2), while in eastern ones the oblique-case /elluy/ (fem./elley/) in its normal function is free to alternate with **sų-** in replacing a singular nominal, even though here too the plural /elloru/ is obligatory.

Adjectival structures

5. The adjective phrase

5.1 Adjectives as heads. The inflectional suffixes on the adj., being mere surface markers of case/number/gender agreement, are reduced so as to copy just three cases (nom., acc., obl.), the two numbers, and the two genders

Table 2.2 Southern, Eastern, and Italo-Western pronouns.

Personal			CRom	So		Ea	It-W
Local	1st Sg	Nom	ęgo	/ego (S)[8]		eu (S)	εo ~ yo
		Acc	me(nę)[9]	mene	(O)	mene (O)	me(ne)
		Obl	mi(ę)	mie		+Obl mie	mi
	2nd Sg	Nom	tu	tu (S)		tu (S)	tu
		Acc	te(nę)	tene	(O)	tene (O)	te(ne)
		Obl	ti(ę)	tie		+Obl tie	ti
	1st Pl	Nom	nos			noi	nos
		Acc		nois			
		Obl	nobis			+Obl nowe	
	2nd Pl	Nom	wos			woi	wos
		Acc		bois			
		Obl	wobis			+Obl wowe	
Substitute	Masc Sg	Nom	illę			ellu	elle ~ elli
		Acc	illu				ellu
		Obl	illui			+Obl elluy	elluy
	Fem Sg	Nom	illa			ella	ella
		Acc					
		Obl	illęi			+Obl elley	ellεy
	Masc Pl	Nom	illi			elli	elli
		Acc	illos				ellos
		Obl	illoru			+Obl elloru	elloru
	Fem Pl	Nom	illę			elle	elle
		Acc	illas				ellas
		Obl	illoru			+Obl elloru	elloru
	Masc Sg	Nom	ipsę	issu			epse
		Acc	ipsu				epsu
	Fem Sg	Nom	ipsa	issa			epsa
		Acc					
	Masc Sg	Nom	ipsi	issos			epsi
		Acc	ipsos				epsos
		Obl	ipsoru	issoru (IO)			
	Fem Pl	Nom	ipsę	issas			epse
		Acc	ipsas				epsas
		Obl	ipsoru	issoru (IO)			
	Rflx	Acc	se(nę)	sene		sene	se(ne)
		Obl	si(ę)	sie		+Obl sie	si
Abstract (neutralized Nom/Acc only)		D-1	istu	(ku)istu		(akkw)estu	(akkw)estu ~ (ku)estu
		D-2	ipsu	(ku)issu			(akkw)essu ~ kutestu[10]
		D-3	illu	(ku)illu		(akkw)ellu	(akkw)ellu ~ (ku)ellu
		ANA	ok	(ec)có			akkó ~ (eč)čók/

(masc. and fem.). Where the case-distinctions themselves are reduced dialectally, the agreement suffixes decrease accordingly.[12]
There are still two morphophonemic classes, viz.

• Those with suffixal shapes matched to those of the ụ-stems for masculine agreement and of the **a**-stems for feminine agreement—thus **bọnụ-**$_{41}$ with masculine forms like those of **kẹlụ-**$_{73}$, i.e. /bọnụs, bọnụ, bọni, bọnos/, and fem. forms like those of **kasa-**$_{262}$ or (ambigene) **ọssụ-**$_{319}$, i.e. /bọna, bọnẹ, bọnas/.

• Those with suffixal shapes matched to those of the **ẹ**-stems for gender agreement—thus **fọrtẹ-**$_{190}$ shows masc. forms like those of **kanẹ-**$_{70}$, i.e. /fọrtis, fọrtẹ, fọrti, fọrtes/, and fem. forms like those of **florẹ-**$_{184}$, i.e. /fọrtẹ, fọrtes/.[13]

Verbal structures

8. The verb phrase

8.0 Internal structure of the verb phrase. The formula for the underlying structure of the CRom verb phrase (VP) is

VP → (Negator) (Aspect) Head

We thus have here, as a consequence of the loss of the attribute (Voice) from the Latin VP, an instance of restructuring at the underlying level. For the resultant shift of Voice to different constituency in the grammar of CRom, see below at 10.3.

8.1 Verbs as heads. Although the surface formula for the CRom verb as a grammatical word remains the same as in Latin, the optional suffixes are reduced to three orders: (1) tense/mood suffixes, (2) concord suffixes, (3) the infinitive and gerundial suffixes.[14] The first two orders are treated below under clause modality (9.5), the third under dependent clauses (13.1-2). The morphological classification of the verb remains based, as in Latin, on the final vowel phoneme of the stem: there are three tense-vowel conjugations (**a**-stems, **e**-stems, **i**-stems) and one lax-vowel conjugation (**ẹ/ị**-stems).

8.2 The perfective aspect. The Latin perfective suffix had already been subjected to considerable wear and tear in popular speech, being weakened

174 / Stage 2: The grammar of the Common Romance language

even to zero in the Ā-stems and Ī-stems; CRom perfective forms for **ama-** hence include /amaịt/ or /amawt/ < AMĀVIT, /amariṭ/ < AMĀVERIT, /amarat/ < AMĀVERAT, /amassẹt/ < AMĀVISSET, /amassẹ/ < AMĀVISSE.

Diachronically, the reduced forms opaquely embodying the perfective marker remain viable in CRom dialects wherever they also carry a person/ number concord suffix (e.g. /amassẹnt/); but the perfective form of the infinitive, having become indistinguishable functionally from /amassẹ/ < perf. past tense AMĀVISSEM, disappears. As a result, in southern and Italo-western dialects, the surviving perfective paradigm becomes indistinguishable functionally from a tense in the modality system of clause structure; this will be clarified under clause structure at 9.5. In these dialects, compensatorily, the perfective constituent of the VP comes to be expressed periphrastically through cleavage of a VP with transitive head **abe-** (< HABĒ- 'avoir/haber') plus object plus equivalent complement, as illustrated herewith (with function above the line and filler-form below it):

Head of VP	+	Object	+	Equivalent		Head of VP	+	Object	+	Equivalent
abe-		Nominal		Participle		**abe-**		Nominal		Participle
Perfective	+	Head of VP	+	Object		Perfective	+	Head of VP	+	Object
Suffix		Any V$_{tr}$		Nominal		**abe-** + -tụ →		Any V$_{tr}$		Nominal

A concrete example, here cited in a clause with present-tense modality but with subject omitted:

/abẹt ịllas lịttẹras skriptas   abẹt ịllas lịttẹras skriptas
skripsịt ịllas lịttẹras   abẹt skriptụ ịllas lịttẹras/

Meanwhile, a model for the dialectal perfective with intransitive verbs had existed since Latin, in both the deponent verb (e.g. NĀTUS ESSE 'être né/haber nacido') and the passive of the transitive verb (e.g. AMĀTUS ESSE 'avoir été aimé/haber sido amado'). Now, in southern and Italo-western dialects the use of **ẹssẹ-** as both perfective and passive Aux becomes a case of complementary distribution: perfective with intransitives, passive with transitives, thus:

Perf → **abe-**/__ trans
       ẹssẹ-/__ intrans

Pass → **ẹssẹ-**/__ trans

Clausal structures

9. The clause: A general overview

9.0 Internal structure of the clause. The formula for the underlying structure of the CRom clause (Cl) is

Cl → ±Subject ±Modality +Predicate ±Complement(s) (Modifier)

We see here two restructurings at the underlying level—one resulting from the loss, in popular Latin, of the attribute (Interrogator); and the other from a reordering which assigns the predicate a basic position immediately after the subject (typologically 'SVO') rather than final in the clause ('SOV').

9.2 Subjects. Diachronically, a nominal subject remains invariably marked by the nominative case in those Italo-western dialects which preserve the nom./acc. distinction; in southern and eastern dialects, with case distinction obliterated except for the eastern optional oblique, the function of subject is unmarked, other than by its position.[15]

9.3 Complements. Diachronic changes in CRom complements are as follows.

9.3.1 Objects. A nominal object of a trans-1 or trans-2 verb continues to be marked by the accusative case in those Italo-western dialects which preserve the nom./acc. distinction. In southern dialects with lost case-marking, a nominal object is marked only by its postpredicate position.[16] In eastern dialects, object nominals with [+anim] head come to be marked by a functor in the shape of the prep. **pęr** stripped, of course, of the semantic feature(s) it has elsewhere as a transitive adverb.[17]

9.3.2 Datives. As the general norm, dative nominals come to be marked by **a**, the reflex of Lat AD, basically a prep. but doubling here as a functor (cf. also note 17). After this **a**, the case-marking (if any) is, of course, accusative. Instead of giving way to the prep.-like functor, however, the CRom oblique-case suffix is retained in the following instances, varying by dialects.

In southern dialects, the substitute pronoun **ips-** retains, as syntactic alternant in dative function, the oblique-plural form (as /issoru/).

In Italo-Western dialects (except some Iberian ones), the substitute pronoun **ịll-** similarly keeps the oblique singular form (as the alternants /elluy/, f. /ellɛy/) as well as the oblique plural form (as /elloru/).

In eastern dialects, not only the oblique substitutes (as /elluy, elley, elloru/) but also the definite-article and demonstrative determiners set forth in 1.3 above remain viable in dative function.[18]

9.3.3 Equivalents. Equivalent complements are either nominals or adjectivals. Nominal equivalents are marked to match object nominals casewise after a trans-4 predicate, or to match subject nominals after a linking predicate, in conformity with the case-marking system (or absence thereof) that any given dialect has. An adjectival equivalent is inflected to agree with the object or the subject, whichever it is matching, in number, gender, and (if any) case, just as they agree with the head noun within a CNP.

9.5 Modality: The tense/mood system. This slot in the clause, underlyingly ordered just ahead of the predicate, is filled by a suffix of tense/mood which hops to the first verboid element to its right, be it the head of the predicate verbal or, if present, the perfective suffix (or Aux, after the dialectal changes reported in 8.2).

The CRom tense/mood system remains the same, morphologically, as it was in Latin, but it becomes affected by sweeping diachronic changes. With tense and mood packaged as they are in a single portmanteau suffix, and with the morphemic contrast between indicative and subjunctive mood all but eliminated in independent clauses, and with the decaying perfective suffix further clouding the morphology, the system becomes so opaque that it breaks down dialectally along the lines we shall now trace.

• The future tense, with part of its evolving paradigm overlapping with the perfective present indicative in some stem-classes (e.g. /amabit/ vs. /amawit/, with /b/ and /w/ starting to coalesce) and with the present subjunctive in others (e.g. /duka/ or /dormya/, with 1st-sg. **-m** reduced to zero), disappears without a trace from all dialects. Its replacement takes two forms: (i) in scattered Italo-western dialects (of Dalmatia and Iberia), a continuation of the perfective future as nonperfective (e.g. /amare-/ or /dormire-/), and (ii) in all dialects, despite the competition of (i) in those few, a periphrastic, or modal, future resulting from a clause-uniting shift, as shown herewith:

$$\frac{\text{Modality}}{\text{Pres. indic.}} + \frac{\text{Predicate}}{\text{Verbal}} + \frac{\text{Object}}{\text{[Clause]}} \rightarrow \frac{\text{Modality}}{\text{Pres. indic.} + \text{Fut. Aux.}} + \frac{\text{Predicate}}{\text{Verbal}} + \left(\frac{\text{Object}}{\text{Nominal}}\right)$$

[19]

A concrete example, here cited with subject omitted as irrelevant:

/abyo + skribere litteras/ → /abyo skribere + litteras/

structured like

/abyo + litteras/   /skribo + litteras/

As a result, the modality constituent will be restructured in each of the descendent languages, as we shall see for It-W in Stage 3.

• The 'future perfect' (i.e. +Perf+Fut), the 'imperfect subjunctive' (i.e. −Perf+Past+Subj), and the 'perfect subjunctive' (i.e. +Perf+Pres+Subj) all merge form-wise at least in the regular verbs (e.g. /amare-/, /dormire-/ . . .); this form persists either as the simple future (instead of the perfective future, cf. just above), or as the imperfect subjunctive in southern dialects, or as the perfect subjunctive in eastern dialects.

• The '(present) perfect indicative' survives everywhere although, while retaining its perfective status in eastern, it becomes simply a new tense (call it PRETERITE) in southern and Italo-western dialects.

• The 'pluperfect indicative' (i.e. +Perf+Past+Indic) survives only in some Italo-western dialects, and becomes along with the preterite another new tense (call it PLUPERFECT) in the modality system; in other dialects it is lost altogether.

• The 'pluperfect subjunctive' is merely lost in southern, but it shifts to replace its missing indicative *mood* counterpart in eastern and its missing imperfect *tense* counterpart in Italo-western.

As a result of these diverse changes, the tense/mood component of the modality system will be restructured in each of the descendent languages, as exemplified by token **a**-stem **ama-** with 1st-sg P/N suffix:

Southern			Eastern				Italo-Western		
	Indic	Subj			Indic	Subj		Indic	Subj
Pres	amo	ame	−Perf	Pres	amo	ame	Pres	amo	ame
Impf	amaba	amare		Past		amawa	Impf	amawa	amasse
Pret		amay	+Perf	Pres	amay	amare	Pret		amay
				Past		amasse	Plup		amara
							Fut		amare

10. Special types of clauses

10.1 Passive clauses. As a result of the morphological changes already detailed in Stage 2, the CRom passive clause is restructured from the Latin one in terms of the following description: (1) it has a nominal as subject, naming the entity undergoing the predicated action; (2) it has any modality; (3) it has a verbal containing the linking verb **ęsse**-[20] as predicate; (4) it has an adjectival as equivalent complement, expressing the action and, optionally, its agent. The head of the adjectival equivalent is the [+pas] participial adj. derived from a transitive verb, and its own agentive complement is a PrepP. In Latin, with the passive voice built into the predicate verbal, the agentive expression had been merely an adverbial modifier in the clause, consisting of the prep. AB ∼ Ā plus an ablative-marked nominal or, rather less usually, PER plus an accusative-marked nominal. Now restructured as the adverbial complement of the passive participle, with A(B) becoming indistinguishable from A(D), CRom favors the available **pęr** or, in eastern dialects at least, **de**.

10.4 Imperative clauses. In CRom these consist, as in Latin, of (1) a P-2 local pronoun as subject, (2) a null modality, (3) a predicate ± complement(s); they never cooccur with a perfective predicate. When the subject is **tu**, concord on the predicate verb is marked by mere absence of inflection; with the subject **wos**, the concord suffix is -**tę**—thus, e.g. /plora (tu)/, /plorate (wos)/.

Prohibitions addressed to **tu** continue to be expressed with **non** plus the infinitive suffix on the verb in southern and eastern dialects. This type /non plorare/ and the alternative with hortatory subjunctive modality /non plores/ both survive in Italo-western dialects, the latter being preferred in Iberia and southern Gallia. In prohibitions to **wos**, the mere negated imperative type /non plorate/ comes to pair off with /non plorare/, while /non ploretis/ matches /non plores/ in those Italo-western dialects which favor the latter.

Clauses and discourse

11. Movement and reduction transformations

11.1 Extraposition of subjects and complements. In CRom, nominal subjects are distinguishable from nominal complements by the persistence of the nom./acc. case opposition to the extent detailed earlier (1.2.2). The movement of clause constituents for reasons of discourse (topicalization, focus, new/old, etc.) is still practicable to some extent, though far less so than in Latin. On the other hand, while the pragmatic reduction of subjects remains viable and unchanged through full deletion, the reduction of complements and even of modifiers develops much more extensively and comes to have formal consequences in all the descendents of CRom. Let us detail the diachronic changes entailed.

11.3 Reduction of complements/modifiers. A new form-class of PRO-COMPLEMENTS is created in all dialects of CRom by virtue of a cleavage of the personal and abstract pronouns, in their accusative and oblique case forms, into (i) normally stressed (tonic) pronouns and (ii) unstressed (atonic), clitic pro-complements. The pronouns convey new information, while the pro-complements convey no new information and are mere trace-forms cross-referring to items present elsewhere in the context of discourse. In CRom the atonic alternants that give rise to the pro-complements are already intertonic unless clause-final, thus in a sense enclitic to some constituent of the clause; now they become uniquely clitic to the head of the predicate verbal, forming one phonological word with it and—regardless of the presence/position of other constituents—normally *pro*clitic as in (say) /égǫ te‿ámo/, but *en*clitic if by reason of subject-deletion the verbal stands first in the clause, as in (say) /ámo‿te/ or /áma‿me/. The fact remains that they are moved to that position transformationally and are therefore not to be regarded as a constituent function within the predicate at the basic level.

In addition to the aforementioned pronouns, in southern and Italo-Western dialects certain demonstrative adverbs functioning as oblique complements or as modifiers cleave likewise into stressed adverbs (proper) and unstressed clitic pro-complements in accordance with the same reduction principle. Table 2.3, which displays the formal genesis of the pro-complements in the same fashion as Table 2.2 shows the continuation of the pronouns, includes the three adverbs affected.

Synchronically, the pro-complement systems of the three descendent languages are then as follows.

Southern			Eastern			
Comp.	Filler	Reduces to				Reduces to
Object / Dative	Local	1st Sg → **mi** 2nd Sg → **ti** 1st Pl → **nos** 2nd Pl → **bos**	Object	Local		1st Sg → **me** 2nd Sg → **te**
	Rflx	→ **si**		Reflx		→ **se**
Object	Masc. Nomnl	Sg → **llu** Pl → **llos**	Dative	Local		1st Sg → **mi** 2nd Sg → **ti**
	Fem. Nomnl	Sg → **lla** Pl → **llas**		Rflx		→ **si**
Dative	Sg. / Pl. Nominal	→ **lli** → **llis**	Object / Dative	Local		1st Pl → **no** 2nd Pl → **wo**
Oblique / Modifier	de-Advbial other Advl	→ **nde** → **bi**	Object	Masc. Nomnl		Sg → **llu** Pl → **lli**
				Fem. Nomnl		Sg → **lla** Pl → **lle**
			Dative	Sg. Pl.	Nominal	→ **lli** → **lle**[27]

180 / Stage 2: The grammar of the Common Romance language

Italo-Western		
Comp.	Filler	Reduces to
Object, Dative	Local	1st Sg → me ~ mi[28] 2nd Sg → te ~ ti 1st Pl → nos 2nd Pl → wos
	Rflx	→ se ~ si
Object	Masc. Nomnl	Sg → lo Pl → los ~ li
	Fem. Nomnl	Sg → la Pl → las ~ le
Dative	Sg. Pl. Nominal	→ li ~ le → lis
Oblique Modifier	de-Adverbial a-Adverbial	→ (e)nde → i ~ ki ~ wi

Table 2.3 Southern, Eastern, and Italo-Western pro-complements.

		CRom	So	Ea	It-W
Personal pro-complements					
Local 1st Sg	Acc	**me(ne)**	/...	me	me
	Obl	**mi(e)**	mi	mi	mi
2nd Sg	Acc	**te(ne)**	...	te	te
	Obl	**ti(e)**	ti	ti	ti
1st Pl	Acc	**nos**	nos	no	nos
2nd Pl	Acc	**wos**	bos	wo	wos
Substitute pro-complements					
Masc Sg	Acc	i̯llu̯	llu[24]	llu	lu[25]
	Obl	i̯lli[21]	lli	lli	li
Fem Sg	Acc	i̯lla	lla	lla	la
	Obl	i̯lle̯[22]	...	...	le
Masc Pl	Nom	i̯lli	...	lli	li
	Acc	i̯llos	llos	...	los
	Obl	i̯llis[23]	llis	...	lis
Fem Pl	Nom	i̯lle̯	...	lle	le
	Acc	i̯llas	llas	...	las
	Obl	i̯llis[23]	llis	...	lis
Rflx	Acc	**se(ne)**	...	se	se
	Obl	**si(e)**	si	si	si
Demonstrative adverb					
			bi		wi
		(e̯kk)i[26]	...	...	(k)i
		i̯nde̯	nde	...	(e)nde/

Dependent clauses

12. Dependent clauses with full modality

12.0 Introduction. The general disappearance of the subjunctive mood from independent clauses changes a subjunctive modality in an embedded clause from unconditioned to conditioned—conditioned, that is, by the presence of the feature [+res] elsewhere in the matrix clause (cf. Stage 1, 12). For embedded clauses where the modality—unconditioned or conditioned, as the case may be—is unreduced, the CRom complementizer **kwǫ** (< QUOD) continues in eastern dialects but is generally replaced by **kwį** (< QUID, originally a Q-word) in southern and Italo-western ones. In indirect yes/no questions it remains **si**, the same complementizer as also serves to introduce the protasis in a conditional clause. Wherever a dependent clause modality is conditioned to be in the subjunctive mood, the complementizer **kwǫ** disappears everywhere, giving way to **kwį** in southern and Italo-western dialects and to **si** in eastern ones—the latter a shift whereby **si** in indirect questions and conditional clauses is in turn replaced by **de**.[29]

12.3 Conditional clauses. In conditional clauses—with the protasis functioning as modifier within the larger construction—the modality of protasis and apodosis are still congruent with respect to tense, i.e. both present, both imperfect, or both future. However, as the inherited future indicative weakens and dies away (cf. 9.5.1), in Italo-western dialects it gives way to the present indicative in the protasis rather than to the new modal future (formed with the present of **abe**-) favored in the apodosis. Everywhere, when [+res] is present and the whole clause expresses a hypothetical, doubtful, or contrary-to-fact condition, the time dimension is neutralized and the imperfect subjunctive alone functions in both the protasis and the apodosis. Here, however, in Italo-western dialects the new modal future begins to appear in the apodosis with the Aux **abe**- (or its equivalent) carrying a *past* tense: the imperfect /awéwa/ in the west, or the new preterite /ábwi/ in Italia. And although we shall continue to call it the modal future (or future mode), this structure is the genesis of the so-called 'conditional tense' of several contemporary Romance grammars.

12.4-6 Relative clauses. In relative clauses, i.e. dependent clauses functioning as modifiers within an NP or an AdvP, the CRom Q-words which serve to reduce an underlyingly repeated head (±attribute) are **kwi** (< QUĪ) as subject; **kwį ~ kwę** (< merged QUID and QUAE) as object; **kuy** (< CŪI) as dative; an adjectival **kuyų** (< CUIUS, pronoun in genitive case) as genitive modifier; **kwęn** (<stressed QUEM) as [+anim] object of preposition; **kwalę** (< QUĀLE-) as [±anim] object of prep.; the adverbs **kwando** and **kwomo** (the last < QUŌMODŌ). From among this array of forms, **kwi** and **kwį** merge as /ki/ in southern dialects (where case is lost); **kwi** gives way to **kwį** or **kwalę** in eastern dialects, **kuy** is lost from southern ones; **kuy** and **kuyų** both lose out to the oblique case of **kwalę** in eastern ones.

13. Dependent clauses with reduced modality

13. The reduction of modality in an embedded CRom clause consists in deleting the tense/mood and attaching to the predicate VP the infinitive suffix or the gerund suffix as a marker of this reduction. No complementizer is required.

13.1 The infinitive suffix -rę. The infinitive suffix **-rę** occurs when the embedded clause is functioning as subject, as object, or as equivalent complement, or as object of a prep. in an (adverbial) oblique complement or modifier, all within the matrix clause. The construction in view can occur only when the subject of the embedded clause (i) is obligatorily deleted from a lower clause as subject because it is coreferent with an object or dative in the matrix clause, or from a lower clause as object (including object of a prep.) because it is coreferent with the matrix subject; or (ii) is an underlying [+human] yet unspecified subject that does not surface in any case.

Of special interest in this frame of reference are those particular subject-deleted lower clauses which function as objects in the matrix. One lexical subset of verbs in the trans-1 subcategory including, noteworthily, **pǫte-, debe-, wǫle-** (and possibly others such as **sǫle-**), becomes eligible in all dialects for an optional transformation whereby the matrix verb moves into the modality position, occupying the slot created in the underlying structure by the modal Aux of futurity **abe-** as established in 9.5 of Stage 2, while the dependent verb, once reduced to its infinitive form, moves up to the position of head verb, with the result that on this cycle two clauses have become united into one. This clause union can actually be detected only when a clitic pro-complement is present, because the pro-complement can be clitic to the lower VP—as in, say, /tu + pǫtis + awdir(e)⌣me/—or it can 'climb' and become clitic to the one and only VP of the united clause as in /tu + me⌣pǫtis awdire/.

Likewise, clause union is effected with the causative verbs **fakę-** or **laksa-**, so that /tu + me⌣fakis punirę/—in which the **me** is the reduced object of the originally dependent (and subjectless) predicate—patterns the same as /tu + me⌣fakis suffrirę/, in which **me** represents the reduced object of the matrix verb **fakę-**.

13.2 The gerund suffix -ndo. The gerund suffix **-ndo** occurs when the embedded clause is functioning as modifier denoting manner or circumstances, but only when (as with the infinitive suffix) the subject of the embedded clause is obligatorily deleted because coreferent with the matrix subject—as in /illi intrant kurrendo/—or if the lower subject is [+human] but unspecified—as in /illu appetitu wenit (kom)edendo/.

Here again, one lexical subset of verbs in the intrans-1 subcategory including, noteworthily, **sta-, wade-, weni-,** and possibly others, becomes eligible in southern and Italo-western dialects for an optional clause-union transformation whereby the matrix verb moves into the modality position as a modal Aux denoting progressivity, while the dependent verb, once reduced to its gerund form, moves up to the position of head verb. Again, this clause union is perceptible only when a pro-complement is present and is clitic either to the lower VP (as in, say, /tu non stas + askultando‿me/) or to the one-and-only VP of the united clause (as in /tu non me‿stas askultando/).

14. Dependent clauses in expressions of comparison

14. In comparisons of *in*equality, the complementizer for the reduced attributive clause is: in southern dialects, the inherited **kwa** (< QUAM); in eastern dialects, either **kwa** or **de + kwantu** (shifted from original use in comparisons of *e*quality); in all Italo-western dialects, **kwi** displacing **kwa**, and in some, just **kwi** or the inherited **de** for symmetrical comparisons and **de kwantu** for asymmetricals. In comparisons of *e*quality, **kwantu** persists everywhere, though with increasing competition in Italo-western dialects from **kwomo** (< QUŌMODO) and even **kwi**.

Diachronic recapitulation. Herewith a summary of the dialectal changes noted in the grammar of Common Romance which affect the underlying structural formulas and/or the constituent systems, and which therefore must be taken into account in the restructuring of one or another of the three descendent languages, namely, Southern, Eastern, and Italo-Western Romance.

• In the structure of the NP: (a) case is lost altogether in southern dialects; nominative and accusative merge phonologically and functionally in eastern dialects; oblique is retained in eastern but replaced by the accusative in Italo-western dialects (except in the ProP); (b) certain of the personal and abstract pronouns, in their acc. and obl. forms, cleave into separate sets of tonic pronouns and of atonic, clitic pro-complements, in all dialects; (c) in the demonstrative determiners, INT is shifted out of the system in southern and Italo-western, D-2 is lost in eastern dialects, while tonic/atonic cleavages produce definite and indefinite articles in all dialects.

- In the structure of the AdvP: certain demonstrative adverbs cleave into separate sets of tonic adverbs proper and atonic, clitic pro-complements, in southern and Italo-western dialects.

- In the structure of the VP: (Aspect) shifted to become part of the tense system in clause modality, then replaced periphrastically, in southern and Italo-western dialects.

- In the structure of the clause: (a) the tense/mood system of the constituent (Modality) changes as follows:
Future indicative lost phonologically, and replaced periphrastically in all dialects.
Future perfect, imperfect subjunctive, and perfect subjunctive merge phonologically, the resultant form persisting functionally as (i) simple future in some Italo-western dialects, (ii) as imperfect subjunctive in southern dialects, (iii) as perfect subjunctive in eastern dialects.
Perfect indicative retained in eastern, becomes preterite tense in southern and Italo-western dialects.
Pluperfect indicative lost in southern and eastern, becomes pluperfect tense in Italo-western dialects.
Pluperfect subjunctive lost in southern, becomes pluperfect indicative in eastern and imperfect subjunctive in Italo-western dialects.
(b) The periphrastic future is added to the modality system in all dialects, as an optional component of (Mode) privileged to cooccur with the present or imperfect (except in eastern dialects) indicative only.

Notes for Stage 2

1. The plural **-i** of masc. ę-stems, analogical to that of ų-stems, comes to be favored over the inherited *-**es**, in order to preserve the pattern of a four-way contrast in all masculines.

2. In each of the three classes there remain a minority of [−par] stems such as this, and among them a very few (nonfeminines) which are also [−sig], e.g. **ominę**$_{-222}$ with NmSg /ǫmǫ/, or **leonę**$_{-250}$ with /leǫ/, or **nominę**$_{-305}$ with /nomę/.

3. In this [−par] stem, both /mųlyę/ and /mųlyęrę/ alternate freely in the singular.

4. This identity of singular forms is uniquely characteristic of [−par] ambigenes; cf. also **temporę**$_{-431}$ with /tęmpųs/ or **kapitę**$_{-64}$ with /kapųt/.

5. Some, but not all, of the It-W items have the inherited -ę in the NmSg; also, as accusative alternants reserved for dative function, certain relics of the CRom genitive/dative case forms, viz. /-estųy (-εy, -orų)/ and /-ellųy (-εy, -orų)/.

6. Italian subdialects also make up a D-2 /ku-te-est-/ by interpolating the local clitic **te** into the second D-1 variant above.

7. The eastern DA may already be taken as enclitic to the first of the other CNP constituents. In the remaining dialects it precedes the head noun.

8. The parenthesized letters indicate functions, not forms: (S) for subject, (O) for other than subject, (DO) for direct object (= object complement), (IO) for indirect object (= dative complement). In the eastern column, +Obl indicates a form.

9. The variants **menę, tenę, senę** are believed to reflect fusions of the pronoun with the Lat interrogative clitic -NE (cf., for example, MĒNE AMĀS 'm'aimes-tu?'), remaining in variable use after the general loss of -NE as an interrogator.

10. For this particular D-2 variant, cf. note 6.

11. The reduction is therefore old enough to feed the rule that the weakening final nasal is variably retained (or merges with /-n/?) in monosyllables (perhaps with nonlow nucleus—e.g. REM, QUEM > CRom **ręn, kęn**?), thus producing /mun, tun, sun/ as against /ma, ta, sa/ etc. like, say, /ya/ (< IAM$_{121}$).

12. In eastern dialects, agreement with oblique and nonoblique is the same except with feminine singular heads—e.g. −Obl /bǫna/ as against +Obl /bǫnę/, the latter identical with ±Obl plural /bǫnę/.

13. Evidence is lacking as to the timing—relative to the split of CRom—of the shift from **-a** to **-ɛ/-i** in agreement with ambigene plurals such as /lǫka/ or /tęmpǫra/; cf. 1.2.2.

14. The gerundial suffix is what survives of the Latin derived nominal or adjectival gerund(ive), which had full case inflection on the derivational suffix -NDU- (see 13.2).

15. Everywhere, the singular local pronouns as subjects surface as **ęgǫ** and **tu**, which may be taken as nominative forms in Italo-western dialects, but as mere syntactic alternants in southern and eastern dialects.

16. And also, in the case of the singular local pronouns, by the syntactic alternants **menę ~ mię** and **tenę ~ tię**; cf. the analogous alternations in eastern dialects.

17. In exactly analogous fashion, the prep. **a** (< Latin AD) as functor begins to mark [+anim] nominal objects in southern dialects and even in a few Italo-western ones—which are likewise losing case distinction along with the nominative suffixes. In this situation the marking is identical to that for datives (see just below).

18. In NPs with the determiner carrying the eastern oblique suffix, the head noun remains also suffixally marked only if it is feminine singular, as, for example, in /kase/ (< Lat CASAE) as against /kasa/, or /flori/ (< Lat FLŌRĪ) as opposed to /flore/.

19. The verbs eligible to become the future Aux are **abe-** or **debe-** for

southern, **wǫle-** for eastern, **abe-** or **wǫle-** for Italo-western dialects (the latter in Rhaetia).

20. The linking verb **fi-** (< Lat FIERI 'devenir/hacerse', typically preferred to passive forms of FACERE$_{162}$), which already in Latin had served alongside ESSE as the perfective passive Aux, as had VENIRE$_{456}$ also to some extent, became amalgamated with **ęssę-** (with forms of both surviving in a single new paradigm) in eastern dialects; both **fi-** and **vęni-** persisted as alternants to **ęssę-** in some Italo-western dialects of Italia and Rhaetia.

21. As the unstressed variant, this inherited reflex of the CLat dative form ILLĪ generally won out over the popular stressed by-form ILLŪI.

22. Again as the unstressed variant, this analogized form, possibly harking back to a popular Latin ILLAE, prevailed as a separate feminine form in the It-W dialects only.

23. Yet again as the unstressed variant, this inherited reflex of the CLat dative plural ILLĪS took preference over that of the genitive plural.

24. It is to be noted that in southern dialects the unstressed variants of the CRom **ịll-** paradigm are perpetuated in complementation with the stressed variants of the **ịps-** paradigm.

25. In the l-initial It-W forms, the geminating coda /l/ is lost with the rest of the elided initial syllable. Such is not the case in either southern or eastern dialects, however; both Sardinian and Roumanian descendents betray reflexes of the original geminate lateral.

26. Reflex of popular Latin (ECCE) HIC. The stressed form of this adverb in CRom is, variably by dialects, **ękkí ~ akkwí ~ kụí**.

27. With the expected /llis/ merging formally with the sg. /lli/ by reason of final /s/-loss, the contrasting /lle/ of the object-reducing paradigm is assigned also this dative-reducing role, for nominals of either gender.

28. The variants differ by dialects. Thus, for example, some Italian dialects have **mi** in both object and dative function, while western and other Italian dialects have **me** in both.

29. Eventually, also **de** + **kwǫ**, the apparent genesis of Rou *dacă*.

Stage 3: The grammar of Italo-Western Romance, together with diachronic changes in its Italo-Dalmatian and Western dialects

Nominal structures

1. The common-noun phrase

1.2 Gender and inflection of nouns

1.2.1 Gender. All the ambigenes become masculines in western dialects. Some of them remain [ambi] in Italo-Dalmatian dialects, though the type of **kɔrpus**$_{93}$ (see Table 2.1 in Stage 2) also becomes [masc].

1.2.2 Inflection. There are just two cases to be marked: the nominative and the accusative. Table 3.1 displays some sample nouns.

Diachronically, case is lost from Italo-Dalmatian dialects, while it is retained in some (but not all) western dialects. The surface formula for the

Table 3.1 Italo-Western noun morphology.

	Stem	NomSg	AccSg	NomPl	AccPl
Masculine	**kɛlu-**	/kɛlus	kɛlu	kɛli	kɛlos
	kane-	kanes	kane	kani	kanes
	kɔrpu-	kɔrpus	kɔrpu	kɔrpi	kɔrpos
	baron-	baro	barone	baroni	barones
Feminine	**kasa-**		kasa	kase	kasas
	flore-		flore		flores
	nɔyte-		nɔyte		nɔytes
Ambigene	**ɔwu-**	ɔwus	ɔwu		ɔwa
	ɔssu-	ɔssus	ɔssu		ɔssa
	braččhu-	braččus	braččhu		bračča/

CN in Italo-Dalmatian (and some western) dialects thus becomes the same as for Southern Romance—namely, CN → Stem (±Number suffix).

1.3 Determiners in the CNP

1.3.1 Adjectival/adverbial words. Within this lexical set, the demonstratives and articles undergo divergent dialectal developments, as shown herewith:

	It-We	It-Dal	We
D-1	(akkw)est- ~ (ku)est- ~ (eč)čest-	(ku)est-	(ak)est- ~ (e)čest-
D-2	(akkw)eps- ~ kutest-	kutest-	(ak)es- ~ akeys-[1]
D-3	(akkw)ell- ~ (ku)ell- ~ (eč)čell-	(ku)ell-	akel- ~ (e)čel-
DA	(el)l- ~ (es)s-	ll-	(e)l- ~ (e)s-
IA	un-	un-	un-

3. The pronoun phrase

3.1 Pronouns as heads. It seems descriptively adequate to claim that the It-We system of personal pronouns, both local and substitute, have *retained* the CRom oblique case instead of losing it as have the nouns (and nonpersonal pronouns, evidently). Diachronically in the dialects, however, all pronominal as well as nominal dative complements come to be marked with the prep.-like functor *a*, so that the formal contrast between accusative and oblique pronouns is neutralized as merely accusative. In Table 3.2 in Stage 3, the It-Dal column reflects total loss of case, the (S) thus standing for 'subject' and the (O) for 'object' (including 'object of prep.')—forms in complementation relative to their function in the clause structure. The We column reflects the ongoing two-case system shared by most western dialects.

The abstract pronouns, unmarked for case (cf. Table 2.2 in Stage 3), develop in Italo-Dalmatian dialects as D-1 /kuesto/, D-2 /kotesto/, D-3 /kuello/; in western dialects as D-1 /(ak)estu/, D-2 /(ak)esu/, D-3 /(ak)elu/; also ANA: It-Dal /ččo/, We /čo ~ akó/.

In addition to the pronouns thus far accounted for, Italian dialects add a series of PERSONAL DEMONSTRATIVE pronouns by the following diachronic process. Some It-We dialects of CRom, at least in Italia, had preserved the oblique-marked determinative adjective forms D-1 ịstuy (-ẹy, -orụ) and D-3 ịlluy (-ẹy, -orụ), increasingly often in CNPs with deleted head, e.g. ịstuy [ọmọ] → ịstuy. The displaced stress in these forms led to elision of the initial vowel, to yield /stuy/, etc. as well as /lluy/ etc. (as in the corresponding pronouns); it is *after* this apocopation that the forms in view obligatorily take

Table 3.2 Italo-Dalmatian and Western personal pronouns.

		It-We	It-Dal		We
Local 1st Sg	Nom	εo ~ yo	/εo	(S)	εo ~ yo
	Acc	me(ne)	me(ne)	(O)	me ~ mi
	Obl	mi			
2nd Sg	Nom	tu	tu	(S)	tu
	Acc	te(ne)	te(ne)	(O)	te ~ ti
	Obl	ti			
1st Pl	Nom Acc Obl	nos	noy		nos
2nd Pl	Nom Acc Obl	wos	woy		wos
Substitute					
Masc Sg	Nom	elle ~ elli	eʎʎi	(S)	ele ~ eli
	Acc	ellu	lluy	(O)	luy
	Obl	elluy			
Fem Sg	Nom	ella	ella	(S)	ela
	Acc				ela ~ lεy
	Obl	ellεy	llεy	(O)	
Masc Pl	Nom	elli	eʎʎi	(S)	eli
	Acc	ellos	lloro	(O)	elos ~ loru
	Obl	elloru			
Fem Pl	Nom	elle	elle	(S)	elas
	Acc	ellas	lloro	(O)	elas ~ loro
	Obl	elloru			
Masc Sg	Nom	epse			
	Acc	epsu	essu		
Fem Sg	Nom	epsa	essa		
	Acc				
Masc Pl	Nom	epsi	essi		
	Acc	epsos			
Fem Pl	Nom	epse	esse		
	Acc	epsas			
Reflex	Acc	se(ne)	se(ne)		se ~ si/
	Obl	si			

the demonstrative prefix and become pronouns—i.e. no longer privileged to 'determine' a deleted head but rather functioning as heads themselves. The resulting blends are D-1 /kustuy, -εy, -oro/, D-2 /kutestuy, -εy, -oro/, and D-3 /kuluy, -εy, -oro/.[2]

4. Reduction of possessive genitive modifiers in higher CNPs

4. The apocopated alternants **m- t- s-** of **mε- to- so-** (< CRom **m(ẹ)- t(ụ)- s(ụ)-**) survive only in some western dialects as possessive articles constrained to occupy the determiner slot of the CNP, in mutual exclusion with demonstratives or articles. To replace a plural nominal, Italo-Dalmatian and some western dialects come to use the reflexes of It-We **elloru** instead of **so-**.

Verbal structures

8. The verb phrase

8.2 The perfective aspect. While the formula for the internal structure of the It-We VP remains the same as in CRom, the perfective constituent is restructured in the form of Aux **awe-/esse-** plus participle suffix on the head. There are no diachronic changes to record in the dialects.

Clausal structures

9. The clause: General

9.5 Modality. While the formula for the internal structure of the It-We clause remains as in CRom, the modality constituent is restructured as Modality → Tense (±Mode). The tenses are five: present, imperfect, preterite, pluperfect, future (the latter being the inherited perfective future, and not viable in all dialects). There is but one mode: that of futurity, distinct from the future tense and manifested by Aux **awe-** plus the infinitive suffix on the head; this optional future mode is limited to cooccurrence with just the present or the imperfect tense.[3] We must note that MODE is not the same as MOOD. What we have termed the 'tense/mood' slot in the Latin and CRom modality is now reduced merely to TENSE, for the inherited indicative and subjunctive moods have fallen into complementary distribution. In CRom the subjunctive mood had occurred in three environments: (1) in prohibitions (i.e. negative clauses addressed to **tu** or **wos**; see Stage 2, 10.4), (2) in independent clauses with optative/hortatory meaning (see Stage 1, 9.5.1), and (3) in embedded clauses wherever triggered by the feature [+res] in the matrix clause (see Stage 1, 12.2). Now in It-We it disappears morphemically by virtue of the restructuring of imperative clauses (see 10.3 in Stage 3) and remains only as a conditioned, automatic variation of tense in dependent clauses (see also 12.1-2 in Stage 3). The [±subjunctive] morphophonemic alternation occurs with just two of the tenses, present and imperfect; it is still manifested via the inherited portmanteau suffixes, so that e.g. present-tense /ama-/ alternates to /ame-/, and imperfect-tense /amawa-/ to /amasse-/, in the [+subj]- triggering environment.

10. Special types of clauses

10.4 Imperative clauses. Imperative clauses and prohibitive clauses are amalgamated in It-W as imperative clauses, with or without a negated predicate. In this restructuring, the subjunctive mood (or, in some dialects, the infinitive suffix) embodied in prohibitions loses its morphemic status and becomes, in the absence of a modality, merely a component of the P/N agreement suffix required in the surface structure. The diachronic process leading to the restructuring may be illustrated graphically as follows:

(1) In clauses with subject **tu**:

$$\text{CRom} \begin{bmatrix} \text{Imperative} \\ \text{Proh.} \end{bmatrix} \begin{bmatrix} \text{(We)} \\ \text{(It)} \end{bmatrix} \begin{array}{l} \textbf{plora} \qquad\qquad + \text{P/N -}\emptyset > \\ \textbf{plora} + \text{subj -}\textbf{e} + \text{P/N -}\textbf{s} > \\ \textbf{plora} + \text{inf -}\textbf{re} + \text{P/N -}\emptyset > \end{array}$$

$$\left. \begin{array}{l} \textbf{plora} + \text{P/N -}\emptyset \text{ /plora/} \\ \textbf{plora} + \text{P/N -}\textbf{es} \text{ /plores/} \\ \textbf{plora} + \text{P/N -}\textbf{re} \text{ /plorare/} \end{array} \begin{array}{l} \_\text{-neg} \\ \_\text{+neg} \end{array} \right\} \begin{array}{l} \text{It-W} \\ \text{Imper.} \end{array}$$

(2) In clauses with subject **wos**:

$$\text{CRom} \begin{bmatrix} \text{Imperative} \\ \text{Proh.} \begin{bmatrix} \text{(We)} \\ \text{(It)} \end{bmatrix} \end{bmatrix} \begin{array}{l} \textbf{plora} \qquad\qquad + \text{P/N -}\textbf{te} > \\ \textbf{plora} + \text{subj -}\textbf{e} \ + \text{P/N -}\textbf{tes} > \\ \textbf{plora} + \text{zero } (\emptyset) + \text{P/N -}\textbf{te} > \end{array}$$

$$\left. \begin{array}{l} \textbf{plora} + \text{P/N -}\textbf{te} \text{ /plorate/} \\ \textbf{plora} + \text{P/N -}\textbf{etes} \text{ /ploretes/} \\ \textbf{plora} + \text{P/N -}\textbf{te} \text{ /plorate/} \end{array} \begin{array}{l} \_\text{-neg} \\ \_\text{+neg} \end{array} \right\} \begin{array}{l} \text{It-W} \\ \text{Imper.} \end{array}$$

Into the new It-W ±negative imperative clause may also be amalgamated the CRom hortatory subjunctive clause with subject **nos**, with or without negation, thus: CRom hort. **(non) plora** + subj. + P/N **-mos** > **(non) plora** + P/N **-emos** /ploremos/ It-W imp.

Clauses and discourse

11. Reduction transformations

11.3 Reduction of complements/modifiers. Table 3.3 displays the It-W pro-complements as developed diachronically in the dialects.

Table 3.3 Italo-Dalmatian and Western pro-complements.

	It-We	It-Dal dcts.	We dcts.
Object Dative	me ~ mi te ~ ti nos wos se ~ si	/me ~ mi te ~ ti no ~ či wo ~ wi se ~ si	me te nos wos se
Object	lu li ~ los la le ~ las	lo li la le	lu los la las
Dative	li ~ le lis	ʎi	li ~ le lis
Oblique Modifier	(e)nde ki ~ wi ~ i	n(d)e či ~ wi	ende i/

Dependent clauses

12. Dependent clauses with full modality

12. With the above restructuring of prohibitive and hortatory subjunctive clauses as imperative clauses without modality, the only remaining independent subjunctive clause is the optative, as exemplified in reflexes of, e.g. Latin VĪVAT RĒX. This construction may now be reanalyzed as the reduction of a higher clause with a predicate expressing a wish, hope, or the like: the matrix verb is lexically unspecified, though assumedly transitive and definitely transmitting the feature [+res]; the subjunctive clause is functioning as object within the higher clause, and in the surface output all but the embedded clause itself is deleted. Motivation for this shift is doubtless to be found in the fact that, variably, a complementizer marking the underlying construction also surfaces in the form of **kwe**, as reflected in French *Que Dieu nous soit en aide!* or Spanish *Que lo haga Jorge.*[4]

12.4-6 Relative clauses. In relative clauses, the set of Q-words serving to reduce a nominal head is the same in It-We as in CRom. From this array of forms, **kwi** is lost from It-Dal dialects (along with case in nouns), as well as **kwɛne** and **kuyu** (both supplanted by **kuy**); on the other hand, **kuy** is lost from western dialects.

14. Dependent clauses in expressions of comparison

14. In comparisons of inequality, the alternate It-We complementizer **de** gives way to the prevalent **kwe** in western dialects.

Diachronic recapitulation. A summary of the dialectal changes noted in the grammar of Italo-Western Romance which affect the underlying structural formulas and/or constituent systems, and which therefore must be taken into account in the restructuring of either of the two descendent languages, namely, Italo-Dalmatian and Western Romance.

• In the structure of the NP: (a) case is lost altogether in Italo-Dalmatian, while it is retained in some (though not all) western dialects; (b) oblique merges with accusative in Italo-western ProPs; (c) a set of personal demonstrative pronouns develops in Italian subdialects.

• In the structure of the clause: (a) the tense/mood system of the constituent (Modality) is reduced to tense alone through the functional neutralization of the indicative and subjunctive moods; (b) prohibitive and hortatory subjunctive clauses are integrated into the imperative type of clause, which is thus expanded to ±negative, with **nos** added to the set of occurrent pronominal subjects.

Notes for Stage 3

1. This by-form results from a dialectal shift of the coda-plus-onset sequence /-ps-/ to /-ks-/ in It-W prior to the coda /k/ > /y/ change in Rule D-10. Cf. modern Catalan *aqueix* /əkɛš/; also Sp *caja*, Po *caixa*, from Latin CAPSA 'caisse' (also 'châsse').

2. The oblique western forms /(e)čestuy/ etc. and /(e)čeluy/ etc., which ultimately give rise to Francian *cestui, celui* never do become pronouns in

the present scheme; they remain syntactic variants of the determiners *cest, cel*.

3. The preterite instead of the imperfect in some, though not all, Italian dialects.

4. There are traces of UT or QUOD used in just this way even in Latin, and eastern dialects of CRom took to using their favored complementizer **si** (cf. Stage 2, 12). To this day, Roumanian has its **să** obligatorily in such clauses (e.g. *Dumnezeu să vă binecuvînteze!* 'Que Dieu vous bénisse! (Eastern Romance had also merged its hortatory subjunctive clause with the construction in view, as evidenced by Ro *să nu uităm* 'n'oublions pas/no olvidemos', instead of amalgamating it with the imperative clause, as in It-W.)

Stage 4:
The grammar of Shifted[1] Western Romance, together with diachronic changes in its Northwestern and Southwestern dialects

Nominal structures

1. The common-noun phrase

1.3 Determiners in the CNP

1.3.1 Adjectival/adverbial words. Within this lexical set, the demonstratives and articles are now:

D-1 (ak)est- ~ (e)čest-
D-2 (ak)es- ~ akeys-
D-3 akel- ~ (e)čel-
DA   (e)l- ~ (e)s-
IA   un-

Of these items, southwestern dialects retain all five, though without the demonstrative variants with initial **(e)č-**; northwestern dialects lack the D-2 demonstrative altogether, perhaps having lost it already in It-W, and they also lack the DA variant with **-s-**, which will survive only in dialects of East Ibero-Romance.

Clausal structures

9. The clause

9.5 Modality. The Aux of the future mode, at least wherever it is **ave-**, variably precedes or follows the head verb within the predicate VP, as in either the normal /áyo kantáre/ or the transposed /kantár(e) áyo/ 'je chanterai/cantaré' etc. In all dialects of ShW, the Aux when postposed comes to be fused, i.e. SYNCRETIZED, with the infinitive head into a single word with just one stress. Thus, for example, with the present tense, /kantár(e) + áyo/ > /kantaráyo/, etc., or with the imperfect tense, /kantár(e) + avéa/ > /kantaréa/, etc. In northwestern dialects of Gallia, the transposition and consequent fusion is invariable and leads to the morphological and functional absorption of the inherited future tense /kantáre-/, which therefore is lost from the tense system. In southwestern dialects (and in northwestern dialects of Rhaetia where the Aux is **vɔle-**), the constituents of the modality remain tactically separate and keep the basic order (e.g. /áyo (de) kantáre/) as well as the extraposition (e.g. /kantáre áyo/), the latter remaining in competition with the syncretic /kantaráyo/;[2] with this variability the old future tense resists absorption by the future mode and is in a position to assume one or another new function in later modality systems.[3]

Diachronic recapitulation. A summary of the dialectal changes noted in the grammar of Shifted Western Romance which affect the underlying structural formulas and/or constituent systems, and which must therefore be taken into account in the restructuring of one of the descendent languages, namely, Northwestern Romance. (Neither of the changes noted entails restructuring of the other descendent language, namely, Southwestern Romance.)

• In the structure of the NP: loss of demonstrative determiner D-2 from northeastern dialects.

• In the structure of the clause: loss of future tense from the modality system in northeastern dialects.

Notes for Stage 4

1. Data are extremely scant for differentiating the grammars of Unshifted and Shifted from that of Western itself. Chiefly noteworthy is the fact that case is lost from unshifted dialects, while it is retained in most (though not Iberian) shifted dialects. The underlying formula for the NP, and the surface formula for the CN, in UnshW are therefore to be restructured the same as for Southern Romance and Italo-Dalmatian Romance, while they remain unchanged in ShW.
2. Cf. Portuguese to this day, with structures like *cantá-lo-ei* 'je le chanterai/lo cantaré', with a clitic pro-complement in the middle of the VP.
3. For example, it will shift to become a new subjunctive alternant, namely, that for present tense + future mode, in West Ibero-Romance.

Appendix 1:
A corpus of Romance lexical items

	GLOSS	SPANISH	PORTUGUESE	CATALAN	OCCITAN	PROTO-SWR
1	'acheter, comprar'	compra /kompra/	compra /kõpra/	compra /komprə/	compra /kumpro/	kompra
2	'affiler, afilar'	afila /afila/	afia /afia/	afila /əfilə/	afila /afilo/	_____
3	'âge, edad'	edad /edad/	idade /idade/	edat /ədat/	edat /edat/	_____
4	'aider, ayudar'	ayuda /ayuda/	ajuda /ažuda/	ajuda /əžudə/	ajuda /aǧüdo/	_____
5	'aigu, agudo'	agudo /agudo/	agudo /agudu/	agut /əgut/	agut /agüt/	_____
6	'ail, ajo'	ajo /axo/	alho /aʎu/	all /aʎ/	alh /al/	_____
7	'aimer, amar'	ama /ama/	ama /ama/	ama /amə/	aima /aymo/	± a(y)ma
8	'aire, era'	era /era/	eira /eyra/	era /erə/	aira /ayro/	_____

A corpus of Romance lexical items / 199

KEY to symbols used in conjuction with the blanks provided under the headings 'Proto-SWR (PSW)', 'Proto-Romance (PRom)', and 'Classical Latin (CLat)'.
Question mark (?) in center: PSW form unreconstructible; no entry to be made.
Question mark (?) at left: PRom form unreconstructible; to be filled in by extrapolation from CLat.
Asterisk (*) in center: item nonexistent in CLat.
Asterisk (*) at left: reconstructed PSW or PRom form to be filled in despite lack of item in one or another input language.
Dagger (†): reconstructed PSW or PRom form to be filled in despite failure of one or another input language to fit the correspondence.
Plus-or-minus (±) or double blank: reconstructed PSW or PRom to be filled in as doublets.
≠ between PRom and CLat: PRom and CLat forms do not fully match.
-R in Roumanian column: no Roumanian cognate.

OLD FRENCH	ITALIAN	ROUMANIAN	SARDINIAN	PROTO-ROMANCE	CLASSICAL LATIN
compre /kumprə/	compra /kompra/	cumpără /kúmpərə/		? _____	_____
afile /afilə/	affila /affila/	-R		? _____	_____ *
ae /əe/	età /etá/	-R	edade /edade/	? _____	_____
ajue /aǧüə/	aiuta /ayuta/	ajută /ažutə/		† _____	_____
agu /agü/	acuto /akuto/	acut /akut/		† _____	_____
ail /aʎ/	aglio /aʎʎo/	ai /ay/	azu /aẓẓu/	_____	_____
aime /ɛymə/	ama /ama/	-R	ama /ama/	_____	_____
aire /ɛyrə/	aia /aya/	arie /árie/	(arzola) /arẓ-/	? _____	_____

200 / Appendix 1

	Gloss	Spanish	Portuguese	Catalan	Occitan	Proto-SWR
9	'âme, alma'	alma /alma/	alma /alma/	ànima /ánimə/	arma /armo/	?
10	'ami, amigo'	amigo /amigo/	amigo /amigu/	amic /əmik/	amic /amik/	
11	'amour, amor'	amor /amor/	amor /amor/	amor /əmó/	amor /amú/	
12	'ample, ancho'	ancho /ančo/	ancho /ãšu/	ample /amplə/	ample /ample/	?
13	'an, año'	año /año/	ano /anu/	any /añ/	an /an/	
14	'âne, asno'	asno /asno/	asno /aznu/	ase /azə/	ase /aze/	?
15	'anneau, anillo'	anillo /aniʎo/	anel /anɛl/	anell /əneʎ/	anèl /anɛl/	?
16	'antique, antiguo'	antiguo /antigwo/	antigo /ãtigu/	antic /əntik/	antic /antik/	
17	'août, agosto'	agosto /agosto/	agosto /agostu/	agost /əgost/	agost /agust/	
18	'appeler, llamar'	llama /ʎama/	chama /šama/	clama /klamə/	clama /klamo/	?
19	'apprendre, aprender'	aprende /aprende/	aprende /aprẽde/	aprèn /əprɛn/	apren /apren/	
20	'arçon, arzón'	arzón /arθon/	arção /arsãw/	arçó /ərsó/	arçon /arsú/	
21	'arène, arena'	arena /arena/	areia /areya/	arena /ərɛnə/	arena /areno/	
22	'argile, arcilla'	arcilla /arθiʎa/	argila /aržila/	argila /əržilə/	argila /arğilo/	?
23	'aube, alba'	alba /alba/	alva /alva/	alba /albə/	alba /albo/	
24	'autre, otro'	otro /otro/	outro /owtru/	altre /altrə/	altre /altre/	awtro altro
25	'aveugle, ciego'	ciego /θyego/	cego /sɛgu/	cec /sek/	cec /sek/	cɛgo cego
26	'avril, abril'	abril /abril/	abril /abril/	abril /əbril/	abril /abril/	
27	'bain, baño'	baño /baño/	banho /bañu/	bany /bañ/	banh /ban/	
28	'baise, besa'	besa /besa/	beija /beyža/	besa /bezə/	baisa /bayzo/	
29	'baiser, beso'	beso /beso/	beijo /beyžu/	bes /bes/	bais /bays/	
30	'balai, escoba'	escoba /eskoba/	escova /eskova/	. . .	escoba /eskubo/	* eskova

A corpus of Romance lexical items / 201

Old French	Italian	Roumanian	Sardinian	Proto-Romance	Classical Latin
ame /anmə/	anima /ánima/	inimă /ínimə/	anima /ánima/		
ami /ami/	amico /amiko/		amigu /amigu/		
amor /amur/	amore /amore/	-R	amore /amore/		
ample /amplə/	ampio /ampyo/		ampru /ampru/	*	
an /an/	anno /anno/	an /an/	annu /annu/		
asne /asnə/	asino /ásino/	-R		?	
anel /anɛl/	anello /anɛllo/	inel /inel/	aneddu /aneddu/		
anti(f) /anti/	antico /antiko/	-R		?	
aost /əust/	agosto /agosto/		austu /austu/		≠
claime /klɛymə/	chiama /kyama/	chiamă /kyamə/	giama /ǧama/		
apren- /aprɛn-/	**apprende** /**apprende**/	aprinde /aprinde/	apprende /apprende/		
arçon /arcuŋ/	arcione /arčone/	-R		?	*
areine /arɛynə/	arena /arena/	-R	arena /arena/		
argile /arǧilə/	argilla /arǧilla/		argidda /argidda/	*	
aube /awbə/	alba /alba/	albă /albə/	alba /alba/		*
autre /awtrə/	altro /altro/			?	
. . .	cieco /čɛko/			?	
avril /avril/	aprile /aprile/		abrile /abrile/		
bain /bɛyñ/	bagno /bañño/		banzu /banẓu/		≠
baise /bɛyzə/	bacia /bača/		basa /basa/		
baisier /bɛyzyɛr/	bacio /bačo/		basu /basu/		
. . .	scopa /skopa/	-R	iscoba /iskoba/	?	

	Gloss	Spanish	Portuguese	Catalan	Occitan	Proto-SWR
31	'banc, escaño'	escaño /eskaño/	escano /eskanu/	. . .	. . .	* _____
32	'barbe, barba'	barba /barba/	barba /barba/	barba /barbə/	barba /barbo/	_____
33	'battre, batir'	bate /bate/	bate /bate/	bat /bat/	bat /bat/	_____
34	'beaucoup, mucho'	mucho /mučo/	muito /mũytu/	molt /mol/	molt /mult/	? _____
35	'beau-frère, cuñado'	cuñado /kuñado/	cunhado /kuñadu/	cunyat /kuñat/	conhat /kuñat/	_____
36	'beau-père, suegro'	suegro /swegro/	sogro /sogru/	sogre /sɔgrə/	sògre /sogre/	_____
37	'bien, bien'	bien /byen/	bem /bẽ/	bé /be/	ben /be/	_____
38	'blanc, blanco'	blanco /blanko/	branco /brãku/	blanc /blaŋ/	blanc /blank/	? _____
39	'boire, beber'	bebe /bebe/	bebe /bɛbe/	beu /bɛw/	beu /bew/	_____
40	'bois, leña'	leña /leña/	lenha /leña/	llenya /ʎeñə/	lenha /leño/	_____
41	'bon, bueno'	bueno /bweno/	bom /bõ/	bo /bɔ/	bon /bu/	_____
42	'bouche, boca'	boca /boka/	boca /boka/	boca /bokə/	boca /buko/	_____
43	'bouillir, bullir'	bulle /buʎe/	bole /bɔle/	bulleix /buʎɛš/	bol /bul/	? _____
44	'bras, brazo'	brazo /braθo/	braço /brasu/	braç /bras/	braç /bras/	_____
45	'canne, caña'	caña /kaña/	cana /kana/	canya /kañə/	cano /kano/	_____
46	'carré, cuadrado'	cuadrado /kwadrado/	quadrado /kwadradu/	quadrat /kwədrat/	cairat /kayrat/	_____
47	'cent, ciento'	ciento /θyento/	cento /sẽtu/	cent /sen/	cent /sent/	_____
48	'cep, cepo'	cepo /θepo/	cepo /sepu/	cep /sɛp/	cep /sep/	_____
49	'cerf, ciervo'	ciervo /θyerbo/	cervo /sɛrvu/	cervo /sɛrbu/	cèrvi /sɛrbi/	† _____
50	'certain, cierto'	cierto /θyerto/	certo /sɛrtu/	cert /sɛrt/	cèrt /sɛrt/	_____
51	'chaîne, cadena'	cadena /kadena/	cadeia /kadeya/	cadena /kədɛnə/	cadena /kadeno/	_____
52	'chair, carne'	carne /karne/	carne /karne/	carn /kar/	carn /kar/	_____

A corpus of Romance lexical items / 203

Old French	Italian	Roumanian	Sardinian	Proto-Romance		Classical Latin
. . .	scanno /skanno/	scaun /skawn/		?		
barbe /barbə/	barba /barba/	barbă /barbə/	barba /barba/			
bat- /bat-/	batte /batte/	bate /bate/				
mout /mut/	molto /molto/	mult /mult/				
. . .	cognato /koññato/	cumnat /kumnat/	connadu /konnadu/		≠	
suire /süyrə/	suocero /swɔ́čero/	socru /sokru/	sogru /sogru/	?		
bien /byɛŋ/	bene /bɛne/	bine /bine/	bene /bene/	†		
blanc /blank/	bianco /byanko/			?		*
beiv- /beyv-/	beve /beve/	bea /bẹa/	bie /bie/			
leigne /leyñə/	legna /leñña/	lemn /lemn/	linnu /linnu/		≠	
bon /boŋ/	buono /bwɔno/	bun /bun/	bonu /bonu/			
boche /bučə/	bocca /bokka/	bukă /bukə/	bucca /bukka/			
bol- /bul-/	bolle /bolle/		buddi /buddi/	?		
braz /brac/	braccio /bračČo/	braț /brac/	brazzu /braccu/			
chane /čanə/	canna /kanna/	-R	canna /kanna/			
carre /karre/	quadrato /kwadrato/			?		
cent /cɛnt/	cento /čɛnto/	-R	chentu /kentu/			
cep /cɛp/	ceppo /čeppo/	cep /čep/		?		
cerf /cɛrf/	cervo /čɛrvo/	cerb /čerb/	cherbu /kerbu/			
certain /cɛrtɛyŋ/	certo /čɛrto/			?		
chaeine /čəeynə/	catena /katena/	-R	cadena /kadena/			
charn /čarn/	carne /karne/	carne /karne/				

Gloss		Spanish	Portuguese	Catalan	Occitan	Proto-SWR
53	'champ, campo'	campo /kampo/	campo /kãpu/	camp /kam/	camp /kamp/	
54	'chanson, canción'	canción /kanθyon/	canção /kãsãw/	cançó /kənsó/	cançon /kansú/	†
55	'chanter, cantar'	canta /kanta/	canta /kãta/	canta /kantə/	canta /kanto/	
56	'char, carro'	carro /kaʀo/	carro /kaʀu/	carro /kaʀu/	carri /kaʀi/	†
57	'charte, carta'	carta /karta/	carta /karta/	carta /kartə/	carta /karto/	
58	'chasser, cazar'	caza /kaθa/	caça /kasa/	caça /kasə/	caça /kaso/	
59	'chat, gato'	gato /gato/	gato /gatu/	gat /gat/	gat /gat/	
60	'château, castillo'	castillo /kastiʎo/	castelo /kastɛlu/	castell /kəsteʎ/	castèl /kastɛl/	
61	'châtier, castigar'	castiga /kastiga/	castiga /kastiga/	castiga /kəstigə/	castiga /kastigo/	
62	'chausser, calzar'	calza /kalθa/	calça /kalsa/	calça /kalsə/	calça /kalso/	
63	'chauve, calvo'	calvo /kalbo/	calvo /kalvu/	calb /kalp/	calvet /kalbet/	?
64	'chef, cabo'	cabo /kabo/	cabo /kabu/	cap /kap/	cap /kap/	
65	'chemin, camino'	camino /kamino/	caminho /kamiñu/	camí /kəmí/	camin /kamí/	
66	'cher, caro'	caro /karo/	caro /karu/	car /kar/	car /kar/	
67	'cheval, caballo'	caballo /kabaʎo/	cavalo /kavalu/	cavall /kəbaʎ/	caval /kabal/	
68	'cheveu, cabello'	cabello /kabeʎo/	cabelo /kabelu/	cabell /kəbɛʎ/	cabel /kabel/	
69	'chèvre, cabra'	cabra /kabra/	cabra /kabra/	cabra /kabrə/	cabra /kabro/	
70	'chien, can'	can /kan/	cão /kãw/	ca /ka/	can /ka/	
71	'chose, cosa'	cosa /kosa/	cousa /kowza/	cosa /kɔzə/	causa /kawzo/	
72	'chou, col'	col /kol/	couve /kowve/	col /kɔl/	caul /kawl/	?
73	'ciel, cielo'	cielo /θyelo/	céu /sɛw/	cel /sɛl/	cèl /sɛl/	
74	'cime, cima'	cima /θima/	cima /sima/	cima /simə/	cima /simo/	

A corpus of Romance lexical items / 205

Old French	Italian	Roumanian	Sardinian	Proto-Romance	Classical Latin
champ /čamp/	campo /kampo/	cîmp /kɨmp/	campu /kampu/		
chançon /čancuŋ/	canzone /kancone/			?	
chante /čantə/	canta /kanta/	cîntă /kɨntə/	canta /kanta/		
char /čar/	carro /karro/	car /kar/	carru /karru/		
chart(r)e /čartə/	carta /karta/	-R	carta /karta/		
chace /čacə/	caccia /kačča/		cazza /kacca/		*
chat /čat/	gatto /gatto/	-R	gattu /gattu/		*
chastel /častɛl/	castello /kastɛllo/		casteddu /kasteddu/		
chastie /častiə/	castiga /kastiga/	ciştigă /kɨštigə/			
chauce /čawcə/	calza /kalca/		calza /kalca/		≠
chauf /čawf/	calvo /kalvo/	-R		?	
chief /čyɛf/	capo /kapo/	cap /kap/	cabu /kabu/		≠
chemin /čəmiŋ/	cammino /kammino/	-R	caminu /kaminu/		*
chier /čyɛr/	caro /karo/	-R	caru /karu/		
cheval /čəval/	cavallo /kavallo/	cal /kal/	caddu /kaddu/		
chevel /čəvɛl/	capello /kapello/			?	
chievre /čyɛvrə/	capra /kapra/	capră /kaprə/	craba /kraba/		
chien /čyɛŋ/	cane /kane/	ciine /kɨyne/	cane /kane/		
chose /čozə/	cosa /kɔsa/			?	*
chol /čol/		-R		?	
ciel /cyɛl/	cielo /čɛlo/	cer /čer/	chelu /kelu/		
cime /cimə/	cima /čima/	-R	chima /kima/		

	Gloss	Spanish	Portuguese	Catalan	Occitan	Proto-SWR
75	'cinq, cinco'	cinco /θinko/	cinco /sīku/	cinc /siŋ/	cinc /sink/	
76	'cinquante, cincuenta'	cincuenta /θinkwenta/	cinqüenta /sīkwĕta/	cinquanta /siŋkwantə/	cinquanta /sinkanto/	
77	'cire, cera'	cera /θera/	cera /sera/	cera /sɛrə/	cera /sero/	
78	'clair, claro'	claro /klaro/	claro /klaru/	clar /kla/	clar /klar/	?
79	'clef, llave'	llave /ʎabe/	chave /šave/	clau /klaw/	clau /klaw/	?
80	'coeur, corazón'	corazón /koraθon/	coração /korasãw/	cor /kɔr/	còr /kor/	?
81	'colombe, paloma'	paloma /paloma/	pomba /pōba/	coloma /kuloma/	colomba /kulumbo/	?
82	'combien, cuanto'	cuanto /kwanto/	quanto /kwãtu/	quant /kwan/	quant /kant/	
83	'commencer, comenzar'	comienza /komyenθa/	começa /komɛsa/	comença /kumɛnsə/	comença /kumenso/	?
84	'conche, cuenca'	cuenca /kwenka/	conca /kōka/	conca /kɔŋkə/	conca /kunko/	
85	'connaître, conocer'	conoce /konoθe/	conhece /koñese/	koneix /kunɛš/	coneis /kuneys/	?
86	'conseil, consejo'	consejo /konsexo/	conselho /kōseʎu/	consell /kunsɛʎ/	conselh /kunsel/	
87	'conter, contar'	cuenta /kwenta/	conta /kōta/	conta /kɔntə/	conta /kunto/	
88	'contre, contra'	contra /kontra/	contra /kōtra/	contra /kontrə/	contra /kuntro/	
89	'coq, gallo'	gallo /gaʎo/	galo /galu/	gall /gaʎ/	gal /gal/	
90	'cor, cuerno'	cuerno /kwerno/	corno /kornu/	corn /kɔr/	còrn /kor/	
91	'corbeau, cuervo'	cuervo /kwerbo/	corvo /korvu/	corb /kɔrp/	còrb /korp/	
92	'corde, cuerda'	cuerda /kwerda/	corda /kɔrda/	corda /kɔrdə/	còrda /kordo/	
93	'corps, cuerpo'	cuerpo /kwerpo/	corpo /korpu/	cos /kɔs/	còs /kos/	?
94	'côte, cuesta'	cuesta /kwesta/	costa /kɔsta/	costa /kɔstə/	còsta /kosto/	
95	'cou, cuello'	cuello /kweʎo/	colo /kɔlu/	coll /kɔʎ/	còl /kol/	
96	'coudre, coser'	cose /kose/	cose /kɔze/	cos /kos/	cos /kus/	

A corpus of Romance lexical items / 207

Old French	Italian	Roumanian	Sardinian	Proto-Romance	Classical Latin
cinc /cink/	cinque /činkwe/	cinci /činč/	chimbe /kimbe/	?	
cincante /cinkantə/	cinquanta /cinkwanta/		chimbanta /kimbanta/		≠
cire /cirə/	cera /čera/	ceară /čarə/	chera /kera/		
clair /kler/	chiaro /kyaro/	chiar /kyar/	giaru /ǧaru/		
clef /klef/	chiave /kyave/	cheie /kyeye/	giae /ǧae/		
cuer /kör/	cuore /kwɔre/		coro /koro/	?	
colom /kulum/	colombo /kolombo/		columbu /kolumbu/	?	
cant, quant /kant/	quanto /kwanto/		cantu /kantu/		
comence /komɛncə/	comincia /kominča/		cominza /kominca/	?	*
conche /kunčə/	conca /konka/	-R	conca /konka/		
conois- /konoys-/	conosce /konošše/	cunoaşte /kunwašte/	konnosche /konnoske/	?	
conseil /kunsεʎ/	consiglio /konsiʎʎo/	-R	consizu /konsiẓẓu/		
conte /kuntə/	conta /konta/	-R	conta /konta/		≠
contre /kuntrə/	contra /kontra/		contra /kontra/		≠
jal /ǧal/	gallo /gallo/	-R		?	
corn /korn/	corno /kɔrno/	corn /korn/	corru /korru/		
corp /korp/	corbo /kɔrbo/	corb /korb/	corbu /korbu/		≠
corde /kordə/	corda /kɔrda/	coardă /kwardə/	corda /korda/		
cors /kors/	corpo /kɔrpo/	corp /korp/	corpus /korpus/	†	≠
coste /kostə/	costa /kɔsta/	coastă /kwastə/	costa /kosta/		
col /kol/	collo /kɔllo/	-R		?	
cos- /kuz-/	cuče /kuče/	coase /kwase/	cosi /kosi/	?	≠

	Gloss	Spanish	Portuguese	Catalan	Occitan	Proto-SWR
97	'couleur, color'	color /kolor/	côr /kor/	color /kuló/	color /kulù/	
98	'coupe, copa'	copa /kopa/	copa /kɔpa/	copa /kopə/	copa /kupo/	
99	'cour, corte'	corte /korte/	corte /korte/	cort /kort/	cort /kurt/	
100	'courir, correr'	corre /koRe/	corre /kɔRe/	corre /koRə/	cor /kur/	
101	'couronne, corona'	corona /korona/	coroa /koroa/	corona /kuronə/	corona /kuruno/	
102	'courroie, correa'	correa /koRea/	correia /koReya/	corretja /kuRɛdžə/	correja /kuRegŏ/	
103	'court, corto'	corto /korto/	curto /kurtu/	curt /kurt/	cort /kurt/	
104	'couteau, cuchillo'	cuchillo /kučiʎo/	cutelo /kutɛlu/	coltell /kulteʎ/	cotèl /kutɛl/	?
105	'coûter, costar'	cuesta /kwesta/	custa /kusta/	costa /kostə/	costa /kusto/	?
106	'couvert, cubierto'	cubierto /kubyerto/	coberto /kobɛrtu/	cobert /kubɛrt/	cobèrt /kubɛrt/	
107	'couvrir, cubrir'	cubre /kubre/	cobre /kɔbre/	cobre /kɔbrə/	cuèrp /kɛrp/	?
108	'craindre, temer'	teme /teme/	teme /tɛme/	tem /tɛm/	tem /tem/	
109	'croire, creer'	cree /kree/	crê /kre/	creu /krɛw/	cretz /krec/	?
110	'croître, crecer'	crece /kreθe/	crece /krɛse/	creix /krɛš/	creis /kreys/	krece / kreyse
111	'croix, cruz'	cruz /kruθ/	cruz /krus/	creu /krɛw/	crotz /kruc/	
112	'cru, crudo'	crudo /krudo/	cru /kru/	cru /kru/	cru /krü/	krudo / kru
113	'cruel, cruel'	cruel /kruel/	cruel /kruɛl/	cruel /kruɛl/	crusèl /krüzɛl/	?
114	'cueillir, coger'	coge /koxe/	colhe /kɔʎe/	cull /kuʎ/	cuèlh /kɛl/	
115	'cuir, cuero'	cuero /kwero/	coiro /koyru/	cuir /kuyr/	cuèr /kɛr/	±
116	'cuire, cocer'	cuece /kweθe/	coze /kɔze/	cou /kɔw/	còtz /koc/	
117	'cuisine, cocina'	cocina /koθina/	cozinha /koziña/	cuina /kuinə/	cosina /kuzino/	
118	'cuisse, muslo'	. . .	coxa /koša/	cuixa /kušə/	cuèissa /kɛyso/	?

A corpus of Romance lexical items

Old French	Italian	Roumanian	Sardinian	Proto-Romance	Classical Latin
color /kulör/	colore /kolore/	culoare /kulware/	colore /kolore/		
cope /kupə/	coppa /koppa/	-R	cuppa /kuppa/		
cort /kurt/	corte /korte/		corte /korte/		
cor- /kur-/	corre /korre/		curre /kurre/		
corone /kuronə/	corona /korona/		corona /korona/		
correie /kuʀeyə/	correggia /korreġġa/		corria /korria/		
cort /kurt/	corto /korto/			?	
coutel /kutɛl/	coltello /koltɛllo/	-R		?	
coste /kustə/	costa /kɔsta/		costa /kosta/	?	
covert /kuvɛrt/	coperto /kopɛrto/		cobertu /kobertu/		
cuevre /kövrə/	copre /kɔpre/	coperă /kópera/	cobere /kóbere/		≠
. . .	teme /teme/	teme /teme/	time /time/		
crei- /krey-/	crede /krede/	crede /krede/	cree /kree/		
creis- /kreys-/	cresce /krešše/	creşte /krešte/	cresche /kreske/		
croiz /kroyc/	croce /kroče/	cruce /kruče/			
cru /krü/	crudo /krudo/	crud /krud/	cruu /kruu/		
cruel /krüɛl/	crudele /krudele/			?	
cueill- /köʎ-/	coglie /kɔʎʎe/	culege /kuleğe/		?	
cuir /küyr/	cuoio /kwɔyo/		corzu /korẓu/	?	
cuis- /küyz-/	cuoce /kwɔče/	coace /kwače/	coghe /koge/		
cuisine /küyzinə/	cucina /kučina/	-R	coghina /kogina/		
cuisse /küysə/	coscia /kɔšša/	coapsă /kwapsə/	cossa /kossa/	?	

Gloss		Spanish	Portuguese	Catalan	Occitan	Proto-SWR
119	'cul, culo'	culo /kulo/	cu /ku/	cul /kul/	cuòl /küol/	?
120	'degré, grado'	grado /grado/	grau /graw/	grau /graw/	gras /gras/	?
121	'déjà, ya'	ya /ya/	já /ža/	ja /ža/	ja /ǧa/	
122	'dent, diente'	diente /dyente/	dente /děte/	dent /den/	dent /dent/	
123	'dépit, despecho'	despecho /despečo/	despeito /despeytu/	despit /dəspit/	despièch /despyɛč/	
124	'devoir, deber'	debe /debe/	deve /dɛve/	deu /dɛw/	deu /dew/	
125	'dieu, dios'	dios /dyos/	deus /dews/	deu /dew/	dièu /dyɛw/	?
126	'dire, decir'	dice /diθe/	dize /dize/	diu /diw/	ditz /dic/	
127	'dix, diez'	diez /dyeθ/	dez /dɛs/	deu /dɛw/	dètz /dɛc/	
128	'doigt, dedo'	dedo /dedo/	dedo /dedu/	dit /dit/	det /det/	
129	'dommage, daño'	daño /daño/	dano /danu/	dany /dañ/	dam /dam/	
130	'donner, dar'	da /da/	dá /da/	da /da/	da /da/	
131	'donner, donar'	dona /dona/	doa /doa/	dona /donə/	dona /duno/	
132	'dormir, dormir'	duerme /dwerme/	dorme /dɔrme/	dorm /dɔrm/	dòrm /dorm/	
133	'douleur, dolor'	dolor /dolor/	dor /dor/	dolor /duló/	dolor /dulú/	
134	'doux, dulce'	dulce /dulθe/	doce /dose/	dolç /dols/	doç /dus/	du(l)ce do(l)ce
135	'douze, doce'	doce /doθe/	doze /doze/	dotze /dodzə/	dotze /duʒe/	?
136	'droit, derecho'	derecho /derečo/	direito /direytu/	dret /drɛt/	drech /dreč/	?
137	'dur, duro'	duro /duro/	duro /duru/	dur /dur/	dur /dür/	
138	'échapper, escapar'	escapa /eskapa/	escapa /eskapa/	escapa /əskapə/	escapa /eskapo/	
139	'échelle, escala'	escala /eskala/	escala /eskala/	escala /əskalə/	escala /eskalo/	eskala eskaʟa
140	'école, escuela'	escuela /eskwela/	escola /eskɔla/	escola /əskɔlə/	escòla /eskolo/	

A corpus of Romance lexical items

OLD FRENCH	ITALIAN	ROUMANIAN	SARDINIAN	PROTO-ROMANCE	CLASSICAL LATIN
cul /kül/	culo /kulo/	cur /kur/	culu /kulu/		
degre /dəgre/	grado /grado/	grad /grad/		±	
ja /ǧa/	già /ǧa/		ja /ya/		
dent /dɛnt/	dente /dɛnte/	dinte /dinte/	dente /dente/		
despit /dɛspit/	dispetto /dispɛtto/	-R	dispettu /dispettu/		
deiv- /deyv-/	deve /deve/	-R		?	
dieu /dyö/	dio /dio/	zeu /zew/	deus /deus/	?	
dis- /diz-/	dice /diče/	zice /ziče/			
diz /dic/	dieci /dyɛči/	zece /zeče/	deghe /dege/	†	
dei /dey/	dito /dito/	deget /déget/		?	
dam /dam/	danno /danno/	daună /dawnə/		?	
...	da /da/	dă /də/	da /da/		
done /donə/	dona /dona/		dona /dona/		
dorm- /dorm-/	dorme /dɔrme/	doarme /dwarme/	dormi /dormi/		
dolor /dulör/	dolore /dolore/		dolore /dolore/		
douz /duc/	dolce /dolče/	dulce /dulče/	dulche /dulke/		
doze /duẓə/	dodici /dódiči/		doighi /dóigi/	?	
dreit /dreyt/	diretto /diretto/	drept /drept/	derettu /derettu/	?	
dur /dür/	duro /duro/	dur /dur/	duru /duru/		
eschape /ɛsčapə/	scappa /skappa/	scapă /skapə/		±	*
eschiele /ɛsčyɛlə/	scala /skala/	scară /skarə/	iscala /iskala/	±	
escole /ɛskolə/	scuola /skwɔla/		iscola /iskola/	±	

212 / Appendix 1

Gloss		Spanish	Portuguese	Catalan	Occitan	Proto-SWR	
141	'écouter, escuchar'	escucha /eskuča/	escuta /eskuta/	escolta /əskoltə/	escota /eskuto/	?	
142	'écrire, escribir'	escribe /eskribe/	escreve /eskrɛve/	escriu /əskriw/	escriu /eskriw/		
143	'écrit, escrito'	escrito /eskrito/	escrito /eskritu/	escrit /əskrit/	escrit /eskrit/		
144	'écu, escudo'	escudo /eskudo/	escudo /eskudu/	escut /əskut/	escut /esküt/		
145	'enfer, infierno'	infierno /infyerno/	inferno /ĩfɛrnu/	infern /infɛr/	infèrn /infɛr/		
146	'enfler, hinchar'	hincha /inča/	incha /ĩša/	infla /inflə/	enfla /enflo/	?	
147	'entendre, entender'	entiende /entyende/	entende /ẽtẽde/	entén /ənten/	entén /enten/		
148	'entrer, entrar'	entra /entra/	entra /ẽtra/	entra /ɛntrə/	intra /intro/		
149	'épais, espeso'	espeso /espeso/	espesso /espesu/	espès /əspɛs/	espés /espes/		
150	'épée, espada'	espada /espada/	espada /espada/	espasa /əspazə/	espasa /espazo/	espada espaza	
151	'épi, espiga'	espiga /espiga/	espiga /espiga/	espiga /əspigə/	espiga /espigo/		
152	'épine, espina'	espina /espina/	espinha /espiña/	espina /əspinə/	espina /espino/		
153	'époux, esposo'	esposo /esposo/	esposo /espozu/	espòs /əspɔs/	espos /espus/		
154	'espérer, esperar'	espera /espera/	espera /espɛra/	espera /əspɛrə/	espera /espero/		
155	'ais, eje'	eje /exe/	eixo /eyšu/	eix /eš/	ais /ays/		
156	'étoile, estrella'	estrella /estreʎa/	estrela /estrɛla/	estrella /əstreʎə/	estèla /estɛlo/	?	
157	'étoupe, estopa'	estopa /estopa/	estopa /estopa/	estopa /əstopə/	estopa /estupo/		
158	'être, estar'	está /está/	está /está/	está /əstá/	está /está/		
159	'étroit, estrecho'	estrecho /estrečo/	estreito /estreytu/	estret /əstrɛt/	estrech /estreč/		
160	'face, haz'	haz /aθ/	face /fase/	faç /fas/	fàcia /fasyo/	?	
161	'faim, hambre'	hambre /ambre/	fome /fɔme/	fam /fam/	fam /fam/	?	
162	'faire, hacer'	hace /aθe/	faze /faze/	fa /fa/	fa /fa/	(f)aʒe (f)a	

Old French	Italian	Roumanian	Sardinian	Proto-Romance	Classical Latin
escoute /ɛskutə/	ascolta /askolta/	ascultă /askultə/	isculta /iskulta/		≠ ≠
escriv- /ɛskriv-/	scrive /skrive/	scrie /skrie/	iscrie /iskrie/	±	
escrit /ɛskrit/	scritto /skritto/		iscrittu /iskrittu/	±	
escu /ɛskü/	scudo /skudo/	scut /skut/	iscudu /iskudu/	±	≠ ≠
enfern /ɛnfɛrn/	inferno /infɛrno/		inferru /inferru/	?	
enfle /ɛnflə/	enfia /enfya/			?	
entend- /ɛntɛnd-/	intende /intɛnde/	întinde /ɨntinde/	intende /intende/		
entre /ɛntrə/	entra /entra/		intra /intra/		
espes /ɛspɛs/	spesso /spesso/			±	
espee /ɛspeə/	spada /spada/		ispada /ispada/	±	≠
espi /ɛspi/	spiga /spiga/	spic /spik/	ispiga /ispiga/	?	
espine /ɛspinə/	spina /spina/	spin /spin/	ispina /ispina/	±	
espos /ɛspus/	sposo /sposo/	-R	isposu /isposu/	±	
espeire /ɛspeyrə/	spera /spera/		ispera /ispera/	±	
ais /ɛys/	asse /asse/	-R	asse /asse/		
esteile /ɛsteylə/	stella /stella/	stea /stea/	isteddu /isteddu/	?	
estope /ɛstupə/	stoppa /stoppa/	-R	istuppa /istuppa/	±	
. . .	sta /sta/	stă /stə/	istá /istá/	±	
estreit /ɛstreyt/	stretto /stretto/			?	
face /facə/	faccia /faččа/	faţă /facə/		*	≠
faim /fɛym/	fame /fame/			?	
fai- /fɛy-/	fa /fa/	face /fače/	faghe /fage/	±	

214 / Appendix 1

	Gloss	Spanish	Portuguese	Catalan	Occitan	Proto-SWR
163	'faire mal, doler'	duele /dwele/	dói /dɔy/	dol /dɔl/	dòl /dol/	
164	'fait, hecho'	hecho /eč̌o/	feito /feytu/	fet /fet/	fach /fač/	± _____
165	'farine, harina'	harina /arina/	farinha /fariña/	farina /fərinə/	farina /farino/	± _____
166	'faux, falso'	falso /falso/	falso /falsu/	fals /fals/	fals /fals/	
167	'faux, hoz'	hoz /oθ/	fouce /fowse/	falç /fals/	falç /fals/	(f)awce (f)alce
168	'fée, hada'	hada /ada/	fada /fada/	fada /fadə/	fada /fado/	± _____
169	'femme, hembra'	hembra /embra/	fêmea /fêmia/	fembra /fɛmbrə/	femna /femno/	?
170	'femme, mujer'	mujer /muxer/	mulher /muʎɛr/	muller /muʎé/	molhèr /muʎέ/	
171	'fendre, hender'	hiende /yende/	fende /fẽde/	fen /fen/	fend /fen/	± _____
172	'fer, hierro'	hierro /yeRo/	ferro /fɛRu/	ferro /fɛRu/	fèrre /fɛRe/	± _____
173	'fête, fiesta'	fiesta /fyesta/	festa /fɛsta/	festa /festə/	fèsta /fɛsto/	
174	'feu, fuego'	fuego /fwego/	fogo /fogu/	foc /fɔk/	fòc /fok/	
175	'feuille, hoja'	hoja /oxa/	folha /fɔʎa/	fulla /fuʎə/	fuèlha /fɛʎo/	± _____
176	'fève, haba'	haba /aba/	fava /fava/	fava /fabə/	fava /favo/	± (f)ava
177	'fiel, hiel'	hiel /yel/	fel /fɛl/	fel /fɛl/	fèl /fɛl/	± _____
178	'fièvre, fiebre'	fiebre /fyebre/	febre /fɛbre/	febre /febrə/	fèbre /fɛbre/	
179	'fil, hilo'	hilo /ilo/	fio /fiu/	fil /fil/	fil /fil/	± _____
180	'fille, hija'	hija /ixa/	filha /fiʎa/	filla /fiʎə/	filha /fiʎo/	± _____
181	'fils, hijo'	hijo /ixo/	filho /fiʎu/	fill /fiʎ/	filh /fil/	± _____
182	'fin, fin'	fin /fin/	fim /fi/	fi /fi/	fin /fi/	
183	'flamme, llama'	llama /ʎama/	chama /šama/	flama /flamə/	flama /flamo/	?
184	'fleur, flor'	flor /flor/	flor /flor/	flor /flo/	flor /flur/	?

A corpus of Romance lexical items / 215

OLD FRENCH	ITALIAN	ROUMANIAN	SARDINIAN	PROTO-ROMANCE	CLASSICAL LATIN
duel- /döl-/	duole /dwɔle/	doare /dware/	dole /dole/		
fait /fɛyt/	fatto /fatto/	fapt /fapt/	fattu /fattu/		
farine /farinə/	farina /farina/		farina /farina/		
faus /faws/	falso /falso/			?	
fauz /fawc/	falce /falče/	falce /falče/	falche /falke/		
fee /feə/	fata /fata/	-R	fada /fada/		≠
feme /fɛnmə/	femmina /fɛmmina/		fèmina /fɛmina/	?	
moillier /muʎyɛr/	moglie /moʎʎe/	muiere /muyere/	muzere /muẓẓere/		
fend- /fɛnd-/	fende /fɛnde/	-R		?	
fer /fɛr/	ferro /fɛrro/	fier /fyer/	ferru /ferru/		
feste /fɛstə/	festa /fɛsta/	-R	festa /festa/		≠
feu /fö/	fuoco /fwɔko/	foc /fok/	fogu /fogu/		
fueille /föʎə/	foglia /fɔʎʎa/	foaie /fwaye/	foza /foẓẓa/		≠
feve /fevə/	fava /fava/	-R	fa /fa/		
fiel /fyɛl/	fiele /fyɛle/	fiere /fyere/	fele /fele/		≠
fievre /fyɛvrə/	febbre /fɛbbre/			?	
fil /fil/	filo /filo/	fir /fir/	filu /filu/		
fille /fiʎə/	figlia /fiʎʎa/	fie /fie/	fiza /fiẓẓa/		
fil /fiʎ/	figlio /fiʎʎo/	fiu /fiw/	fizu /fiẓẓu/		
fin /fiŋ/	fine /fine/		fine /fine/		
flame /flamə/	fiamma /fyamma/		fiamma /fyamma/	*	
flor /flör/	fiore /fyore/	floare /flware/	fiore /fyore/		

216 / Appendix 1

	Gloss	Spanish	Portuguese	Catalan	Occitan	Proto-SWR
185	'floc, copo'	...	froco /frɔku/	floc /flok/	floc /fluk/	?
186	'foi, fe'	fe /fe/	fé /fɛ/	fe /fɛ/	fe /fe/	
187	'foin, heno'	heno /eno/	fenu /fenu/	fe /fɛ/	fen /fe/	(f)eno (f)eNo
188	'fontaine, fuente'	fuente /fwente/	fonte /fõte/	font /fɔn/	font /funt/	
189	'force, fuerza'	fuerza /fwerθa/	força /fɔrsa/	força /fɔrsə/	fòrça /forso/	
190	'fort, fuerte'	fuerte /fwerte/	forte /fɔrte/	fort /fɔrt/	fòrt /fort/	
191	'four, horno'	horno /orno/	forno /fornu/	forn /for/	forn /fur/	±
192	'fourche, horca'	horca /orka/	forca /forka/	forca /forkə/	forca /furko/	±
193	'fourmi, hormiga'	hormiga /ormiga/	formiga /formiga/	formiga /furmigə/	formiga /furmigo/	±
194	'frais, fresco'	fresco /fresko/	fresco /fresku/	fresc /frɛsk/	fresc /fresk/	
195	'frein, freno'	freno /freno/	freio /freyu/	fre /frɛ/	fren /fre/	
196	'front, frente'	frente /frente/	fronte /frõte/	front /frɔn/	front /frunt/	
197	'fruit, fruta'	fruta /fruta/	fruta /fruta/	fruita /fruytə/	frucha /früčo/	
198	'fuir, huir'	huye /uye/	foge /fɔže/	fuig /fuč/	fug /füč/	?
199	'fumée, humo'	humo /umo/	fumo /fumu/	fum /fum/	fum /füm/	±
200	'fumer, fumar'	fuma /fuma/	fuma /fuma/	fuma /fumə/	fuma /fümo/	
201	'garder, guardar'	guarda /gwarda/	guarda /gwarda/	guarda /gwardə/	garda /gardo/	
202	'geler, helar'	hiela /yela/	geia /žeya/	gela /ʒɛlə/	gèla /ǰɛlo/	
203	'geline, gallina'	gallina /gaʎina/	galinha /galiña/	gallina /gəʎinə/	galina /galino/	
204	'gendre, yerno'	yerno /yerno/	genro /žẽru/	gendre /ʒɛndrə/	gendre /ǰendre/	?
205	'gens, gente'	gente /xente/	gente /žẽte/	gent /ʒen/	gent /ǰent/	?
206	'gland, landre'	landre /landre/	lande /lãde/	glan /glan/	aglan /aglá/	?

A corpus of Romance lexical items / 217

OLD FRENCH	ITALIAN	ROUMANIAN	SARDINIAN	PROTO-ROMANCE	CLASSICAL LATIN
floc /flok/	fiocco /fyɔkko/	floc /flok/	fioccu /fyokku/	*	
fei /fey/	fede /fede/	-R		?	
fein /feyŋ/	fieno /fyɛno/	fîn /fɨn/	fenu /fenu/		
font /funt/	fonte /fonte/			?	
force /forcə/	forza /fɔrca/		forza /forca/		*
fort /fort/	forte /fɔrte/	foarte /fwarte/	forte /forte/		
forn /furn/	forno /forno/	-R	furru /furru/		
forche /furčə/	forca /forka/	furcă /furkə/	furca /furka/		
formie /furmiə/	formica /formika/		formiga /formiga/	?	
freis /freys/	fresco /fresko/	-R	friscu /frisku/		*
frein /freyŋ/	freno /freno/	frîu /frɨw/	frenu /frenu/		
front /frunt/	fronte /fronte/	frunte /frunte/	fronte /fronte/		
fruit /früyt/	frutta /frutta/	frupt /frupt/		?	
fui- /füy-/	fugge /fuǧǧe/	fuge /fuǧe/	fui /fui/		≠
fumee /fümeə/	fumo /fumo/	fum /fum/	fumu /fumu/	?	
fume /fümə/	fuma /fuma/		fuma /fuma/		
garde /gardə/	guarda /gwarda/	-R		?	*
giele /ǧyɛlə/	gela /ǧela/		gela /gela/		≠
geline /ǧəlinə/	gallina /gallina/	găină /gəinə/			
gendre /ǧɛndrə/	genero /ǧɛnero/	ginere /ǧinere/	génneru /génneru/		≠
gent /ǧɛnt/	gente /ǧɛnte/	ginte /ǧinte/		*	
glant /glant/	ghianda /gyanda/	ghindă /gində/		?	

Gloss	Spanish	Portuguese	Catalan	Occitan	Proto-SWR
207 'goût, gusto'	gusto /gusto/	gosto /gostu/	gust /gust/	gost /gust/	
208 'goutte, gota'	gota /gota/	gota /gota/	gota /gotə/	gota /guto/	
209 'gouverner, gobernar'	gobierna /gobyerna/	governa /govɛrna/	governa /gubɛrnə/	govèrna /gubɛrno/	
210 'grain, grano'	grano /grano/	grão /grãw/	gra /gra/	gran /gra/	
211 'grand, grande'	grande /grande/	grande /grãde/	gran /gran/	grand /grant/	
212 'gros, grueso'	grueso /grweso/	grosso /grɔsu/	gros /grɔs/	gròs /gros/	
213 'guerre, guerra'	guerra /gɛʀa/	guerra /gɛʀa/	guerra /gɛʀə/	guèrra /gɛʀo/	
214 'gueule, gola'	gola /gola/	gola /gɔla/	gola /golə/	gola /gulo/	
215 'guise, guisa'	guisa /gisa/	guisa /giza/	guisa /gizə/	guisa /gizo/	
216 'hausser, alzar'	alza /alθa/	alça /alsa/	alça /alsə/	alça /also/	
217 'haut, alto'	alto /alto/	alto /altu/	alt /al/	alt /alt/	
218 'herbe, hierba'	hierba /yerba/	herva /ɛrva/	herba /ɛrbə/	èrba /ɛrbo/	
219 'heure, hora'	hora /ora/	hora /ɔra/	hora /ɔrə/	ora /uro/	
220 'hier, ayer'	ayer /ayer/	. . .	ahir /əi/	ièr /yɛr/	?
221 'hiver, invierno'	invierno /imbierno/	inverno /īvɛrnu/	hivern /ibɛr/	ivèrn /ibɛr/	±
222 'homme, hombre'	hombre /ombre/	homem /ɔmẽ/	home /ɔmə/	òme /ome/	?
223 'huit, ocho'	ocho /očo/	oito /oytu/	vuit /buyt/	uèch /ɛč/	
224 'île, isla'	isla /isla/	ilha /iʎa/	illa /iʎə/	illa /illo/	?
225 'jeu, juego'	juego /xwego/	jogo /žogu/	joc /žɔk/	jòc /ǧok/	?
226 'jouer, jugar'	juega /xwega/	joga /žɔga/	joga /žɔgə/	jòga /ǧogo/	?
227 'joug, yugo'	yugo /yugo/	jugo /žugu/	jou /žow/	jo /ǧu/	?
228 'jour, dia'	dia /dia/	dia /dia/	dia /diə/	. . .	* dia

A corpus of Romance lexical items / 219

OLD FRENCH	ITALIAN	ROUMANIAN	SARDINIAN	PROTO-ROMANCE	CLASSICAL LATIN
gost	gusto	gust	gustu		
/gust/	/gusto/	/gust/	/gustu/		
gote	gotta	gută	gutta		
/gutə/	/gotta/	/gutə/	/gutta/		
governe	govɛrna	-R	guverna		
/guvɛrnə/	/govɛrna/		/guberna/		
grain	grano	grîu			
/grɛyŋ/	/grano/	/grɨw/		?	
grant	grande	-R			
/grant/	/grande/			?	
gros	grosso	gros			
/gros/	/grɔsso/	/gros/			
guerre	guerra	-R			
/gɛʀə/	/gwɛrra/			?	*
gole	gola	gură	gula		
/gölə/	/gola/	/gurə/	/gula/		
guise	guisa	-R			
/gizə/	/gwisa/			?	*
hauce	alza	înalță	alza		
/hawcə/	/alca/	/-alcə/	/alca/	‡	*
haut	alto	înalt	altu		
/hawt/	/alto/	/-alt/	/altu/	‡	
erbe	erba	iarbă	erba		
/ɛrbə/	/ɛrba/	/yarbə/	/erba/		
ore	ora	oară	ora		
/örə/	/ora/	/warə/	/ora/		
ier	ieri	ieri	eris		
/yɛr/	/yɛri/	/yery/	/eris/	?	
ivern	inverno		jerru		
/ivɛrn/	/invɛrno/		/yerru/	±	
ome	uomo	om	ómine		
/omə/	/wɔmo/	/om/	/ómine/	?	
uit	otto	opt	otto		
/üyt/	/ɔtto/	/opt/	/otto/		
isle	isola		isula		
/islə/	/isola/		/ísula/	*	
gieu	giuoco	joc			
/ǧö/	/ǧwɔko/	/žok/		*	
joe	giuoca	joacă			
/ǧuə/	/ǧwɔka/	/žwakə/		*	
jo(u)	giogo	jug	juu		
/ǧu/	/ǧogo/	/žug/	/yuu/		
di	di	zi	die		≠
/di/	/di/	/zi/	/die/	±	≠

Gloss		Spanish	Portuguese	Catalan	Occitan	Proto-SWR
229	'juin, junio'	junio /xunio/	junho /žuñu/	juny /žuñ/	junh /ǧün/	?
230	'jument, yegua'	yegua /yegwa/	egua /ɛgwa/	egua /egwə/	èga /ɛgo/	
231	'lac, lago'	lago /lago/	lago /lagu/	llac /ʎak/	lac /lak/	
232	'lacs, lazo'	lazo /laθo/	laço /lasu/	llaç /ʎas/	laç /las/	
233	'laine, lana'	lana /lana/	lã /lã/	llana /ʎanə/	lana /lano/	
234	'laisser, dejar'	deja /dexa/	deixa /deyša/	deixa /dešə/	daisa /dayso/	
235	'lait, leche'	leche /leče/	leite /leyte/	llet /ʎet/	lach /lač/	
236	'laitue, lechuga'	lechuga /lečuga/	leituga /leytuga/	lletuga /ʎətugə/	lachuga /lačügo/	
237	'lance, lanza'	lanza /lanθa/	lança /lãsa/	llança /ʎansə/	lança /lanso/	
238	'langue, lengua'	lengua /lengwa/	língua /lĩgwa/	llengua /ʎengwə/	lenga /lengo/	
239	'lapin, conejo'	conejo /konexo/	coelho /koeʎu/	conill /kuniʎ/	conilh /kunil/	
240	'large, largo'	largo /largo/	largo /largu/	llarc /ʎark/	larg /lark/	
241	'larme, lágrima'	lágrima /lágrima/	lágrima /lágrima/	llágrima /ʎágrimə/	lágrema /lágremo/	?
242	'laver, lavar'	lava /laba/	lava /lava/	llava /ʎabə/	lava /labo/	
243	'lettre, letra'	letra /letra/	letra /letra/	lletra /ʎɛtrə/	letra /letro/	
244	'lever, llevar'	lleva /ʎeba/	leva /lɛva/	lleva /ʎebə/	lèva /lɛbo/	?
245	'lier, ligar'	liga /liga/	liga /liga/	lliga /ʎigə/	liga /ligo/	
246	'lieu, luego'	luego /lwego/	logo /lɔgu/	lloc /ʎɔk/	lòc /lok/	
247	'lièvre, liebre'	liebre /lyebre/	lebre /lɛbre/	llebre /ʎebrə/	lèbre /lɛbre/	
248	'lin, lino'	lino /lino/	linho /liñu/	lli /ʎi/	lin /li/	
249	'linceul, lenzuelo'	lenzuelo /lenθwelo/	lençol /lẽsɔl/	llençol /ʎənsɔl/	lençòl /lensol/	±
250	'lion, león'	león /leon/	leão /leãw/	lleó /ʎəó/	leon /leú/	

Old French	Italian	Roumanian	Sardinian	Proto-Romance	Classical Latin
juin /ǧüyñ/	giugno /ǧuñño/	-R		?	
ieue /yɛwə/	...	iapă /yapə/	ebba /ebba/	?	
lai /lɛy/	lago /lago/	lac /lak/	lagu /lagu/		
laz /lac/	laccio /lačč̌o/	-R	lazzu /laccu/		
laine /lɛynə/	lana /lana/	lînă /lɨnə/	lana /lana/		
laisse /lɛysə/	lascia /lašša/		lassa /lassa/	?	
lait /lɛyt/	latte /latte/	lapte /lapte/	latte /latte/		
laitue /lɛytüə/	lattuga /lattuga/	lăptucă /ləptukə/	lattuga /lattuga/		≠
lance /lancə/	lancia /lanča/		lanza /lanca/		
lengue /lɛŋgə/	lingua /lingwa/	limbă /limbə/	limba /limba/		≠
conil /koniʎ/	coniglio /koniʎʎo/	-R		?	
larc /lark/	largo /largo/	larg /larg/	largu /largu/		
larme /larmə/	lacrima /lákrima/	lacrimă /lákrimə/	lágrima /lágrima/		
leve /levə/	lava /lava/	lă /lə/			
letre /lɛtrə/	lettera /léttera/		littera /littera/		
lieve /lyɛvə/	leva /lɛva/	ia /ya/	leba /leba/	†	
leie /leyə/	lega /lega/	leagă /leagə/	lia /lia/		≠
lieu /lyö/	luogo /lwɔgo/	loc /lok/	logu /logu/		
lievre /lyɛvrə/	lepre /lɛpre/	iepure /yépure/		?	
lin /liŋ/	lino /lino/	in /in/	linu /linu/		
linçuel /lincöl/	lenzuolo /lenzwɔlo/			?	
lion /liuŋ/	leone /leone/		leone /leone/		

	Gloss	Spanish	Portuguese	Catalan	Occitan	Proto-SWR
251	'lit, lecho'	lecho /lečo/	leito /leytu/	llit /ʎit/	lièch /lyɛč/	
252	'loi, ley'	ley /ley/	lei /ley/	llei /ʎey/	lei /ley/	
253	'lombe(s), lomo'	lomo /lomo/	lombo /lõbu/	llom /ʎom/	lom /lum/	±
254	'long, luengo'	luengo /lwengo/	longo /lõgu/	...	long /lunk/	*
255	'louer, loar'	loa /loa/	louva /lowva/	lloa /ʎoə/	lausa /lawzo/	?
256	'loup, lobo'	lobo /lobo/	lobo /lobu/	llop /ʎop/	lop /lup/	
257	'lumière, lumbre'	lumbre /lumbre/	lume /lume/	llum /ʎum/	lum /lüm/	±
258	'lumière, luz'	luz /luθ/	luz /lus/	...	lutz /lüc/	*
259	'lune, luna'	luna /luna/	lua /lua/	lluna /ʎunə/	luna /lüno/	
260	'mai, mayo'	mayo /mayo/	maio /mayu/	maig /mač/	mai /may/	
261	'main, mano'	mano /mano/	mão /mãw/	ma /ma/	man /ma/	
262	'maison, casa'	casa /kasa/	casa /kaza/	casa /kazə/	casa /kazo/	
263	'majeur, mayor'	mayor /mayor/	maior /mayɔr/	major /məžó/	major /mağú/	?
264	'mal, mal'	mal /mal/	mal /mal/	mal /mal/	mal /mal/	
265	'mauvais, malo'	malo /malo/	mau /maw/	mal /mal/	mal /mal/	
266	'mâle, macho'	macho /mačo/	macho /mašu/	mascle /masklə/	mascle /maskle/	?
267	'manche, manga'	manga /manga/	manga /mãga/	mánega /mánəgə/	marga /margo/	?
268	'marché, mercado'	mercado /merkado/	mercado /merkadu/	mercat /mərkat/	mercat /merkat/	
269	'mari, marido'	marido /marido/	marido /maridu/	marit /mərit/	marit /marit/	
270	'mars, marzo'	marzo /marθo/	março /marsu/	març /mars/	març /mars/	
271	'marteau, martillo'	martillo /martiʎo/	martelo /martɛlu/	martell /mərteʎ/	martèl /martɛl/	
272	'menace, amenaza'	amenaza /amenaθa/	ameaça /ameasa/	amenaça /əmənasə/	menaça /menaso/	±

A corpus of Romance lexical items / 223

Old French	Italian	Roumanian	Sardinian	Proto-Romance	Classical Latin
lit /lit/	letto /lɛtto/	-R	lettu /lettu/		
lei /ley/	legge /lɛğğe/	lege /leğe/			
lombe /lumbə/	lombo /lombo/	-R	lumbu /lumbu/		
lonc /luŋk/	lungo /lungo/	lung /lung/	longu /longu/		≠
loe /luə/	loda /lɔda/	laudă /lawdə/		*	
leu /lö/	lupo /lupo/	lup /lup/			≠
lumiere /lümyɛrə/	lume /lume/	lume /lume/		?	
. . .	luce /luče/		lughe /luge/	*	
lune /lünə/	luna /luna/	lună /lunə/	luna /luna/		
mai /mɛy/	maggio /mağğo/	-R	maju /mayu/		
main /mɛyŋ/	mano /mano/	mînă /mɨnə/	manu /manu/		≠
chiese /čyɛzə/	casa /kasa/	casă /kasə/			
maior /mayör/	maggiore /mağğore/	-R	majore /mayore/	*	
mel /mel/	male /male/		male /male/		
mel /mel/	malo /malo/			?	
masle /maslə/	maschio /maskyo/	mascur /máskur/		?	
manche /mančə/	manica /mánika/	mîneca /mɨnekə/	mániga /mániga/		
marchie /marčye/	mercato /merkato/	-R		?	
mari /mari/	marito /marito/			?	
marz /marc/	marzo /marco/				
martel /martɛl/	martello /martɛllo/	-R	marteddu /marteddu/		*
menace /mənacə/	minaccia /mináčča/			?	

224 / Appendix 1

	Gloss	Spanish	Portuguese	Catalan	Occitan	Proto-SWR
273	'mer, mar'	mar /mar/	mar /mar/	mar /mar/	mar /mar/	
274	'merci, merced'	merced /merθed/	mercê /mersé/	mercè /mərsέ/	mercé /mersé/	mercede mercé
275	'mesure, mesura'	mesura /mesura/	mesura /mezura/	mesura /məzurə/	mesura /mezüro/	
276	'mettre, meter'	mete /mete/	mete /mɛte/	met /mɛt/	met /met/	
277	'mi-, medio'	medio /medyo/	meio /meyu/	mig /mič/	mièg /myɛč/	?
278	'miel, miel'	miel /myel/	mel /mɛl/	mel /mɛl/	mèl /mɛl/	
279	'mille, mil'	mil /mil/	mil /mil/	mil /mil/	mil /mil/	
280	'mois, mes'	mes /mes/	mès /mes/	mes /mɛs/	mes /mes/	
281	'monnaie, moneda'	moneda /moneda/	moeda /moeda/	moneda /munɛdə/	moneda /munedo/	
282	'mont, monte'	monte /monte/	monte /mõte/	mont /mon/	mont /munt/	
283	'mordre, morder'	muerde /mwerde/	morde /mɔrde/	. . .	mòrd /mort/	*
284	'mort, muerte'	muerte /mwerte/	morte /mɔrte/	mort /mɔrt/	mòrt /mort/	
285	'mort, muerto'	muerto /mwerto/	morto /mɔrtu/	mort /mɔrt/	mòrt /mort/	
286	'mou, muelle'	muelle /mweʎe/	mole /mɔle/	moll /mɔ /	mòl /mol/	
287	'mouche, mosca'	mosca /moska/	mosca /moska/	mosca /moskə/	mosca /musko/	
288	'moulin, molino'	molino /molino/	moinho /moiñu/	molí /mulí/	molin /muli/	
289	'mourir, morir'	muere /mwere/	morre /mɔʀe/	mor /mɔr/	mòr /mor/	
290	'mouvoir, mover'	mueve /mwebe/	move /mɔve/	mou /mow/	mòu /mow/	
291	'muet, mudo'	mudo /mudo/	mudo /mudu/	mut /mut/	mut /müt/	
292	'mur, muro'	muro /muro/	muro /muru/	mur /mur/	mur /mür/	
293	'mûr, maduro'	maduro /maduro/	maduro /maduru/	madur /mədú/	madur /madü/	
294	'naître, nacer'	nace /naθe/	nasce /nase/	neix /neš/	nais /nays/	nace nayse

A corpus of Romance lexical items / 225

OLD FRENCH	ITALIAN	ROUMANIAN	SARDINIAN	PROTO-ROMANCE	CLASSICAL LATIN
mer /mer/	mare /mare/	mare /mare/	mare /mare/		
merci /mɛrci/	mercede /merčede/	-R		?	
mesure /məzürə/	misura /misura/	măsură /məsurə/			
met- /mɛt-/	mette /mette/			?	
mi /mi/	mezzo /mɛẓẓo/	miez /myez/	mesu /mesu/		
miel /myɛl/	miele /myɛle/	miere /myere/	mele /mele/		≠
mil /mil/	mille /mille/	mie /mie/		±	
meis /meys/	mese /mese/		mese /mese/		
moneie /moneyə/	moneta /moneta/			?	
mont /munt/	monte /monte/	munte /munte/	monte /monte/		≠
mord- /mord-/	morde /mɔrde/	-R		?	
mort /mort/	morte /mɔrte/	moarte /mwarte/	morte /morte/		
mort /mort/	morto /mɔrto/	mort /mort/	mortu /mortu/		
mol /mol/	molle /mɔlle/	moale /mwale/	modde /modde/		
mosche /musčə/	mosca /moska/	muscă /muskə/	musca /muska/		
molin /muliŋ/	molino /molino/		molinu /molinu/		*
muer- /mör-/	muore /mwɔre/	moare /mware/		?	
muev- /möv-/	muove /mwɔve/	-R		?	
mu /mü/	muto /muto/	mut /mut/	mudu /mudu/		
mur /mür/	muro /muro/		muru /muru/		
meur /məür/	maturo /maturo/		maduru /maduru/		
nais- /nɛys-/	nasce /našše/	naște /našte/	nasche /naske/		

Gloss		Spanish	Portuguese	Catalan	Occitan	Proto-SWR	
295	'nef, nave'	nave /nabe/	nave /nave/	nau /naw/	nau /naw/		
296	'neige, nieve'	nieve /nyebe/	neve /nɛve/	neu /nɛw/	nèu /nɛw/		
297	'neuf, nueve'	nueve /nwebe/	nove /nɔve/	nou /nɔw/	nòu /now/		
298	'neuf, nuevo'	nuevo /nwebo/	novo /novu/	nou /nɔw/	nòu /now/		
299	'nez, nariz'	nariz /nariθ/	nariz /naris/	nas /nas/	nas /nas/	?	
300	'nid, nido'	nido /nido/	ninho /niñu/	niu /niw/	nis /nis/	?	
301	'nier, negar'	niega /nyega/	nega /nɛga/	nega /negə/	nèga /nɛgo/		
302	'noeud, nodo'	nodo /nodo/	nó /nɔ/	nus /nus/	notz /nuc/	?	
303	'noir, negro'	negro /negro/	negro /negru/	negre /nɛgrə/	negre /negre/		
304	'noix, nuez'	nuez /nweθ/	noz /nɔs/	nou /now/	notz /nuc/		
305	'nom, nombre'	nombre /nombre/	nome /nome/	nom /nɔm/	nom /num/	nom(br)e nɔm(br)e	
306	'notre, nuestro'	nuestro /nwestro/	nosso /nɔsu/	nostre /nɔstrə/	nòstre /nostre/	±	
307	'nu, nudo'	nudo /nudo/	nu /nu/	nu /nu/	nud /nüt/	nudo nu	
308	'nuit, noche'	noche /noče/	noite /noyte/	nit /nit/	nuèch /nɛč/	?	
309	'oeil, ojo'	ojo /oxo/	olho /oʎu/	ull /uʎ/	uèlh /ɛl/		
310	'oeuf, huevo'	huevo /webo/	ovu /ovu/	ou /ɔw/	uòu /yow/		†
311	'oeuvre, obra'	obra /obra/	obra /ɔbra/	obra /ɔbrə/	òbra /obro/		
312	'oignon, cebolla'	cebolla /θeboʎa/	cebola /sebola/	ceba /sɛbə/	ceba /sebo/	ceboʟa ceba	
313	'ombre, sombra'	sombra /sombra/	sombra /sõbra/	ombra /ombrə/	ombra /umbro/	±	
314	'onde, onda'	onda /onda/	onda /õda/	ona /onə/	onda /undo/	±	
315	'ongle, uña'	uña /uña/	unha /uña/	ungla /unglə/	ongla /unglo/	?	
316	'onze, once'	once /onθe/	onze /õze/	onze /onzə/	onze /unze/		

A corpus of Romance lexical items

Old French	Italian	Roumanian	Sardinian	Proto-Romance	Classical Latin
nef /nef/	nave /nave/		nae /nae/		
neif /neyf/	neve /neve/	nea /nea/	nie /nie/		≠
nuef /nöf/	nove /nɔve/	nouă /nowə/	noe /noe/	†	
nuef /nöf/	nuovo /nwɔvo/	nou /now/	nou /nou/		
nes /nes/	naso /naso/	nas /nas/	nasu /nasu/		
ni /ni/	nido /nido/	-R		?	
nie /niə/	nega /nega/	-R		?	
neu /nö/	nodo /nodo/	nod /nod/			
neir /neyr/	nero /nero/	negru /negru/		?	
noiz /noyc/	noce /noče/		nughe /nuge/		
nom /num/	nome /nome/	nume /nume/	nómene /nómene/	±	
nostre /nostrə/	nostro /nɔstro/	nostru /nostru/	nostru /nostru/		
nu /nü/	nudo /nudo/			?	
nuit /nüyt/	notte /nɔtte/	noapte /nwapte/	notte /notte/		
ueil /öʎ/	occhio /ɔkkyo/	ochi /oky/	oju /oyu/		
uef /öf/	uovo /wɔvo/	ou /ow/	ou /ou/		≠
uevre /övrə/	opera /ɔpera/	-R	óbera /óbera/		
...	cipolla /čipolla/	ceapă /čapə/	chibudda /kibudda/	?	
ombre /umbrə/	ombra /ombra/	umbră /umbrə/	umbra /umbra/		
onde /undə/	onda /onda/	undă /undə/	unda /unda/		
ongle /uŋglə/	unghia /ungya/	unghie /ungye/	ungia /unǧa/		
onze /unẓə/	undici /úndiči/		úndighi /úndigi/	?	

	GLOSS	SPANISH	PORTUGUESE	CATALAN	OCCITAN	PROTO-SWR
317	'or, oro'	oro /oro/	ouro /owru/	or /ɔr/	aur /awr/	
318	'oreille, oreja'	oreja /orexa/	orelha /oreʎa/	orella /ureʎə/	aurelha /awreʎo/	
319	'os, hueso'	hueso /weso/	osso /osu/	os /ɔs/	òs /os/	
320	'ours, oso'	oso /oso/	urso /ursu/	os /os/	ors /urs/	o(r)so u(r)so
321	'ouvert, abierto'	abierto /abyerto/	aberto /abɛrtu/	obert /ubɛrt/	obèrt /ubɛrt/	abɛrto obɛrto
322	'ouvrir, abrir'	abre /abre/	abre /abre/	obre /ɔbrə/	òbre /obre/	
323	'païen, pagano'	pagano /pagano/	pagão /pagãw/	pagá /pəgá/	pagan /pagá/	
324	'paille, paja'	paja /paxa/	palha /paʎa/	palla /paʎə/	palha /paʎo/	
325	'pain, pan'	pan /pan/	pão /pãw/	pa /pa/	pan /pa/	
326	'paître, pacer'	pace /paθe/	pasce /pase/	peix /peš/	pais /pays/	pace payse
327	'paix, paz'	paz /paθ/	paz /pas/	pau /paw/	patz /pac/	
328	'palais, palacio'	palacio /palaθyo/	paço /pasu/	palau /pəlaw/	palatz /palac/	?
329	'pan, paño'	paño /paño/	pano /panu/	pany /pañ/	pan /pan/	
330	'parent, pariente'	pariente /paryente/	parente /parẽte/	parent /pəren/	parent /parent/	
331	'paroi, pared'	pared /pared/	parede /parede/	paret /pərɛt/	paret /paret/	
332	'part, parte'	parte /parte/	parte /parte/	part /part/	part /part/	
333	'pas, paso'	paso /paso/	passo /pasu/	pas /pas/	pas /pas/	
334	'passer, pasar'	pasa /pasa/	passa /pasa/	passa /pasə/	passa /paso/	
335	'payer, pagar'	paga /paga/	paga /paga/	paga /pagə/	paga /pago/	
336	'peau, piel'	piel /pyel/	pele /pɛle/	pell /peʎ/	pèl /pɛl/	pɛl pɛLe
337	'pécher, pecar'	peca /peka/	peca /pɛka/	peca /pɛkə/	peca /peko/	
338	'pêcher, pescar'	pesca /peska/	pesca /pɛska/	pesca /pɛskə/	pesca /pesko/	

A corpus of Romance lexical items / 229

OLD FRENCH	ITALIAN	ROUMANIAN	SARDINIAN	PROTO-ROMANCE	CLASSICAL LATIN
or /or/	oro /ɔro/	aur /awr/			
oreille /orɛʎə/	orecchia /orekkya/	ureche /urekye/	orija /oriya/		
os /os/	osso /ɔsso/	os /os/	ossu /ossu/		≠
ors /urs/	orso /orso/	urs /urs/	ursa /urs-/		
overt /uvɛrt/	aperto /apɛrto/			?	
uevre /övrə/	apre /apre/			?	
paien /payɛŋ/	pagano /pagano/	păgîn /pəgɨn/			
paille /paʎə/	paglia /paʎʎa/	paie /paye/	paza /paẓẓa/		
pain /pɛyŋ/	pane /pane/	pîine /pɨyne/	pane /pane/		
pais- /pɛys-/	pasce /pašše/	paște /pašte/	pasche /paske/		
paiz /pɛyc/	pace /pače/	pace /pače/	paghe /page/		
palaiz /palɛyc/	palazzo /palacco/	părat /pərac/		?	
pan /paŋ/	panno /panno/	-R	pannu /pannu/		
parent /parɛnt/	parente /parɛnte/	părinte /pərinte/	parente /parente/		
parei /parey/	parete /parete/	perete /perete/		?	
part /part/	parte /parte/	parte /parte/	parte /parte/		
pas /pas/	passo /passo/	pas /pas/	passu /passu/		
passe /pasə/	passa /passa/		passa /passa/		*
paie /pɛyə/	paga /paga/	-R	paga /paga/		≠
pel /pɛl/	pelle /pɛlle/	piele /pyele/	pedde /pedde/		
peche /pɛčə/	pecca /pekka/		pecca /pekka/		≠
pesche /pɛsčə/	pesca /peska/		pisca /piska/		

Gloss		Spanish	Portuguese	Catalan	Occitan	Proto-SWR
339	'peine, pena'	pena /pena/	pena /pena/	pena /pɛnə/	pena /peno/	
340	'pelle, pala'	pala /pala/	pá /pa/	pala /palə/	pala /palo/	
341	'penser, pensar'	piensa /pyensa/	pensa /pẽsa/	pensa /pensə/	pensa /penso/	
342	'perdre, perder'	pierde /pyerde/	perde /pɛrde/	pert /pɛrt/	pèrd /pɛrt/	
343	'peser, pesar'	pesa /pesa/	pesa /pɛza/	pesa /pɛzə/	pesa /pezo/	
344	'peu, poco'	poco /poko/	pouco /powku/	poc /pɔk/	pauc /pawk/	
345	'pièce, pieza'	pieza /pyeθa/	peça /pɛsa/	peça /pesə/	pèça /pɛso/	
346	'pied, pie'	pie /pye/	pé /pɛ/	peu /pew/	pè /pɛ/	?
347	'pierre, piedra'	piedra /pyedra/	pedra /pɛdra/	pedra /pedrə/	pèira /peyro/	
348	'place, plaza'	plaza /plaθa/	praça /prasa/	plaça /plasə/	plaça /plaso/	?
349	'plaie, llaga'	llaga /ʎaga/	chaga /šaga/	...	plaga /plago/	?
350	'plain, llano'	llano /ʎano/	chão /šãw/	pla /pla/	plan /pla/	?
351	'plaindre, plañir'	plañe /plañe/	plange /plãže/	plany /plañ/	planh /plan/	?
352	'plainte, llanto'	llanto /ʎanto/	pranto /prãtu/	plany /plañ/	planh /plan/	?
353	'plaire, placer'	place /plaθe/	praze /praze/	plau /plaw/	platz /plac/	?
354	'plante, llanta'	llanta /ʎanta/	chanta /šãta/	planta /plantə/	planta /planto/	?
355	'plein, lleno'	lleno /ʎeno/	cheio /šeyu/	ple /plɛ/	plen /ple/	?
356	'pleuvoir, llover'	llueve /ʎwebe/	chove /šɔve/	plou /plow/	plòu /plow/	?
357	'plomb, plomo'	plomo /plomo/	chumbo /šũbu/	plom /plom/	plomb /plump/	?
358	'ployer, llegar'	llega /ʎega/	chega /šega/	plega /plɛgə/	plega /plego/	?
359	'pluie, lluvia'	lluvia /ʎubya/	chuva /šuva/	pluja /plužə/	plueja /plɛǧo/	?
360	'poil, pelo'	pelo /pelo/	pelo /pelu/	pel /pɛl/	pel /pel/	

Old French	Italian	Roumanian	Sardinian	Proto-Romance	Classical Latin
peine /peynə/	pena /pena/	-R	pena /pena/		
pele /pelə/	pala /pala/	-R	pala /pala/		
pense /pɛnsə/	pensa /pɛnsa/	-R	pensa /pensa/		≠
perd- /pɛrd-/	perde /pɛrde/	pierde /pyerde/	perde /perde/		
peise /peyzə/	pesa /pesa/	pasă /pasə/	pesa /pesa/		
peu, po(u) /pö/	poco /pɔko/		pagu /pagu/	?	
piece /pyɛcə/	pezza /pɛcca/	-R	pezza /pecca/		*
pie /pyɛ/	piede /pyɛde/		pe /pe/	*	
pierre /pyɛʀə/	pietra /pyɛtra/	piatră /pyatrə/	preda /preda/		
place /placə/	piazza /pyacca/			?	
plaie /plɛyə/	piaga /pyaga/	plagă /plagə/		*	
plain /plɛyŋ/	piano /pyano/	-R	pianu /pyanu/	*	
plaign- /plɛyñ-/	piange /pyanǧe/	plînge /plɨnǧe/	pianghe /pyange/		
plainte /plɛyntə/	pianto /pyanto/		piantu /pyantu/	?	
plais- /plɛyz-/	piace /pyače/	place /plače/	piaghe /pyage/		
plante /plantə/	pianta /pyanta/		pyanta /pyanta/	*	
plein /pleyŋ/	pieno /pyɛno/		pienu /pyenu/		
pluev- /plöv-/	piove /pyɔve/	plouă /plowə/	pioe /pyoe/		≠
plomb /plump/	piombo /pyombo/	plumb /plumb/		?	
pleie /pleyə/	piega /pyɛga/	pleacă /plęakə/		?	
pluie /plüyə/	pioggia /pyɔǧǧa/	ploaie /plwaye/		?	
peil /peyl/	pelo /pelo/	păr /pər/	pilu /pilu/		

	GLOSS	SPANISH	PORTUGUESE	CATALAN	OCCITAN	PROTO-SWR
361	'poing, puño'	puño /puño/	punho /puñu/	puny /puñ/	punh /pün/	
362	'poire, pera'	pera /pera/	pera /pera/	pera /pɛrə/	pera /pero/	
363	'poisson, peje'	peje /pexe/	peixe /peyše/	peix /pɛš/	peys /peys/	
364	'pis, pecho'	pecho /peČo/	peito /peytu/	pit /pit/	pièch /pyɛČ/	
365	'poivre, pebre'	pebre /pebre/	. . .	pebre /pɛbrə/	pebre /pebre/	*
366	'pondre, poner'	pone /pone/	põe /põy/	pon /pon/	pon /pun/	
367	'pont, puente'	puente /pwente/	ponte /põte/	pont /pɔn/	pont /punt/	
368	'porc, puerco'	puerco /pwerko/	porco /porku/	porc /pɔrk/	pòrc /pork/	
369	'porte, puerta'	puerta /pwerta/	porta /pɔrta/	porta /pɔrtə/	pòrta /porto/	
370	'pouvoir, poder'	puede /pwede/	pode /pɔde/	pot /pɔt/	pòt /pot/	
371	'pré, prado'	prado /prado/	prado /pradu/	prat /prat/	prat /prat/	
372	'prendre, prender'	prende /prende/	prende /prẽde/	pren /prɛn/	pren /pren/	
373	'prix, precio'	precio /preθyo/	preço /presu/	preu /prɛw/	prètz /prɛc/	?
374	'prouver, probar'	prueba /prweba/	prova /prɔva/	prova /prɔbə/	pròva /probo/	
375	'puits, pozo'	pozo /poθo/	poço /posu/	pou /pow/	potz /puc/	
376	'quand, cuando'	cuando /kwando/	quando /kwãdu/	quan /kwan/	quant /kant/	
377	'quarante, cuarenta'	cuarenta /kwarenta/	quarenta /kwarẽta/	quaranta /kwərantə/	quaranta /karanto/	
378	'quart, cuarto'	cuarto /kwarto/	quarto /kwartu/	quart /kwart/	quart /kart/	
379	'quatre, cuatro'	cuatro /kwatro/	quatro /kwatru/	quatre /kwatrə/	quatre /katre/	
380	'quel, cual'	cual /kwal/	qual /kwal/	qual /kwal/	qual /kal/	
381	'quérir, querer'	quiere /kyere/	quere /kɛre/	. . .	quèr /kɛr/	*
382	'queue, cola'	cola /kola/	cauda /kawda/	coa /koə/	coa /kuo/	?

A corpus of Romance lexical items / 233

Old French	Italian	Roumanian	Sardinian	Proto-Romance	Classical Latin
poing /poyñ/	pugno /puñño/	pumn /pumn/			
peire /peyrə/	pera /pera/	pară /parə/	pira /pira/		≠
peisson /peysuŋ/	pesce /pešše/	pește /pešte/	pische /piske/	†	
piz /pic/	petto /pɛtto/	piept /pyept/	pettus /pettus/	†	≠
peivre /peyvrə/	pepe /pepe/	-R		?	
pon- /pun-/	pone /pone/	pune /pune/	pone /pone/		
pont /punt/	ponte /ponte/	punte /punte/	ponte /ponte/		
porc /pork/	porco /pɔrko/	porc /pork/	porcu /porku/		
porte /portə/	porta /pɔrta/	poartă /pwartə/	porta /porta/		
pue- /pö-/	può /pwɔ/	poate /pwate/	pode /pode/		
pre /pre/	prato /prato/	-R	pradu /pradu/		
pren- /prɛn-/	prende /prende/	prinde /prinde/	prende /prende/		
priz /pric/	prezzo /prɛcco/	preț /prec/		?	
prueve /prövə/	prova /prɔva/	-R		?	
puiz /püyc/	pozzo /pocco/	puț /puc/	puzzu /puccu/	?	
quant, cant /kant/	quando /kwando/	cînd /kɨnd/	cando /kando/		
quarante,ca- /karantə/	quaranta /kwaranta/			?	
quart, cart /kart/	quarto /kwarto/	-R		?	
quatre,catre /katrə/	quattro /kwattro/			?	
quel /kel/	quale /kwale/	care /kare/	cale /kale/		
quier- /kyɛr-/	chiede /kyɛde/	cere /čere/	chere /kere/		
coe /köə/	coda /kɔda/	coadă /kwadə/	coa /koa/	?	

	GLOSS	SPANISH	PORTUGUESE	CATALAN	OCCITAN	PROTO-SWR
383	'fromage, queso'	queso /keso/	queijo /keyžu/	...	...	* _____
384	'quinze, quince'	quince /kinθe/	quinze /kīze/	quinze /kinzə/	quinze /kinze/	_____
385	'quoi, qué'	qué /ke/	quê /ke/	què /kɛ/	que /ke/	_____
386	'racine, raiz'	raiz /ʀaiθ/	raiz /ʀais/	...	raiç /ʀais/	* _____
387	'raison, razón'	razón /ʀaθon/	razão /ʀazãw/	raó /ʀəó/	rason /ʀazú/	_____
388	'rayon, rayo'	rayo /ʀayo/	raio /ʀayu/	raig /ʀač/	raia /ʀayo/	_____ ?
389	'reine, reina'	reina /ʀeyna/	rainha /ʀaiña/	reina /ʀeynə/	rèina /ʀɛyno/	_____ ?
390	'répondre, responder'	responde /ʀesponde/	responde /ʀespõde/	respòn /ʀəspɔn/	respond /ʀespunt/	_____
391	'rire, reir'	ríe /ʀie/	ri /ʀi/	riu /ʀiw/	ritz /ʀic/	_____ ?
392	'rive, riba'	riba /ʀiba/	riba /ʀiba/	riba /ʀibə/	riba /ʀibo/	_____
393	'rivière, rio'	río /ʀio/	rio /ʀiu/	riu /ʀiw/	riu /ʀiw/	_____ ?
394	'roi, rey'	rey /ʀey/	rei /ʀey/	rei /ʀey/	rei /ʀey/	_____
395	'rompre, romper'	rompe /ʀompe/	rompe /ʀõpe/	romp /ʀom/	romp /ʀump/	_____
396	'rompu, roto'	roto /ʀoto/	roto /ʀotu/	...	rot /ʀut/	* _____
397	'rond, redondo'	redondo /ʀedondo/	redondo /ʀedõdu/	rodó /ʀudó/	redond /ʀedunt/	_____ ?
398	'roue, rueda'	rueda /ʀweda/	roda /ʀɔda/	roda /ʀɔdə/	roda /ʀodo/	_____
399	'sac, saco'	saco /sako/	saco /saku/	sac /sak/	sac /sak/	_____
400	'sain, sano'	sano /sano/	são /sãw/	sa /sa/	san /sa/	_____
401	'saint, santo'	santo /santo/	santo /sãtu/	sant /san/	sant /sant/	_____
402	'saluer, saludar'	saluda /saluda/	saúda /sauda/	saluda /səludə/	saluda /salüdo/	_____
403	'salut, salud'	salud /salud/	saúde /saude/	salut /səlut/	salut /salüt/	_____
404	'sang, sangre'	sangre /sangre/	sangue /sãge/	sanc /saŋ/	sang /sank/	_____

A corpus of Romance lexical items / 235

Old French	Italian	Roumanian	Sardinian	Proto-Romance	Classical Latin
. . .	cacio /kačo/	caş /kaš/	casu /kasu/	?	
quinze /kinẓə/	quindici /kwindiči/			?	
quei /key/	che /ke/	ce /če/		?	
racine /ʀacinə/	radice /radiče/	rădăcină /rədəčinə/	raichina /raikina/	?	
raison /ʀɛyzuŋ/	ragione /rağone/	-R		?	
rai /ʀɛy/	raggio /rağğo/	rază /raz-/	raju /rayu/	?	
reine /ʀəinə/	regina /režina/	regină /režinə/		?	
respond- /ʀɛspund-/	risponde /risponde/	răspunde /rəspunde/		?	
ri- /ʀi-/	ride /ride/	rîde /ride/	rie /rie/		
rive /ʀivə/	ripa /ripa/			*	
. . .	rio /rio/	rîu /riw/	riu /riu/	?	
rei /ʀey/	re /re/	rege /reğe/	rege /rege/	?	
romp- /ʀump-/	rompe /rompe/	rupe /rupe/		±	≠
rot /ʀut/	rotto /rotto/	rupt /rupt/		*	
reont /ʀəunt/	rotondo /rotondo/	rotund /rotund/		?	
roe /ʀuə/	ruota /rwɔta/	roată /rwatə/	roda /roda/		
sac /sak/	sacco /sakko/	sac /sak/	saccu /sakku/		
sain /sɛyŋ/	sano /sano/		sanu /sanu/		
saint /sɛynt/	santo /santo/		santu /santu/	?	
salue /salüə/	saluta /saluta/	sărută /sərutə/	saluda /saluda/		
salu /salü/	salute /salute/		salude /salude/		
sanc /saŋk/	sangue /sangwe/	sînge /sinğe/	sámbene /sámbene/	±	

Gloss	Spanish	Portuguese	Catalan	Occitan	Proto-SWR
405 'sauter, saltar'	salta /salta/	salta /salta/	salta /saltə/	salta /salto/	
406 'sauver, salvar'	salva /salba/	salva /salva/	salva /salbə/	salva /salbo/	
407 'saveur, sabor'	sabor /sabor/	sabor /sabor/	sabor /səbó/	sabor /sabú/	
408 'savon, jabón'	jabón /xabon/	sabão /sabãw/	sabó /səbó/	sabon /sabú/	†
409 'sec, seco'	seco /seko/	seco /seku/	sec /sɛk/	sec /sek/	
410 'seigneur, señor'	señor /señor/	senhor /señor/	senyor /səñó/	senhor /señú/	
411 'sein, seno'	seno /seno/	seio /seyu/	si /si/	sen /se/	
412 'sel, sal'	sal /sal/	sal /sal/	sal /sal/	sal /sal/	
413 'selle, silla'	silla /siʎa/	sela /sɛla/	sella /seʎə/	sèla /sɛlo/	
414 'semer, sembrar'	siembra /syembra/	semeia /semeya/	sembra /sɛmbrə/	semena /semeno/	?
415 'sept, siete'	siete /syete/	sete /sɛte/	set /sɛt/	sèt /sɛt/	
416 'serpent, sierpe'	sierpe /syerpe/	serpe /sɛrpe/	serp /sɛrp/	sèrp /sɛrp/	
417 'servir, servir'	sirve /sirbe/	serve /sɛrve/	serveix /sərbɛš/	servis /serbis/	?
418 'seul, solo'	solo /solo/	só /sɔ/	sol /sol/	sol /sul/	
419 'six, seis'	seis /seys/	seis /seys/	sis /sis/	sièis /syɛys/	?
420 'soie, seda'	seda /seda/	seda /seda/	seda /sɛdə/	seda /sedo/	
421 'soif, sed'	sed /sed/	sede /sede/	set /sɛt/	set /set/	
422 'soleil, sol'	sol /sol/	sol /sɔl/	sol /sol/	solelh /sulel/	?
423 'somme, sueño'	sueño /sweño/	sono /sonu/	son /sɔn/	sòm /som/	?
424 'somme, suma'	suma /suma/	suma /suma/	suma /sumə/	soma /sumo/	
425 'sonner, sonar'	suena /swena/	soa /soa/	sona /sɔnə/	sona /suno/	
426 'sourd, sordo'	sordo /sordo/	surdo /surdu/	sord /sort/	sord /surt/	

OLD FRENCH	ITALIAN	ROUMANIAN	SARDINIAN	PROTO-ROMANCE	CLASSICAL LATIN
saute /sawtə/	salta /salta/	saltă /saltə/	salta /salta/		
sauve /sawvə/	salva /salva/		salba /salba/		*
savor /savör/	sapore /sapore/	-R	sabore /sabore/		
savon /savuŋ/	sapone /sapone/	săpun /səpun/	sabone /sabone/		≠
sec /sɛk/	secco /sekko/	sec /sek/	siccu /sikku/		
seignor /sɛyñör/	signore /siññore/			?	
sein /seyŋ/	seno /seno/			?	
sel /sel/	sale /sale/	sare /sare/	sale /sale/		
sele /sɛlə/	sella /sɛlla/	şea /ša/	sedda /sedda/		
seme /sɛmə/	semina /sémina/	seamănă /seámənə/	sémena /sémena/	?	
set /sɛt/	sette /sɛtte/	şapte /šapte/	sette /sette/		
serpent /sɛrpɛnt/	serpe /sɛrpe/	şarpe /šarpe/	serpente /serpente/		
serv- /sɛrv-/	serve /sɛrve/		serbi /serbi/		
sol /söl/	solo /solo/		solu /solu/		
sis /sis/	sei /sɛy/	şase /šase/	ses /ses/		
seie /seyə/	seta /seta/	-R	seda /seda/		*
sei(f) /sey/	sete /sete/	sete /sete/	sidis /sid-/		
soleil /solɛʎ/	sole /sole/	soare /sware/	sole /sole/	†	
some /somə/	sonno /sonno/	somn /somn/	sonnu /sonnu/		
some /somə/	somma /somma/	sumă /sumə/	summa /summa/		
sone /sonə/	suona /swɔna/	sună /sunə/	sona /sona/		
sort /surt/	sordo /sordo/	surd /surd/	surdu /surdu/		

238 / Appendix 1

	GLOSS	SPANISH	PORTUGUESE	CATALAN	OCCITAN	PROTO-SWR
427	'sueur, sudor'	sudor /sudor/	suor /suor/	suó /suó/	susor /süzú/	___?___
428	'sûr, seguro'	seguro /seguro/	seguro /seguru/	segur /səgú/	segur /segű/	
429	'tailler, tajar'	taja /taxa/	talha /taʎa/	talla /taʎə/	talha /taʎo/	
430	'taureau, toro'	toro /toro/	touro /towru/	tor /tɔr/	taure /tawre/	
431	'temps, tiempo'	tiempo /tyempo/	tempo /tẽpo/	temps /tems/	temps /tens/	___?___
432	'tendre, tierno'	tierno /tyerno/	tenro /tẽʀu/	tendre /tɛndrə/	tendre /tendre/	___?___
433	'tenir, tener'	tiene /tyene/	tem /tẽ/	té /te/	ten /te/	
434	'terre, tierra'	tierra /tyeʀa/	terra /tɛʀa/	terra /tɛʀə/	tèrra /tɛʀo/	
435	'tête, cabeza'	. . .	testa /tɛsta/	testa /testə/	tèsta /tɛsto/	* ___
436	'tisser, tejer'	teje /texe/	tece /tɛse/	teixeix /təšɛš/	tèis /tɛys/	___?___
437	'toile, tela'	tela /tela/	teia /teya/	tela /tɛlə/	tela /telo/	
438	'tomber, caer'	cae /kae/	cai /kay/	cau /kaw/	catz /kac/	___?___
439	'tordre, torcer'	tuerce /twerθe/	torce /tɔrse/	torça /tɔrsə/	tòrç /tors/	
440	'toujours, siempre'	siempre /syempre/	sempre /sẽpre/	sempre /semprə/	sempre /sempre/	
441	'tour, torre'	torre /toʀe/	torre /toʀe/	torre /toʀə/	tor /tur/	
442	'tourner, torna'	torna /torna/	torna /tɔrna/	torna /tornə/	torna /turno/	
443	'tout, todo'	todo /todo/	todo /todu/	tot /tot/	tot /tut/	
444	'tracer, trazar'	traza /traθa/	traça /trasa/	traça /trasə/	traça /traso/	
445	'treize, trece'	trece /treθe/	treze /treze/	tretze /trɛdzə/	tretze /treẓe/	___?___
446	'trente, treinta'	treinta /treynta/	trinta /trĩta/	trenta /trentə/	trenta /trento/	___?___
447	'trésor, tesoro'	tesoro /tesoro/	tesouro /tezowru/	tresor /trəzó/	. . .	
448	'trois, tres'	tres /tres/	três /tres/	tres /trɛs/	tres /tres/	

A corpus of Romance lexical items

Old French	Italian	Roumanian	Sardinian	Proto-Romance	Classical Latin
suor /süör/	sudore /sudore/	sudoare /sudware/	suore /suore/		
seur /səür/	sicuro /sikuro/	-R	seguru /seguru/		
taille /taʎə/	taglia /taʎʎa/	taie /taye/			*
tor /tor/	toro /tɔro/	taur /tawr/	trau /trau/		
tens /tɛns/	tempo /tɛmpo/	timp /timp/	tempus /tempus/	†	≠
tendre /tɛndrə/	tenero /ténero/	tînăr /tɨnər/		?	
tien- /tyɛn-/	tiene /tyɛne/	ţine /cine/	tene /tene/		
terre /tɛʀə/	terra /tɛrra/	ţară /carə/	terra /terra/		
teste /tɛstə/	testa /tɛsta/	ţastă /castə/	testa /testa/		*
tis- /tis-/	tesse /tɛsse/		tesse /tesse/	?	
teile /teylə/	tela /tela/		tela /tela/		
chie- /čyɛ-/	cade /kade/	cade /kade/		*	
tord- /tord-/	torce /tɔrče/	toarce /twarče/	torche /torke/		
sempre /sɛmprə/	sempre /sɛmpre/		sémpere /sémpere/		
tor /tur/	torre /torre/	-R	turre /turre/		
torne /turnə/	torna /torna/	toarnă /twarnə/	torra /torra/		
tot /tut/	tutto /tutto/	tot /tot/	tottu /tottu/	?	
trace /tracə/	traccia /tračča/	-R	trazza /tracca/		*
tre(i)ze /trɛẓə/	tredici /trédiči/		tréighi /tréigi/	?	
trente /trɛntə/	trenta /trenta/		trinta /trinta/	?	
tresor /trəzor/	tesoro /tesɔro/	-R		?	
treis /treys/	tre /tre/		tres /tres/		

240 / Appendix 1

	Gloss	Spanish	Portuguese	Catalan	Occitan	Proto-SWR
449	'un, uno'	uno /uno/	um /ū/	un /un/	un /ün/	
450	'vache, vaca'	vaca /baka/	vaca /vaka/	vaca /bakə/	vaca /bako/	
451	'vaincre, vencer'	vence /benθe/	vence /vẽse/	venç /bɛns/	venç /bens/	
452	'val, valle'	valle /baʎe/	vale /vale/	vall /baʎ/	val /bal/	
453	'valoir, valer'	vale /bale/	vale /vale/	val /bal/	val /bal/	
454	'veine, vena'	vena /bena/	veia /veya/	vena /bɛnə/	vena /beno/	
455	'vendre, vender'	vende /bende/	vende /vẽde/	ven /bɛn/	vend /bent/	
456	'venir, venir'	viene /byene/	vem /vẽ/	ve /be/	ven /be/	
457	'vent, viento'	viento /byento/	vento /vẽtu/	vent /ben/	vent /bent/	
458	'ventre, vientre'	vientre /byentre/	ventre /vẽtre/	ventre /bentrə/	ventre /bentre/	
459	'ver, gusano'	. . .	verme /vɛrme/	verm /bɛrm/	vèrm /bɛrm/	* _____
460	'vert, verde'	verde /berde/	verde /verde/	verd /bɛrt/	verd /bert/	
461	'vêtir, vestir'	viste /biste/	veste /vɛste/	vesteix /bəstɛš/	vestis /bestis/	? _____
462	'vie, vida'	vida /bida/	vida /vida/	vida /bidə/	vida /bido/	
463	'vieux, viejo'	viejo /byexo/	velho /veʎu/	vell /bɛʎ/	vièlh /byɛl/	
464	'vif, vivo'	vivo /bibo/	vivo /vivu/	viu /biw/	viu /biw/	
465	'vigne, viña'	viña /biña/	vinha /viña/	vinya /biñə/	vinha /biño/	
466	'vin, vino'	vino /bino/	vinho /viñu/	vi /bi/	vin /bi/	
467	'vingt, veinte'	veinte /beynte/	vinte /vĩte/	vint /bin/	vint /bint/	† _____
468	'vivre, vivir'	vive /bibe/	vive /vive/	viu /biw/	viu /biw/	
469	'voie, vía'	vía /bia/	via /via/	via /biə/	via /bio/	
470	'voile, velo'	velo /belo/	véu /vɛw/	vel /bɛl/	vel /bel/	

A corpus of Romance lexical items / 241

Old French	Italian	Roumanian	Sardinian	Proto-Romance	Classical Latin
un /üŋ/	uno /uno/	un /un/	unu /unu/		
vache /vačə/	vacca /vakka/	vacă /vakə/	bacca /bakka/		
veinc- /veyŋk-/	vince /vinče/		vinche /binke/		
val /val/	valle /valle/	vale /vale/	badde /badde/		
val- /val-/	vale /vale/	-R	bale /bale/		
veine /veynə/	vena /vena/	vînă /vɨnə/	vena /bena/		
vend- /vɛnd-/	vende /vende/	vinde /vinde/	bende /bende/		
vien- /vyɛn-/	viene /vyɛne/	vine /vine/	bene /bene/		≠
vent /vɛnt/	vento /vɛnto/	vînt /vɨnt/	ventu /bentu/		
ventre /vɛntrə/	ventre /vɛntre/	-R	bentre /bentre/		
verm /vɛrm/	verme /vɛrme/	vierme /vyerme/	verme /berme/		
vert /vɛrt/	verde /verde/	verde /verde/	virde /birde/		
vest /vɛst-/	veste /vɛste/		vesti /besti/		
vie /viə/	vita /vita/	vită /vitə/	vida /bida/		
vieil /vyɛʎ/	vecchio /vɛkkyo/	vechi /veky/			≠
vif /vif/	vivo /vivo/	viu /viw/	biu /biu/		
vigne /viñə/	vigna /viñña/	vie /vie/	vinza /binʓa/		
vin /viŋ/	vino /vino/	vin /vin/	vinu /binu/		
vint /vint/	venti /venti/		vinti /binti/	?	
viv- /viv-/	vive /vive/	-R			
veie /veyə/	via /via/	-R	via /bia/		≠
veile /veylə/	velo /velo/	văl /vəl/		?	

242 / Appendix 1

	Gloss	Spanish	Portuguese	Catalan	Occitan	Proto-SWR
471	'voir, ver'	ve /be/	vê /ve/	veu /bɛw/	vetz /bec/	?
472	'voisin, vecino'	vecino /beθino/	vizinho /viziñu/	vei /bəi/	vesin /bezí/	
473	'voix, voz'	voz /boθ/	voz /vɔs/	veu /bɛw/	votz /buc/	
474	'voler, volar'	vuela /bwela/	voa /voa/	vola /bɔlə/	vòla /bolo/	
475	'votre, vuestro'	vuestro /bwestro/	vosso /vɔsu/	vostre /vɔstrə/	vòstre /bostre/	†

SUBSET of Latin lexical items (not in corpus) for downtracing.

	Latin	Gloss
S1	ADFLĀ-	'trouver, hallar'
S2	AEQUĀLE-	'égal, igual'
S3	AQUA	'eau, agua'
S4	AQUILA	'aigle, águila'
S5	AUDĬ-	'ouīr, oir'
S6	AUSĀ-	'oser, osar'
S7	BOVE-	'boeuf, buey'
S8	CALIDU-	'chaud, caliente'
S9	CAMERA	'chambre, cámara'
S10	CATHEDRA	'chaire, cadera'
S11	BASSIĀ-	'baisser, bajar'
S12	BASSU-	'bas, bajo'
S13	CAMBIĀ-	'changer, cambiar'
S14	CAMĪSIA	'chemise, camisa'
S15	CARRICĀ-	'charger, cargar'
S16	CILIU-	'cil, ceja'
S17	CĪVITĀTE-	'cité, ciudad'
S18	CLĀVU-	'clou, clavo'
S19	COMEDE-	'manger, comer'
S20	COMPLĒ-	'accomplir, cumplir'
S21	DICTU-	'dit, dicho'
S22	DUO	'deux, dos'
S23	DUPLU-	'double, doble'

Old French	Italian	Roumanian	Sardinian	Proto-Romance		Classical Latin
vei- /vey-/	vede /vede/	vede /vede/		?		
veisin /veyziŋ/	vicino /vičino/	vecin /večin/	bighinu /biginu/		≠	
voiz /voyc/	voce /voče/		boghe /boge/			
vole /volə/	vola /vɔla/		vola /bola/	?		
vostre /vostrə/	vostro /vɔstro/	vostru /vostru/	bostru /bostru/		≠	

S24	EXĪ-	'sortir, salir'
S25	FASCE-	'faisse, haz'
S26	FASCIA	'faisseau, faja'
S27	FEBRUĀRIU-	'février, febrero'
S28	FERĪ-	'blesser, herir'
S29	FOCĀCIU-	'fouace, hogaza'
S30	FRĀTRE-	'frère, hermano'
S31	FRAXINU-	'frêne, fresno'
S32	FRĪGE-	'frire, freir'
S33	FRĪGIDU-	'froid, frío'
S34	GEMMA	'jaune, yema'
S35	GENUCULU-	'genou, hinojo'
S36	GINGĪVA-	'gencive, encía'
S37	GYPSU-	'gypse, yeso'
S38	HODIĒ-	'-'hui, hoy'
S39	HOSPITE-	'hôte, huésped'
S40	IMPLĒ-	'emplir, henchir'
S41	GAUDIU-	'joie, gozo'
S42	IĀNUĀRIU-	'janvier, enero'
S43	INGENIU-	'engin, ingenio'
S44	IŪDICE-	'juge, juez'
S45	IŪLIU-	'juillet, julio'
S46	IUNGE-	'joindre, uñir'

S47	IUNCTU-	'joint, junto'
S48	IUVENE-	'jeune, joven'
S49	LATERE-	'côté, lado'
S50	LEGE-	'lire, leer'
S51	LĪBERU-	'libre, libre'
S52	LONGĒ	'loin, lejos'
S53	LUCTĀ-	'lutter, luchar'
S54	MACRU-	'maigre, magro'
S55	MAGIS	'mais, más'
S56	MAGISTRU-	'maître, maestro'
S57	MĀTRE-	'mère, madre'
S58	MELIŌRE-	'meilleur, mejor'
S59	MĒNSA	'table, mesa'
S60	MINUS	'moins, menos'
S61	NEPŌTE-	'neveu, nieto'
S62	NŌBILE-	'noble, noble'
S63	NUMERU-	'nombre, número'
S64	MANDŪCĀ-	'manger, comer'
S65	OPERĀRIU-	'ouvrier, obrero'
S66	OFFERE-	'offrir, ofrecer'
S67	PAGĒNSE-	'pays, país'
S68	PAUPERE-	'pauvre, pobre'
S69	PEDICULU-	'poux, piojo'
S70	PĒIŌRE-	'pire, peor'
S71	PERĪCULU-	'péril, peligro'
S72	PLAGIA	'plage, playa'
S73	PLŌRĀ-	'pleurer, llorar'
S74	PLŪS	'plus, más'
S75	POPULU-	'peuple, pueblo'
S76	PARABOLA	'parole, palabra'
S77	PATRE-	'père, padre'
S78	PREHĒNSU-	'pris, preso'
S79	PROFECTU-	'profit, provecho'
S80	PULSĀ-	'pousser, pujar'
S81	QUATTUORDECIM	'quatorze, catorce'
S82	QUINTU-	'quint, quinto'
S83	PRECĀ-	'prier, rogar'
S84	RECIPE-	'recevoir, recibir'
S85	ROGĀ-	'prier, rogar'
S86	RUBEU-	'rouge, rojo'
S87	RUSSU-	'roux, rojo'
S88	SAGITTA	'flèche, saeta'

S89	SAPE-	'savoir, saber'
S90	SEQUE-	'suivre, seguir'
S91	SENTĪ-	'sentir, sentir'
S92	SIGILLU-	'sceau, sello'
S93	SONU-	'son, son'
S94	SPATULA	'épaule, espalda'
S95	SPECULU-	'miroir, espejo'
S96	STANNU-	'étain, estaño'
S97	SŪDĀ-	'suer, sudar'
S98	SUFFERE-	'souffrir, sufrir'
S99	TABULA	'table, mesa'
S100	TALPA	'taupe, topo'
S101	TINGE-	'teindre, teñir'
S102	TRAHE-	'traire, traer'
S103	TREPALIU-	'travail, trabajo'
S104	TRUCTA	'truite, trucha'
S105	URTĪCA	'ortie, ortiga'
S106	TĪTIŌNE-	'tison, tizón'
S107	VERMICULU-	'vermeil, bermejo'
S108	VICE-	'fois, vez'
S109	VOLE-	'vouloir, querer'

Appendix 2
Independent projects in diachronic phonology and morphosyntax

Diachronic Phonology Project No. 1: The changes in underlying systems which lead from the phonology of Eastern Romance, to be restructured after the split of Common Romance, to the phonological system of Romanian as described syncronically in Volume 1. A specific history of the Roumanian language will need to be utilized in order to identify one or more of the language changes and splits in the relevant branch of the *Stammbaum*. Hypothetical intermediate nodes in this still-to-be-constructed branch would be Balkan Romance, Common Roumanian (with Daco-, Istro-, Macedo-, and Megleno-Roumanian dialects), and Old (Daco-)Roumanian. (See Bibliography.)

Diachronic Phonology Project No. 2: The changes in underlying systems which lead from the phonology of Italo-Dalmatian, as it would be restructured after the split of Italo-Western, to the phonological system of Italian as described synchronically in Volume 1. A specific history of the Italian language will need to be utilized in order to identify language changes and splits in the relevant branch of the *Stammbaum*. Hypothetical intermediate nodes would be (1) Italo-Romance, or Common Italian—with northeastern (including Friulian), central, and southern dialects, (2) Central Italian, (3) (Old) Tuscan. (See Bibliography. Note: The inclusion of Friulian in Italo-Romance, rather than in Rhaeto-Romance as traditionally, as well as that of northwestern Italian lects (Lombard, Piedmontese, Ligurian) in Shifted Western Romance rather than in Italo-Romance, is discussed in Agard 1980.)

Diachronic Morphosyntax Project No. 1: The underlying and superficial changes which lead from the grammar of Eastern Romance, as restructured after the split of Common Romance, to the grammar of Roumanian as described synchronically in Volume 1. A specific history of the Roumanian language will need to be utilized in order to formulate one or more of the intermediate stages in the development, e.g. Balkan Romance, Common Roumanian (comprising Daco-, Istro-, Macedo-, and Megleno-Roumanian dialects) and Old (Daco-)Roumanian. (See Bibliography.)

Diachronic Morphosyntax Project No. 2: The underlying and superficial changes which lead from the grammar of Italo-Dalmatian Romance, as restructurable after the split of Italo-Western Romance, to the grammar of Italian as described synchronically in Volume 1. A specific history of the Italian language will need to be utilized in order to identify intermediate stages in the development, e.g. Common Italian (with northeastern, central, and some southern dialects), Central Italian, (Old) Tuscan. (See Bibliography.)

Diachronic Morphosyntax Project No. 3: The underlying and superficial changes which lead from the grammar of Northwestern Romance, as restructurable after the split of Shifted Western, to the grammar of French as described synchronically in Volume 1. A detailed history of the French language will need to be consulted in relation to the intermediate nodes in the *Stammbaum* determined by phonological developments as set forth specifically in Agard (1980), i.e. Gallo-Rhaetian, Oïl, Central Oïl, Franco-Orléanais, Francian. (See Bibliography.)

Diachronic Morphosyntax Project No. 4: The underlying and superficial changes which lead from the grammar of Southwestern Romance, as restructurable after the split of Shifted Western, to the grammars of Spanish and of Portuguese as described synchronically in Volume 1. Detailed histories of both languages will need to be consulted in relation to the intermediate nodes in the *Stammbaum* determined by phonological developments as set forth in Part Two of the present volume—i.e. West Ibero-Romance (Chapter 7), Castilian and Galician (Chapter 8), Burgalese then North Castilian (Chapter 9), Portuguese (Chapter 10). (See Bibliography.)

Appendix 3
A *Stammbaum* of the Romance languages

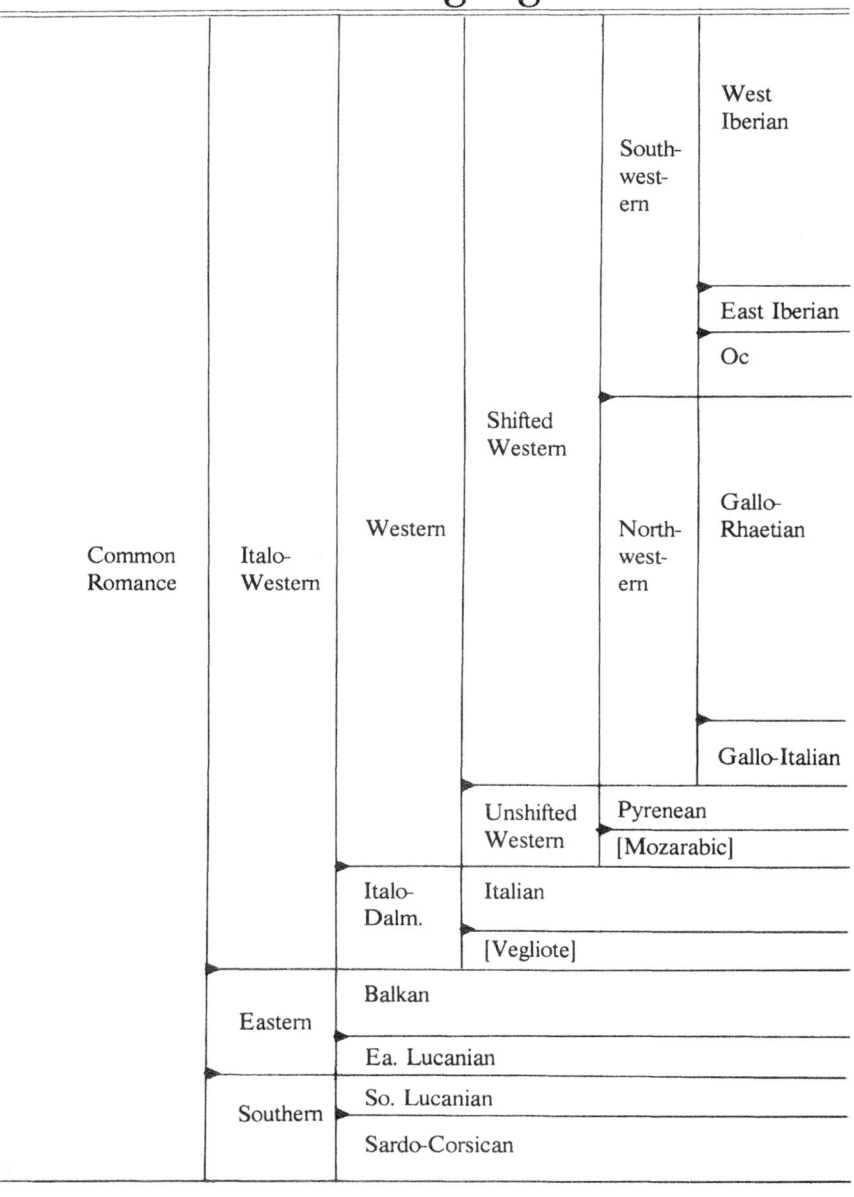

A *Stammbaum* of the Romance languages / 251

Galician			Portuguese → Gallegan	**Portuguese**
Asturo-Leonese			Various lects	
Castilian	Burgalés	South Castilian	Sephardic, New World Sp	**Spanish**
		North Castilian	Old World Sp	
	[Toledano]			
			Catalan →	**Catalan**
			Gascon, Occitan, Provençal et al.	
Oïl	So. Ea. Oïl		Franco-Provençal, Franche-Comtois	
	Cent. Oïl	So. Cent. Oïl	Francien → Orléanais	**French**
		No. Cent. Oïl	Norman, Picard	
	No. Ea. Oïl		Walloon, Lorrain	
	West Oïl		Angevin, Poitevin et al.	
West Rhaetian			Romansh lects	
East Rhaetian			Engadine lects	
			Genoese, Lombard, Piedmontese et al.	
			Aragonese, Béarnais	
			Tuscan → other Ital lects	**Italian**
			Daco-Roumanian → other Rou lects	**Roumanian**
			Castelmezzano	
			Nova Siri et al.	
			Logudorese, Campidanese et al.	

Bibliography

Note. The majority of the titles listed in the present bibliography are diachronically oriented, and for each major language they contain at least one historical grammar (covering both phonology and morphosyntax) and one etymological dictionary. Also included under each of the five languages described in Volume 1 is one nonhistorical grammar of the transformational-generative school, mainly for optional use in rounding out a synchronic knowledge in connection with one or another of the independent study projects suggested in Appendix 3. The entries are mainly books, most of which in turn offer lengthy bibliographies. Shorter articles included are very few, and are confined to ones with precise relevance to a crucial or controversial issue. The entire bibliography makes no claim to exhaustiveness.

Comparative Romance in general:

Agard, F.B. 1975. Toward a taxonomy of language split (Part 1: Phonology). Leuvense Bijdragen 64:293–312.
Bec, Pierre. 1970. Manuel pratique de philologie romane. Paris.
Belardi, Walter. 1979. Dal latino alle lingue romanze. Rome.
Bergquist, M.F. 1981. Ibero-Romance: Comparative phonology and morphology. Washington, D.C.: University Press of America.
Bourciez, Édouard. 1967a. Éléments de linguistique romane. 5th ed. Paris.
Camproux, Charles. 1979. Les langues romanes. Paris.
Canfield, D.L., and J.C. Davis. 1975. An introduction to Romance linguistics. Carbondale, Ill.: Southern Illinois University Press.
Contreras, Heles. 1962–63. Una clasificación morfo-sintáctica de las lenguas románicas. Romance Philology 16:261–68.
Diez, Friedrich. 1887. Etymologisches Wörterbuch der romanischen Sprachen. 5th ed. Bonn.
Elcock, W.D. 1960. The Romance languages. London and New York: Faber and Faber.
Francescato, Giuseppe. 1973. Rumeno, dalmatico, ladino, italiano: premesse e prospettive per una classificazione. Studii și cercetări lingvistice 24:529–37.

Hall, R.A. Jr. 1950. The reconstruction of Proto-Romance. Lg. 26:6–27.
———. 1974. External history of the Romance languages. New York: American Elsevier. (Has extensive bibliography.)
———. 1976. Proto-Romance phonology. New York: American Elsevier.
———. 1983. Proto-Romance morphology. Amsterdam: John Benjamins.
Jaeggli, Osvaldo. 1982. Topics in Romance syntax. Dordrecht, Netherlands.
Lausberg, Heinrich. 1956–62. Romanische Sprachwissenschaft. Berlin. 4 vols. (Spanish translation, 1965. Lingüística románica. Madrid.)
Leonard, C.S. Jr. 1970. The Romance 'Stammbaum' in the West. Romance Philology 33:261–76.
———. 1978. Umlaut in Romance: an essay in linguistic archaeology. Grossen-Linden, W. Germany: Hoffmann.
Lüdtke, Helmut. 1956. Die strukturelle Entwicklung des romanischen vokalismus. Bonn.
———. 1965. Le vie di comunicazione dell'impero romano e la formazione dei dialetti romanzi. Atti del X Congresso Internazionale di Linguistica e Filologia Romanza 1103–09.
Malkiel, Yakov. 1960. A tentative typology of Romance historical grammars. Lingua 9:321–416.
Manoliu-Manea, Maria. 1971. Gramatica comparată a limbilor romanice. București.
Martinet, André. 1964. Économie des changements phonétiques. 2nd ed. Berne.
Mendelhoff, Henry. 1969. A manual of comparative Romance linguistics: Phonology and morphology. Washington, D.C.: Catholic University of America Press.
Meyer-Lübke, Wilhelm. 1890–1902. Grammatik der romanischen Sprachen. Leipzig. 4 vols. French translation, 1890–1906. Grammaire des langues romanes. Paris (reprinted 1925, New York).
———. 1909. Einführung in das Studium der romanischen Sprachwissenschaft. 2nd ed. Heidelberg. Spanish translation by Américo Castro 1926. Introducción a la lingüística románica. Madrid.
Muljačić, Žarko. 1967. Die Klassifikation der romanischen Sprachen. Romanistisches Jahrbuch 18:23–37.
Otero, C.P. 1971. Evolución y revolución en romance. Barcelona.
Pei, Mario. 1949. A new methodology for Romance classification. Word 5:135–46.
Pop, Sever. 1956–57. Encyclopédie de la philologie romane: langues et dialectes de la Romania. Louvain.
Posner, Rebecca. 1966. The Romance languages. Garden City, N.Y.: Anchor Books.
———, ed. 1981. Trends in Romance linguistics and philology. The Hague.
Rohlfs, Gerhard. 1966–. Romanische Philologie. 2nd ed. 2 vols. Heidelberg.

Romeo, Luigi. 1968. The economy of diphthongization in early Romance. The Hague.
Schürr, Friedrich. 1956. La diphtongaison romane. Revue de Linguistique Romane 20:107–44, 161–248.
Straka, Georges. 1956. La dislocation linguistique de la Romania et la formation des langues romanes à la lumière de la chronologie relative des changements phonétiques. Revue de Linguistique Romane 20:249–67.
Tagliavini, Carlo. 1972. Le origini delle lingue neolatine. 6th ed. Bologna.
von Wartburg, Walther. 1950. Die Ausgliederung der romanischen Sprachräume. 2nd ed. French translation, 1967. La fragmentation linguistique de la Romania. Strasbourg. Spanish translation, 1952. La fragmentación lingüística de la Romania. Madrid.
―――. 1951. Die Entstehung der romanischen Völker. 2nd ed. Tübingen. French translation of 1st ed. 1941. Les origines des peuples romans. Paris.

French (including Old French):

Agard, F.B. 1980. The genealogy of the French language. In: Contributions to historical linguistics. Edited by van Coetsem and Waugh. Leiden.
Baldinger, K., J.-D. Gendron, and G. Straka. 1972–. Dictionnaire étymologique de l'ancien français. Tübingen and Paris.
Bourciez, Édouard and Jean. 1967b. Phonétique française: étude historique. Paris.
Brunot, Ferdinand, and Charles Bruneau. 1905–69. Histoire de la langue française des origines à nos jours. 13 vols. Paris.
Dauzat, Albert. 1964. Nouveau dictionnaire étymologique et historique. Paris.
Ewert, Alfred. 1938. The French language. London: Faber and Faber.
Foulet, Lucien. 1919. Petit syntaxe de l'ancien français. Paris.
Haudricourt, André, and Alphonse Juilland. 1949. Essai pour une histoire structurale du phonétisme français. Paris.
Kayne, R.S. 1975. French syntax: The transformational cycle. Cambridge, Mass.: MIT Press.
Nyrop, Kristoffer. 1899–1930. Grammaire historique de la langue française. 6 vols. Copenhagen.
Pope, M.K. 1934. From Latin to Modern French with especial consideration of Anglo-Norman. Manchester: Manchester University Press.
Rickard, Peter. 1974. A history of the French language. London: Hutchinson.
Schwan, E., D. Behrens, and O. Bloch. 1932. Grammaire de l'ancien français. 4th ed. Leipzig.
von Wartburg, Walther. 1934. Évolution et structure de la langue française. Leipzig.

Italian:

Devoto, Giacomo. 1936. Storia della lingua di Roma. Bologna.
Grandgent, C.H. 1927. From Latin to Italian. Cambridge, Mass.: Harvard University Press.
Migliorini, Bruno. 1960. Storia della lingua italiana. Firenze.
Pei, Mario. 1941. The Italian language. New York: Columbia University Press.
Pfister, Max. 1979–. Lessico etimologico italiano. Wiesbaden.
Prati, Angelico. 1951. Vocabolario etimologico italiano. Milano.
Rohlfs, Gerhard, 1949–54. Historische Grammatik der italienischen Sprache und ihrer Mundarten. Bern. Italian translation, 1966–69. Grammatica storica della lingua italiana e dei suoi dialetti. Torino.
Saltarelli, Mario. 1970. La grammatica generativa trasformazionale, con introduzione alla fonologia, sintassi e dialettologia italiana. Firenze.

Latin (including 'Vulgar Latin'):

Allen, J.H., and J.B. Greenough. 1878. A Latin grammar. Boston: Ginn.
Bennett, C.E. 1907. The Latin language: A historical outline of its sounds, inflections and syntax. Boston: Allyn and Bacon.
Coşeriu, Eugenio. 1954. El llamado 'latín vulgar' y las primeras diferenciaciones romances. Montevideo.
Grandgent, C.H. 1905. An outline of the phonology and morphology of Vulgar Latin. Boston: D.C. Heath.
Hill, A.A. 1958. Introduction to linguistic structures. [Appendix B is a structural sketch of Latin.] New York: Harcourt, Brace.
Maurer, T.H. Jr. 1959. Gramática do latim vulgar. Rio de Janeiro.
Palmer, L.R. 1961. The Latin language. 3rd ed. London: Faber and Faber.
Väänänen, Veikko. 1967. Introduction au latin vulgaire. 2nd ed. Paris.

Portuguese:

Bueno, F. da Silveira. 1955. A formação histórica da língua portuguesa. Rio de Janeiro and São Paulo.
———. 1963. Grande dicionàrio etimológico-prosódico da língua portuguesa. São Paulo.
Machado, J.P. 1967. Dicionàrio etimológico da língua portuguesa. Lisboa.
Mattoso Câmara, Joaquim jr. 1972. The Portuguese language. Chicago: University of Chicago Press.
Perini, M.A. 1976–. A gramática gerativa: introdução ao estudo da sintaxe portuguesa. Belo Horizonte.

Silva Neto, Serafim. 1952. História da língua portuguesa. Rio de Janeiro.
Teyssier, Paul. 1980. Histoire de la langue portugaise. Paris.
Williams, E.B. 1968. From Latin to Portuguese: Historical phonology and morphology of the Portuguese language. 2nd ed. Philadelphia.

Roumanian:

Caragiu-Marioțeanu, Matilda. 1968. Fono-morfologia aromână: studiu de dialectologie structurală. București.
Cioranescu, Alexandre. 1958. Diccionario etimológico rumano. Tenerife, Spain.
Densusianu, Ovidiu. 1901–38. Histoire de la langue roumaine. 2 vols. Paris.
DuNay, André. 1977. The early history of the Rumanian language. Lake Bluff, Ill.: Jupiter Press.
Nandriș, Grigore. 1951. The development and structure of Rumanian. Slavonic and East European Review 30:7–39.
―――. 1963. Phonétique historique du roumain. Paris.
Petrovici, Emil. 1964. Unitatea dialectală a limbii române. Studii și cercetări lingvistice 15:431–43. French translation, 1964. L'unité dialectale de la langue roumaine. Revue Roumaine de Linguistique 9:375–88.
Pușcariu, Sextil. 1905. Etymologisches Wörterbuch der rumänischen Sprache. Heidelberg.
―――. 1940. Limba română. București.
Rosetti, Alexandru. 1956. Limba romînă în secolele al XIII-lea-al XVI-lea. București.
―――. 1968. Istoria limbii române de la origini pînă în secolul al XVII-lea. București.
―――. 1973. Brève histoire de la langue roumaine. The Hague.
Vasiliu, Emanuel and Sanda Golopenția-Eretescu. 1973. Sintaxa transformațională a limbii române. București. English translation: The transformational syntax of Romanian. The Hague.

Spanish:

Agard, F.B. 1976. The genealogy of Modern Spanish. In: Proceedings of the Second International Conference on Historical Linguistics. Edited by W.M. Christie. Amsterdam.
Alonso, Amado. 1955–69. De la pronunciación medieval a la moderna en español. 2 vols. Madrid.
Burt, J.R. 1980. From phonology to philology: An outline of descriptive and historical Spanish linguistics. Washington, D.C.: University of America Press.
Canfield, D.L. 1962. La pronunciación del español en América. Bogotá.

Corominas, Juan. 1954–57. Diccionario crítico etimológico de la lengua castellana. 4 vols. Madrid.
_____. 1961. Breve diccionario etimológico de la lengua castellana. Madrid.
D'Introno, Francesco. 1979. Sintaxis transformacional del español. Madrid.
Entwistle, W.J. 1962. The Spanish language, together with Portuguese, Catalan and Basque. 2nd ed. London: Faber and Faber.
García de Diego, Vicente. 1946. Manual de dialectología española. Madrid.
_____. 1970. Gramática histórica española. Madrid.
Lapesa, Rafael. 1959. Historia de la lengua española. 2nd ed. New York.
Menéndez Pidal, Ramón. 1956. Orígenes del español. 4th ed. Madrid.
_____. 1966. Manual elemental de gramática histórica española. 12th ed. Madrid.
Spaulding, R.K. 1943. How Spanish grew. Berkeley and Los Angeles: University of California Press.
Zamora Vicente, 1967. Dialectología española. 3rd ed. Madrid.

Other languages (Catalan, Dalmatian (Vegliote), Gallo-Italian, Lucanian, Occitan, Pyrenean (Aragonese, Bearnese), Rhaetian (Friulian, Ladin), Sardinian, Sicilian):

Badia i Margarit, Antoni. 1951. Gramática histórica catalana. Barcelona.
Bartoli, M.G. 1910. Das Dalmatische: altromanische Sprachreste von Veglia bis Ragusa und ihre Stellung in der appenino-balkanischen Romania. 2 vols. Vienna.
Battisti, Carlo. 1962. Le valli ladine dell'Alto Adige e il pensiero dei linguisti italiani sulla unità dei dialetti ladini. Firenze.
Bec, Pierre. 1973a. La langue occitane. Paris.
_____. 1973b. Manuel pratique d'occitan moderne. Paris.
Elcock, W.D. 1938. De quelques affinités phonétiques entre l'aragonais et le béarnais. Paris.
Ferguson, Thaddeus. 1972. The evolution of the stressed vowel system of Vegliote. In: Studies in honor of Mario Pei. Edited by Fisher and Gaeng. Chapel Hill, N.C.: The University of North Carolina Press.
Francescato, Giuseppe. 1967. Dialettologia friulana. Udine, Italy.
Gartner, Theodor. 1910. Handbuch der rätoromanischen Sprache und Literatur. Halle.
Hadlich, R.L. 1965. The phonological history of Vegliote. Chapel Hill, N.C.: The University of North Carolina Press.
Leonard, C.S. Jr. 1964. Proto-Rhaeto-Romance and French. Lg 40:23–32.
_____. 1969. A reconstruction of Proto-Lucanian. Orbis 18:439–84.

Mazzola, M.L. 1976. Proto-Romance and Sicilian. Lisse, Netherlands.
Saunders, Gladys. 1975. A comparative study of the Gallo-Italian dialects. Ann Arbor, Mich.: University Microfilms (on demand).
Wagner, M.L. 1941. Historische Lautlehre des Sardischen. Halle/S.
_____. 1951. La lingua sarda: storia, spirito, forme. Bern.
_____. 1957–64. Dizionario etimologico sardo. Heidelberg.

www.ingramcontent.com/pod-product-compliance
Ingram Content Group UK Ltd.
Pitfield, Milton Keynes, MK11 3LW, UK
UKHW041916140426
5217IPUK00013B/185